MW00909868

FINANCIAL ACCOUNTING
FOR HOSPITALITY MANAGEMENT

FINANCIAL ACCOUNTING FOR HOSPITALITY MANAGEMENT

Elisa S. Moncarz, CPA
Nestor de J. Portocarrero, CPA

School of Hospitality Management
Florida International University
Miami, Florida

VNR VAN NOSTRAND REINHOLD
———————— New York

Copyright © 1986 by Van Nostrand Reinhold
Library of Congress Catalog Card Number 86-3563
ISBN 0-87055-505-7

All rights reserved. No part of this work covered by the
copyright hereon may be reproduced or used in any
form or by any means—graphic, electronic, or
mechanical, including photocopying, recording, taping,
or information storage and retrieval systems—without
written permission of the publisher.

All personal and company names used in this work are
intended to be fictitious and, accordingly, any similarity
to any living person or actual company is purely
coincidental, except where indicated.

Material from Financial Accounting Standards Board
publications, copyright © by Financial Accounting
Standards Board, High Ridge Park, Stamford,
Connecticut 06905, U.S.A. Reprinted (or quoted) with
permission. Copies of the complete documents are
available from the FASB.

Van Nostrand Reinhold
115 Fifth Avenue
New York, New York 10003

Van Nostrand Reinhold International Company Limited
11 New Fetter Lane
London EC4P 4EE, England

Van Nostrand Reinhold
480 La Trobe Street
Melbourne, Victoria 3000, Australia

Nelson Canada
1120 Birchmount Road
Scarborough, Ontario M1K 5G4, Canada

16 15 14 13 12 11 10 9 8 7 6 5 4

Library of Congress Cataloging-in-Publication Data

Moncarz, Elisa S.
  Financial accounting for hospitality management.

  Bibliogrpahy: p.
  Includes index.
  1. Hotels, taverns, etc.—Accounting.
2. Restaurants, lunch rooms, etc.—Accounting.
I. Portocarrero, Nestor de J.   II. Title.
HF5686.H75M66   1986   657'.837   86-3563
ISBN 0-87055-505-7

Contents

[handwritten annotation: only applicable to business uses reversing entry]

Preface

Financial Accounting for Hospitality Management is designed to provide students with a proper merging of basic accounting theory and practice and is tailored for the special needs of the hospitality service industries. Much of the specific content of this book is the result of the authors' extensive experience as professional accountants, and as professors in the accounting and finance program of the School of Hospitality Management at Florida International University.

In our pioneering effort to develop an introductory course to management accounting for the hospitality industry—which is offered by the aforementioned school—it became evident that existing books dealing with introductory accounting were not suitable for students of hospitality management. These books frequently focus on techniques, tools, and procedures that are mostly applicable to manufacturing firms without giving full attention to the unique characteristics of hospitality firms. Such books do not cover the basic areas of major concern to hospitality management. Thus, this book was written with the express aim of correcting this major deficiency.

A greater need for a thorough understanding of accounting by hospitality management personnel has arisen as businesses have been confronted with inflationary trends, recessions, high interest costs, and other major factors that have acted to hinder economic growth over the past decade. Recent statistics and forecasts indicate that the hospitality industry will face a continuing economic challenge in the future. The emphasis on management's ability to face future economic uncertainties, such as slower economic growth and increased government regulations, will remain. Indeed, the manner in which hospitality management deals with these issues will make the difference between business success and failure.

In addition to these economic challenges, there are some distinctive characteristics of the hospitality industry which also have placed a greater demand for middle- and top-echelon hospitality managers to acquire the operational and financial expertise necessary to aid them in more effectively performing their duties now as well as in meeting the challenges of the future. This book gives full recognition to the unique needs of the hospitality industry.

INTENDED AUDIENCE

This book is primarily designed to meet the needs of the undergraduate student with little or no previous exposure to accounting who is majoring in hospitality management. It will also be instructive and useful for those already working in the hospitality field, who want to gain insight into the accounting aspects of the industry as well as develop a better understanding of the uses of accounting information. Similarly, it is suitable as a teaching vehicle in management development programs.

As noted above, the text has been built on the assumption that the reader has no previous accounting education. Accordingly, the book is intended for use by students in first-semester accounting courses offered by four-year hospitality management education programs. In addition, the book is well suited for use by junior colleges offering hospitality-related programs leading to an associate degree. It is also suitable as a reference book for graduate students of hospitality management who have had limited exposure to business and accounting.

Since the chapters are, for the most part, independent of each other (especially those in Parts III and IV), the book can be easily adapted to the requirements of any appropriate accounting course in a hospitality management program by omitting or extending several chapters.

ORGANIZATION OF MATERIAL

At the outset, the text provides an overview of the hospitality service industries. This is done by focusing on the nature, major characteristics, recent trends, and future outlook for the major segments of the industry. The presentation of the text material is then divided into four major parts:

Part	Title	Chapters
I	The Accounting Framework	1–4
II	The Accounting Cycle and Procedures	5–10
III	Financial Statements	11–13
IV	Selected Topics	14–19

Part I is designed to provide a groundwork for the accounting process which is addressed in Part II. Accounting terms and basic accounting concepts are covered as part of this fundamental groundwork. Hospitality industry examples supplement textual material to aid in the learning process. In order to introduce the student to the business background of accounting, a review of the different forms of legal organizations used in the hospitality industry has been included in the last chapter in Part I.

Part II is devoted exclusively to the accounting process—the accounting cycle—using a step-by-step examination of each of the stages used in the accounting cycle of a service-type business. Considerable attention is given to the proper matching of expenses against revenues in the understanding of the adjustment process.

Part III deals primarily with the major financial statements—the balance sheet, the statement of income, and the statement of changes in financial position. An in-depth review of the balance sheet and the statement of income based on the Uniform System of Accounts for Hotels is included. A complete set of financial statements of an actual hospitality firm are examined in Chapter 13. In this manner, the concepts and procedures associated with the statement of changes in financial position are reviewed.

Several special topics are presented in the fourth and final part of the text. These include inventory, property and equipment, responsibility accounting, corporation accounting, and financial analysis. The objective is to develop student expertise in these areas and provide limited practice in using accounting information for managerial purposes.

Assignment material may be selected from questions, exercises, and problems at the end of most chapters to accommodate a wide variety of student comprehension and interest. Questions provide a review of the key ideas and major points covered in the text, whereas exercises and problems are more comprehensive in scope and, for the most part, are arranged in order of increasing difficulty. An Instructor's Solution Manual containing responses to all questions, and solutions to all exercises and problems, is available to adopters.

An extensive glossary and an index, appearing at the end of the book, serve as useful reference tools by enabling readers to locate key accounting and business terms easily.

SPECIAL FEATURES OF THIS BOOK

In addition to a comprehensive coverage of financial and managerial topics geared to the hospitality industry, which is presented in a clear and concise format, this textbook offers other important features:

1. A step-by-step analysis of the different stages of the accounting cycle for a hospitality service firm.
2. A discussion of appropriate provisions of the wage–hour law and tax laws affecting the hospitality industry.
3. An in-depth examination of the statement of income based on the Uniform System of Accounts for Hotels (Seventh Revised Edition).
4. The use of a chart of accounts based on the Uniform System of Accounts for Hotels in the discussion of responsibility accounting. (The chart of accounts is included as the Appendix.)
5. An emphasis on the "why" and "how" of accounting concepts and procedures.
6. A thorough review of the financial statements and footnotes of an actual company in the hospitality industry—La Quinta Motor Inns, Inc.
7. A review of the major disclosures found on financial statements of hospitality firms.
8. Full recognition, where appropriate, of current pronouncements of the Financial Accounting Standards Board and the American Institute of Certified Public Accountants.

In general, this book is expected to meet a very important need in the hospitality industry. Students pursuing a career in hospitality management will, by using this book, acquire sufficient understanding of accounting to enable them to pursue further studies on the use of accounting information for decision-making purposes. Moreover, these future hospitality managers should acquire a broad-based understanding of why their accounting skills and understanding are so essential to the success of the hospitality industry organization.

ACKNOWLEDGMENTS

The authors are grateful to the many individuals and organizations for the assistance and encouragement that they gave during the writing of this book. First, we want to thank all our students who provided us with the motivation to undertake this major endeavor. We also wish to express our deep appreciation to Dr. Anthony G. Marshall, dean of the School of Hospitality Management of Florida International University, for his support and encouragement during the preparation of this work. Ms. Harriet Damon Shields deserves a special acknowledgment for the many hours she spent in providing valuable editorial and production assistance.

In addition, we express our thanks to the American Institute of Certified Public Accountants, the Financial Accounting Standards Board, the Hotel Association of New York, and Laventhol & Horwath for their permission to use materials from their publications. We are also indebted to La Quinta Motor Inns, Inc., Restaurant Associates Industries, Inc., Delta Air Lines, Inc., Wendy's International, Inc., and Denny's, Inc. for providing us with copies of their financial statements.

Finally, we wish to express our sincere appreciation to our spouses Dr. Raul Moncarz and Maria Esperanza Portocarrero, and to our children for their patience and understanding. They provided us with the inspiration needed to bring this book to a successful completion. This book is dedicated to them.

ELISA S. MONCARZ
NESTOR de J. PORTOCARRERO

FINANCIAL ACCOUNTING
FOR HOSPITALITY MANAGEMENT

Introduction to the Hospitality Service Industries

Even in our most remote past, whenever people have ventured forth from the relative safety of their homes, villages, or cities, to reach a distant location, passing over unfamiliar terrain, they have needed shelter at night and food and water to restore their energies. The uncertainty and risk involved in early travel probably made it a rather dangerous undertaking. Although the major motivations for modern travel are tourism and business, the needs of travelers have not changed—they still need a way to get there, a place to stay, and something to eat.

Rendering hospitality services thus involves satisfying some of humanity's most basic needs. Because of this, offering hospitality to travelers has in many cultures been considered a matter of high moral duty. Early travelers were offered food and lodging by local residents as a matter of tradition. Eventually, trade followed, trade routes developed, and regular rest stops grew up along them.

THE NATURE OF THE HOSPITALITY INDUSTRY

It is rather difficult today to define the hospitality industry precisely. We could fall back on its original meaning and say that it includes all enterprises that provide a means of travel and/or lodging and food for the traveler. Yet, in our present complex society there is an overlap between, on the one hand, the entertainment industry, the health care industry, and the educational industry, and, on the other hand, what might be called the strictly hospitality functions of providing travelers with transportation, lodging, and food. The lack of a clear-cut distinction between industries becomes evident when we try to answer questions such as these:

- Is a hospital, which provides food and lodging, as well as health care, part of the hospitality industry or strictly part of the health care industry?
- Is a celebrity performing in a hotel part of the entertainment industry or part of the hospitality industry?
- Is foodservice at a public spectacle, such as a football game, part of the entertainment industry or part of the hospitality industry?
- Are student boarding houses or school foodservice contracts part of the educational industry or part of the hospitality industry?

Because of the ambiguities, there is no generally acceptable definition of the hospitality industry. However, the nature of the industry can be analyzed

1

by identifying its main structures (or segments) and focusing on the unique characteristics of these segments.

As previously noted, the hospitality industry originated out of the traveler's need for three basic services: (1) transportation, (2) lodging, and (3) food. Although the form in which these needs are satisfied has evolved considerably over time, the basic needs remain. Therefore, the hospitality industry includes activities that satisfy or help satisfy any of these basic needs of the traveler. Initially, the needs for food and lodging outside the home were intimately associated with the concept of travel. Today, although the travel aspect of the industry is stronger than ever, the foodservice aspect has taken on an independent existence. For example, we can now go to eat in a restaurant in a hospital or a school without traveling. In fact, it is not uncommon to have meals brought to the home by a catering service. Thus we see that—while they still include the three basic elements travel, food, and lodging—the services rendered by the industry have undergone some transformation.

Given the preceding description of the types of services that are currently called hospitality services, what types of activities can be considered as an integral part of the hospitality industry today? Among the activities that fall fully and clearly within the hospitality industry are

1. Travel
   - airlines
   - railroads
   - bus lines
   - passenger ships (both destination and cruise oriented)
2. Travel support activities
   - travel agencies
   - taxi services
   - car rentals
   - mobile home parks
   - boat rentals
3. Lodging
   - commercial hotels (for tourist or business travelers)
   - resort hotels
   - residential hotels (boarding houses and homes for the aged)
   - hostels
   - motels
   - campgrounds
4. Foodservices
   - full-service restaurants
   - banquet services
   - fast-food restaurants
   - cafeterias
   - snack bars
   - drive-ins
   - coffee shops
   - vending machines
   - meal delivery services
   - foodservices associated with other hospitality activities (such as in-flight foodservice)
5. Recreation
   - clubs
   - amusement parks

- camping facilities
- entertainment centers

Those activities that cross industry lines, in that they contain some non-hospitality-type-services, fall into the following categories:

1. Health related
    - hospitals
    - sanitariums
    - convalescent centers
2. Education related
    - foodservice for schools
    - boarding facilities for schools
3. Public spectacle related
    - foodservice associated with entertainment industry activities

Figure I.1 provides an approximate idea of how hospitality industry sales are divided among the three basic services that have traditionally been associated with the industry.

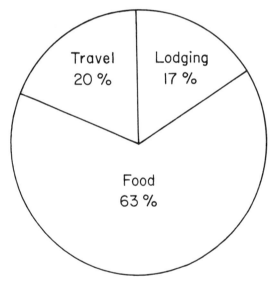

Figure I.1. Pie chart showing how sales of the three basic services of the hospitality industry are distributed.

Source: Somerset R. Waters, "Travel Industry World Yearbook—The Big Picture—1983." Child & Waters, Inc., New York, NY, p. 33.

COMMON CHARACTERISTICS OF HOSPITALITY INDUSTRY FIRMS

Although we cannot define the hospitality industry precisely, we can list some general characteristics applicable to the industry as a whole, or to major segments within the industry:

1. The hospitality industry is primarily devoted to selling services that people go to the hospitality establishment to receive. Passengers board the airline's airplane, guests travel to hotels, and diners enter restaurants. One might think that the sale of food in a restaurant is primarily the sale of a

tangible product; but actually only about 33% of every dollar spent at a restaurant pays for the cost of food. The rest is used to pay for services such as purchasing, cooking and serving the food, as well as creating an appropriate atmosphere in the restaurant.

2. Between 30 and 40% of a hospitality firm's costs consist of salaries, wages, and related items. This should not be surprising if we consider that the sale of services is the industry's main source of revenue and services usually must be rendered personally.

3. Hospitality firms tend to require large capital investment. Considerable sums of money are needed to construct hotels, motels, airplanes, ships, and restaurants. This, in turn, forces hospitality firms to seek huge amounts of financing. Not only is there a need for large capital investments in the industry, but usually these are investments in items that cannot be put to alternative uses, should their intended use prove to be unprofitable. Buildings designed as hotels cannot be efficiently used as factories, used airplanes bring a fraction of what they cost because ever more fuel-efficient airplanes are being developed, etc. Capital investment in the hospitality industry is thus a risky all-or-nothing matter.

4. As in the case with some other industries, the sales of hospitality firms tend to be cyclical. Furthermore, there are at least three types of cycles, and in some cases four, to contend with. First, there is the weekly cycle. People tend to eat out and travel more on weekends. Second, there is the seasonal cycle. As shown in Figure I.2, Americans tend to take more vacation trips in the months of July and August. The third type of cycle that affects the hospitality industry is the business cycle. Because vacation travel is considered a luxury, it is part of the discretionary expenditures that households eliminate first when incomes decline. Fourth and last, restaurants have an additional cycle to contend with: the daily cycle. Depending on the type of restaurant, most of a restaurant's business is concentrated at the normal mealtimes.

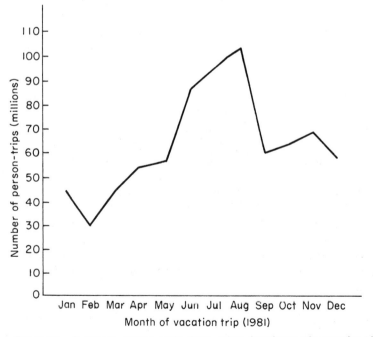

Figure I.2. Seasonal vacation cycle chart—when Americans take vacation trips.
Source: Somerset R. Waters, "Travel Industry World Yearbook—The Big Picture—1983." Child & Waters, Inc., New York, NY, p. 39.

These cycles make it more difficult for a hospitality firm to program its major cost category, namely, labor. They also oblige firms in the industry to have excess idle capacity during the slow part of their cycles. Building only to satisfy minimum demand would hinder hospitality firms from taking full advantage of their cycle peaks and would expose them to losing clients to the competition during these peaks.

Of course, not all hospitality firms are affected equally by these cycles. Hospitality services associated with schools and hospitals are not affected much by economic cycles and there is very little unpredictability in their daily, weekly, and seasonal cycles.

RECENT TRENDS IN THE HOSPITALITY INDUSTRY

From 1960 to the present the hospitality industry has experienced the greatest growth in its history. During this period airline passengers were introduced to the jet airplane; the interstate highway system was developed, providing fertile ground for Kemmons Wilson's (founder of Holiday Inns) widespread application of the motel (motor–hotel) concept; the fast-food segment matured during this period as pizza, Mexican, and dietetic fast-food chains joined the traditional hamburger stand; and computers helped to revolutionize the marketing process.

Indeed, the concept of "marketing" as a profession was raised to an art during this era. The resort vacation travel chain was stimulated with the success of Club Med, and the idea of time-sharing was introduced. The major U.S. hotel chains expanded into practically every corner of the globe, even into Eastern Europe, often transforming the local economies where they were established. This overseas expansion was accompanied by the development of the concept of the hotel management contract and the birth of the travel and entertainment credit card. The readily accessible credit provided by the credit card, plus the proliferation of tours, which were brought within the reach of almost everyone's pocketbook, gave great impetus to travel. The Caribbean basin became a fully developed vacation destination. Furthermore, hotel design was revolutionized by Kemmons Wilson's roadside inn, William Tabler's concentration on functional hotels, and John Portman's multistory atrium concept.[1] Finally, to fund this incredible growth, the use of what has been called "creative financing" was introduced.

All of this occurred within approximately 25 years. Unfortunately, this period also marked the dilution of the impact of such hotel personalities as Conrad Hilton, Ernest Henderson, J. Willard Marriott, Kemmons Wilson, and Howard Johnson. Their imprint on the hospitality industry continues through the corporations they created, but they no longer lend the flamboyance of their personalities to the industry. Perhaps the hospitality industry is now too large for the influence of any one person to be felt significantly, and this in itself is an important recent development in the industry. It is an undesirable consequence of growth, since the image of hospitality can best be conveyed by the warmth and exuberance of individuals, something very difficult for an institution to duplicate.

A phenomenal wave of expansion in the hospitality industry began after the end of World War II with the development of the interstate highway

[1]Kemmons Wilson was the founder of Holiday Inns; William Tabler designed most of the Hilton Hotels and developed the rule of thumb for construction costs—$1,000 cost for every $1 of room rate; John Portman developed the open lobby "atrium" concept.

system in the United States, which provided the framework upon which to build large hotel and restaurant chains, whose size permitted them later to expand overseas. Kemmons Wilson first identified the need for a chain of roadside inns (motels) to provide travelers on the interstate highways with service of a recognized quality standard. The Holiday Inn sign came to represent quality that a traveler could rely on. Additionally, these motels were located along the highways making it unnecessary to fight city traffic after a long day's drive in order to reach a midtown hotel.

Those motels gave rise to an architectural style based on functionalism and simplicity. Usually the traveler could drive right up to the door of the room. This was also an efficient design from the motel's point of view since no bell-hops were required.

The restaurant chains also experienced rapid growth as the increasingly mobile U.S. populace needed places to eat along the way. As the interstate highway system grew in importance, the railroad system declined, as did the downtown hotel. Because of the recognized standard of quality offered by national motel chains, the number of "mom and pop" motor inns also diminished considerably. However, the large amount of capital required to build these motel chains was raised by the use of franchising, which provided some small operators the opportunity to participate in this new growth. Nevertheless, the majority of family-run operations were put out of business, with the result that between 1958 and 1983, the number of hotel/motels decreased from approximately 70,000 to 55,000, while the number of rooms available increased by about 500,000.[2]

The next step forward in the industry came with the introduction of jet air travel. This contributed to the expansion of hotel and restaurant chains overseas, to such an extent that U.S. hotel chains called themselves "innkeepers for the world." Hotels overseas were being built so fast that in one year, 1963, Hilton International doubled in size. There are now more than nine million tourist quality hotel/motel rooms worldwide, of which approximately six million are located abroad. As of 1983, there were 90 Sheraton hotels abroad, 210 Holiday Inns, 90 Hilton Internationals, and 110 Intercontinental Hotels, of which eight properties are in Eastern European countries. This internationalization has also applied to foreign chains, such as Trusthouse Forte (British), Meridien Hotels (French), New Otani (Japanese), Dunfey Group (Irish), Swisshotel (Swiss), and Four Seasons Hotels (Canadian), which have also expanded beyond the confines of their home countries.

In the meantime, during the period of postwar affluence, the entire Caribbean basin became a tourist haven with luxurious hotels dotting the islands, principally Puerto Rico. Along with William Tabler's functional and efficient inner-city hotels, Morris Lapidus was creating hotels of extravagant and almost outlandish opulence in tourist locales, such as Miami. Air conditioning became a standard in hotel rooms. The packaged tour became commonplace, no longer accessible only to the very wealthy as it had been in the early part of the century. Credit cards increased the ease with which travel could be financed, as Carte Blanche, Diners Club, and American Express, among others, sought to enroll every eligible American, and then expanded abroad.

Resort chains, such as Club Med, promised their patrons familiar surroundings in a new vacation spot every year, and casinos were legalized in Atlantic

[2]Mort Weiser, The rise of hotel chains and expansion of markets. *Travel Weekly* 25th Anniversary Issue (May 31, 1983), p. 189.

City, the first place after Nevada to do so. Other special interest resorts developed as the industry competed for the attention of skiers, golfers, tennis players, and even orchid lovers.

Airlines introduced computers into the reservation process, facilitating the making of airline connections and the selection of the most economical routes. Total sales of airplane seats increased as interconnected computer reservation systems allowed airlines to refer passengers to their competitors when their own planes were full, thus better serving the interest of the traveling public.

A traveler could now plan a trip more quickly and efficiently. The hotel segment of the industry could not overlook this innovation and soon had computerized reservation systems of its own. The first such system was the Holidex I of Holiday Inns, introduced in 1964. It only reported which motels had rooms available, but did not indicate the type of room. Later systems maintained lists of guests' names and the names under which reservations had been made, as well as the types of rooms available in each hotel/motel. Most recently, the Westron System of Westin Hotels has enabled the guest to enter information in any order and maintains a complete history of all changes made in each reservation, thus reducing the possibility of misunderstanding. Now, hotel reservation systems are interconnected with airline reservation systems, finally allowing hospitality industry firms to sell fully integrated travel services to the public.

The next logical step was for vertical integration within the industry, as airlines attempted to own and operate hotel chains. For example, American Airlines purchased the Americana Hotels, United Airlines purchased Westin Hotels, and TWA purchased Hilton International. However, the management talents required to run an airline proved quite different from those required to operate a hotel chain, and divestiture followed not long after the acquisition of the hotel chains. The benefits of vertical integration within the hospitality industry continue to be enticing, and the suggestion has been made that the hospitality industry should be called the "transpitality" (transportation and hospitality) industry.[3]

Throughout this era of growth, the travel agency segment of the industry also experienced a resurgence. Twenty-five years ago hotels viewed travel agents as unncessary and often were unwilling to pay them for their services. With the access to business clients and to hotels and airlines that computers have provided to travel agencies, they can no longer be ignored as an industry segment. This is especially true as the travel and lodging sectors of the industry feel the need to work together more closely. The travel agency is the natural go-between, providing travelers with an overview of the many alternatives available to them. More than 80% of all domestic tourists and more than 50% of all international travelers used a travel agent in 1980.[4]

Another economic outgrowth of the last 25 years has been the evolution of sales skills into marketing skills. The term *marketing* began to appear on managers' calling cards in the 1960s and was the product of the increased competition that the postwar expansion generated in the industry. The problem of finding adequate food and lodging faced by the prewar traveler was transformed into the problem of choosing among the almost overwhelming array of possible alternatives. This need to choose was imposed on the traveler from the very moment that planning the trip began, as computers presented

---

[3]John Palmer, The transpitality industry. *International Journal of Hospitality Management 3*, No. 1 (1984), pp. 19–23.

[4]"Travel Market Yearbook" (1982), pp. 77, 80.

quality categories and alternative routes by which to select and reach the final destination.

The hospitality industry was forced to respond to the marketplace the way other consumer industries had learned to do. If it targeted the entire spectrum of travelers, a hospitality firm was likely to miss all travelers, as its competitors zeroed in on specific types of travelers and lured them away successfully. The catchphrase in sales became "market segmentation," which involved analyzing the total market to determine the different needs of the various types of travelers and then deciding which market segments the firm wished to service. Some of the market segments identified were

1. The business traveler
   * economy
   * first class
2. The convention market
   * business
   * special interest groups (e.g., American Legion)
3. The tourist traveler
   * economy
   * luxury
   * special interest (e.g., sports, intellectual pursuits)
4. The diner seeking
   * luxury table restaurants
   * economy table restaurants
   * fast-food service
5. The market for catered meals

Hospitality firms concentrating on specific segments of the market were able to offer services and amenities that would fill the needs of specific types of travelers better than a firm devoted to serving all travelers in general.

Newly developed market research techniques enabled firms to analyze the market and then later to evaluate how effectively they were reaching their targeted market segments. This feedback allowed hospitality firms to fine tune their salesmanship to a degree unheard of before. By using these techniques, for instance, Ramada Inns was able to make the decision to build the Ramada Renaissance Hotel chain to service the first-class travel market. This segmentation of the market also helped the familiar cozy country inns (some dating from before the turn of the century) to survive by reaching out for the traveler interested in Americana.

The traditional approach of the hospitality industry to sales remained the same. This approach was eloquently expressed by William Prigge, who for 25 years traveled worldwide, opening Hilton hotels, when he stated that the three most important factors in sales were (1) empathy for customers' problems, (2) anticipation of their needs, and (3) timing. The new marketing tools enabled the industry to exploit these three factors with greater precision for an ever-growing number of market segments.

THE FUTURE OF THE HOSPITALITY INDUSTRY

Two main factors augur continued rapid growth for the hospitality industry in the United States, which will, in turn, generate growth in the industry on a worldwide basis:

1. The average age of the U.S. population is expected to increase by 1990, as a result of a disproportionate increase in the 25–44-year-old and 65-and-over categories.[5] The former age group is composed of middle-level executives and is the age group that spends the most on traveling. This group consists of postwar baby boom infants, who are now reaching middle age.

Although the 65-and-over category has not been as traditionally travel prone, the upcoming group will be composed of retirees of America's most accelerated period of growth, and hence will be more affluent than earlier groups in this age category. They will have more social security, more pensions, and more savings. Furthermore, although they travel less frequently than people of younger age, they tend to take longer trips since they have more free time.[6]

2. The second factor favoring growth in the hospitality industry is the increasing automation being introduced into U.S. manufacturing industries. At some point, the increases in worker productivity that result from the robotization of the manufacturing process should enable workers to have more free time, a portion of which will be spent traveling.

The travel industry, with sales of $191 billion in 1981, became the second largest retail business in the United States.[7] Furthermore, the rate of growth in international tourism is approximately twice that of the gross national product (GNP).[8] It is estimated that approximately 600,000 net new rooms will be needed in the early 1990s to service this growth.[9] This will place continued demands on the part of the hospitality industry for (1) trained personnel and (2) capital.

Already in the 1984 economic recovery more than two million new jobs were created in the fast-food industry. As automation has increased, the proportion of workers in the service sector of the U.S. economy has increased from 53% in the 1950s to 70% in 1984, to an expected 73% in the 1990s.[10] Service industries are devoted to serving people, but the implication is that this service must be rendered by people. In the hospitality industry, machines do not serve people, people serve people. As Sinclair Lewis expressed it, to be a hotel keeper,

> you've got to learn a lot . . . you'll have to learn manners—learn to be poker-faced with guys that would take advantage of you. You'll have to know all about china and silver and glass and linen and brocade and the best woods for flooring and furniture. A hotel manager has to be a certified public accountant, a professor of languages, a quickaction laundryman, a plumber, a heating engineer, a carpenter, a swell speechmaker, an authority on the importance of every tinhorn state senator or one-night stand lecturer that blows in and expects to have the red carpet already hauled out for him. He's got to set a table like a Vanderbilt. If you can do all this, you'll have a good time.[11]

Because it is an industry of people serving people, automation cannot be counted on to increase productivity as much in this industry as in the man-

[5]Two billion travelers forecast by 2000 A.D. *Florida Hotel and Motel News* (Aug. 1984), p. 22.

[6]Consumer demographics—The changing of America. *Lodging Hospitality* (Feb. 1983), p. 38.

[7]Somerset R. Waters, "Travel Industry World Yearbook, The Big Picture—1983." Child & Waters, Inc., New York, NY, p. 29.

[8]*Ibid.,* p. 15.

[9]John Lesure, Hotels break ground with financing methods. *Travel Weekly* 25th Anniversary Issue (May 31, 1983), p. 210.

[10]A remarkable job machine. *Time Magazine* (June 25, 1984), p. 52.

[11]Sinclair Lewis, "Work of Art." Doubleday, Doran & Co., Inc., Garden City, NY (1935), p. 71. Copyright 1934. Sinclair Lewis; Copyright renewed 1962 Michael Lewis. Reprinted by permission of the estate of Michael Lewis.

ufacturing industries. There will therefore be a strong demand for workers in the industry through the mid-1990s.

As for capital, it is estimated that about $40 billion[12] will be needed between 1984 and 1995 to provide the required 600,000 room net increase, as well as the restaurants and transportation facilities that go along with this increase in rooms. This means that managers will have to be adept not only in the operational aspects of management (maximizing sales and controlling costs), but also in financial management. They will have to be conversant with the language of business: accounting. Just as U.S. companies discovered that it was awkward to send managers abroad who did not speak the local language, so is it also awkward and risky to enter the business world without knowing its language. Ellsworth Statler visited Cornell in 1925 and everyone was aghast when he said to one of the classes of students, ". . . You're wasting your time here. You don't have to learn this stuff to be a hotelman. When I have an engineering problem, I hire an engineer. I don't know a damn thing about the British Thermal Units, and there's no reason for you to, either. Go on home and get a job."[13] Given his initial attitude, it speaks all the more eloquently in favor of formal schooling for hotel managers that, in a speech given the following day, after going over the school curriculum and participating in some exercises, he said, "I am converted. Meek[14] can have any damn thing he wants." It is worth noting that many recognized undergraduate hotel school programs include at least four required accounting courses in their curriculums.

[12]Two billion travelers forecast by 2000 A.D. *Florida Hotel and Motel News* (Aug. 1984), p. 22.
[13]Floyd Miller, "Statler, America's Extraordinary Hotelman." The Statler Foundation, Ithaca, NY (1968).
[14]Howard B. Meek, first head of the School of Hotel Management at Cornell University, Ithaca, NY.

The Accounting Framework

I

Accounting as the Basis for Management Decisions

Accounting is a system for collecting, summarizing, analyzing, and reporting, in monetary terms, information concerning an organization, and supplying that information to decision-makers. The information provided by the accounting system must be useful and relevant to the users of the accounting data, who are generally classified into two categories: (1) the organization's management, that is, those individuals charged with the responsibility for directing the operations of the business enterprise, and (2) outsiders, that is, investors, creditors, government, employees, credit unions, and others interested in certain financial aspects of the business.

This book will focus on the accounting system from the point of view of the hospitality manager as the user of accounting information. We shall not, however, discuss the managerial uses of accounting information in the hospitality field until the student has a good understanding of what accounting information is and why it is essential for the successful operation of lodging, foodservice, and travel organizations.

As a starting point, this chapter examines the major features and the basic objectives of both the accounting system and hospitality organizations. Additionally, some key terms and concepts are introduced. Finally, we discuss the hospitality manager's need for accounting information.

ACCOUNTING: THE LANGUAGE OF BUSINESS

The main purpose of accounting is to provide the information necessary to the organization's management to enable it to plan and control its business activities. Implicit in this objective is the idea that accounting is another important management tool. Accordingly, accounting has been referred to as "the language of business" because it is the primary means of communicating business information.

Learning accounting is like learning a new language. If hospitality managers are to make effective use of accounting information, they must acquire an adequate understanding of the accounting system, including its nature and limitations. Because good decisions require proper analysis of accounting data, the hospitality manager who lacks training in accounting is unable to identify all the pertinent elements of the decision-making process, and thus it is highly doubtful that he or she can function as an effective manager.

USERS OF ACCOUNTING INFORMATION

As stated earlier, the principal user of accounting information is the organization's management. The type of accounting data needed by hospitality managers depends on a number of factors, such as the location and class of the operation. For instance, the manager of a small motel operation requires less accounting information than the manager of a large hotel chain, who is far removed from direct contact with day-to-day operations. However, regardless of the type of accounting data needed, every hospitality firm uses accounting information to measure business success and to select the best possible alternative in attaining company objectives.

Present and prospective hospitality investors need information on how well a firm is doing before they decide whether or not to sell or buy company stock. At the same time, bankers and other hospitality creditors are concerned with granting and renewing credit to hospitality organizations, and depend largely on accounting data for the evaluation of the risks involved in making loans and extending credit. Due to the capital-intensive nature of the hospitality industry, it becomes extremely important for hospitality organizations to maintain themselves in good financial condition in view of the aforementioned evaluations conducted by both investors and creditors—the main suppliers of funds.

It is interesting to note that external users of accounting information view the organization's management as information providers. Investors, creditors, and other users of accounting information have certain expectations about how the management of the hospitality firm should perform. When they receive accounting data describing how management has actually performed, they use these data as the basis for making economic decisions. Consequently, hospitality managers are held responsible for the accounting data used by outside parties.

THE DISTINCTION BETWEEN MANAGEMENT ACCOUNTING AND FINANCIAL ACCOUNTING

Management accounting is concerned with the internal uses of accounting information by the manager. Financial accounting, on the other hand, provides information for both internal and external uses and is based on a set of principles and a number of ground rules designed to enhance and clarify communication between the business and parties external to the business.

The two kinds of accounting are obviously related, in three basic ways:

1. All accounting is essentially financial in nature, in that it is stated in "terms of money."
2. Management is responsible for the content of both management and financial accounting reports.
3. Both management and financial accounting rely upon the accounting information system.

Based on the foregoing, it is obvious that the use of managerial data must be preceded by an adequate understanding of financial accounting.

ORGANIZATIONS AND THEIR STRUCTURE

Before studying how accounting is used in business, we must first discuss the nature of business. Organizations can be defined as distinct entities—a person or persons—with stated purposes operating in some definable environment. A university providing educational services is an organization, as are an attorney offering legal services and a motel operation providing lodging and food services.

All of the different types of organizations operate in an environment by interacting with each other in various kinds of quid pro quos (something for something). These quid pro quos, or equal exchanges of values between organizations, are known in accounting as business transactions. For example, a hotel maid, as an employee, provides cleaning services in return for a paycheck from the hotel organization (employer).

Accounting deals with the essence of business activity: economic exchange interaction between organizations. In accounting, we have to decide for which organization we are accounting. It is desirable at this point to discuss the basic structure and objectives of the hospitality organization.

The primary purpose toward which the hospitality organization works is to provide services to the general public. A hotel operation offers lodging and foodservices for a fee. Similarly, a travel agency provides travel services and receives in return a commission fee. Hence, the common objective of all hospitality firms is to provide services with a mind to earning a profit. The management of the firm is charged with the responsibility of conducting the day-to-day activities according to established goals that the organization desires to achieve, such as good reputation and dependability; but the primary objective is to achieve an adequate return on the investment made by the owners of the company.

In planning, controlling, and carrying out specific functions within the organization, there are three different levels of management: top management, middle management, and lower management. The president and vice president(s) of the company, as members of top management, guide the overall direction of the hospitality firm while relying on middle and lower management to plan, coordinate, and control at their management levels in keeping with the established policies of the organization. In this connection, line and staff unit relationships govern the basic structure of the organization. Line authority is directly related to the specific goals and objectives of the organization. The staff units, on the other hand, exist to provide services to other units and to top management.

Consider the organization chart of Apache Hotel, a medium-sized hotel operation, shown in Figure 1.1. This chart tells us, for example, that the general manager has line authority over all departments of the operation. He or she has the overall responsibility for seeing that services are offered timely and properly. The manager of each unit has line authority over the staff. For example, in this chart we see that the chef has line authority over cooks, baker, and pastry chef, and also has the final responsibility for food preparation. If there are any problems in the area of food preparation, the chef is expected to be aware of them and take appropriate corrective action. In turn, the chef is responsible to the food and beverage director, who, in turn, is responsible to the general manager for the overall performance of the food and beverage department.

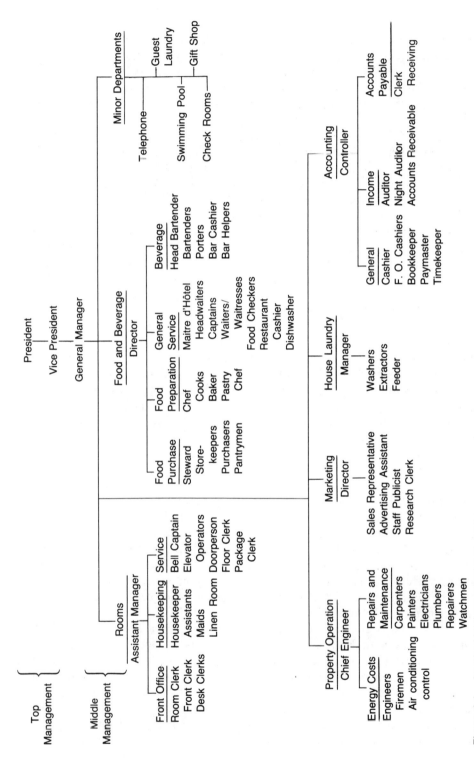

Figure 1.1. Apache Hotel organizational chart.

16

ACCOUNTING AS AN INFORMATION SYSTEM

Information is one basic resource that hospitality organizations use in managing their affairs. In addition to accounting, which is a very significant part of the management information system, hospitality managers also rely on data from related fields in their decision-making process, including economic, marketing, and personnel information.

Just as management can be viewed as a system, accounting can also be seen from a systems viewpoint.

Figure 1.2 shows, the inputs to the accounting system are source documents (checks, sales, purchase invoices, etc.) that serve as evidence that a business transaction took place. For that reason, business transactions have been regarded as the raw material of the accounting system. It is self-evident that understanding business transactions is essential in learning accounting, that is, knowing what happened with reference to a specific event, all of which requires the clear identification of the values of what is given and received as a result of the business transaction. For instance, if a restaurant borrows $20,000 from a bank for 30 days, the restaurant has received cash with a value of $20,000. On the other hand, the restaurant has given written promise to repay the $20,000 in 30 days, the value of which must aggregate the same dollar amount.

Once business transactions are identified, they are recorded and summarized to show the progress and position of the firm. This is accomplished by completing the sequence of steps known as the accounting cycle. In effect, the accounting cycle involves the processing of the raw material of the accounting system (business transactions) in order to get the output or end product, which is information to management in the form of financial statements and other accounting reports.

The basic steps of the accounting cycle include a recording phase, commonly referred to as bookkeeping, which is often confused with the overall accounting function. Accounting, however, goes beyond the bookkeeping function, which is mechanical in nature. Accounting's analytical function is primarily the design of specific accounting systems and the preparation, analysis, and interpretation of accounting data as presented in the financial statements produced by the accounting system.

Input ----------→ Process ------------→ Output
Source Documents   Reduction of Data   Information to Management
                        (Accounting Cycle)

Figure 1.2.   The accounting system.

FINANCIAL STATEMENTS

Financial statements (the output or end product of the accounting system) represent means of transmitting to management and other interested parties a concise picture of the profitability and financial condition of a business entity. The two major financial statements are the balance sheet and the statement of income. Together these two statements summarize all the business transactions included in the detailed accounting records of the company.

The balance sheet shows the financial position of a company at a particular point in time. It will answer questions such as what amounts are owned by the company (assets) or what amounts are owed by the company (liabilities). It is also referred to as a position statement or statement of condition. Furthermore, it is of great interest to management and outsiders as an indicator of the financial strength of the firm.

The statement of income reflects the results of the operations of a company during a specific period of time, better known as the accounting period—a month, a quarter, a year. It will indicate whether management has achieved its primary objective—earning an adequate profit for the owners of the company during the accounting period.

In addition to the balance sheet and the income statement, there is a third basic financial statement, the statement of changes in financial position. The latter summarizes the financing and investing activities of management during the accounting period. Also, it is used by hospitality managers in the planning of future investment projects, as well as in making major financing decisions, which are of utmost importance to the hospitality industry as a result of its large capital requirements.

The three aforementioned financial statements are prepared in accordance with a set of conventions called generally accepted accounting principles (GAAP). These principles, and the related concepts to which they are directed, represent the foundation of accounting. They will be discussed in more detail later.

Because of the unique features of the hospitality industry, and particularly departmentalized operations for some segments of the industry, some industry associations have developed uniform systems of accounts to be used in the preparation of financial statements. In Part III, we shall discuss in some detail the basic guidelines underlying the preparation of the statement of income according to the uniform system of accounts for hotels, which underwent a major revision in 1977 and has been approved by the American Hotel and Motel Association.

THE HOSPITALITY MANAGER'S NEED FOR ACCOUNTING INFORMATION

As we have already noted, it would be impossible for a hospitality industry organization to carry out and fulfill its basic goals without good accounting information. To give a specific example of how accounting information aids hospitality management, consider the following situation:

Felippe Inn is a medium-sized motel operation, headed by Ms. Henley, its general manager. The company employs 65 people, who are working toward the principal objective of the organization—earning an adequate profit by providing lodging and food services. Felippe Inn owns land and a building in which the motel operates, and also the furniture and fixtures used in its operations. Additionally, it has cash in a bank account, office and housekeeping supplies, and food that is offered for sale. All of these items represent the resources that Felippe Inn needs to conduct its business.

What accounting information is needed by Ms. Henley in order to conduct business activities and make the necessary economic decisions of the Felippe Inn organization? In essence, she needs accounting information to direct daily operations, to plan future operations, and to select the best alternative in the solution of operational problems. Specifically, she will need to know the contribution of each department of the motel to total earnings, the amounts owed by customers, the amounts owed to each purveyor and the date payment is due, the amount of cash in the bank at any particular time, and the future cash requirements of the motel. These are just some examples of the type of accounting information required by Ms. Henley for directing a smooth operation. Without receiving adequate accounting information, on a timely basis, Ms. Henley's decisions may fail to achieve the basic objectives of Felippe Inn.

→The higher the level of authority and responsibility, the greater the need for accounting information. Nevertheless, middle and lower management are also dependent upon accounting records in decision-making. For instance, the housekeeper of Felippe Inn needs to know what supplies are on hand and what items are needed so that additional quantities can be ordered.

Sometimes, hospitality management relies upon the expertise of professional accountants to meet its need for accounting information. The Certified Public Accountant (CPA) is the recognized professional accountant. Required to hold a CPA certificate indicating the attainment of specific educational and professional criteria, the passing of the CPA examination, and complying with ethical and technical standards enforced by this profession, the CPA furnishes auditing, tax, and other accounting services. While CPAs are also engaged to provide advice and consultation on various management problems, they do not make management decisions.

In summary, the primary aim of accounting is to provide useful and relevant information to management as an aid to decision-making. On this basis, hospitality managers are not interested in accounting as an end in itself, but as a necessary step toward using financial statements and other accounting information for decision-making purposes.

Regardless of the degree of assistance provided by professional accountants, the knowledge of accounting so indispensable to the successful operation of the hospitality firm requires that each manager possess an adequate accounting background.

QUESTIONS

1. What is accounting?
2. What is the main purpose of accounting?
3. Name and describe which groups are the primary users of accounting information.
4. What is the main difference between management accounting and financial accounting?
5. What are the similarities between financial accounting and management accounting?
6. Describe how accounting information can be used by a hospitality firm as a basis for making business decisions.
7. What is an organization?
8. What is the main objective of a hospitality organization?
9. What is the output or end product of the accounting system?
10. Name and describe the basic financial statements.
11. Why must a hospitality manager have a basic understanding of the accounting system?
12. Who is responsible for the information contained in the financial statements? *OWNER*
13. What is the input of the accounting system? *SOURCE DOCU.*
14. What is a business transaction? *ANY ACCOUNTING ENTRY*
15. Contrast bookkeeping and accounting.

EXERCISES

1. What financial statement(s) would you use to verify each of the following:
   (a) The earnings of Apache Hotel decreased 50% during the year.
   (b) Apache Hotel invested $100,000 in a new convention hall during the current accounting period.
   (c) Apache Hotel borrowed $80,000 to make the above investment.
   (d) Apache Hotel sold an old freezer at a profit during the current accounting period.
   (e) Apache Hotel repaid $10,000 during the current accounting period.
2. Name five potential users of financial statements and indicate why they may be interested in them.
3. Name five source documents and explain their function.
4. Identify three business transactions for the Apache Hotel. Explain why these transactions might affect the balance sheet and/or the income statement of Apache Hotel and state the value(s) received and given for each transaction.

PROBLEMS

1. The Apache Hotel operates a parking lot on some adjacent land, which it rents from its owner under a five-year lease agreement dated January 1, 1984. Consider the following information:
   (1) Apache Hotel installed a lighting system on the parking lot at a cost of $10,000, on January 5, 1984.
   (2) Rent payments on the lease are $12,000 per year.
   (3) Apache Hotel paid an attendant on an hourly basis according to the number of hours punched on his time card. During 1985, this payment amounted to $12,000.
   (4) The electricity paid for lighting the parking lot amounts to $11,000 per year.
   (5) The hotel spent $2,000 during 1984 to repair the parking lot. It borrowed the money from Second National Bank and paid $200 interest on the loan in 1985.
   (6) During 1985, 36,500 cars used the parking lot, paying an average of $1.00 per car. The parking attendant gave each customer a receipt.
   (7) The Apache Hotel sold a fixed number of parking spaces to another hotel on the other side of the lot for a $9,600 yearly fee. During 1985, monthly invoices of $800 were sent to the hotel.

   Required:
   (a) Describe all of the transactions you can identify for the year ending December 31, 1985, that are strictly related to the operations of the parking lot.
   (b) Name the source documents that are likely to be involved in each transaction.
   (c) Determine the parking lot's results of operations for the year ending December 31, 1985 (i.e., did it make or lose money?)
   (d) Were there any transactions that took place in 1984 but were not repeated in 1985? Do these transactions benefit the parking lot during 1985? What would you call these items?
   (e) Prepare a balance sheet strictly for the Apache Hotel's parking lot as of December 31, 1984.
   (f) Prepare a balance sheet for the parking lot as of December 31, 1985. What would be an appropriate name for the difference between the amount of assets the parking lot owns and the amount of money it owes (i.e., liabilities)?
2. (a) List the assets or resources of a hypothetical person (possibly a friend of yours). Then list all the person's debts (the amounts you think they owe).
   (b) Calculate the difference between what they own and what they owe. Decide on a name to be used for this difference.
   (c) What is the accounting name for the two lists you made in (a) and for the difference you calculated in (b)?

3. **(a)** List as many sources of imaginary income as you can think of for a hypothetical person (possibly a friend).
   (b) List as many amounts spent to earn the aforementioned income (i.e., expenses) as you can think of for this same person.
   (c) Calculate the difference between the person's income and expenses.
   (d) What are (a), (b), and (c) above called in accounting language when you put them together?

4. Visit a fast-food hamburger restaurant. List as many resources (assets) as you think the restaurant owns and give them estimated values. Approximate their actual values as closely as you can. Then list all the debts (liabilities) you think they have, indicating specific amounts. Calculate the difference between these two lists. Determine an appropriate name for this difference.

   What is the accounting name for what you have created above?

5. Visit another fast-food restaurant. List all the sources of income you think it has and indicate specific amounts for each type of income. Be as realistic as you can.

   Now list all of the amounts spent to earn the aforementioned income (i.e., expenses) you can think of. Indicate specific amounts. Again, try to be as realistic as you can.

   Calculate the difference between these two lists. Are the expenses on your list greater than the income, or is the income greater than the expenses?

   What is the accounting name for what you have created above?

2

Basic Accounting Concepts

Simultaneously with the recognition of accounting as a system that provides the financial information necessary for making certain business decisions, the need arises for guidelines to ensure the usefulness and reliability of this accounting information.

In Chapter 1, we saw that the main purpose of accounting is to accumulate information concerning the financial activities of a business organization in a manner that will permit its meaningful summarization in the form of financial statements. Obviously, there cannot be widespread understanding of financial statements unless they are prepared in conformity with a body of generally accepted rules or conventions.

These rules or conventions are called generally accepted accounting principles, better known by their initials GAAP. There are several basic concepts toward which all GAAP are oriented. GAAP interpret the manner of applying these concepts in specific accounting situations, thereby providing the basis for accounting practice.

In this chapter, we first describe the major reference sources used to decide whether or not a particular accounting treatment has substantial authoritative support and thus merits application as a GAAP. In so doing, we review the main organizations authorized to formulate GAAP. We then explain seven of the basic accounting concepts on which GAAP are based, and which relate principally to the preparation of one of the two basic financial statements to be dealt with in this text—the balance sheet. The dual-aspect concept of accounting, in particular, is the subject of extensive review, which results from the fact that all business transactions have a dual aspect, which is part of the fundamental accounting equation.

We demonstrate that the balance sheet, the ultimate presentation format for business transactions, is also based on the dual-aspect concept as reflected in the fundamental accounting equation.

The remaining basic accounting concepts, those more directly applicable to the income statement, will be covered in Chapter 3.

GENERALLY ACCEPTED ACCOUNTING PRINCIPLES

In essence, GAAP are those principles which have received substantial support from an authoritative source. The primary organization responsible for developing GAAP in the United States in the past has been the American Institute of Certified Public Accountants (AICPA). Although the 1933 and 1934 securities laws gave the U.S. Securities and Exchange Commission (SEC)[1] the authority and responsibility for the development of GAAP, the

---

[1]A Federal agency responsible for protecting the interests of investors in publicly held companies.

SEC informally delegated most of this responsibility to the AICPA. Nevertheless, the SEC has been exerting an ever-increasing influence upon the development of accounting principles, especially in the recent past, because of a growing feeling that the accounting profession has not acted at all times in the best interests of improved financial disclosure. As a result, the SEC has become more involved in the development of its own acceptable accounting principles as formulated in Regulation S-X and in the SEC Accounting Releases.

Up to 1973 GAAP were most heavily influenced by the Accounting Principles Board (APB) of the AICPA. From 1973 to the present, the Financial Accounting Standards Board (FASB) has been primarily responsible for developing GAAP. The FASB, which is part of the Financial Accounting Foundation, an institution that is independent of all professional accounting groups, was created by the AICPA as a successor to the APB, which was disbanded in 1973, in order to improve the confidence of investors and other users of financial statements. Since the APB was composed of accounting professionals who donated their efforts on a part-time basis, the output of the APB was in many instances insufficient to satisfy the members of the business and investment communities.

The APB issued 31 opinions and 15 accounting research studies prior to its dissolution. At this writing (1985), the FASB has issued over 80 statements. All opinions, research studies, and statements issued by the APB and the FASB are currently part of GAAP and therefore are considered to have authoritative support unless they have been superseded by a subsequent FASB pronouncement. The FASB is constantly responding to new accounting problems as they arise by amending and enlarging the body of GAAP.

Although entities in the hospitality industry are not legally required to conform to GAAP, there is a strong presumption of misrepresentation in the financial statements if an entity does not. In fact, the financial statements of most hospitality industry firms of any substantial size are examined by independent certified public accountants (CPAs) who are required to issue an opinion regarding the fairness of presentation in these statements. If the CPA's opinion is to be unqualified, it must include a clear affirmation of the financial statements' conformity with GAAP. Material departures from GAAP must be spelled out in the CPA's opinion letter accompanying the financial statements. Thus, they become a matter of public knowledge, affecting how investors, creditors, and other interested parties view the company.

BASIC ACCOUNTING CONCEPTS

As already mentioned, there is an underlying structure of concepts from which all GAAP are derived. They provide the basis for accounting practice and consequently referred to as basic features, principles, postulates, fundamentals, or conventions. The seven basic accounting concepts underlying the preparation of the balance sheet are:

1. Business entity concept
2. Money measurement concept
3. Objectivity concept
4. Going-concern concept
5. Cost concept

6. Conservatism concept

7. Dual-aspect concept

BUSINESS ENTITY CONCEPT

The business entity concept indicates that a hospitality organization will be viewed, for accounting purposes, as a unit independent from its owners. In other words, the firm is considered an economic unit that stands on its own and therefore, when recording financial information, the activities of the hospitality firm must be kept separate and distinct from personal finances of its owners.

For example, the personal automobile of a hotel owner (Mr. X) should not be included among the resources owned by the hotel organization. X Hotel should be recognized as a separate entity in its own right, separate and distinct from Mr. X, its owner. Although Hotel X and Mr. X may not be separate entities from the legal standpoint, the resources assigned to Hotel X for its exclusive use must be accounted for as if they belong to Hotel X separately from Mr. X's other personal resources.

The debts of a business must also be reported separately from the debts of the owner. This means that even if there is no legal distinction between Hotel X and Mr. X, only those debts of Mr. X that are directly related to the hotel business may be included in the hotel's financial statements.

MONEY MEASUREMENT CONCEPT

Accounting is concerned with the recording of facts that can be expressed in monetary terms. Without such a standard of measure, accounting reports would not be very meaningful, for they would include such diverse items as 8 trucks, 18,000 square feet of building space, and 100 acres of land, with no statement of their value in terms of a common monetary unit.

In the United States, financial statements are expressed in terms of U.S. dollars. This common denominator enables the quantification of the effects of a wide variety of financial transactions. Use of the dollar as a measuring unit assumes that it is an unchanging yardstick, a stable measuring unit. Unfortunately, we all know that a 1986 dollar does not have the same purchasing power as a 1970 or 1960 dollar. The rather significant inflation (increase in prices resulting in decreased purchasing power of the dollar) of the late 1970s and early 1980s has created concern over the validity of considering the dollar a stable measuring unit.

Several techniques have been devised (and more proposals are currently under review) to adjust financial statements in order to compensate for the changing value of the dollar. However, at this writing, GAAP still requires the use of the money measurement concept. Only very large, publicly held hospitality industry entities are required to disclose in supplementary form the effect of inflation on the financial statements (in accordance with experimental Statement No. 33, 1979, issued by the FASB).

OBJECTIVITY CONCEPT

In order to ensure the necessary reliability of the information disclosed in financial statements, the accounting measurements must be objective and verifiable, that is, free from bias and subject to verification by an independent third party, usually an auditor. Some accounting measurements are very easily verified, but many measurements on financial statements contain elements of judgment and thus need to be systematized so that others repeating the same rational process will obtain the same measurement results. In any event, the amounts reported should not be biased by the subjective judgments of management.

For instance, objective verifiable evidence in processing the purchase of inventory will include a vendor's invoice showing that the purchase was actually made.

GOING-CONCERN CONCEPT

In the absence of evidence to the contrary, the assumption we make in the accounting process is that the hospitality entity will continue in operation indefinitely. It follows, therefore, since the business is not to be sold or liquidated, that there is no need to record current replacement values (market values) or liquidating values.

The going-concern concept, also known as the continuity concept, influences the measurement process. Under this assumption, we show the resources owned by the business (land, buildings) at their original cost inasmuch as they are not going to be sold. Instead, we assume that these resources are used in the regular operations of the business. Hence, the current resale value of these resources is irrelevant in the measurement process.

When there is good reason to believe that the going-concern concept is no longer applicable to a particular firm, then management is required to measure the resources owned by the business at their liquidating value. Using liquidation values is seldom justified—a firm must be in partial or total liquidation before a firm's resources may be so valued.

COST CONCEPT

The cost concept is very closely related to the going-concern concept. It states that cost is the proper basis for the accounting of the resources owned by the hospitality organization. These resources are called assets.

Assets represent future values (resources), owned by the business. Cost is defined as the price paid to acquire an asset. The acquisition cost of an asset will remain in the accounting records until the asset is sold, expires, or is consumed by the business.

For example, a piece of land acquired by a hotel in 1970 for $100,000 would appear on the balance sheet at its acquisition cost until sold by the hotel. If in 1987 the land could be sold for $150,000, no change would be made in the accounting records to reflect this fact. The land would still appear on the balance sheet at its acquisition cost of $100,000.

It follows from the cost concept that the amounts at which assets are listed in the accounting records do not indicate what these assets are worth except at the time they are acquired. In fact, at the initial recording of a transaction historical cost usually is the same as the fair market value. However, as time passes, the cost and fair market value will more than likely differ due to changes in a particular market or to inflationary and recessionary trends in the economy as a whole.

CONSERVATISM CONCEPT

Conservatism represents a departure from the cost principle when convincing evidence exists that cost cannot be recovered. It is a judgment exercised in evaluating uncertainties, in order to avoid self-serving exaggeration.

In a technical sense, conservatism means selecting the method of measurement that yields the least favorable immediate results. Traditionally, this attitude has been reflected in the working rule, "Anticipate no gains, but provide for all possible losses."

In applying the conservatism concept, assets are to be written up (recorded at a higher value) only upon an exchange, but they might be written down (recorded at a lower value) without an exchange. For instance, consider lower-of-cost-or-market rules in recording food or beverage inventories. Inventories are written down when replacement costs decline, but they are not written up when replacement costs increase.

The conservatism concept, however, should not be used to justify an unwarranted reduction in the asset costs and earnings of an entity. An example of this is provided by the FASB in its Statement of Accounting Concept No. 2, issued in May, 1980. This statement interprets the conservatism concept in the specific area of estimates of future events. According to the statement, if two estimates of future payment, one greater than the other, are equally likely to occur, conservatism requires the use of the lesser estimate. If, however, the greater future payment estimate is more likely to happen, it will be more objective to use the greater estimate rather than the lesser. Consequently, the application of the conservatism concept does require the use of prudent judgment in evaluating the uncertainties and risks inherent in business situations. A deliberate understatement of the assets and earnings of the firm, which goes contrary to the facts as they are likely to evolve, should be avoided.

DUAL-ASPECT CONCEPT: THE FUNDAMENTAL ACCOUNTING EQUATION

The dual-aspect concept is based on the fact that there are ownership claims to all things of value. This can be expressed in the form of the fundamental accounting equation:

$$Assets = Equities$$

If a hospitality entity buys a car for $5,000 cash, the asset's value is recorded as $5,000. The entity has the right of ownership over the car for an equal amount of $5,000. This ownership right is called the owner's equity in the car. If, however, the entity borrows $3,000 to buy the car, then the lender of this money has a claim against the car in the amount of $3,000. At the same time, the owner's claim is reduced to $2,000 ($5,000 − $3,000). The claims of lenders against the assets of a firm are called liabilities. After taking into account the claims of lenders, the fundamental accounting equation becomes

$$Assets = Liabilities + Owners' equity$$

If we substitute the amounts from our hypothetical car purchase, the equation will be expressed as

$$Assets = Liabilities + Owners' equity$$
$$\$5,000 \text{ (car)} = \$3,000 \text{ (amount borrowed)} + \$2,000$$

As we can see, all assets of the business are claimed by someone—either by the owners or by outside parties, known as creditors.

Assets are all the resources owned by the hospitality entity. These may consist of money (cash), land, buildings, equipment, and other property or property rights. Liabilities are the claims of creditors (lenders) against the assets of the hospitality firm. Creditors have a claim against these assets until amounts they loan to the entity have been repaid. Examples of liabilities include accounts payable (amounts owed to suppliers) and notes payable (amounts owed to the bank).

Owners' equity represents the claims of the owners of the hospitality organization. It is also referred to as capital or stockholders' equity, depending on the type of legal organization used by the entity. (This will be explained in detail in Chapter 4.) The owners' equity can be determined at any time by subtracting the liabilities from the assets. The fundamental accounting equation can be rearranged in the following manner:

$$\text{Owners' equity} = \text{Assets} - \text{Liabilities}$$

This illustrates the residual nature of owners' equity. That is, owners have claims on the assets of the hospitality business *only* after the creditors' claims have been fully satisfied.

At the inception of a hospitality firm's life, the owners' equity is represented by the original investment made by the owners in the business. Subsequently, owners' equity may increase with additional owners' investments. Further, an entity makes a profit when it earns more assets than it consumes. This net increase in assets belongs to the owners of the entity, so that earning a profit also increases the owners' equity of an entity. On the other hand, since losses produce a net decrease in the assets of an entity, they diminish owners' equity. We can say that business profits belong to the owners and business losses must be absorbed by the owners. In other words, owners reap the fruits of profits earned by the entity, but must also bear the brunt of losses. Accordingly, when a firm earns assets, we say that it is receiving revenue, whereas when a firm consumes assets we say that it is incurring expenses. Usually, a hospitality firm earns assets by selling food and beverages or by selling a service, such as temporary lodging. Revenues and expenses can be said to be logical extensions of owners' equity. Revenues represent an increase in the entity's assets resulting from the sale of goods or services and consequently, they will increase owners' equity. In the process of earning these revenues, assets are consumed, resulting in a corresponding decrease in owners' equity. Thus, expenses represent the costs incurred by the hospitality entity in earning revenues and tend to decrease owners' equity. Similarly, when assets earned are distributed to the owners of the firm in some form (usually money), this also logically produces a decrease in owners' equity.

The fundamental accounting equation forms the basis of the double-entry accounting system. All transactions will have a dual effect on the equation, maintaining its equality *at all times*. The sum of the claims of creditors and owners must always equal the total assets of a hospitality industry entity.

Therefore, a transaction that increases an asset must, in turn, increase a liability or owners' equity and/or decrease another asset. For example, if Aric's Motel borrowed $2,000 from a bank, the assets (cash) of the business would increase $2,000, while the liabilities (notes payable) would also increase by $2,000. If Aric's Motel buys a refrigerator for cash, one asset (cash) decreases while another asset (equipment) increases. In both instances, the fundamental accounting equation remains in balance.

Effect of Transactions on the Fundamental Accounting Equation

As noted before, business transactions affect elements on both sides of the fundamental accounting equation equally. Thus, while the total assets of a business may increase or decrease, the change will always be accompanied by a corresponding change in liabilities and/or owners' equity. In accounting, this condition of equality must always exist. To illustrate the fundamental accounting equation further, we analyze the following three transactions for CB Motel:

> June 1: (a) Mr. Carlton Bober invested $100,000 cash in the business.
> (b) CB Motel paid $1,000 cash for housekeeping supplies.
> (c) CB Motel purchased $30,000 worth of furniture and equipment on account.

Transaction (a)—Invested Cash. Mr. Carlton Bober made a contribution or investment of cash to start his CB Motel business. The dual-aspect of this event is that CB Motel now has an asset, cash, of $100,000, and Mr. Bober, the owner, has a claim against this asset, also of $100,000. This transaction would be shown as follows:

$$\frac{\text{Assets} \quad = \text{Liabilities} + \text{Owner's equity}}{100,000 \text{ (cash)} = \quad 0 \quad + \quad 100,000}$$

Transaction (b)—Paid Cash for Housekeeping Supplies. CB Motel purchased housekeeping supplies for cash, exchanging one asset for another. The total amount of assets did not change, but now there are two assets, cash and housekeeping supplies inventory. Owner's equity was not affected by this transaction. The effects of transactions (a) and (b) on the fundamental accounting equation are shown below:

	Assets	=	Liabilities	+	Owner's equity
(a)	Cash + Housekeeping = supplies		0	+	100,000
	+100,000 + 0				
(b)	−1,000 + 1,000	=	0	+	0
	+99,000 + 1,000	=	0	+	100,000

$$\underbrace{100,000}_{\text{Assets}} = \underbrace{100,000}_{\text{Equities}}$$

Transaction (c)—Purchase of Furniture and Equipment on Account. CB Motel purchased furniture and equipment on credit. An asset (furniture and equipment) is increased and a liability (accounts payable) also increases. The owner's equity is not affected. The overall effect on the fundamental accounting equation of the CB Motel produced by the transactions is shown below:

	Assets			= Liabilities + Owner's equity	
	Cash	Housekeeping supplies	Furniture & equipment	Accounts payable	
(a)	+100,000			=	0 + 100,000
(b)	−1,000	+ 1,000		=	0 + 0
(c)			+30,000	= +30,000 +	0
	99,000	+ 1,000	+30,000	= 30,000 +	100,000

$$\underbrace{130,000}_{\text{Assets}} = \underbrace{130,000}_{\text{Equities}}$$

We can now see how the property values (assets) of a hospitality firm can be determined at any point in time by adding the claims of creditors (liabilities) and the claims of owners (owners' equity) against these assets. It is also evident that at every step of the accounting process, the equality of the fundamental accounting equation is maintained.

We can now begin to understand why the fundamental accounting equation is the basis for the preparation of one of the basic financial statements—the balance sheet. The balance sheet is often referred to as "the position statement" because it reflects the financial position of a company at a single point in time. This statement includes the assets of the firm and the claims against those assets (liabilities and owners' equity) on a specific date. In the above illustration, the balance sheet of CB Motel as of June 3, 1987 would show the following information summarized according to the fundamental accounting equation:

CB MOTEL
Balance Sheet
June 3, 1987

Assets		Liabilities & Owner's Equity	
Cash	$ 99,000	Liabilities	
Housekeeping supplies		Accounts payable	$ 30,000
inventory	1,000	Owner's equity	
Furniture and equipment	30,000	Carlton Bober, capital	100,000
Total assets	$130,000	Total liabilities & owner's equity	$130,000

ILLUSTRATIVE PROBLEM

We continue analyzing the effect of typical transactions on the fundamental accounting equation by reviewing several transactions for a newly formed restaurant. These business transactions are events that affect the financial condition of the business. They are explained below and analyzed in Table 2.1.

Mr. David Ricardo and Ms. Lisa Montcalm formed a partnership, David and Lisa's Restaurant, which was engaged in several transactions during the first two weeks of operations. These transactions are presented on pp. 32 and 33. (Refer to Table 2.1 for the analysis of the effect of each of these transactions on the fundamental accounting equation.)

TABLE 2.1. Transaction Analysis for David and Lisa's Restaurant (Dates as Indicated)

Date, Feb., 1987	Transaction	Cash	Accounts receivable	Food inventory	Prepaid expenses	Land	Equipment	Accounts payable	Notes payable	Mortgages payable	Ricardo capital	Montcalm capital	Revenue/(expense)	
							Assets			**Liabilities**			**Owners' Equity**	
1.	Owners' invested cash	10,000									5,000	5,000		
2.	Borrowed $30,000 from bank	+30,000 / 40,000							+30,000 / 30,000		5,000	5,000		
3.	Paid one month's rent	−2,000 / 38,000							30,000		5,000	5,000	−2,000 / (2,000)	Rent expense
4.	Purchased food inventory on a COD basis	−2,000 / 36,000		+2,000 / 2,000					30,000		5,000	5,000		
5.	Sales for first week	+500 / 36,500	+500 / 500	2,000					30,000		5,000	5,000	(2,000) +1,000 / (1,000)	Food sales
6.	Prepaid beverage license fee	−1,200 / 35,300	500	2,000	+1,200 / 1,200				30,000		5,000	5,000	(1,000)	
7.	Cost of food sold	35,300	500	−400 / 1,600	1,200				30,000		5,000	5,000	−400 / (1,400)	Cost of food sold
8.	Prepaid insurance premium	−2,400 / 32,900	500	1,600	+2,400 / 3,600				30,000		5,000	5,000	(1,400)	
9.	Purchased land	−2,000 / 30,900	500	1,600	3,600	+20,000 / 20,000			30,000	+18,000 / 18,000	5,000	5,000	(1,400)	
10.	Cash received for first week's credit card sales	+285 / 31,185	−300 / 200	1,600	3,600	20,000			30,000	18,000	5,000	5,000	−15 / (1,415)	Credit card fees
11.	Purchased kitchen equipment on account	31,185	200	1,600	3,600	20,000	+2,000 / 2,000	+2,000 / 2,000	30,000	18,000	5,000	5,000	(1,415)	
12.	Sales for second week	+1,200 / 32,385	+1,300 / 1,500	1,600	3,600	20,000	2,000	2,000	30,000	18,000	5,000	5,000	+2,500 / 1,085	Food sales
13.	Cost of food sold	32,385	1,500	−1,000 / 600	3,600	20,000	2,000	2,000	30,000	18,000	5,000	5,000	−1,000 / 85	Cost of food sold
	Closing balance	32,385	1,500	600	3,600	20,000	2,000	2,000	30,000	18,000	5,000	5,000		

Total assets: 60,085

Total liabilities and owners' equity: 60,085

1. Mr. Ricardo and Ms. Montcalm invested $5,000 each to start David and Lisa's Restaurant. The total investment of $10,000 is deposited in a bank account opened in the name of the restaurant. The asset (cash) and the owners' equity are increased.

2. A bank loan of $30,000 is negotiated and the proceeds of the loan are deposited in the organization's bank account. A note is issued by the bank calling for annual interest of 12%. An asset (cash) increases and a liability (notes payable) also increases.

3. A lease is signed, for a fully equipped building for two years, with the right to renew for two additional years. The annual cost is $24,000, payable monthly in advance. The first month's rent ($2,000) is paid. An asset (cash) decreases and an expense (rent expense) increases, causing a corresponding indirect decrease in owners' equity.

4. Food inventory is purchased for $2,000. Supplies require cash payment by new accounts, and so payment is collect on delivery (COD). An asset (food inventory) is received in exchange for another asset (cash).

5. Sales for the first week were $1,000: $500 in cash, $300 paid by credit cards, and $200 on open account. Assets (cash and accounts receivable) increased and revenues (food sales) increased, resulting in an indirect increase in owners' equity. Accounts receivable reflects the future value received by the restaurant in the form of the customer's understanding to pay for the food and services received when due, according to the applicable credit terms.

6. A beverage license application is filed. The year's fee is $1,200 payable with the application. Since David and Lisa's Restaurant is making an advance payment for an item having a future value to the business (the right to sell alcoholic beverages for the specified time period), they are acquiring an asset. This type of asset is commonly referred to as a prepaid expense because payment is made before the expense is incurred. It will become an ordinary expense gradually as its benefits are consumed by the restaurant in the generation of revenues, which will occur as the license expires during the course of the year. Consequently, this transaction results in one asset (prepaid expenses) being exchanged for another asset (cash).

7. Food costing $400 was consumed in making the sales for the first week. An asset (food inventory) is decreased and expenses (cost of food sold) increased due to the consumption of the food in producing the aforementioned sales. The increase in expenses will cause an indirect decrease in owners' equity inasmuch as expenses decrease owners' equity.

8. David and Lisa's Restaurant purchased a two-year fire insurance and liability policy for $2,400, paying cash. Again, the business has acquired a future value—two-year insurance protection—by making an advance payment. Thus, the insurance protection bought with the $2,400 premium is an asset that falls within the previously described asset category of prepaid expenses. Consequently, one asset (prepaid expenses) is exchanged for another asset (cash).

9. The partners agree to purchase a future building site. The cost is $20,000. They pay $2,000 down and give a 10-year, 15% mortgage for the balance. One asset (land) increases, another asset (cash) decreases for the cash paid out, and a liability (mortgages payable) increases as a result of the written promise to repay the mortgage loan in 10 years.

10. The credit card company sends a $285 check in payment for credit card sales during the first week ($300). The remaining $15 is the 5% fee the

2. Prepare a balance sheet for Handy Andy's fast-food parlor at August 31, 1985 from the following accounts (Andrew Runn is the owner of the company):

Andrew Runn's capital	$87,000	Land	$40,000
Taxes payable	5,000	Prepaid expenses	4,000
Accounts receivable	15,000	Cash	10,000
Notes payable	25,000	Accounts payable	22,000
Equipment	10,000	Building	98,000
Inventory	12,000	Mortgage payable	50,000

3. State whether each of the following can be used as conclusive evidence that the company is earning a profit. Explain.
   (a) Increase in total assets.
   (b) Increase in accounts receivable.
   (c) Increase in owner's equity.
   (d) Increase in net income.
   (e) Increase in cash.

4. A company has the following assets and liabilities at the beginning of the year:

Assets	$430,000
Liabilities	$280,000

Calculate assets, liabilities, and owners' equity after taking into account the following transactions:
(a) A liability of $10,000 was paid off.
(b) Kitchen equipment worth $25,000 was exchanged for vehicles worth $25,000.
(c) The owner deposited $30,000 in the company's bank account.
(d) The company earned $50,000.
(e) The company purchased equipment for $20,000 in cash plus a note payable of $23,000.

5. Give an example of a transaction that might have the following effect:
   (a) Increase owners' equity and decrease a liability.
   (b) Decrease an asset and decrease a liability.
   (c) Decrease owners' equity and decrease an asset.
   (d) Increase one asset and decrease another asset.
   (e) Increase an asset and increase a liability.

PROBLEMS

1. (a) Prepare a schedule similar to the one in Table 2.1. Use multicolumn accounting paper. Create accounts as needed, placing the name of each account at the head of a column. Then list the following transactions of the Carlton Beach Amusement Park, owned by Mr. Frank Carlton, indicating the effect of each transaction in the appropriate columns. If a transaction has no effect on the account listed in a column, enter a zero in that column.
   (1) Mr. Carlton invests $50,000 in cash and $30,000 in equipment.
   (2) The amusement park sells $15,000 worth of tickets for cash.
   (3) Salaries of $3,000 are paid.
   (4) Rent in the amount of $1,000 is paid.
   (5) A new ride is purchased for $25,000; of this amount $15,000 is paid in cash and a note payable is signed for the balance.
   (6) A $6,000 electricity invoice was received. It will be paid next month.
   (7) A $500 invoice for water was received and paid.
   (8) Tour tickets worth $3,000 are sold on credit.
   (9) Two old cars worth a total of $6,000 are exchanged for an air conditioner for the Funny House.
   (10) Office supplies worth $500 are purchased for cash; half will be consumed this period.
   (11) Advertising worth $1,000 was purchased, half in cash and half on account.

(12) Mr. Carlton withdraws $2,500.

(13) Invoices for $3,500 are paid by the amusement park.

(14) A $3,600 invoice for a full year's insurance policy ($300 per month) was received and paid.

(15) Accounts receivable worth $2,000 were collected.

(16) The $10,000 note payable in (5) expired and was renewed.

(b) Prepare a balance sheet for the Carlton Beach Amusement Park.

2. Below are pictured several balance sheets of the Tastee Bun Hamburger Stand, a sole proprietorship organized by John Carland on September 1, 1985. Describe the original transactions and subsequent changes reflected in the following balance sheets.

(a) September 1, 1985

Assets		Liabilities & Owner's Equity	
Cash	$40,000	Liabilities	
Equipment	20,000	Notes payable	$15,000
		Total liabilities	15,000
		Owner's equity	
		John Carland's capital	45,000
		Total owner's equity	45,000
Total assets	$60,000	Total liabilities & owner's equity	$60,000

(b) September 4, 1985

Assets		Liabilities & Owner's Equity	
Cash	$ 15,000	Liabilities	
Land	50,000	Notes payable	$15,000
Building	80,000	Mortgages payable	100,000
Equipment	20,000	Total liabilities	115,000
		Owner's equity	
		John Carland's capital	50,000
		Total owner's equity	50,000
Total assets	$165,000	Total liabilities & owner's equity	$165,000

(c) September 8, 1985

Assets		Liabilities & Owner's Equity	
Cash	$ 15,000	Liabilities	
Inventory	9,000	Accounts payable	$ 9,000
Land	50,000	Notes payable	15,000
Building	80,000	Mortgages payable	100,000
Equipment	20,000	Total liabilities	124,000
		Owner's equity	
		John Carland's capital	50,000
		Total owner's equity	50,000
Total assets	$174,000	Total liabilities & owner's equity	$174,000

(d) September 12, 1985

Assets		Liabilities & Owner's Equity	
Cash	$ 20,000	Liabilities	
Accounts receivable	10,000	Accounts payable	$ 9,000
Inventory	2,000	Notes payable	15,000
Land	50,000	Mortgages payable	100,000
Building	80,000	Total liabilities	124,000
Equipment	20,000	Owner's equity	
		John Carland's capital	58,000
		Total owner's equity	58,000
Total assets	$182,000	Total liabilities & owner's equity	$182,000

(e) September 17, 1985

Assets		Liabilities & Owner's Equity	
Cash	$ 15,000	Liabilities	
Accounts receivable	10,000	Accounts payable	$ 9,000
Inventory	2,000	Notes payable	15,000
Land	50,000	Mortgages payable	100,000
Building	80,000	Total liabilities	124,000
Equipment	20,000	Owner's equity	
		John Carland's capital	53,000
		Total owner's equity	53,000
Total assets	$177,000	Total liabilities & owner's equity	$177,000

(f) September 25, 1985

Assets		Liabilities & Owner's Equity	
Cash	$ 8,000	Liabilities	
Accounts receivable	10,000	Accounts payable	$ 7,000
Inventory	2,000	Notes payable	10,000
Land	50,000	Mortgages payable	100,000
Building	80,000	Total liabilities	117,000
Equipment	20,000	Owner's equity	
		John Carland's capital	53,000
		Total owner's equity	53,000
Total assets	$170,000	Total liabilities & owner's equity	$170,000

(g) September 27, 1985

Assets		Liabilities & Owner's Equity	
Cash	$ 13,000	Liabilities	
Accounts receivable	5,000	Accounts payable	$ 7,000
Inventory	2,000	Notes payable	10,000
Land	50,000	Mortgages payable	100,000
Building	80,000	Total liabilities	117,000
Equipment	20,000	Owner's equity	
		John Carland's capital	53,000
		Total owner's equity	53,000
Total assets	$170,000	Total liabilities & owner's equity	$170,000

(h) September 30, 1985

Assets		Liabilities & Owner's Equity	
Cash	$ 10,000	Liabilities	
Accounts receivable	5,000	Accounts payable	$ 9,000
Inventory	7,000	Notes payable	10,000
Land	50,000	Mortgages payable	100,000
Building	80,000	Total liabilities	119,000
Equipment	20,000	Owner's equity	
		John Carland's capital	53,000
		Total owner's equity	53,000
Total assets	$172,000	Total liabilities & owner's equity	$172,000

3. Explain each of the transactions in the table on the next page using the identifying letters in the left-hand column. If there is more than one possible explanation, state them all. Then prepare a simple balance sheet from this worksheet.

		Assets			Liabilities	Owner's equity
	Cash	Accounts receivable	Inventories	Property & equipment	Accounts payable	Smith's capital
(a)	+55,000	0	0	+15,000		+70,000
(b)	−40,000	0	0	+60,000	+20,000	0
	15,000	0	0	75,000	20,000	70,000
(c)	+5,000	+5,000	0	0	0	+10,000
	20,000	5,000	0	75,000	20,000	80,000
(d)	−5,000	0	+15,000	0	+10,000	0
	15,000	5,000	15,000	75,000	30,000	80,000
(e)	−5,000	0	0	0	−5,000	0
	10,000	5,000	15,000	75,000	25,000	80,000
(f)	+15,000	0	0	0	0	+15,000
	25,000	5,000	15,000	75,000	25,000	95,000
(g)	0	0	−8,000	0	0	−8,000
	25,000	5,000	7,000	75,000	25,000	87,000
(h)	+3,000	−3,000	0	0	0	0
	28,000	2,000	7,000	75,000	25,000	87,000
(i)	−5,000	0	0	0	0	−5,000
	23,000	2,000	7,000	75,000	25,000	82,000
(j)	+15,000	0	0	−15,000	0	0
	38,000	2,000	7,000	60,000	25,000	82,000

4. John Fisher graduated from Florida International University School of Hospitality Management. Upon graduation John decided to start a take-out restaurant. In the process of doing this he executed the transactions listed below.
   (a) Prepare a schedule similar to the one in Table 2.1. Create accounts as needed on multicolumn accounting paper by placing the name of each account at the head of a column. List the following transactions on this schedule, indicating the effect of each transaction in the appropriate columns. If a transaction has no effect on the account listed in a column, enter a zero.
      (1) As the initial investment in the company John Fisher deposited $150,000 in the company's bank account.
      (2) The company purchased $5,000 worth of food and beverages for future consumption. The purchase was made with 20% cash and 80% credit.
      (3) The company purchased equipment for $2,000 cash.
      (4) The company purchased land for $40,000 and a building for $90,000, by making a $30,000 down payment and signing a mortgage note payable in the amount of $100,000 for the balance
      (5) Sales during the first week were $5,000, all cash.
      (6) Food and beverages worth $1,500 were consumed in making these sales.
      (7) Office supplies worth $300 were purchased for cash.
      (8) Paid salaries in the amount of $600.
      (9) Received an invoice for water of $50 and paid on the same day.
      (10) Received the electricity invoice for $200, but did not pay it immediately.
      (11) Sold $1,500 worth of food and beverages to a local business on credit.
      (12) Consumed $500 worth of food and beverages in making the above sale.
      (13) Paid $2,000 of invoices that were due.
      (14) Took advantage of a discount price and paid a trash collection fee of $1,200 for the entire year. At the time this amount was recorded, one month's service had already been received.
      (15) Collected $750 on previous credit sales.
      (16) John Fisher withdrew $1,000 from the company's bank account for his personal use.
   (b) Prepare a balance sheet for the restaurant.

3

Measuring Business Income:
Basic Concepts

As we know, the income statement reports upon the profitability of a business entity for a specified period of time. It is used to convey to hospitality management and other interested parties whether or not the firm achieved its principal objective—that of earning a profit for its owners. Accordingly, the income statement is considered a primary report of most importance to all financial statement users, especially management, since it shows the progress of the organization during a particular period of time.

The income statement, the main focus of which is the measurement of business income, summarizes the revenues earned and the expenses incurred during the period as the basis for determining net income. Net income is the difference between revenues earned and expenses incurred during the stated period. A net loss results if expenses exceed revenues.

In Chapter 2, we discussed seven basic accounting concepts related principally to the preparation of the balance sheet. The purpose of this chapter is to explain the remaining five basic accounting concepts, those most directly related to the measurement of business income. They serve as guidelines for the proper recognition of revenues and expenses and thus are emphasized in the preparation of the second basic financial statement—the income statement.

We first discuss the measurement of business income through analysis of its main components, namely, revenues and expenses. Then we cover the five associated basic accounting concepts:

1. Time period concept
2. Realization concept
3. Matching concept
4. Consistency concept
5. Materiality concept

In the course of our discussion, we shall point out how the accrual basis of accounting establishes the criteria for recognition of revenues and expenses and thus is of crucial importance in the measurement of business income. This chapter also deals with the cash basis and the tax basis of accounting for income.

Additionally, we illustrate a simple income statement format using the information provided by the transactional analysis problem presented in Chapter 2 (Table 2.1). Finally, a more complete income statement format adapted from APB Opinion No. 9 is presented as our authoritative source of GAAP. (More comprehensive information concerning the income statement appears in Chapter 12.)

THE MEASUREMENT OF BUSINESS INCOME

The measurement of business income is the main focus of the income statement, which summarizes revenues and expenses over a stated period of time. Hence, the determination of the point in time when each revenue and expense should be recognized and the allowable amount of revenue and expense are of crucial importance in determining the net income or net loss for the period. In order to establish guidelines for recognizing revenues and expenses, we must examine the characteristics of revenues and expenses in greater detail.

The prime objective of a hospitality firm is to earn a profit (net income) for its owners, thereby providing an adequate return on the owners' investments in the business (return on investment, ROI). This objective is achieved primarily by providing services to its customers. A hotel firm offers lodging, food, and telephone services, among others; a restaurant provides a dining experience to its patrons; a club offers to its members the use of the swimming pool, tennis courts, golf courses, and so on. All these examples illustrate the revenues earned by hospitality-oriented organizations by providing services to customers. Consequently, when a company sells its services (or goods), assets (mainly cash or accounts receivable) are received by the company in exchange. As we already know, assets received in exchange for goods and services sold are called revenues. Revenues will result in a corresponding increase in net income and ultimately in owners' equity.

The hospitality firm has to use certain items in operating the business and providing the aforementioned services to its customers. These items represent the costs of doing business, or expenses, and include the cost of goods and services consumed (incurred) in generating revenues. For instance, a travel agency consumes the services of its employees (salary and wage expenses), the service of a utility company (electricity expense), and so on.

An income statement is prepared by listing the revenues earned during the period and the expenses incurred in earning those revenues during the same period. The basic accounting concepts relating to the measurement of income must serve as guidelines for the proper recognition of revenues and expenses, thereby ensuring accuracy and uniformity of income measurement.

TIME PERIOD CONCEPT

Even though business activities are considered to continue forever (in accordance with the going-concern concept discussed in Chapter 2), the income statement reports revenues, expenses, and resulting net income only for a convenient segment of time. The main reason for subdividing the life of an enterprise this way is to provide management and other users of accounting information with periodic reports that will serve as a basis on which to evaluate the firm's progress.

The segment of time selected to measure the results of operations of a hospitality organization is called the accounting period. It may cover one month, three months (a quarter), or one year, and represents the interval of time over which the transactions are recorded and summarized in order to prepare the basic financial statements, which is done at the end of the period. Whereas the balance sheet, as we saw, is prepared as of the last date of the accounting period, the income statement includes the business activity over the entire accounting period being reported on. Because of this, the income statement is considered a flow statement. For external reporting purposes, the accounting period is usually one year, which may or may not coincide with the calendar year. When a 12-month period other than a calendar year is used, it is called a fiscal year. Usually when a fiscal year accounting period is selected, it is based on an entity's natural business year. A natural business year ends when business activity is at its lowest point, thereby facilitating the measurement of business income.

Accounting statements for periods shorter than one year are called interim statements and are used primarily for internal management information purposes. Many hotels and restaurants prepare monthly and/or quarterly interim statements. Also, publicly held companies (those owned by the general public) are required to submit quarterly statements to the SEC in addition to their annual reports.

In sum, the time period concept states that the results of operations will be measured over specific intervals of time.

THE REALIZATION CONCEPT

The realization concept dictates the recognition of revenue. It requires that revenue be recognized at the time it is earned, which generally occurs when a sale of a product is made (formally, when title to goods is transferred) or services are rendered: "Recognition is the process of formally recording or incorporating an item in the financial statements of an entity."[1]

Based on the realization concept, the receipt of cash is not a determining factor in the recognition of revenues. Revenues are to be assigned to the accounting period in which they are earned, regardless of when cash is actually collected. For instance, the sale of a hotel room on credit terms (on account) will be recognized as revenue by the hotel in the period when the customer receives the services, as opposed to the period when cash is actually collected. When the hotel customer pays the amount due (at some future date), the amount collected is not considered revenue, but is treated instead as an exchange of two assets (a decrease in accounts receivable and an increase in cash).

In practice, the moment when revenue must be recognized is often called the point of sale and is subject to the following conditions:

- The earning process is essentially complete.
- Its exchange value can be objectively determined.

Based on the realization principle, revenues received in advance may not be recognized in the current period. Customers' deposits, for example, do not fulfill the requirements for revenue recognition since the earnings process is not essentially complete. Thus, when a hotel receives a deposit to be applied against a future reservation, the deposit does not represent revenue, but is considered unearned income (deferred income) since services have not yet been rendered. It represents an increase in assets (cash) and liabilities (unearned income). When the customer applies a deposit to an actual room rental, then and only then will the revenue be recognized by the hotel.

Occasionally, problems arise in applying the realization concept to practical situations. One typical example of a difficult revenue recognition situation in

[1]Financial Accounting Standards Board, *Statement of Financial Accounting Concepts No. 3,* "Elements of Financial Statements of Business Enterprises" (Dec. 1980), Par. 83.

the hospitality industry is accounting for franchise fee revenue. Generally, the sale of a franchise results in the receipt by the hotel or restaurant chain of an initial fee plus a percentage of annual gross revenue over the life of the franchise in exchange for granting certain rights and performing specified services such as assistance in site selection or supervision of construction activity. The initial fee may call for a down payment at the time of signing the franchise agreement and the balance in equal installments over a specified future period. In deciding when the initial fee revenue should be recognized, several alternatives are available:

1. When the cash is received (cash basis)
2. At the inception of the franchise (when the agreement is signed)
3. Spread over the life of the franchise agreement
4. When substantial performance has occurred.

Current accounting authorities require alternative (4), which normally has taken place when the franchise begins operation. This alternative seems to fulfill the revenue recognition criteria better than the others based on the assumption that the earnings process is virtually complete when a franchisee opens for business.

MATCHING CONCEPT—THE ACCRUAL BASIS OF ACCOUNTING

The matching concept deals with the recognition of expenses. Just as revenues are to be recognized when earned (the realization concept), the matching concept calls for expenses to be recognized when consumed (incurred) in the process of generating revenues. Furthermore, expenses are to be matched (offset) against the revenues they helped produce during each accounting period. As with revenues, expenses are recognized when incurred, regardless of whether or not cash is paid out. Salaries and wages, for example, are recognized as expenses in the period the employee services are received, even though this might not be the same period in which payment for those services is made.

Although expenses recognition will normally follow revenue recognition, as noted earlier, some problems do occur in determining when certain revenues are to be recognized. Furthermore, it may also be difficult to determine exactly which expenses have been incurred in producing revenues in a given accounting period. This means that perfect matching is quite difficult to achieve. Nonetheless, it is essential to match revenues and expenses over time in order to ensure the proper measurement of periodic business income.

In the process of recognizing expenses, one of the problems encountered is that not all costs can be directly assigned to specific revenues. Some expenses may only have an indirect relationship with revenues. Three different standards can be applied to determine whether an expense should be recognized in the current period, as follows:

1. The expense is directly associated with revenues of the period.
2. The expense is directly associated with the accounting period itself.
3. The expense cannot be associated with the revenues of future periods.

Use of the first standard for recognizing expenses implies a direct relationship between expenses and revenues. This direct relationship may also be considered causal in nature. For instance, a commission paid by a hotel for a particular booking should be reported as an expense in the same period that the revenue from the room sale is reported.

Use of the second standard relates to the recognition of expenses that are not directly associated with specific revenue transactions but have contributed to the earning of revenues in general. Thus, they are said to be "costs of doing business." General and administrative costs such as general insurance or professional fees may not be directly associated with any one sale during the period. Nevertheless, these expenses are essential to the operation of the hospitality service firm. Some of these expenses may benefit several accounting periods and may therefore require allocation to the periods that they benefit. For example, an annual insurance premium paid in advance (prepaid insurance) must be allocated as an expense to the monthly periods that it benefits. We cover the systematic allocation of these costs in later chapters.

Use of the third standard for recognizing expenses implies that even though an expense does not produce a benefit in the current accounting period, it is reported as an expense simply because it cannot be associated with the revenue of future periods. In other words, there is an immediate recognition of a *de facto* consumption of an item that does not benefit the current or future periods. The expensing of spoiled food held in inventory is an example of the immediate recognition of an expense that cannot be associated with revenues of the current or future periods. Assets (food inventory) have been consumed (spoiled) without producing revenues since the food cannot be sold in the current or future periods.

Application of the matching concept in the measurement of income is at the heart of the accrual basis of accounting. The determination of periodic business income is based upon the proper matching of expenses incurred during the period against the revenues they help earn. The process of expense recognition can also be visualized in terms of offsetting efforts (expenses) against the rewards (revenues) of the period. This results in the determination of business success (net income) or failure (net loss) for the specified period of time.

CONSISTENCY CONCEPT

The consistency concept requires an entity to give the same accounting treatment to similar events in successive accounting periods. Only when this concept is applied can meaningful comparisons be made between periods. Consistent application of accounting methods and procedures increases the usefulness of financial statements to a firm by facilitating the identification of trends within the firm.

It should be noted that consistent application of accounting methods and procedures does not, in and of itself, allow comparisons among different firms. Diversity in utilizing accounting methods and procedures is acceptable among different firms as long as the methods and procedures used are compatible with GAAP. Within each individual firm, however, consistency in their application is imperative.

The concept of consistency does not, however, preclude all changes in accounting methods and procedures. If there is good reason for changing procedures it should be done. Such changes may be needed to adapt to a changing environment or to conform to new pronouncements of the FASB or the SEC. If a change is deemed necessary, however, the responsibility for justifying it lies with management: "The nature of and justification for a change in accounting principle and its effect on net income should be disclosed in the financial statements of the period in which the change is made. The justification for the change should explain clearly why the newly adopted accounting principle is preferable."[2]

Changes in accounting methods and procedures should therefore not be taken lightly.

MATERIALITY CONCEPT

Accounting only deals with significant information—there is no reason to be concerned with what is not important. Therefore insignificant items are not considered in applying the basic accounting concepts. To determine materiality, the size of an item must be considered in relation to the size of the business (i.e., within the economic environment of the firm). An item that is material to one firm may not be material to another.

Consider the following example: A travel agency acquires 20 pencils at a cost of $3 for use in its office. In theory, the acquisition of these items represents an acquired future value (an asset). However, since the amount is considered insignificant, the $3 would be charged to current operations (expensed) and would be included on the income statement of the period as part of miscellaneous expenses. This concept permits a firm to account for amounts that it considers immaterial, in the most efficient and economic manner, rather than the one that is most theoretically correct.

Management is responsible for determining materiality. The decision of what is and what is not material calls for the exercise of judgment and common sense, within the context of a particular firm. Therefore, the relative importance of any event must be evaluated in relation to the firm where it occurs, and this requires prudent judgment.

Expensing $2,000 worth of miscellaneous equipment may be considered immaterial for a very large publicly held company such as McDonald's Corporation. The same amount, however, would be considered material for a small restaurant or hotel and should be recorded as an asset.

OTHER CONCEPTS OF INCOME MEASUREMENT

The accrual basis is considered the most accurate basis of income determination since it provides for the matching of revenues during each accounting period. This accounting method conforms to GAAP, but other bases of income determination are also encompassed by GAAP in certain circumstances. We discuss two of these here: the cash basis of accounting and the tax basis of income determination.

[2]American Institute of Certified Public Accountants, *Accounting Principles Board Opinion No. 20*, "Accounting Changes" (July 1971), Par. 17.

Cash Basis of Accounting

Under the cash basis of accounting, revenues are recognized and recorded only when cash is received (cash revenues), while expenses are recognized only when payment is made (cash expenses). Although the cash basis is generally considered unacceptable for financial reporting purposes, it might be permissible for certain small businesses that do in fact operate primarily on the cash basis. For example, a small restaurant selling for cash only (no credit sales) and paying wages and supplies with cash may use the cash basis instead of the accrual basis.

Obviously, the cash basis of accounting is far simpler than the accrual basis. All that needs to be recorded and reported on the statement of income are the excess of cash receipts over cash disbursements representing the cash basis income for the period. Nonetheless, the cash basis of accounting is only permitted by GAAP when revenues and expenses materially coincide with cash receipts and cash payments.

Tax Basis of Income Measurement

Income measured for tax purposes is governed by regulations established principally by the U.S. Congress, the tax courts, and the Internal Revenue Service. The goals of these regulations are significantly different from the goals of financial reporting based on GAAP. These regulations are based on the tax code, which has been influenced by political pressures, court decisions, and sound public policy. The purpose of the tax code is to provide different legal methods of calculating net income for the payment of taxes, not all of which are compatible with GAAP, but that encourage taxpayers to behave in ways that are beneficial to the country socially or economically.

While net income is determined by the proper application of GAAP, taxable income is based on the tax code. Taxable income, as shown on a tax return filed with the government, may not agree with earnings before taxes as reported on a hospitality firm's income statement. For example, the interest earned on municipal bonds is included as revenue for the purpose of calculating net income. However, it is excluded from revenues when calculating taxable income because the tax code exempts from taxation all interest paid by municipalities on the money they borrow. The impact of the tax code on various financial aspects of a firm will be discussed in later chapters.

ILLUSTRATIVE INCOME STATEMENT

The information used in the transactional analysis for David and Lisa's hypothetical restaurant (Table 2.1) will be used again here to demonstrate how an income statement can be prepared. In the process of doing so, the effect of revenue and expenses on owners' equity will be considered in order to understand why these income statement elements are subdivisions of owners' equity.

Although we illustrated the preparation of the balance sheet in Chapter 2 by directly referring to the transactional analysis worksheet, in practice the income statement is normally prepared first. It is necessary first to calculate the amount of net income (revenues less expenses), which is then added to the beginning owners' equity. By adding net income to beginning owners' equity we calculate the amount of owners' equity at the end of the accounting period covered by the income statement.

In Table 2.1, revenues are indicated by a plus (+) sign and expenses are indicated by a minus (−) sign based on the fact that revenues increase owners' equity whereas expenses have the effect of decreasing it. Accordingly, net income will increase owners' equity; on the other hand, net loss will decrease owners' equity.

The income statement for David and Lisa's Restaurant is shown below:

DAVID AND LISA'S RESTAURANT
Income Statement
For the Period Ended February 13, 1987

Revenues		
Food sales		$3,500
Total revenues		3,500
Expenses		
Cost of food sold	$1,400	
Rent	2,000	
Credit card fees	15	
Total expenses		3,415
Net income		$ 85

COMPREHENSIVE INCOME STATEMENT ILLUSTRATION

The income statement for David and Lisa's Restaurant is an oversimplified version of an actual income statement. A more comprehensive income statement is presented in Figure 3.1, based on an adaptation of the illustrative income statement format included in APB Opinion No. 9. (The income statement will be covered in greater depth in Chapter 12.)

BB HOSPITALITY COMPANY
Statement of Income
Years Ended December 31, 1985 and 1984

	1985	1984
Revenues		
Net sales	$84,600	$75,600
Other income	80	100
Total revenues	84,680	75,700
Costs and expenses		
Cost of goods sold	20,000	16,000
Operating, general, and administrative expenses	45,000	42,000
Interest expense	1,000	800
Other deductions	100	70
Income tax	5,400	4,130
Total costs and expenses	71,500	63,000
Net income	$13,180	$12,700

Figure 3.1. Example of a comprehensive income statement.
Source: Adapted from APB Opinion No. 9, p. 134, December, 1966.

Comments: In Figure 3.1, the presentation of two successive years (1985 and 1984) permits a comparison of the company's performance between years, and thus enhances the use of financial statements for decision-making purposes. Note also that the income tax is considered an expense of doing business for the corporate form of legal organization, which will be discussed in Chapter 4, and is the most prevalent form of business organization in the United States. Some of the factors to be taken into account in calculating income taxes as well as alternative ways of showing income tax on the income statement will be covered in later chapters.

QUESTIONS

1. What is the purpose of the income statement?
2. List the basic accounting concepts that are most applicable to the income statement.
3. What is the name of the segment of time selected for measuring results of operations? What is the standard length of time period for external reporting purposes?
4. Why is the income statement considered a flow statement?
5. What is an interim statement?
6. Is every cash receipt a revenue? Is every cash expenditure an expense? Explain.
7. Does the consistency concept mean that all firms must use the same GAAP in preparing their financial reports? Explain.
8. What is the most important factor in determining whether or not a specific amount is material?
9. What is income before taxes called when it is calculated according to the Internal Revenue Code?
10. How do we calculate owners' equity at the end of the accounting period?
11. How does net income affect owners' equity? How does a net loss affect owners' equity? Explain.
12. How does the matching concept relate to the realization concept?

EXERCISES

1. Prepare an income statement based on the following items:

Rent expense	$ 100	Supplies expense	$ 55
Insurance	50	Payroll expense	200
Utilities	90	Laundry expense	45
Sales	1,100	Cost of food sold	350
Interest expense	55	Interest income	90

2. Below is given the amount of Carl Rahn's (the owner) capital at the beginning and end of an accounting period. Subsequently certain transactions are presented that occurred during the period. Explain the effect of these transactions on owner's equity.

Beginning owner's equity	$1,235
Ending owner's equity	$2,466

(a) The company purchased a refrigerator for $560 cash.
(b) Carl Rahn took home the old refrigerator, which was recorded on the books of the company at $300 but had a current resale value of $350.
(c) Carl Rahn deposited $1,000 in cash in the company's bank account. The company signed a note promising to pay it back in 6 months.

   (d) Carl Rahn withdrew $250 from the company's bank account for his own
       personal use.
   (e) Carl Rahn brought a new sign he had at home to the business for its exclusive
       use. The sign had a current market value of $1,400.
   (f) Carl Rahn invested an additional $1,000 in the business.
   (g) The company borrowed $10,000 to buy land.
   (h) The company reflected a $619 loss from operations during the period.
3. The following is an abbreviated balance sheet for the Cargill Restaurant, which
   is owned and operated by Fred Cargill:

Assets		Liabilities & Owner's Equity	
Food and beverage inventories	$150,000	Liabilities	
		Notes payable	$100,000
		Owner's equity	
		Fred Cargill's capital	50,000
Total assets	$150,000	Total liabilities & owner's equity	$150,000

   If the restaurant sold all of its food and beverage inventories for
   (a) $100,000
   (b) $150,000
   (c) $200,000
   what would its balance sheet and income statement look like, assuming there
   were no other transactions?
4. (a) What basis of accounting is the statement below structured upon?
   (b) Could it be used as an income statement for the month of March? Explain.
   (c) Convert the statement into an income statement and explain what changes
       you made.

SOLE BROTHERS FISH RESTAURANT
Statement of Cash Receipts and Expenditures
For the Month Ending March 1988

Receipts	
Cash sales	$181,000
Collections on credit sales	17,500
Owners' investment	6,000
Total receipts	204,500
Expenditures	
Inventory purchases (cash)	$180,000
Owners' withdrawals	3,000
Payment of accounts payable	15,000
Payroll expense	55,000
Utilities expense (including a $1,000 deposit)	2,500
Rent for March, April, May, current year	3,000
Total expenditures	258,500
Excess of expenditures over receipts	($ 54,000)

   Note: Credit sales during March amounted to $32,000, and $65,000 of inventory
was consumed during the month.
5. A balance sheet for the Far Away Travel Agency as of July 1, 1989 is presented at
   the top of the following page. The travel agency is a partnership business owned
   equally by Mark and Claudia Ferguson.

FAR AWAY TRAVEL AGENCY
Balance Sheet
As of July 1, 1989

Assets		Liabilities & Owners' Equity	
Cash	$ 11,656	Liabilities	
Accounts receivable	46,209	Accounts payable	$ 3,313
Advertising and office supplies	5,348	Mortgage payable	115,000
Prepaid expenses	2,000	Total liabilities	118,313
Property and equipment	132,300	Owners' equity	
Deposits	800	M. Ferguson capital	40,000
		C. Ferguson capital	40,000
		Total owners' equity	80,000
Total assets	$198,313	Total liabilities & owners' equity	$198,313

(a) Prepare a balance sheet and income statement reflecting the following transactions for the month of July.

July 1 Mark and Claudia Ferguson each invested an additional $10,000 in the business.

3 The agency purchased $3,210 worth of advertising brochures on account. One half of these new brochures were consumed during the month of July.

15 Commission earned amounted to $10,500. No payments on these commissions were received during July.

16 Collections on accounts receivable amounted to $29,000.

18 July rent of $1,000 for certain equipment had been paid in advance during June.

25 Utilities bills amounting to $980 were received but not paid.

28 Commissions of $4,675 were paid to others.

29 Accounts payable amounting to $1,671 were paid.

31 Salaries of $3,000 were paid.

(b) What wording will you use to specify the balance sheet and income statement dates? Why?

PROBLEMS

1. The balance sheet for the Marseille Restaurant, owned by Mr. N. D. Gestion, is presented below at May 1, 1987.

MARSEILLE RESTAURANT
Balance Sheet
As of May 1, 1987

Assets		Liabilities & Owner's Equity	
Cash	$ 20,000	Liabilities	
Accounts receivable	10,000	Accounts payable	$ 15,000
Inventory	5,000	Mortgages payable	120,000
Property & equipment	145,000	Total liabilities	135,000
		Owner's equity	
		N. D. Gestion's capital	45,000
Total assets	$180,000	Total liabilities & owner's equity	$180,000

(a) Head up a worksheet as follows:

Transcription description	Assets			Liabilities	Owner's equity	
	Cash	A/R	Inventory	A/P	Revenues	Expenses
Purchase inventory on credit			+1,000	+1,000		

(b) Indicate the effect of each of the following transactions on the basic accounting equation by completing the worksheet.

(c) Prepare a balance sheet as of May 31, 1988, and an income statement for the month of May 1988 for Marseille Restaurant.

   1. Purchased $1,000 of inventory on credit.
   2. Sales are made in the amount of $7,000, of which $3,000 are credit sales, the balance are cash sales.
   3. Inventory in the amount of $2,300 is consumed in making these sales.
   4. Collections on accounts receivable amounted to $6,000.
   5. Paid $1,000 for equipment rental.
   6. Received water invoice for $150.
   7. Paid payroll of $3,600.
   8. Received interest income of $200.
   9. Cash sales amounted to $6,000.
  10. Consumed $3,600 worth of inventory in making these sales.
  11. Purchased $3,000 of inventory, of which $500 is on account, the balance for cash.
  12. The electricity invoice for $280 is received and paid the same day.
  13. Supplies worth $50 are purchased and used the same day.
  14. Accounts payable in the amount of $5,000 are paid.
  15. A $500 invoice for the current month's insurance is received. It will be paid next month.

2. (a) Describe each of the transactions of the Ship's Hull Restaurant (owned by Mr. Hull) indicated in the table below and identified by number in the left-hand column.

(b) Prepare a balance sheet and income statement for the restaurant based on these transactions.

Note: Assume revenues are generated by food sales.

| Assets | | Liabilities | | Owner's equity | | | |
| | | | | Capital | Revenue | Expenses | |
Name	Amount	Name	Amount			Name	Amount
1. Cash	+20,000			+20,000			
2. Equipment	+30,000						
Cash	−10,000	Notes payable	+20,000				
3. Land & building	+130,000	Mortgages payable	+100,000	+30,000			
4. Inventory	+20,000						
Cash	−10,000	Accounts payable	+10,000				
5. Cash	+15,000				+30,000		
Accounts receivable	+15,000						
6. Inventory	−9,000					Cost of sales	+9,000
7. Cash	−8,000					Payroll	+8,000
8.		Accounts payable	+1,000			Utilities	+1,000
9. Prepaid rent	+2,000						
Cash	−2,000						
10. Cash	+3,000	Unearned revenue	+3,000				
11. Cash	−4,000	Accounts payable	−4,000				

| | Assets | | Liabilities | | Owner's equity | | | |
| | | | | | Capital | Revenue | Expenses | |
Name	Amount	Name	Amount			Name	Amount
12. Cash	+7,000						
Accounts receivable	−7,000						
13.		Accounts payable	+500			Supplies	+500
14.		Accounts payable	+800			Laundry	+800
15. Equipment	−5,000						
Cash	+2,000	Notes payable	−3,000				
16. Cash	−2,500			−2,500			
Totals (1–16)	+186,500		+128,300	+47,500	+30,000		−19,300

3. Head up a sheet of paper as indicated below and record the following transactions by adding or subtracting them in the appropriate columns. Place the name of the asset, liability, or owner's equity item for which you are making an entry in the column headed "name" and the letter representing the transaction in the column marked "transaction." Then prepare a balance sheet and income statement reflecting the results of these transactions.

	Assets		Liabilities		Owner's equity	
Transaction	Name	Amount	Name	Amount	Name	Amount

(a) Jim Stiel, the owner, invests $20,000 in cash in his catering business—Jim Stiel's Catering. He also contributes a refrigerator, with a market value of $600, to the business.

(b) The business entity paid the rent for the building it occupies. It has a one-year lease. A payment of $500 for the current month and another payment of $500 for the twelfth month was made.

(c) Purchased supplies for $200 on credit.

(d) Borrowed $1,000 from the bank against a note payable.

(e) Rendered catering services amounting to $7,000, of which 40% of the sales are credit sales, the remainder cash sales.

(f) Purchased food and beverages worth $5,000 on account.

(g) Consumed $3,000 from food and beverage inventory in making the sales specified in (e).

(h) Consumed 50% of the supplies purchased in (c) in the current accounting period.

(i) Paid payroll of $2,200.

(j) Received water invoice for $150.

(k) Jim Stiel withdraws $800 in cash for his personal use.

(l) Received and paid an electricity invoice for $280.

(m) Collected $1,600 of the accounts receivable.

(n) Paid $2,100 of the accounts payable.

(o) Paid $200 of the notes payable.

(p) Jim Stiel withdraws $1,500 for his personal use.

4. Indicate the basic accounting concept(s) applicable in each of the following situations. Explain the reason why the transaction might not be properly recorded.

(a) Land is recorded at $100,000, what it cost 10 years ago, even though its current market value is $300,000.

(b) A motel owner gave her manager a $200 petty cash fund to cover cash expenditures but failed to determine how much of these funds had been spent when she prepared the financial statements.

(c) A travel agency pays two months' rent in advance and records the entire payment as "rent expense."

(d) A hotel owner has decided to liquidate his hotel and requests his accountant to record the hotel's assets on the balance sheet at their current market value.

(e) Food and beverage inventory purchased for $7,000 last year is now worth only $5,000. The accountant tells the restaurant manager that she must mark it down by $2,000 on the company's accounting books.

(f) Joe Mix has two cars that belong to him. He wants to include them in the balance sheet of his Mix'em-Up Restaurant Company so that it will appear the company has more assets.

(g) A catering contract was signed by a restaurant with a local tour bus company. The owner of the restaurant requested his accountant to include some future sales from this catering contract in the restaurant's current income statement to improve corrent earnings.

(h) A hotel has extended credit to several guests and the invoices sent them are still unpaid. In the past the manager has never included the invoices as part of the hotel's sales until payment was received.

(i) The owner of a travel agency does not want to prepare formal financial statements even though it has been a year since the agency was created. The owner says she knows it is not doing well and so wants to postpone preparation of financial statements until results will be favorable.

(j) A large airline with $200 million in sales has customarily recorded equipment purchases of $1,000 or less as an expense. In order to avoid having to report a loss in the current period, management is considering changing this policy so that all equipment purchases above $200 will be included in the equipment asset account, and then switching back next year to the previous $1,000 cut-off amount.

Types of Business Organizations

Although accounting for assets and liabilities is basically the same in all forms of business organizations, there are major differences in the owners' equity section of the balance sheet for the main types of business enterprises. Furthermore, deciding which type of business organization is best for a particular hospitality firm entails a general understanding of the main features and characteristics of each, as well as a recognition of the many financial and legal implications, which will have a major impact upon the firm's basic purposes and aspirations.

The three common types of business organizations are the sole proprietorship, the partnership, and the corporation. Many small hotels, restaurants, and travel agencies are first organized as sole propriertorships or partnerships. Nevertheless, the corporate form predominates among businesses in the United States in terms of dollar volume. There might be fewer hospitality corporations, but they transact more business than all the partnerships and proprietorships combined.

The objective of this chapter is to identify and analyze the main characteristics of the three basic types of legal organization. We will start by discussing the sole propriertorship form of business organization. We do this by examining the main advantages and disadvantages of each and the major differences between them. We also illustrate the presentation of the owners' equity section of a balance sheet for all three types of business organization. Corporate accounting will receive more extensive and exclusive coverage in Chapter 17.

THE SOLE PROPRIETORSHIP

A sole proprietorship is a business owned by a single person. Typically, the individual proprietor originally finances the hotel or restaurant by using his or her personal savings, supplemented by bank or government loans.

The proprietorship form of legal organization is the simplest form of organization for a hospitality firm since no formal procedures are needed to establish the business. The owner/operator is only required to comply with specific state and/or local licensing laws in order to start selling goods and services to the public. The business entity itself generally has no reporting requirements separate and distinct from those incumbent upon the owner, nor does it have any limitations that the owner would not have. In view of the fact that there is but one owner, the sole proprietorship provides total control over resources and operations. All profits belong to the owner/proprietor, with no need to share them. Moreover, the total control held by the proprietor facilitates the decision-making process, since there is no need to deal with differences of opinion in day-to-day operations, and there are no co-owners to consult in establishing policies or making other business decisions.

The proprietorship is not in and of itself subject to taxation. However, the annual federal and state tax returns filed by the owner must include the income or loss from the business. Thus, the income tax rate applicable to the sole proprietorship is determined on the basis of the owner's total income from all sources and his or her total deductions.

The two principal disadvantages of sole proprietorships are limited life and the unlimited liability of the owner. Upon the death or retirement of the owner, the current business must be dissolved inasmuch as there are normally no provisions for the continuity of the business. Furthermore, unlimited liability makes the owner of a sole proprietorship personally liable for the firm's actions and debts. This means that the owner's personal assets are legally available to satisfy business debts.

Another disadvantage of a sole proprietorship is that it depends solely on its own operations and the financial capabilities of its owner. Since the sole proprietorship is an unincorporated business owned by one individual it becomes very hard to raise large amounts of capital.

As a result of these drawbacks it is almost impossible for a sole proprietorship to expand rapidly. It simply cannot obtain the large amounts of funds necessary for the rapid construction of new hotels, restaurants, and travel agencies or for the renovation of existing ones. It is very difficult for an organization with a limited life, whose assets may serve as collateral for the owner's other businesses, to borrow large sums of money.

ADVANTAGES AND DISADVANTAGES OF SOLE PROPRIETORSHIPS

To summarize, the principal advantages of the sole proprietorship form of legal organization are

1. *Ease of formation.*   Proprietorships are simple to establish since there is no need to comply with the federal and state laws applicable to partnerships and corporations.
2. *Control over operations.*   Because there are no co-owners, the owner/operator has complete control over daily operations, thereby speeding up the decision-making process.
3. *No sharing of profits.*   All the profits of the business belong only to the owner.
4. *Simplicity.*   Proprietorships are subject to less government regulations than partnerships and corporations.
5. *Taxation.*   A proprietorship's income is not subject to separate taxation. However, owners must include the applicable business income or losses in their personal tax returns. Since a corporation's income is taxed twice, once at the corporate level and again when dividends are paid, a sole proprietorship is usually more economical taxwise, if the owner does not wish to leave profits in the business.

The main disadvantages of the sole proprietorship are

1. *Limited life.*   Death or bankruptcy of the owner results in the dissolution of the business.
2. *Unlimited liability.*   The owner is personally liable for the firm's debts and actions.
3. *Difficulty in raising capital.*   Rapid expansion of proprietorship operations is very difficult to achieve because a sole proprietorship does not have access to large amounts of borrowed money or investment by other owners.

THE PARTNERSHIP

A partnership is "an association of two or more persons to carry on as co-owners a business for profit."[1] The partnership form is therefore owned by two or more persons called the partners. It is a somewhat more formal type of legal organization than the sole proprietorship, but much less formal than a corporation. Currently, it is extensively used by small hotels, restaurants, travel agencies, and other hospitality service companies that want to combine the managerial ability, hospitality industry experience, and capital of two or more persons.

While the partnership can be based on an oral understanding between partners, written agreements are highly recommended. The partnership agreement should include, as a minimum, the following:

- Name of partnership and business location
- Name of each partner
- Amount contributed by each partner
- Each partner's salary
- Procedures for dissolution of partnership
- Partnership duration, if applicable
- Procedure for division of profits and losses between partners

Like a proprietorship, a partnership is fairly simple to organize and is subject to few government regulations. It also has limited life. Death, bankruptcy, or withdrawal of a partner results in the dissolution of the business. Similarly, admission of a new partner to an existing partnership either by contribution of capital or by acquisition of an interest from an old partner requires the formation of a new partnership. The law regards the partnership as a proprietorship with more than one owner. A partnership cannot sue or be sued. In addition, it cannot enter into contracts and is not subject to taxation. All business transactions are viewed by the law as acts of the partners as individuals.

The individual partners' actions thus can actually obligate the business if they are performed within the scope of the partnership. Additionally, each partner becomes personally liable for the business actions of the other partners. This feature of partnerships is referred to as mutual agency, which means that each partner is an agent of the company and can enter into contracts and bind the partnership to any contract in the regular course of business.

---

[1]Uniform Partnership Act, Part II, Section 6. The Uniform Partnership Act governs the formation and operation of partnerships. Most states have incorporated this act into their statutes.

Like proprietorships, the partnership form of legal organization has unlimited liability. The partnership is jointly and individually liable for the
debts of the partnership—in other words, in the event that the partnership is
unable to pay its debts, the partners' personal assets will be available to
satisfy creditors' claims.

There are many different ways in which partners can distribute profits or
losses from the business. If there is no prior agreement, the profits are divided
equally among the partners taking into consideration some pertinent factors:

- Each partner's capital contribution
- The time spent by each partner in the business
- Goodwill contribution by each partner
- Each partner's special ability and experience in the field.

As indicated before, partnership income is not subject to taxation, but, all
partners must include their share of profits or losses in their individual tax
returns and pay income taxes using the applicable personal income tax rate.
(Of course, partners can use partnership losses to offset other income on their
personal tax returns.)

ADVANTAGES AND DISADVANTAGES
OF PARTNERSHIPS

The main advantages of the partnership form of business organization are

1. *Ease of formation.*   Partnerships are relatively easy to organize, being
   subject to few government regulations.
2. *Opportunity to combine capital, hospitality industry experience, and managerial ability of two or more persons.*   For this reason, it is a very common form of organization used by small restaurants and hotels.
3. *Partnership income is not subject to taxation.*   Even though individual
   partners must include their individual share of profits or losses from the
   partnership in their personal tax return, the individual income tax is
   generally lower than the corporate tax rate.

The major disadvantages of the partnership form of legal organization are

1. *Limited life.*   Withdrawal, death, or bankruptcy of a partner will result
   in the dissolution of a partnership. Likewise, admission of a new partner
   ends the old partnership relationship.
2. *Unlimited liability.*   Each partner is personally liable to creditors for
   debts incurred by other partners acting for the partnership.
3. *Mutual agency.*   Each partner is an agent of the company and can obligate the partnership for his or her acts within the scope of the partnership business.
4. *Difficulty in raising capital.*   Although it is somewhat easier for partnerships to obtain the capital required for expanding operations than it
   is for proprietorships, it is still difficult to raise huge amounts of partnership capital since the ability to do so is limited by the partners' personal wealth and borrowing power.

THE CORPORATION

A corporation is considered a legal person, separate and distinct from its owner. The most famous definition of a corporation was included in the Dartmouth College Case Decision by Chief Justice John Marshall in 1819: A corporation is "an artificial being, invisible, intangible, and existing only in contemplation of law."[2]

Thus, a corporation is a multiple-owner organization that is recognized as a separate legal entity by law. Accordingly, it can enter into contracts and can sue or be sued. Since the corporation is a legal person, a corporate officer signing a loan as agent for a corporation is not putting personal assets at risk. The corporation is responsible for its own acts to the extent of its own assets only, not those of the individual stockholders. Thus, one of the main reasons for incorporating a partnership or proprietorship is to protect the owners' personal assets from losses beyond the amount invested in the business.

The owners of a corporation are called shareholders or stockholders, inasmuch as the ownership interest in the company is evidenced by readily transferable shares of stock issued (sold) by the corporation. The shareholders of a corporation control the regular operations of the business only indirectly by electing a board of directors, who actually manage the corporation. In this management capacity, the board of directors selects the corporation's officers, who run day-to-day operations as well as establish general corporate policies. This circuitous route notwithstanding, ultimate control of a corporation rests with the shareholders.

Corporations are incorporated under the laws of one of the 50 states or the federal government. Generally, hospitality industry corporations are chartered by the states. They are limited in their activities to those stipulated in the charter. The process of incorporating a hospitality business involves the payment of legal fees, and incorporation fees paid to the state in order to secure the charter. All these payments are referred to as organization costs and are initially recorded as assets since they have a future value to the business.

Unlike the partnership and proprietorship forms of business organization, the corporate form facilitates acquisition of the large amounts of capital needed for expansion. This can be accomplished through the sale of additional shares of stock to new owners by issuing stock certificates representing their interest in the enterprise and the means by which ownership can be easily transferred in the future. Since the borrowing capacity of a profitable corporation is far greater than that of a proprietorship or a partnership because of its limited liability, building new hotels or restaurants, renovating old ones, and purchasing new equipment as means of expanding existing operations are greatly facilitated by using the corporate form of legal organization.

Since corporations have several owners it is usually necessary to establish a management team (which may or may not include one or more owners) to carry on the operations of the business. The members of this management team, composed of corporation officers and employees, act as agents for the corporation and conduct its business as a separate legal person with the same rights, duties, and responsibilities of a natural person. A shareholder (not an officer of the corporation) has no power to bind the corporation to contracts, unlike a partner or a proprietor. Also, shareholders enjoy limited liability,

[2]Dartmouth College v. Woodward, 4 Wheaton (U.S.) 518 (1819).

which means that they are protected from personal losses beyond the amount of their investment. In contrast with partnerships and proprietorships, corporate income is subject to taxation, that is, corporations are required to pay income taxes and file separate tax returns. Shareholders do not have to include their corporation's net income in their personal tax returns except for those earnings actually paid out to them in the form of dividends. Accordingly, corporate income is taxed twice: first the corporation's income, and then the shareholders' dividends.

ADVANTAGES AND DISADVANTAGES OF CORPORATIONS

The advantages of the corporate form of legal organization are

1. *Limited liability.*   The special legal status enjoyed by corporations acts as a barrier to protect the owners/shareholders from losses beyond the amount of their investment.
2. *Indefinite life.*   Unlike proprietorships and partnerships, the life of the corporate form of business organization is not affected by the withdrawal of a shareholder in any way since the corporation is treated legally as if it were a person separate from its owners.
3. *No mutual agency.*   Shareholders who are not legal agents or officers are unable to bind a corporation by their actions. If they own many shares, they may bear a strong influence on its management team, but cannot unilaterally bind the corporation legally without the specific authorization of the corporation itself.
4. *Ease of obtaining additional capital.*   Corporations are aptly structured for borrowing large sums of money. They also have a legal structure that enables them to sell small ownership interests (shares) to the general public.
5. *Ease of transfer of ownership interest.*   Since ownership of the corporation is via shares of stock, it is fairly simple to transfer ownership interest. Shareholders can ordinarily sell their shares to others without obtaining the company's approval, whereas a sole proprietor cannot sell partial interests in a business nor can a partner sell a partnership interest without dissolving the partnership.
6. *Separate legal entity.*   By virtue of its special legal status, a corporation has the power to buy, own, or sell property. Furthermore, it can enter into contracts, and can sue or be sued.

The principal disadvantages of the corporate form of legal organization are

1. *Double taxation.*   Corporate income is initially subject to the payment of income taxes by the corporate entity itself, and then shareholders are required to pay income taxes on the portion of corporate earnings distributed to them in the form of dividends.
2. *More government control.*   Corporations are governed and influenced to a great extent by federal government regulations.
3. *More costly to organize.*   The establishment of a corporation entails the payment of legal fees and state charter fees.
4. *More involved decision-making process.*   In corporations, important business decisions may be quite time consuming. They usually must be

referred up the chain of command, often necessitating the agreement and final approval of the board of directors of the corporation.

5. *Dilution of earnings and control.* A typical corporation has a large number of owners/shareholders, who must share the earnings and control of the corporation with many other owners.

OWNERS' EQUITY IN THE BALANCE SHEET

The form of legal organization determines the manner of reporting owners' equity on the balance sheet. In fact, the accounting and legal differences between the three main forms of business organization are reflected in the owners' equity section of the balance sheet. We shall therefore turn our attention to the balance sheet and discuss the manner of accounting for owners' equity under each form of business enterprise.

Owners' Equity for Proprietorships

Since there is only one owner, it is very simple to account for owner's equity and present it on the balance sheet of the sole proprietorship. Basically there is only a single account, the owner's capital account, to deal with. All entries affecting owner's equity are recorded in this account, which includes owner's investment(s) in the business, withdrawals, and business income or losses. A breakdown of the different sources of changes in the owner's capital account that have occurred from the date of the preceding balance sheet is often included in the company's balance sheet. Nonetheless, a separate statement of owner's capital (or owner's equity) is considered a better presentation. Such a statement might look as follows:

STATEMENT OF OWNER'S CAPITAL
For the Year Ended December 31, 1989

Beginning balance, December 31, 1988	$10,000
Add: Net income for the year 1989	3,000
	13,000
Less: Withdrawals for the year 1989	1,000
Ending balance, December 31, 1989	$12,000

The balance sheet will only show the ending balance of $12,000. As indicated before, the aforementioned detail could also be included on the face of the balance sheet in lieu of preparing a separate statement of owner's capital. It is also often added to the bottom of the income statement. Withdrawals (also called drawings) represent the amount of cash or other property taken by the owner from the business for personal use. They are treated as a reduction of the owner's equity in the business. Proprietors have the power to remove money or other assets from the business for personal use at any time.

Owners' Equity for Partnerships

The owners' equity of a partnership is similar to that of a proprietorship except that there is a separate account for each partner, including the same details as the proprietor's capital account (net income, withdrawals, and investments).

Typically, either the balance sheet or a separate statement of partners' capital would show an individual account for each partner. If there are a large number of partners, only one combined partners' capital account is presented on the balance sheet, and individual partners' capital accounts appear in the statement of partners' capital.

As in the case of a sole proprietorship, each partner's share of partnership profits is added to that partner's capital account. As noted previously, the apportioning of profits is determined in the partnership agreement; in the absence of an agreement, profits are divided equally among the partners.

When one partner contributes more capital or more expertise and reputation to the partnership than the other partners, that partner may be remunerated by the payment of interest or salary. Such payments are deducted as expenses in order to determine the profit to be divided among the partners.

The following is an illustration of a statement of partners' capital for A and B Partnership:

A AND B PARTNERSHIP
Statement of Partners' Capital
For the Year Ended December 31, 1989

	A, capital	B, capital	Total
Beginning balance, December 31, 1988	$50,000	$65,000	$115,000
Add: Net income for the year 1989	25,000	25,000	50,000
Totals	75,000	90,000	165,000
Less: Withdrawals during 1989	12,000	19,000	31,000
Ending balance, December 31, 1989	$63,000	$71,000	$134,000

Note that A and B have agreed to share earnings equally. B, who originally invested more than A, is withdrawing more than A in an effort to equalize his capital investment with that of A eventually.

Owners' Equity for Corporations

Since the owners of a corporation are the shareholders (or stockholders), the owners equity section of a corporate balance sheet is commonly referred to as shareholders' equity (or stockholders' equity). It is divided into two major subdivisions—paid-in-capital and retained earnings—in order to differentiate between the owners'/shareholders' investments in the business and the accumulated earnings retained in the firm since the company's formation.

The paid-in capital represents the sources of invested capital, including common stock, preferred stock, and additional paid-in capital (see below). When a firm has issued only one class of stock it is referred to as common stock (or simply capital stock). Hence, the common shareholders are considered the true owners of the corporation. Some corporations issue another class of stock, preferred stock, as an additional source of capital. The preferred shareholders, as the name implies, have certain preferences on earnings distributions and upon liquidation of the firm.

There may be different types and classes of capital stock (in both common and preferred stock), each having its own special features. For instance, there is par and no-par stock. Most stocks have a par value, which is an arbitrary value assigned to one share of stock either by the corporation or the board of directors. No-par stock has no specific value per share assigned to it. Additional paid-in capital reflects the portion of paid-in capital that exceeds the par value of the capital stock.

Another special feature pertains to preferred stock, which can be cumulative or noncumulative with regard to dividends. When preferred stock is non-cumulative and the board of directors does not declare an annual dividend, the preferred stockholders' right to receive a dividend for that year expires. In the case of cumulative preferred stock, the right to receive each year's dividends never expires and no dividends may be declared on common stock until all dividends in arrears on cumulative preferred stock are paid. As noted before, a more extensive coverage of the different classes and types of capital stock, as well as other aspects of corporate accounting, is given in Chapter 17.

The second source of shareholders' equity is retained earnings. Retained earnings represent the total of all the previous years' net income that has not been distributed as dividends. By not distributing earnings to the shareholders as dividends, the enterprise is in a position to use this retained income as a source of capital for future growth. In fact, for many profitable, fast-growing hospitality firms retained earnings represent a larger portion of shareholders' equity than does invested capital.

All large hospitality corporations and many small ones normally prefer to prepare a separate statement of retained earnings that will itemize the changes that have taken place in retained earnings during the period. This statement is comparable to the statement of owner's capital and the statement of partners' capital. The main items included in the statement of retained earnings are

- Beginning balance
- Net income or net loss for the period
- Dividends declared during the period
- Ending balance

The balance sheet, however, only includes the ending balance of retained earnings. If the amount of accumulated losses exceeds accumulated income, a negative balance will be shown as a reduction of owners' equity. In this case the balance sheet will use the term *deficit* instead of retained earnings. The following is an illustration of a simple statement of retained earnings:

FRB RESTAURANTS, INC.
Statement of Retained Earnings
For the Year Ended December 31, 1989

Beginning balance, December 31, 1988	$65,000
Add: Net income for year 1989	28,000
	93,000
Less: Dividends	8,000
Ending balance, December 31, 1989	$85,000

As stated previously, the ending balance of retained earnings at any point in time reflects the net amount of accumulated income not paid out to shareholders in the form of dividends since the company was first organized. The shareholders' equity section of the corporate balance sheet will list all the aforementioned accounts representing the two sources of owners' equity to the firm: invested capital and retained earnings. It is customary to list each account separately and to include pertinent disclosures required by certain accounting pronouncements, which include the number of authorized shares of common stock and preferred stock (if applicable), the number of issued and outstanding shares, and the class and type of stock.

The following is an illustration of the shareholders' equity section of the FRB Restaurants, Inc. balance sheet as of December 31, 1989:

FRB RESTAURANTS, INC.
Shareholders' Equity
December 31, 1989

Paid-in capital	
Preferred stock, $10 par value;	
authorized, issued, and outstanding 1,000 shares	$ 10,000
Common stock, $1 par value;	
authorized and outstanding 50,000 shares	50,000
Total paid-in capital	60,000
Retained earnings	85,000
Total shareholders' equity	$145,000

The above illustration is a simplified version of the shareholders' equity section of a corporate balance sheet. Many corporations include other equity accounts, such as additional paid-in capital. In our example, the shares of common and preferred stock were sold at par, and so there was no need to present the additional paid-in capital account.

In the remaining chapters, while we shall occasionally include illustrations and problems concerning sole proprietorships and partnerships, our emphasis will be on the corporate form of legal organization since the corporation is the major form of business enterprise in terms of economic power in the United States.

QUESTIONS

1. What are the three main types of business organization?
2. In what section of the balance sheet are the accounting differences between these types of organizations manifested?
3. Name three advantages of the sole proprietorship form of business organization. Name three disadvantages.
4. In what ways does accounting for a partnership differ from accounting for a sole proprietorship?
5. Name three advantages of a partnership. Name three disadvantages.
6. Which is the most important form of business organization in terms of dollar volume in the United States?
7. What is the main difference between the owners' equity section of a corporation's balance sheet and that of a partnership or sole proprietorship?
8. In which type of business organization are the owners not responsible for the business entity's debts? Which type of business entity is considered an entity separate from the owners both legally and accountingwise?
9. Name three advantages of the corporate form of business organization. Name three disadvantages.
10. What types of business organizations are likely to present a statement of owners' capital? a statement of retained earnings?
11. What are three unique characteristics of each of the three forms of business organizations?

EXERCISES

1. (a) Prepare a statement of owners' capital for the Bon Chef Restaurant as of December 31, 1985 based on the following information:

     (1) Each of the three owners (Bill, Mary, and Joe) withdrew $12,000 during the year.

     (2) The net income for the year was $105,000.

     (3) The balance in the owners' capital account on December 31, 1985 was $336,666 invested equally by each owner.

     (4) The balance in the owners' capital account on January 1, 1985 was $267,666.

     (5) Each owner's share of the profits was reported on his or her personal income tax return. There is no formal agreement regarding the division of profits.

  (b) What type of business organization is the Bon Chef Restaurant? Explain.

2. (a) Prepare the owners' capital (owners' equity) section of Sleepwell Motel's 1986 balance sheet based on the following facts:

     (1) The motel's most recent fiscal year ended July 31, 1986.

     (2) The retained earnings as of August 1, 1985 (the beginning of the fiscal year) amounted to $20,000. During the year ended July 31, 1986 it earned $10,000.

     (3) Sold 10,000 shares of common stock at their $5 par value during fiscal year 1983.

     (4) Sold 1,000 shares of $10 preferred stock at par during fiscal year 1984.

  (b) What type of business organization is the Sleepwell Motel? Explain.

3. (a) Based on the following facts, prepare a statement of owners' capital at year end for the Farewell Travel Agency, owned by Peter Fahr.

     (1) It lost $5,000 during the year.

     (2) Peter Fahr withdrew $1,000 during the year.

     (3) The accumulated losses at the end of the year amounted to $15,000.

     (4) Peter Fahr made an additional $5,000 investment during the year.

     (5) Peter Fahr reported the $5,000 loss on his personal income tax return.

  (b) What type of business organization is the Farewell Travel Agency? Explain.

4. The Lafitof Amusement Park is organized as a corporation. Indicate whether the following statements are true or false:

  (a) There are no separate accounts in the owners' equity section for recording the cumulative undistributed earnings and the amounts of invested capital.

  (b) There is no need to have a board of directors since one of the characteristics of a corporation is that it has a management team separate and distinct from the owners.

  (c) A statement of retained earnings can be prepared for the Lafitof Amusement Park.

  (d) The owners are personally liable for all of the corporation's debts.

  (e) The owners must include their portion of the corporation's net income on their personal tax returns.

  (f) The corporation's earnings are only taxed once, except for those earnings declared as dividends.

PROBLEMS

1. The Restful Inn Hotel presents you with the following information:

     (1) The hotel sold 5,000 shares of common stock at their par value of $8 per share.

     (2) The hotel earned a profit of $30,000 in the year ended September 30, 1984.

     (3) Dividends of $8,000 were declared in the year ended September 30, 1985.

     (4) The hotel had an accumulated loss of $20,000 at the end of the year ended September 30, 1983.

     (5) One thousand shares of preferred stock were sold August 1, 1985 at their par value of $10.

(6) The hotel earned a $25,000 profit in the year ended September 30, 1985.

(7) Dividends of $5,000 were declared in the year ended September 30, 1985.

(a) State what kind of business organization the hotel is and explain what leads you to this conclusion.

(b) Prepare the shareholders' equity section of the balance sheet as of September 30, 1985, the end of its fiscal year.

2. Orville Brother is thinking of starting a restaurant and is undecided as to what form of business organization to use. He lists the following facts concerning his future business and asks you to help him make his decision. What form of business organization would you recommend to him? Explain your reasons.

(a) I need to be able to make decisions quickly during the initial stage of my venture.

(b) I want to be able to expand rapidly if my first restaurant is profitable.

(c) I want to be able to start up quickly and do not want to be bothered with many government reporting requirements initially.

(d) I have good credit and I am not afraid of standing behind this new venture with my own assets until it becomes creditworthy on its own.

(e) However, I have heard of many restaurant owners being forced out of business because they were sued by customers who slipped and fell, were fed contaminated food, or were accidentally burned. I feel I can control conditions in my first restaurant, but I am afraid of what can happen when I expand.

(f) In order to expand rapidly I shall need a complete management organization once my first restaurant is successful.

(g) I shall need to raise abundant capital in order to expand rapidly.

(h) Since I want it to grow rapidly, the company will not be distributing any of its earnings for at least 7 or 8 years.

3. Below is presented the owners' equity section of a travel agency's balance sheet.

Shareholders' Equity

Preferred stock, $10 par, 10% cumulative;	
1,000 shares authorized, issued, and outstanding	$ 10,000
Common stock, $5 par; 5,000 shares authorized,	
issued, and outstanding	25,000
Common stock, $3 par; 10,000 shares authorized,	
issued, and outstanding	30,000
Total paid-in capital	65,000
Retained earnings	35,000
Total shareholders' equity	$100,000

Answer the following questions based on the travel agency's shareholders' equity section:

(a) What type of business is it? Why?

(b) How much have the owners invested in the entity?

(c) How much net income has the entity not distributed?

(d) What is the price per share at which the company sold each type of stock?

(e) Which types of stock have voting rights?

(f) What is the total amount of ownership rights of all the owners of the entity?

4. Prepare the Fairview Tour Bus Company's shareholders' equity section and a statement of retained earnings for the year ended August 31, 1986 based on the following information:

(a) 10,000 shares of common stock were sold at $5 par during the fiscal year 1985.

(b) Retained earnings for the year ended August 31, 1986 amounted to $230,000.

(c) Preferred stock in the amount of $150,000 was sold at $10 par during the fiscal year 1986.

(d) Retained earnings as of August 31, 1985 amounted to $185,000.

(e) Dividends amounting to $20,000 were paid out in the 1986 fiscal year.

(f) Dividends of $30,000 were paid out in the 1985 fiscal year.

(g) Net income for the year ended August 31, 1985 amounted to $50,000.

II

Accounting Cycle and Procedures

5

Processing Business Transactions

In order to make full use of accounting information in management decisions, we must know how to analyze the output of the accounting process in order to evaluate the performance and financial condition of the hospitality entity. Understanding accounting depends greatly on the ability to analyze business situations and recognize business transactions when they occur—to "know what happened."

Knowing what happened for accounting purposes requires (1) identification of the value(s) given and the value(s) received in each transaction, and (2) determination of the dollar amounts to be entered in the accounting records in order to record these value exchanges. Once we have analyzed and recorded the business transactions, it is not difficult to summarize data into meaningful categories for management information purposes.

As mentioned in Chapter 1, the accounting system consists of input, processing, and output. The input of the accounting system consists of source documents such as checks, time cards, and purchase and sales invoices, which record the fact that a business transaction has taken place. In this chapter, we shall first explain the nature of these business transactions, and see how they are the raw material of the accounting process. Second, we shall begin to examine the accounting cycle—the multistep actions. The first step of the cycle is the identification and understanding of business transactions through a procedure known as transactional analysis. Finally, we shall introduce the second step of the accounting cycle—journalizing, which is covered in greater detail in Chapter 6.

BUSINESS TRANSACTIONS: THE RAW MATERIAL OF THE ACCOUNTING PROCESS

We learned in Chapter 1 that accounting is a system for collecting, summarizing, analyzing, and reporting (in monetary terms) information about an organization, that is, it is a system for keeping track of value exchanges between organizations. These value exchanges are known in accounting as business transactions. (In Figure 1.2, the source documents proved a record of business transactions.)

Business transactions are events that take place in the life of a business and that result in an equal exchange of values. They may involve investing in the business, selling goods (food and beverages, for example) or services, paying bills, purchasing needed items from vendors, or collecting receivables.

In order to record these transactions, a bookkeeper or accountant must be informed that they have taken place. Source documents will provide such information; that is, they constitute the evidence of completed transactions, which is the basis for processing them in the accounting system. For example, when an established restaurant purchases food or beverage for its inventory, it normally buys on account and receives an invoice, which becomes the basis for processing the purchase transaction. When the invoice is paid, the check issued by the restaurant will serve as proof that a cash payment transaction has been completed. Likewise, employee time cards or time sheets are very important source documents in a hospitality firm due to the labor-intensive nature of the industry. They reflect the expenditure of time as a basis for the processing of payroll transactions.

For each business transaction that occurs, a source document is received or created. These documents not only serve as objective evidence that transactions have taken place, but they also indicate the amounts to be recorded, in keeping with the objectivity concept of accounting. They provide the opportunity to capture all of the information necessary for processing within the accounting system.

We can see how understanding business transactions is basic to the acquisition of accounting knowledge—they are the raw material of the accounting process. For example, in a restaurant, a chef processes raw materials—food ingredients such as vinegar, paprika, raw meat, cooking oil, pepper, and garlic—in order to deliver the final product to the restaurant's customers—a prepared meal. Similarly, the raw material of the accounting process, business transactions (cash receipts, sales, purchases, payments), must be processed by the bookkeeper or accountant through the accounting system in order to obtain its final product—financial statements and other periodic reports for the use of management and other decision-makers.

THE ACCOUNTING CYCLE

The accounting cycle represents the processing stage of the accounting system. This is the stage where business transactions are summarized and analyzed in order to obtain the output of the system.

The accounting cycle consists of seven steps, as shown in Table 5.1. Many hospitality firms operate with annual accounting periods, and thus apply the

TABLE 5.1. The Accounting Cycle

Steps	Comments
1. Identification and analysis of business transactions	Recognition of value(s) received and value(s) given
2. Journalizing	Chronological recording of business transactions in a journal
3. Posting	Transferring the information from the journal to the ledger
4. Taking the trial balance of the general ledger	Ascertaining the equality of account balances in the ledger
5. Adjusting the trial balance	Adjusting account balances at the end of the accounting period to reflect passage of time
6. Preparation of financial statements	Using the financial statement worksheet to prepare the balance sheet and income statement
7. Closing the books	Preparing accounting records for the next accounting period

accounting cycle steps on an annual basis by closing the books once a year. However, most large hospitality firms and some small ones may also prepare interim reports (monthly, quarterly, etc.); thus they will perform these steps for the interim period(s) in addition to the year end.

As we saw in Chapter 3, if the annual accounting period ends on December 31 it is called a calendar year. However, some firms may follow a fiscal year coinciding with their natural business year, in which case the annual accounting period will usually be selected to end when business activity is at its lowest point, thus facilitating the process of preparing financial statements.

IDENTIFICATION OF BUSINESS TRANSACTIONS

All business transactions by definition involve a quid pro quo or equal exchange of values. That is, for every transaction there are one or more values received and one or more values given, and these values are equal. This can be represented by the value exchange equation:

$$\text{values received (vr)} = \text{values given (vg)}$$

To illustrate this concept, we refer again to the three transactions included in Chapter 2.

Transaction (a)—Invested Cash. Mr. Carlton Bober invested $100,000 cash in his new CB Motel business. This transaction results in CB Motel receiving a value, cash in the amount of $100,000, and giving in return an ownership share to the owner, Mr. Bober. Based on the equality of values exchanged we conclude that assets increased $100,000 while owner's equity also increased in the same amount. In terms of the value exchange equation,

$$\text{vr (cash)} = \text{vg (100\% ownership share)}$$
$$\$100,000 = \$100,000$$

Based on the dual aspect of accounting, the effect of this transaction on the fundamental accounting equation was shown to be

$$A = L + OE$$
$$100,000 \text{ (cash)} = 0 + 100,000 \text{ (capital)}$$

where A is assets, L is liability, and OE is owner's equity.

Transaction (b)—Paid Cash for Housekeeping Supplies. CB Motel made a cash payment of $1,000 for the purchase of housekeeping supplies. The value received by the business consists of housekeeping supplies, an asset, with a value of $1,000. The value given in return would be cash, another asset, in the amount of $1,000. Again, in terms of the value exchange equation,

$$\text{vr (housekeeping supplies inventory)} = \text{vg (cash)}$$
$$\$1,000 = \$1,000$$

We had previously expressed this transaction in terms of the fundamental accounting equation as an exchange of the assets cash and housekeeping supplies inventory.

$$0 \begin{cases} +1{,}000 \text{ housekeeping supplies inventory} \\ -1{,}000 \text{ cash} \end{cases} \quad \begin{aligned} A &= L + OE \\ &= 0 + 0 \end{aligned}$$

Transaction (c)—Purchase of Furniture and Equipment on Account. In this transaction CB Motel received furniture and equipment with a value of $30,000 (vr). In return for this vr, CB Motel gave its promise to repay the $30,000 in the future, an accounts payable (A/P). Note that this promise was given in the form of an understanding in the normal course of business by virtue of accepting X company's credit terms as a condition for the purchase of furniture and equipment. It is evident that the vr, furniture and equipment (an asset), is equal to the vg, accounts payable (a liability). This account payable reflects the fact that $30,000 is owed to X company, which now becomes a creditor of CB Motel:

$$\text{vr (furniture \& equipment)} = \text{vg (accounts payable)}$$
$$\$30{,}000 = \$30{,}000$$

Furthermore, the effect of transaction (c) in terms of the fundamental accounting equation is

$$A = L + OE$$
$$+30{,}000 \text{ furniture \& equipment} = +30{,}000 \text{ A/P} + 0$$

In these three examples, we saw how every business transaction involved an equal exchange of values: the value received (vr) was always equal to the value given (vg). In each transaction, there was only one vr and one vg. However, many transactions involve two or more values received and/or two or more values given. In such cases, the equality of values exchanged will still prevail. Let us consider the following transaction:

Transaction (d)—Week's Sales. The sales of CB Motel for the week consisted of $3,000 in cash sales and $5,000 in credit sales. In this case there are two values received, cash and accounts receivable (A/R). An accounts receivable is the promise received from customers to pay a specific amount in the future, in this case $5,000, pursuant to CB Motel's credit terms.

Consequently, transaction (d) involves the combination of two asset values received (cash $3,000 and accounts receivable $5,000) in the amount of $8,000. These values received will equal the value given by CB Motel, services performed (room sales) in the amount of $8,000:

$$\text{vr} = \text{vg}$$
$$\$3{,}000 \text{ cash} + \$5{,}000 \text{ A/R} = \$8{,}000 \text{ room sales}$$
$$\$8{,}000 = \$8{,}000$$

The effect of the above transaction on the fundamental accounting equation is

$$A = L + OE$$
$$3{,}000 \text{ cash} + 5{,}000 \text{ A/R} = 0 + 8{,}000 \text{ room sales}$$
$$+8{,}000 = 0 + 8{,}000$$

To summarize, step 1 of the accounting cycle entails recognizing that a business transaction affecting the financial condition of the hospitality firm took place. This identification process entails a two-stage analysis of each business transaction:

1. Determine the individual value(s) received (vr) and the individual value(s) given (vg) for each transaction. As we already know, all transactions involve an equal exchange of values based upon the quid pro quo (something for something) characteristic inherent in all business transactions. Thus, in every transaction vr = vg.
2. Analyze the effect of each transaction in terms of the fundamental accounting equation. That is, think through the effect of the transaction on assets, liabilities, and owners' equity, including the subdivisions of owners' equity: revenues and expenses.

After all the business transactions occurring in a particular accounting period have been recognized and analyzed, we are in a position to record, sort out, and summarize them. Before going on to these remaining steps of the accounting cycle, we shall enhance our understanding of step 1 by analyzing several business transactions.

TRANSACTIONAL ANALYSIS

Hundreds or even thousands of business transactions may take place every day in an average hospitality firm, the volume depending on the size of the business. Some of the more typical of these transactions are identified and described in Table 5.2, (1) in terms of their effect on the fundamental accounting equation and (2) in terms of their effect on the value exchange equation. The kind of analysis in Table 5.2 is a specific example of transactional analysis in action.

VALUES RECEIVED (DEBITS) AND
VALUES GIVEN (CREDITS):
AN INTRODUCTION TO JOURNALIZING

It is worth noting again that using transactional analysis to comprehend what happened with respect to one transaction or a group of related transactions is crucial and will considerably accelerate the overall learning process.

Having acquired a clear understanding of what happened in the business transactions of a particular period, we are ready to process these transactions through the accounting system. This takes us to step 2: journalizing. Journalizing is the chronological recording of business transactions in a journal, or keeping a business diary to record all values received (vr) and all values given (vg) for each transaction. The journal is often referred to as a "book of original entry" because it is the place where transactions are initially recorded.

We have learned that every transaction involves receiving one or more values and giving one or more values and that the total of values received must equal the total of values given. This is an appropriate point to become acquainted with accounting terminology: values received are called debits and

TABLE 5.2. Hospitality Firm Transactional Analysis

| Typical business transactions | | Effect on fundamental accounting equation | | | | | Values exchanged | | |
Description	Type	A	=	L	+	OE[a]	VR	=	VG
1. Owners' investment in hospitality organization	Invested capital	+cash		0		+owners' capital	Cash or other property		Ownership share (individual, partnership share, or stock)
2. Borrowing money	Borrowed capital	+cash		+notes payable		0	Cash		Promise to pay (notes payable)
3. Purchase inventory (supplies or merchandise inventory) for cash	Purchase	+inventory -cash		0		0	Goods (for sale or to be consumed by hospitality firm)		Cash
4. Purchase inventory (supplies or merchandise inventory) on account	Purchase	+inventory		+A/P		0	Goods		Implied promise to pay (A/P)
5. Cash sales	Sales	+cash		0		+revenue	Cash		Goods (food sales, beverage sales) or services (room sales)
6. Sales on open account	Sales	+A/R		0		+revenue	Promise to pay (A/R)		Goods or services
7. Repay loan or pay for credit purchases	Cash disbursement	-cash		-A/P or notes payable		0	Note or promise to pay		Cash
8. Pay a cash expense	Cash disbursement	-cash		0		-expense	Use of goods or services		Cash
9. Renew bank note	Due date extension on borrowed capital	0		0		0	Continued use of money		Renewal of promise to pay
10. Withdrawal of money by owners	Cash disbursement	-cash		0		-withdrawal	Reduction of ownership share		Cash

[a]Remember that: revenues increase OE and expenses decrease OE.

values given are called credits, and so the value exchange equation can also be written

$$\text{debits} = \text{credits}$$

By accounting convention, debit may be abbreviated to Dr and credit to Cr. In every transaction, therefore, Dr = Cr.

When journalizing business transactions, we record in the journal all values received by debiting the specific asset, liability, owners' equity, revenue, or expense item(s). At the same time we record all values given by crediting the appropriate asset, liability, owners' equity, revenue, or expense item(s). We shall now refer to these items as accounts. An account is a recording format for gathering and summarizing the effect of business transactions. There is a separate account for each type of asset, liability, owners' equity, revenue, and expense. We have already seen that for every transaction recorded in the journal all debits must be equal to all credits. This is necessary to record the equal exchange of values in business transactions. This dual aspect of accounting, more importantly, is the basic premise supporting the double-entry accounting system.

The actual procedures to be followed in journalizing will be discussed in depth in Chapter 6. At this point it is important only to recognize that if we learn how to determine what accounts are to be credited or debited, step 2 of the accounting cycle—journalizing—will become a fairly simple procedure.

Let us consider two examples of how we can determine what accounts need to be debited and what accounts need to be credited in recording business transactions in the journal.

Example 1. Borrowed $10,000 from the ABC Bank, Signing a 90-Day Promissory Note.   A promissory note consists of a written promise to pay a certain sum of money on demand or at a specified future time. In this example there is a written promise to pay ABC bank $10,000 in 90 days from the date the money was borrowed.

The transaction involves a value received (the asset cash) in the amount of $10,000 and a value given (the promise to repay the note) in the same amount. Hence, the cash account is debited and the notes payable account (a liability account) is credited since we debit value(s) received and credit value(s) given.

The journal entry will be shown as follows:

> Dr   Cash   10,000
> Cr   Notes payable   10,000

Notice that the credit entry has been indented. This will be done at all times, as we shall see when we discuss journalizing procedures in Chapter 6.

Example 2. Paid Rent for the Month, $1,000.   The value received (rent expense) denotes that we have received the right to use the rented premises for a period of one month in exchange for the payment of $1,000. The cash asset reflects the value given in this transaction. Therefore, we must debit rent expense (vr) and credit cash (vg) or:

> Dr   Rent expense   1,000
> Cr   Cash   1,000

Note that the effect of this transaction on the fundamental accounting equation is a decrease in cash (an asset) and a decrease in owners' equity. Nonetheless, we do not debit owners' equity. Instead, we debit rent expense since expenses produce decreases in owners' equity and we must have separate account(s) for expenses.

Traditionally, in order to learn how to record business transactions in a journal, students were asked to memorize certain rules (referred to as the rules of debit and credit) without any attempt to understand the logic involved in the development of these rules. It was simply stated that debits and credits had no meaning other than "left" and "right" since, as we shall see, debits are entered on the left side of an account and credits are entered on the right side of an account. However, we feel that to understand accounting it is not only necessary to understand the rules of debit and credit, but more importantly, to understand the logic behind these rules. That is why we used the "equal exchange of values" approach in our initial example of recording transactions in a journal. Understanding the inherent logic in the accounting system facilitates performing the accounting process and comprehending its output.

The general rules of debits and credits are shown in Table 5.3. We can see that increases in asset accounts will be recorded by debiting the proper asset account, whereas decreases in assets will be credited to the proper asset account. This can be easily understood by recognizing that when an asset increases, the hospitality firm receives a value, a resource that will provide future economic benefit. For example, when food inventory is purchased for cash or on credit the firm receives a value, food inventory (an asset), which will have to be debited based on the rules in Table 5.3.

The same rationale applies in the case of expenses. An increase in expenses signifies that a value has been received by the hospitality firm in the past and has been consumed in its operations. Therefore, the specific expense account representing the item consumed by the hospitality firm will be debited to reflect the value received by the business. For instance, when rent expense is incurred it means that the firm has received a value—the use of the rented premises for a particular period—and thus the rent expense account will have to be debited when recording the transaction in a journal.

Insofar as liability, owners' equity, and revenue accounts are concerned, increases will be recorded as credits to the respective accounts. This is based on the fact that one or more values will be given by the hospitality firm when there are increases in any of those accounts. When we make a purchase on credit, for example, the business will have to give a value, in the form of a promise to pay in the future, for the item purchased.

This results in an increase in the liability account, accounts payable. Thus,

TABLE 5.3. **Rules of Debit and Credit**[a]

Account	Debit	Credit
Asset	+	−
Liabilities	−	+
Owners' equity	−	+
Revenue	−	+
Expense	+	−

[a]A plus indicates that an account has increased, and a minus indicates that it has decreased.

we will be crediting accounts payable to recognize the value given, which happens to represent an increase in a liability account.

The rules of debits and credits listed in Table 5.3 can be easily remembered by referring to the fundamental accounting equation:

$$\text{Assets} = \text{Liabilities} + \text{Owners' equity}$$

Dr increases	Cr increases
Cr decreases	Dr decreases

In other words, asset increases are debited. Asset decreases, on the other hand, are credited, based on the fact that the business gives a value any time an asset decreases (in the form of a cash payment, land, furniture, or any other resource owned by the business).

At the same time, increases in liability and owners' equity accounts will be credited, recognizing that the entity has given a value in the form of a promise to pay (liability) or a share in ownership (owners' equity). Conversely, decreases in these accounts will be debited, reflecting the value(s) received by the firm (a return to the firm of any previously given promise to pay, or a return of ownership share).

From the foregoing discussion we can conclude that there are two alternative approaches to journalizing, i.e., the process of identifying the particular accounts to which specific transaction amounts should be debited or credited.

The first approach is based on the logic of value exchanges (values received = values given). This approach is highly recommended because it touches the core of the accounting function: keeping track of value exchanges. The second alternative is based on the fundamental accounting equation. It involves memorizing the rules of debits and credits presented in Table 5.3, and applying them in the process of journalizing. Relating these rules to the fundamental accounting equation should make them easier to remember.

If the student is able to analyze transactions effectively using the first approach, then the second approach is unnecessary. Because it provides a more fundamental understanding of the accounting function, the analysis of value exchanges is to be preferred. The rules of debits and credits method is presented, however, because many students find it easier to assimilate and it is still widely used in the study of introductory accounting.

Regardless of which approach is used, once students have learned to translate business transactions into specific accounts to be debited or credited with appropriate amounts, they will have mastered the journalizing process. This can only be accomplished by practicing the technique in the actual solution of problems.

Chapter 6 will provide the opportunity to put into practice the technique of journalizing. It will expand our coverage of journalizing procedures. A greater variety of transactions will be analyzed and illustrated in the process of explaining how they are to be recorded in the general journal, the simplest and most flexible type of journal.

QUESTIONS

1. What are the three stages of an accounting system? In which stage does the accounting cycle occur?

2. What are the various steps of the accounting cycle? List them in proper sequence.

3. What is transactional analysis? In what part of the accounting cycle does it occur and why is it necessary?

4. What is the function of source documents? Name three source documents.

5. What is meant when it is said that a company operates on a calendar-year basis? On a fiscal-year basis? On a natural-year basis?

6. What is step 1 of the accounting cycle? On what basic accounting concept is it based? Under what circumstances are values received in a business transaction equal to values given?

7. What effect do values received have on the different elements of the fundamental accounting equation?

8. Why is it important to understand "what happened" in a business transaction?

9. How do revenues affect owners' equity? How do expenses affect owners' equity?

10. Define journalizing.

11. What are two different ways of understanding the process of journalizing?

12. State the rules of debits and credits.

13. What is the ultimate objective of the accounting system?

EXERCISES

1. Place the following steps of the accounting cycle in proper sequence and define them:
   (a) Adjusting the trial balance
   (b) Journalizing
   (c) Closing the books
   (d) Transactional analysis
   (e) Taking the trial balance of the general ledger
   (f) Preparing financial statements
   (g) Posting

2. For the following transactions state the values received and the values given:
   (1) $15,000 in cash is invested to start a company.
   (2) The company borrows $5,000.
   (3) Furniture is purchased in the amount of $2,000, paying $1,000 in cash and $1,000 on credit.
   (4) The company pays back $3,000 of the money it borrowed.
   (5) The owner transfers to this company $6,000 worth of equipment that was used by another organization owned by the owner.
   (6) Equipment is sold for $3,000, receiving $2,000 in cash and the balance on account.
   (7) The owner withdraws $1,500 in cash from the company for his personal use.

3. (a) Based on your answers to Exercise 2 indicate the effect of the given transactions on the accounting equation and express the values received and values given in terms of debits and credits. The first transaction is presented below as an example:
      (1) The $15,000 in cash received by the company represents an increase in assets. Increases in assets are recorded as debits. The $15,000 worth of ownership rights given represent an increase in owners' equity. Increases in owners' equity are recorded as credits.
   (b) What general statement can you make concerning the procedure for recording values received and values given?

4. Suggest one transaction that may have caused the changes in the various elements of the accounting equation indicated in each case on the next page.

Assets	= Liabilities +	Owners' equity		
		Investment +	Revenues –	Expenses
(a) +10,000	0	+10,000	0	0
(b) +1,000	0	0	0	0
−1,000				
(c) +5,000	+5,000	0	0	0
(d) +4,000	0	0	+4,000	0
(e) −2,000	0	0	0	+2,000
(f) −1,500	0	−1,500	0	0
(g) 0	+1,000	0	0	+1,000
(h) 0	−2,000	+2,000	0	0
(i) −1,000	−1,000	0	0	0
(j) +1,000	+2,000	−1,000	0	0
(k) +4,000	+3,000	+1,000	0	0

5. For each of the items presented below calculate the missing amount.
   (a) Assets = $35,000, revenues = $15,000, invested capital = $16,000, liabilities = $19,000, expenses = ?
   (b) Expenses = $8,000, invested capital = $4,000, liabilities = $16,000, revenues = $12,000, assets = ?
   (c) Invested capital = $10,000, assets = $110,000, expenses = $35,000, revenues = $40,000, liabilities = ?
   (d) Assets = $112,000, expenses = $560,000, liabilities = $73,000, revenues = $544,000, invested capital = ?
   (e) Assets = $50,000, invested capital = $6,000, liabilities = $46,000, expenses = $10,000, revenues = ?

PROBLEMS

1. Consider the following transactions of the Short Stop Commuter Airline.
   (a) Determine the value(s) received and value(s) given for each transaction.
   (b) Determine the debits and credits needed to record each transaction.
      (1) The owner of the airline invested his light plane, worth $60,000, in exchange for 6,000 shares of $5 par common stock of the new company.
      (2) The owner loaned the company $10,000 in cash in exchange for a note payable.
      (3) The company purchased $4,000 worth of furniture for $3,000 cash, giving a note payable for the balance.
      (4) $2,000 worth of spare parts were purchased on open account with 30-day credit terms.
      (5) $3,000 worth of commuter services were sold on account to a corporation.
      (6) Salaries amounting to $1,500 were paid.
      (7) A 6-month lease was signed for office space at $800 per month.
      (8) The current month's rent was paid and the sixth (last) month's rent was paid, both at the beginning of the month, making a total payment of $1,600.
      (9) An invoice for water amounting to $150 was received but not paid.
      (10) Cash sales amounted to $9,900.
      (11) A $2,000 payment was received on the credit sales previously made.
      (12) Dividends of $3,000 were paid.
      (13) A $1,000 payment was made to creditors of the company.
      (14) An invoice for electricity amounting to $200 was received and paid.
      (15) An invoice for gasoline amounting to $1,200 was received and paid.

2. Prepare a worksheet as shown below and enter the transactions of the Eversweet Coffee Shop listed subsequently. Write the name of the desired account in the appropriate account column and the amount in the corresponding amount column. Indicate increases in an account with a plus (+) and decreases with a minus (−) sign.

	Assets		Liabilities		Owner's equity	
Transaction	Account	Amount	Account	Amount	Account	Amount

   (a) The coffee shop was established as a sole proprietorship with a deposit of $20,000 in its bank account made by the owner, Charles Greener.

   (b) The coffee shop signed a 1-year lease for a location that had previously been used as a coffee shop and was almost fully furnished. The first and last month's rent was paid, a total of $2,000 for the 2 months.

   (c) Some additional furniture and equipment was purchased for the coffee shop. The furniture cost $4,000 and the oven and refrigerator cost $6,000. Of the total $10,000 purchase, one half was paid cash and a note payable was signed for the balance.

   (d) Food and beverages worth $4,000 were purchased on credit.

   (e) Cash sales of $5,000 were made.

   (f) Food and beverages worth $1,500 were consumed in making these sales.

   (g) A local business opened an account and bought $500 on account. $150 worth of food and beverages were consumed in making these sales.

   (h) $1,000 worth of supplies inventory was purchased on credit.

   (i) A $1,300 payment was made on suppliers' accounts.

   (j) An electricity invoice for $200 was received.

   (k) Payroll of $280 was paid to the part-time help.

   (l) A $400 payment was received as part payment on previous credit sales.

   (m) An invoice for water amounting to $200 was received and paid.

   (n) Charles Greener took home $500 worth of unprepared food and withdrew $500 in cash.

   (o) The company paid $2,000 on the note payable it had previously signed.

3. (a) Prepare a worksheet as follows:

		Assets			Liabilities			Owner's equity								
								Investment			Revenues			Expenses		
Transaction	Description	Dr Cr	Acct	Amt	Dr Cr	Acct	Amt	Dr Cr	Acct	Amt	Dr Cr	Acct	Amt	Dr Cr	Acct	Amt

(b) Enter the following transactions of the Kirkshire Restaurant in the appropriate columns. First, describe each transaction in the description column, then enter a Dr or Cr in the Dr/Cr column, followed by the name and amount of the affected account in the next two columns.

1.	Cash	+25,000	J. Kirkshire, capital	+20,000
			Notes payable	+5,000
2.	Food inventory	+8,000	Accounts receivable	+3,000
	Cash	−5,000		
3.	Furniture	+3,000	Notes payable	+7,000
	Equipment	+4,000		
4.	Cash	+2,500	Sales	+2,500
5.	Cost of sales	+750	Food inventory	−750
6.	Cash	−400	Payroll	+400
7.	Accounts receivable	+1,000	Sales	+1,000
8.	Cost of sales	+300	Food inventory	−300
9.	Electricity expense	+200	Accounts payable	+200
10.	Water expense	+100	Cash	−100
11.	Cash	+400	Accounts receivable	−400
12.	Food inventory	−150	Accounts payable	−150
13.	Rent	+350	Cash	−700
	Prepaid rent	+350		
14.	Cash	+600	Customers' deposits	+600
15.	Withdrawals	+1,000	Cash	−1,000

(c) After transcribing all transactions verify that the fundamental accounting equation applies to the column totals of your worksheet.

6

Journalizing, Posting, and Taking a Trial Balance

In the previous chapter we learned how to analyze transactions by comprehending that each transaction involves an equal exchange of values. We also learned that the dual-aspect concept of accounting, which reflects this duality inherent in every transaction, is the concept upon which the accounting rules of debit and credit are based. Ultimately, then, identifying what values are given and what values are received provides a greater understanding of how to record transactions than merely memorizing the rules of debits and credits.

In this chapter we expand our coverage of step 2 of the accounting cycle—journalizing—by learning how to record transactions in the accounting records of the hospitality entity once they have been analyzed. We also learn the use of the general journal, the most generally applicable and most flexible type of journal, and the specific procedures for journalizing.

Next, the procedure for posting from the general journal to the general ledger is covered. The method of calculating account balances in the general ledger accounts is explained, as well as the structure and function of the "T" account format.

Subsequently, the taking of a trial balance of the general ledger is discussed in detail, and the best method of locating and correcting errors made in the accounting process is indicated. Finally, the general ledger format in a computerized accounting system is contrasted with that in a manual system.

To review briefly, as noted before, journalizing (step 2 of the accounting cycle) entails the chronological recording of business transactions in a journal by recording the value(s) received and the value(s) given for each transaction. As also noted, the values received are debited, whereas the values given are credited, and they must be equal in value,

$$Dr = Cr$$

The journal can then be perceived as a business diary that records in chronological order all values received (Dr) and all values given (Cr) while maintaining the basic equality of value exchanges. Therefore, the journal must be designed to accommodate the dual aspect of every transaction. We describe and illustrate in this chapter the use of the general journal in recording business transactions because it is the most flexible journal utilized for general accounting purposes. Nonetheless, there are other journals, known as special-purpose journals, and these are described in Chapter 9.

General Journal

(1)	(2)	(3)	(4)	
Date	Description	Ref	Dr	Cr

Figure 6.1. General journal—sample page setup.

THE GENERAL JOURNAL

Journals are described as books of original entry because they are the first place where transactions are recorded in an accounting system. The general journal is used to gather and record in an orderly fashion all hospitality entity transactions. A sample page of the general journal is shown in Figure 6.1. The general journal (GJ) consists of the following items:

(1) *The date column*—used to show in chronological order when each business transaction took place.
(2) *The description column*—used to indicate the names of the specific accounts being debited and credited as well as an explanation of the transaction.
(3) *The reference column (Ref)*—to be used in transferring information from the journal to the book of final entry (the general ledger) by a procedure, to be explained later, called posting.
(4) *Debit (Dr) and credit (Cr) columns*—used to enter the actual amounts being debited and credited.

Recording Transactions in the General Journal

After this brief familiarization with the general journal format, we are now ready to examine the actual process of journalizing. As explained in Chapter 5, step 1 of the accounting cycle consists in the analysis of each transaction in order to discern what values are received (vr) and what values are given (vg). We explained then that values received are recorded as debits and values given are recorded as credits.

Journalizing consists of entering these debit and credit amounts in the debit and credit columns of the general journal, along with the date of the transaction, the name of each account to be debited or credited, and below this a brief description of the transaction being recorded. This information for each transaction, when completely entered in the general journal, is known as a journal entry.

The actual steps to be followed in recording transactions in the general journal can be summarized as follows (refer to Figure 6.1):

1. We first enter the transaction date by writing the year in small numerals at the top of the date column (1) and the month and day on the first line of the date column. Normally, the year and month are not repeated for subsequent entries made on the same journal page.
2. We record the name(s) and amount(s) of the account(s) debited by enter-

ing the account name(s) in the description column (2) and the amount(s) debited in the Dr column (4). The dollar sign is omitted since it is understood that all amounts are in dollars.

3. We record the name(s) and amount(s) of the account(s) credited by indenting the account name(s) in the description column (2) and entering the amount(s) credited in the Cr column (4). As in step 2, the dollar sign is omitted.
4. We write an explanation of the entire transaction on the next line below the credit entry in the description column (2).
5. As previously stated, after all transactions are recorded we transfer the information from the journal to a book of final entry (the general ledger) by means of posting procedures, step 3 of the accounting cycle. In this regard, we indicate in the Ref column (3) of the general journal the account number(s) being posted as evidence that the posting was actually made. (Posting procedures will be covered later.)
6. Verify that the total of the debits equals the total of the credits, i.e., that the journal entry balances. If it does not balance a review of the original transaction analysis should be made. When only one debit and one credit entry exists this step may seem superfluous. However, in the case of complex journal entries, where more than one debit or credit exist, it will help avoid wasting time later searching for errors due to unbalanced journal entries.

Sample Journal Entry

To illustrate these steps we journalize the following transaction.

April 5, 1985   Mr. Carlton invests $30,000 in his new travel agency, a sole proprietorship, by transferring this amount from his personal bank account to the travel agency's bank account.

The travel agency, an accounting entity separate and distinct from Mr. Carlton himself, receives $30,000 in cash. In exchange it gives to Mr. Carlton ownership rights in the amount of $30,000. The value received, cash, must be debited to the cash account and the value given, ownership rights, is credited to Mr. Carlton's capital account. Figure 6.2 shows how this transaction would be recorded in a general journal. The procedure for preparing the journal entry is as follows:

1. The transaction date, April 5, 1985, is entered in the date column. Since this is the initial journal entry for the year, the year "1985" was written in small numerals above the first line of the date column. Since this is

General Journal

Date 1985	Description	Ref	Dr	Cr
April 5	Cash		30,000	
	Mr. Carlton's Capital			30,000
	Initial capital investment			

Figure 6.2.   Initial travel agency journal entry.

also the first journal entry for the month, April was written on the first line of the date column along with the date. For other entries on this same page the year and month are not repeated.

2. The cash account was debited $30,000. Thus, the name of this account was entered in the description column and the amount of the debit $30,000, in the Dr column. The dollar sign is omitted since it is understood that all amounts are in dollars.

3. Mr. Carlton's capital account was credited $30,000. Thus, the name of the account credited, Mr. Carlton's capital, was entered in the description column. Remember, the names of the accounts being credited are indented to help distinguish them from accounts being debited.

The amount of the credit, $30,000, is entered in the Cr column. As in step 2, the dollar sign is also omitted.

4. An explanation of the transaction was written on the next line following the credit entry. Explanations of transactions should always be brief and to the point. In this case three words suffice to describe the entire nature of the transaction, Initial capital investment.

5. When these amounts are later transferred (posted) to the general ledger, the number of the account(s) to which they are posted will be entered in the Ref column.

6. Since this journal entry has only one credit and one debit it was not necessary to total the debits or the credits in order to verify that they are equal.

ILLUSTRATIVE GENERAL JOURNAL

Now that we understand how to make a journal entry we shall reinforce our new ability by analyzing the process of recording the following 16 varied transactions in the general journal of the Montric Restaurant. The Montric Restaurant is a partnership owned equally by Mr. Montcalm and Mr. Ricardo.

Transactions of the Montric Restaurant—June 1988

1. June 1   Mr. Montcalm and Mr. Ricardo make the initial investment in their restaurant by depositing $2,500 each to open a separate bank account for the new accounting entity, the Montric Restaurant.

2. June 1   A bank loan of $10,000 is granted. The proceeds are deposited in the new entity's bank account. The note payable calls for simple interest at 12% per year (12% APR).

3. June 2   A lease is signed to rent a fully equipped building for use as a restaurant, during one year, with the right to renew for 2 additional years. The annual rental is $12,000.

4. June 3   The first month's rent, amounting to $1,000, is paid.

5. June 4   Food inventory is purchased for $1,800. Since suppliers insist on cash payment from new accounts, the purchase terms are collect on delivery (COD).

6. June 11   Sales for the first week of operations are $4,900. Of these sales $4,500 are in cash, $150 paid through travel and entertainment (T.E.) cards, and $250 on open account to local business.

7. June 11   Food costing $400 was used in making the above sales.

8. June 12 A two-year fire insurance policy is purchased by the restaurant for $960 and is paid in cash.

9. June 13 The restaurant purchases a plot of land on which to construct its own restaurant building. The total cost is $10,000. A down payment of $2,000 is made and a 4-year, 10% mortgage note is given for the balance.

10. June 16 The partners each withdraw $1,000 for their personal use.

11. June 18 Mr. Montcalm takes food costing $50 home for his personal use. The retail price of this food is $140.

12. June 21 Eighty dollars is received in partial payment of sales on open account.

13. June 22 The electricity invoice arrives in the amount of $164. The partners decide to pay it later.

14. June 24 The cook is paid $4 per hour for the 120 hours he has worked.

15. June 28 The $164 electricity invoice is paid.

16. June 30 The water invoice for $40 is received and paid the same day.

Montric Restaurant
Recording 16 Sample Transactions
in the General Journal

As previously stated, these transactions are to be recorded in chronological order according to the date on which the transaction took place. The month will appear only on the first line of the general journal. Thereafter, all entries on the same page will include the day's date only. The year and the month will be repeated in transaction 9 because this will be the first transaction on the second page of the general journal. As always, values received are debited, values given are credited.

Transaction No. 1

June 1, 1988 Mr. Montcalm and Mr. Ricardo make the initial capital investment in their restaurant by depositing $2,500 each to open a separate bank account for the new accounting entity, The Montric Restaurant.

Values Exchanged. An asset, cash in the amount of $5,000, is received by the restaurant in exchange for ownership rights (owners' equity accounts) of $2,500 each given to Mr. Montcalm and Mr. Ricardo. Values received are recorded as debits, values given are recorded as credits.

Rules of Dr and Cr. Asset increases are debited and increases in owners' equity accounts are credited.

Journal Entry

Date 1988	Description	Ref	Dr	Cr
June 1	Cash		5,000	
	Mr. Montcalm's capital Mr. Ricardo's capital			2,500 2,500
	Initial capital investment			

Transaction No. 2

June 1, 1988 $10,000 cash is borrowed and a note is signed.

Values Exchanged.   An asset, cash, in the amount of $10,000, is received by the restaurant in exchange for a promise to pay it back, notes payable (a liability).

Rules of Dr and Cr.   Asset increases are debits and liability increases are credits.

Journal Entry

Date	Description	Ref	Dr	Cr
1	Cash		10,000	
	Notes payable			10,000
	Borrowed $10,000 from bank			

Transaction No. 3

June 2, 1988   A lease on the building is signed.

Values Exchanged.   No values are exchanged. This is merely an agreement to exchange values in the future.

Rules of Dr and Cr.   Not applicable—no transaction.

Journal Entry.   None—no transaction took place.

Transaction No. 4

June 3, 1988 $1,000 is paid for the first month's rent of the leased building.

Values Exchanged.   The restaurant is receiving a service, the use of the building for one month, and gives an asset, cash, in exchange.

Rules of Dr and Cr.   Using rented space represents the consumption of a service, an expense. Increases in expenses are debited since we receive the right to use the premises for a month. An asset, cash, decreases, which is recorded as a credit.

Journal Entry

Date	Description	Ref	Dr	Cr
3	Rent expense		1,000	
	Cash			1,000
	Paid first month's rent			

Transaction No. 5

June 4, 1988 $1,800 worth of food is purchased.

Values Exchanged.   An asset, food, worth $1,800 is received. Another asset of equal value, $1,800 in cash, is given.

Rules of Dr and Cr. The increase in the asset, food inventory, is recorded as a debit, whereas the decrease in the asset, cash, is recorded as a credit.

Journal Entry

Date	Description	Ref	Dr	Cr
4	Inventory—food		1,800	
	Cash			1,800
	Purchased food inventory			

Transaction No. 6
June 11, 1988   First week's sales are $4,900. Cash sales are $4,500 and credit sales $400.

Values Exchanged. Two assets, $4,500 in cash and $400 in agreements to future payments (accounts receivable), are received. Food and related dining services worth $4,900 are given.

Rules of Dr and Cr. An increase in assets, cash and accounts receivable, is debited. Goods and services sold are revenues and revenues should be credited.

Journal Entry

Date	Description	Ref	Dr	Cr
11	Cash		4,500	
	Accounts receivable		400	
	Sales			4,900
	Week's sales			

Transaction No. 7
June 11, 1988   The restaurant consumes food in the amount of $400 in making the week's sales.

Values exchanged. The restaurant receives the use of $400 worth of food. It gives up an asset, food inventory, in exchange.

Rules of Dr and Cr. Assets consumed are expenses. Increases in expenses are debits. Decreases in assets, food inventory in this case, are credits.

Journal Entry

Date	Description	Ref	Dr	Cr
11	Cost of food sold		400	
	Inventory—food			400
	Cost of week's sales			

Transaction No. 8
June 12, 1988   A two-year fire insurance policy is purchased for $960 in cash.

Values Exchanged.   The restaurant receives a future value, insurance coverage during the next two years. In exchange, an asset, $960 in cash, is given.

Rules of Dr and Cr.   The insurance company's commitment to provide insurance coverage during the next two years is an asset that will provide future benefit, a prepaid expense. The increase in the asset, prepaid expenses, is debited. The decrease in the asset, cash, is credited.

Journal Entry

Date	Description	Ref	Dr	Cr
12	Prepaid expenses		960	
	Cash			960
	Purchased fire insurance			

Transaction No. 9
June 13, 1988   Land worth $10,000 is purchased with a $2,000 down payment and an $8,000 mortgage note.

Values Exchanged.   An asset, land, worth $10,000 is received. In exchange another asset, $2,000 in cash, plus a liability, the promise to pay $8,000 in the future, are given.

Rules of Dr and Cr.   One asset, in this case land, increases and should be debited. Another asset, cash, decreases and is credited. A liability, mortgage notes payable, increases and is credited.

Journal Entry

Date 1988	Description	Ref	Dr	Cr
June 13	Land		10,000	
	Cash			2,000
	Mortgages payable			8,000
	Purchased land			

Transaction No. 10
June 16, 1988   Each partner withdraws $1,000.

Values Exchanged.   The restaurant receives a return of ownership rights, recorded through an account called "withdrawals," which will be later netted out against partners' capital accounts. In exchange it gives each partner an asset, $1,000 in cash.

Rules of Dr and Cr.   Withdrawals is a contra-equity account since it reduces partners' capital. Thus, the withdrawals account is debited. The decrease in the asset account, cash, is credited.

Journal Entry

Date	Description	Ref	Dr	Cr
16	Montcalm's withdrawals		1,000	
	Ricardo's withdrawals		1,000	
	Cash			2,000
	Partners' withdrawals			

Transaction No. 11
June 18, 1988 Mr. Montcalm withdraws $50 worth of food.

Values Exchanged. Withdrawals do not have to be made in cash. The restaurant is receiving a $50 reduction in ownership rights and is giving food, with a cost of $50, in exchange. The retail value of the food is not relevant since no retail sale was made.

Rules of Dr and Cr. Again, the contra-equity account withdrawals is increased, resulting in a debit. An asset, inventory—food, is credited, reflecting the asset decrease.

Journal Entry

Date	Description	Ref	Dr	Cr
18	Montcalm's withdrawals		50	
	Inventory—food			50
	Partner's withdrawal			

Transaction No. 12
June 21, 1988 A client made a partial payment of $80 on his open account.

Values Exchanged. The restaurant receives an asset, $80 in cash, and gives a reduction of the amount owing to it (accounts receivable) in exchange.

Rules of Dr and Cr. An asset, cash in this case, is increased. Another asset, accounts receivable, is decreased. Therefore, we debit an asset, cash, and credit an asset, accounts receivable.

Journal Entry

Date	Description	Ref	Dr	Cr
21	Cash		80	
	Accounts receivable			80
	Received payment on open account			

Transaction No. 13
June 22, 1988 An electricity invoice for $164 is received and will be paid later.

Values Exchanged. This is a completed transaction because (1) we have consumed a service (electricity) and (2) we know the value of that service. In return for the electricity received, the restaurant is giving an implied promise to pay in the future, an account payable.

Rules of Dr and Cr. A service consumed is an expense, which is debited. An implied promise to pay is an account payable, a liability, which is recorded as a credit.

Journal Entry

Date	Description	Ref	Dr	Cr
22	Utilities expense		164	
	Accounts payable			164
	Receipt of electricity invoice			

Transaction No. 14
June 24, 1988   The cook is paid wages of $480 ($4 × 120 hours).

Values Exchanged. The cook's services are received and consumed. In exchange, $480 in cash is given to the cook.

Rules of Dr and Cr. A service consumed is an expense, and increases in expenses are debited. Cash, an asset, is decreased and thus is credited.

Journal Entry

Date	Description	Ref	Dr	Cr
24	Payroll expense		480	
	Cash			480
	Paid cook's wages			

Transaction No. 15
June 28, 1988   The $164 electricity invoice is paid.

Values Exchanged. A reduction of amounts owed by the restaurant (accounts payable) is received in exchange for an asset, cash.

Rules of Dr and Cr. Amounts owed are accounts payable, which are liabilities. Decreases in liabilities are debits. Asset decreases are credits. In this case there is a decrease in both an asset, cash, and a liability, accounts payable.

Journal Entry

Date	Description	Ref	Dr	Cr
28	Accounts payable		164	
	Cash			164
	Paid electricity invoice			

Transaction No. 16
June 30, 1988   A $40 water invoice is received and paid the same day.

Values Exchanged.   The use of $40 worth of water is received and consumed in exchange for an asset, cash.

Rules of Dr and Cr.   Services or assets consumed are expenses. Increases in expenses are debits. Cash, an asset, decreases and thus is credited.

Journal Entry

Date	Description	Ref	Dr	Cr
30	Utilities expense		40	
	Cash			40
	Received and paid water invoice			

For the reader's reference the analyses of the above transactions have been summarized in Table 6.1, where the reader may also verify that:

1. Total values received = total values given.
2. Total debits = total credits.
3. The fundamental accounting equation (assets = liabilities + owners' equity) was preserved.

Pages 1 and 2 of the complete general journal of Montric Restaurant appear on the left side of Figure 6.6 (see pp. 102 and 103). Notice that since transaction no. 9 (June 13, 1988) is the first entry on the second page of the general journal, the year and month are repeated.

At this point we have learned (1) to analyze transactions and (2) to journalize them by entering them in a book of original entry called a general journal. Nonetheless, the information included in the journal is not very useful because of the way the information is organized (in chronological order). That is, it is very difficult to determine the effect of all transactions in each account since there might be several entries affecting each account, some of which may be debits and some credits. The next step in the accounting cycle—posting to the general ledger—enables us to overcome this problem.

POSTING TO THE GENERAL LEDGER

Posting to the general ledger—step 3 of the accounting cycle—involves the transfer of the information recorded in the journal to a book of final entry known as the ledger. This is done by copying the debits and credits recorded in the journal in their corresponding accounts in the general ledger.

As stated earlier, the debits and credits entered chronologically in the general journal must be organized and summarized in order to provide meaningful and useful information. This is accomplished through the posting procedures. In this manner, the ledger will serve as a summary of the effect of all business transactions for all accounts.

TABLE 6.1. Analysis of Montric Restaurant's Transactions

Transaction	Assets	Liabilities	Owners' equity			Values exchanged		Accounting entry	
			Capital	Revenues	Expenses	Values received	Values given	Dr	Cr
1. Partners invest $2,500 each in the restaurant	+5,000 cash	0	+2,500 Montcalm's capital +2,500 Ricardo's capital	0	0	$5,000 in cash	Ownership rights $5,000	5,000 cash	2,500 Montcalm's capital 2,500 Ricardo's capital
2. Borrow $10,000 from a bank	+10,000 cash	+10,000 notes payable	0	0	0	$10,000 in cash	Promise to pay $10,000	10,000 cash	10,000 notes payable
3. Lease contract is signed (no transaction involved)	0	0	0	0	0	None	None	None	None
4. $1,000 rent is paid	-1,000 cash	0	0	0	-1,000 rent expense	Use of building for one month with value of $1,000	$1,000 in cash	1,000 rent expense	1,000 cash
5. $1,800 worth of food is purchased COD	-1,800 cash +1,800 food inventory	0	0	0	0	$1,800 worth of food	$1,800 in cash	1,800 food inventory	1,800 cash
6. Cash sales of $4,500, credit sales of $400 are made	+4,500 cash +400 accounts receivable	0	0	+4,900 sales	0	$4,500 received in cash, plus agreement to pay $400 in the future	Food & related services worth $4,900	4,500 cash 400 accounts receivable	4,900 sales
7. Food that cost $400 consumed in making above sales	-400 food inventory	0	0	0	-400 cost of sales	Use of $400 worth of food	$400 reduction in food inventory	400 cost of sales	400 food inventory
8. A two-year fire insurance policy is purchased for $960	-960 cash +960 prepaid expenses	0	0	0	0	Right to future insurance in the amount of $960	$960 in cash	960 prepaid expenses	960 cash

Transaction								
9. Land is purchased for $2,000 cash & an $8,000 mortgage note	−2,000 cash +10,000 land	+8,000 mortgage payable	0	0	0	Land worth $10,000	$2,000 in cash, promise to pay $8,000	10,000 land	2,000 cash 8,000 mortgage payable
10. Each partner withdraws $1,000 for his personal use	−2,000 cash	0	−1,000 Montcalm's withdrawals −1,000 Ricardo's withdrawals	0	0	Return of ownership rights worth $2,000	$2,000 in cash	1,000 Montcalm's withdrawals 1,000 Ricardo's withdrawals	2,000 cash
11. Mr. Montcalm takes $50 worth of food home	−50 food inventory	0	−50 Montcalm's withdrawals	0	0	Return of ownership rights worth $50	$50 reduction in food inventory	50 Montcalm's withdrawals	50 food inventory
12. $80 is received in partial payment of open account	+80 cash −80 accounts receivable	0	0	0	0	$80 in cash	$80 in reduction of accounts receivable	80 cash	80 accounts receivable
13. Received electricity invoice for $164, to be paid later	0	+164 accounts payable	0	0	−164 utilities expense	Use of $164 worth of electricity	Agreement to pay $164 in the future	164 utilities expense	164 accounts payable
14. Cook is paid $480	−480 cash	0	0	0	−480 payroll expense	Services worth $480 rendered by cook	$480 in cash	480 payroll expense	480 cash
15. Electricity invoice is paid, $164	−164 cash	−164 accounts payable	0	0	0	Reduction of amount owed to electric co., $164	$164 in cash	164 accounts payable	164 cash
16. Water invoice for $40 is received and paid	−40 cash	0	0	0	−40 utilities expense	Use of $40 worth of water	$40 in cash	40 utilities expense	40 cash
TOTALS	23,766	18,000	2,950	4,900	20,184	37,038	37,038	37,038	37,038

THE GENERAL LEDGER

The general ledger, the book of final entry, consists of a group of accounts that constitute a hospitality organization's accounting system. It may be a book, a loose-leaf binder, a tray of cards, or magnetic tapes or disks. No matter what its form, the general ledger will summarize the effect of the transactions recorded for each account. An accounting system will have a separate account for each type of asset, liability, owners' equity, revenue, and expense. Typically, the general ledger accounts will appear in financial statement order, that is, first all the asset accounts, then liability and owners' equity accounts, and finally the revenue and expense accounts. The actual number of accounts will vary from operation to operation, depending on the nature of the business as well as on management's need for information.

CHART OF ACCOUNTS

In order to facilitate finding general ledger accounts during journalizing, posting, and preparing financial statements, the hospitality organization normally creates a chart of accounts, which consists of a sequential listing of all the firm's account names and assigned numbers.

The balance sheet asset accounts are listed first, from top to bottom. Then the liability and owners' equity accounts are listed, from top to bottom. In keeping with the fact that revenue and expenses are a subdivision of owners' equity, these income statement accounts are listed after the owners' equity accounts in the same order in which they normally would appear on the income statement.

Account numbers are assigned to the various general ledger accounts in order to facilitate their identification, and the account numbers are entered in the Ref column of the general journal to indicate that the corresponding debit or credit amount has been posted to the appropriate general ledger account.

A simple general ledger (GL) account classification might be as follows:

Type of account	Account numbers
Assets	100 to 199
Liabilities	200 to 299
Owners' equity	300 to 399
Revenues	400 to 499
Cost of sales	500 to 599
Other expenses	600 to 699

Table 6.2 shows the account numbers that will be used to organize the accounts of the Montric Restaurant. The accounts are listed as they would appear on the balance sheet and income statement to assist the reader in visualizing the relationship between account location and account number. Normally, however, the chart of accounts consists of a single listing of accounts in sequential numerical order.

When preparing a chart of accounts some numbers should remain unassigned in each account category (cash, accounts receivable, inventory, etc.) to be utilized later should it be necessary to add new accounts in each category.

TABLE 6.2. Sample Chart of Accounts

Account	Number	Account	Number
Assets		Liabilities	
Cash	101	Accounts payable	201
Accounts receivable	104	Notes payable	205
Notes receivable	106	Mortgages payable	209
Inventory—food	115	Payroll payable	215
Inventory—supplies	119	Taxes payable	230
Prepaid expenses	125	Unearned revenues	251
Land	135	Owners' equity	
Buildings	139	Montcalm's capital	301
Equipment	142	Montcalm's withdrawals	302
Furniture and fixtures	151	Ricardo's capital	306
		Ricardo's withdrawals	307
		Revenues	
		Sales	401
		Expenses	
		Cost of sales	501
		Payroll	606
		Utilities	611
		Rent	616
		Insurance	621

THE "T" ACCOUNT

As indicated before, a general ledger account may take many different forms. Its simplest form, the "T" account format, is used for learning purposes, and sometimes during the subsequent use of accounting data for decision-making purposes. It is, indeed, a very simple method of gathering and summarizing debits and credits in the general ledger.

The "T" account derives its name from its shape, resembling, as it does, the capital letter "T":

(1)	(2)
Cash	**No. 101**
Dr	Cr
(3)	(4)

The "T" account consists of four major parts:

(1) The name of the account
(2) The account number
(3) The left side, known as the debit side (Dr)
(4) The right side, known as the credit side (Cr)

POSTING PROCEDURES

The "T" account format will be utilized to explain the process of posting since this format will be used for learning purposes and in problem solving throughout the text.

The steps used in posting to the general ledger using the "T" account format, starting with the debit postings first, are:

1. Enter the date of the transaction as shown in the journal to the left of the Dr column of the "T" account to be debited.
2. Enter in the debit column of the "T" account the amount of the debit entry as shown in the journal.
3. Enter in the general journal Ref column the number of the general ledger account to which the debit entry was posted. This step will serve as evidence that the journal entry was posted from the journal to the ledger.
4. The preceding three steps are repeated for the credit side of the journal entry, with the exception that we enter the date and amount in the credit column of the general ledger "T" account.

Once all journal entries have been posted from the general journal to the general ledger for a week, month, or any other period of time selected by the hospitality company, we must determine the balance of each account in the general ledger. We shall be guided by the basic rules of debit and credit in the determination of a general ledger account balance. That is, assets and expenses will have a normal debit balance since increases in these accounts are debited. Likewise, liability, owners' equity, and revenue accounts will normally have a credit balance because increases in these accounts are credited.

Accordingly, the balance of each account is found by adding the debits, adding the credits, and subtracting the smaller sum from the larger sum. For asset and expense accounts the larger total will normally be in the debit column, resulting in a debit balance. Similarly, for liability, owners' equity, and revenue accounts, the larger total will normally be in the credit column, resulting in a credit balance.

Figure 6.3 shows the general ledger cash account in "T" account format.

		(1) Cash			**(2)** No. 101	
(3)	Bal.	6/1/88	1,468			
(4)		6/2/88	500	6/3/88	172	**(4)**
		Totals	1,968		172	
(5)	Bal.	6/3/88	1,796			

Figure 6.3. Sample general ledger cash account—"T" format.

The main elements of the cash "T" account are

(1) The name of the account (cash)
(2) The account number (101)
(3) The beginning balance (Bal. 6/1/88)
(4) The transaction dates and amounts debited and credited during the period
(5) The ending balance (Bal. 6/3/88)

Refer to the posting procedures enumerated before and to the determination of an account balance in reviewing Figure 6.3. Since the total debits (including the beginning debit balance) were larger than the total credits, we have an ending debit balance of $1,796 (total debits of $1,968 less total credits of $172).

THE GENERAL LEDGER FORMAT

As pointed out earlier, the "T" account format is, indeed, an excellent teaching tool and thus we shall use it during our discussions and for problem solving throughout the book. However, "T" accounts are not used in practice. An example of a GL account format that has been widely used in practice is shown in Figure 6.4.

Account: Cash (5)			Account No.: 101			
Date 1988	Description	Ref	(6) Dr	Cr	Balance Dr	Cr
June 1	Balance brought forward				1,468	
2	Sales	GJ-1	500			
3	Expenses	GJ-1		172	1,796	

Figure 6.4. General ledger account—ledger page format.

A general ledger page account format generally includes:

(1) The name of the account, to differentiate it from other accounts.
(2) The number of the account, to help identify its nature and its location in the general ledger.
(3) The date column.
(4) A description column.
(5) A reference column to show the source of the information being posted.
(6) Activity columns for posting the debit and credit amounts corresponding to the activity of the period.
(7) Balance columns for determining an updated balance after each transaction.

When the general ledger account format shown in Figure 6.4 is used, two additional steps are required to complete posting procedures:

- A brief description of the transaction under the description column (i.e., sales).
- The source of the posted information in the Ref column using initials from the source book followed by the page number. For instance, a posting from page 1 of the general journal would be indicated by GJ-1.

POSTING ILLUSTRATED

The debit side of the initial transaction of the Montric Restaurant will be posted here as an example of the posting process. The complete transaction is

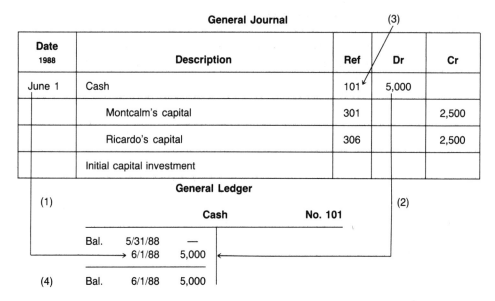

General Journal (3)

Date 1988	Description	Ref	Dr	Cr
June 1	Cash	101	5,000	
	Montcalm's capital	301		2,500
	Ricardo's capital	306		2,500
	Initial capital investment			

General Ledger

(1)   **Cash**   **No. 101**   (2)

Bal.   5/31/88   —
6/1/88   5,000

(4)   Bal.   6/1/88   5,000

Figure 6.5. Montric Restaurant—initial transaction.

shown in a section of the general journal given in Figure 6.5. A description of the process is as follows:

(1) The date of the debit transaction, 6/1/88, is entered on the left-hand side of the general ledger cash "T" account.
(2) The $5,000 debit to cash is entered on the left-hand side of the general ledger cash "T" account.
(3) The number of the cash account, 101, is entered in the general journal Ref column to indicate that the debit has been posted.
(4) The balance is calculated for the cash account as of June 1, 1988. An increase in cash is debited, and so the $5,000 transaction amount is added to the beginning zero balance, resulting in a debit balance of $5,000 as of June 1, 1988.

The credit side of the entry is posted following this same procedure.

All the subsequent entries would be posted in the same manner, by posting either all debit entries first and then all credit entries, or by posting one complete journal entry at a time. The posting of all of Montric Restaurant's transactions using the "T" account format is shown in Figure 6.6. Figure 6.7 shows the general ledger accounts as they would appear in the standard ledger format. In order to reinforce the understanding of the posting process, the reader should trace the remaining entries of the Montric Restaurant from the general journal to the appropriate general ledger accounts in Figure 6.6 (pp. 102 and 103). A comparison of the "T" account format in Figure 6.6 with the ledger page account format in Figure 6.7 (pp. 104 and 105) should also be made.

When all of the transactions for the period have been posted to the appropriate general ledger accounts, these accounts summarize the impact of the period's activity. Before they can serve as the basis for the preparation of financial statements, however, two more steps in the accounting cycle are required. Step 4 of the accounting cycle—taking a trial balance of the general ledger—will be discussed next.

TAKING A TRIAL BALANCE
OF THE GENERAL LEDGER

In order to test the accuracy of debit and credit balances in the general ledger at the end of an accounting period, a trial balance is prepared. This consists of a list of all the general ledger accounts with their current balances as of the last day of the period.

Typically, every time numbers are manipulated, errors and omissions are likely to be made. For instance, a debit entry could have been posted as a credit to the general ledger account. In order to conform to the dual-aspect concept of accounting we have seen that debits must equal credits. We shall now be able to verify the equality of value exchanges (debit balances and credit balances must be equal) by taking a trial balance of the general ledger.

The trial balance will serve as a proof of the arithmetic accuracy of the recording and posting process. Once the balances of the individual ledger accounts have been determined we shall be ready to take the trial balance by listing the individual account names and numbers and their respective debit or credit balances. A trial balance is said to be in balance when debit balances equal credit balances and we are able to assume that no errors were made in the completion of the first four steps of the accounting cycle.

The procedure for taking a trial balance of the general ledger is as follows:

1. Set up a list with all of the general ledger account numbers on the left and names on the right in chart of account order.
2. Set up two columns to the right of this list. The left column should be headed Dr and the right column should be headed Cr.
3. Enter debit balances in the Dr column and credit balances in the Cr column.
4. Total the Dr column and the Cr column. The two totals should be equal, indicating that the trial balance balances.

The trial balance for the Montric Restaurant is shown in Figure 6.8. The accounts payable account does not appear on the trial balance since it has a zero balance. The electricity invoice that was originally entered in the account had been paid prior to the end of the accounting period (June 30, 1988), which is also the balance sheet date.

DISCOVERING ERROR SOURCES

In spite of the assumption of accuracy if the trial balance balances, it does not necessarily mean that there are no errors or omissions. As a method of discovering accounting errors the trial balance has three shortcomings:

1. Equal errors in opposite directions will compensate for each other without unbalancing the trial balance.
2. If a complete journal entry has been omitted entirely or posted twice, the trial balance will still balance because the debits and credits omitted or posted twice are of equal values. That is why it is important not to fill in the Ref column of the general journal until after the debit or credit has actually been posted to the general ledger.
3. Finally, if a debit or a credit is posted to the wrong account, the trial balance will still balance. This is a very difficult type of error to detect and there is no way to avoid it except by being careful.

MONTRIC RESTAURANT
General Journal

Date 1988	Description	Ref	Dr	Cr
June 1	Cash	101	5,000	
	Mr. Montcalm's capital	301		2,500
	Mr. Ricardo's capital	306		2,500
	Initial capital investment			
1	Cash	101	10,000	
	Notes payable	205		10,000
	Borrowed $10,000 from bank			
3	Rent expense	616	1,000	
	Cash	101		1,000
	Paid first month's rent			
4	Inventory—food	115	1,800	
	Cash	101		1,800
	Purchased food inventory			
11	Cash	101	4,500	
	Accounts receivable	104	400	
	Sales	401		4,900
	Week's sales			
11	Cost of food sold	501	400	
	Inventory—food	115		400
	Cost of week's sales			
12	Prepaid expenses	125	960	
	Cash	101		960
	Purchased fire insurance			

Cash No. 101

	Dr			Cr
6/1/88	5,000		6/3/88	1,000
6/1/88	10,000		6/4/88	1,800
6/11/88	4,500		6/12/88	960
6/21/88	80		6/13/88	2,000
			6/16/88	2,000
			6/24/88	480
			6/28/88	164
			6/30/88	40
Totals	19,580		Totals	8,444
Bal.	11,136			

Accounts Receivable No. 104

	Dr			Cr
6/11/88	400		6/21/88	80
Totals	400			80
Bal.	320			

Inventory—Food No. 115

	Dr			Cr
6/4/88	1,800		6/11/88	400
			6/18/88	50
Totals	1,800			450
Bal.	1,350			

Prepaid Expenses No. 125

	Dr
6/12/88	960
Total	960
Bal.	960

Land No. 135

	Dr
6/13/88	10,000
Total	10,000
Bal.	10,000

Accounts Payable No. 201

	Dr			Cr
6/28/88	164		6/22/88	164
Totals	164			164
			Bal.	0

Notes Payable No. 205

		Cr
	6/1/88	10,000
	Total	10,000
	Bal.	10,000

Mortgages Payable No. 209

		Cr
	6/13/88	8,000
	Total	8,000
	Bal.	8,000

General Ledger (T-accounts)

Montcalm's Withdrawals No. 302
6/16/88	1,000	
6/18/88	50	
Total	1,050	
Bal.	1,050	

Montcalm's Capital No. 301
6/1/88	2,500	
Total	2,500	
Bal.	2,500	

Sales No. 401
6/11/88	4,900	
Total	4,900	
Bal.	4,900	

Utilities Expense No. 611
6/22/88	164	
6/30/88	40	
Total	204	
Bal.	204	

Ricardo's Withdrawals No. 307
6/16/88	1,000	
Total	1,000	
Bal.	1,000	

Payroll Expense No. 606
6/24/88	480	
Total	480	
Bal.	480	

Ricardo's Capital No. 306
6/1/88	2,500	
Total	2,500	
Bal.	2,500	

Cost of Food Sold No. 501
6/11/88	400	
Total	400	
Bal.	400	

Rent Expense No. 616
6/3/88	1,000	
Total	1,000	
Bal.	1,000	

General Journal

Date	Account	Ref	Debit	Credit
June 13	Land	135	10,000	
	Cash	101		2,000
	Mortgages payable	209		8,000
	Purchased land			
16	Montcalm's withdrawals	302	1,000	
	Ricardo's withdrawals	307	1,000	
	Cash	101		2,000
	Partners' withdrawals			
18	Montcalm's withdrawals	302	50	
	Inventory—food	115		50
	Partner's withdrawal			
21	Cash	101	80	
	Accounts receivable	104		80
	Received payment on open account			
22	Utilities expense	611	164	
	Accounts payable	201		164
	Receipt of electricity invoice			
24	Payroll expense	606	480	
	Cash	101		480
	Paid cook's wages			
28	Accounts payable	201	164	
	Cash	101		164
	Paid electricity invoice			
30	Utilities expense	611	40	
	Cash	101		40
	Received and paid water invoice			

Figure 6.6. Montric Restaurant—general journal and general ledger in "T" account format. The reader should verify that all postings not indicated by arrows have been made correctly from the general journal to the general ledger.

Cash — Acct. No. 101

Date 1988	Description	Ref	Dr	Cr	Balance Dr	Balance Cr
June 1	Capital	GJ-1	5,000			
1	Bank loan	1	10,000			
3	Expense	1		1,000		
4	Food inv	1		1,800		
11	Sales	1	4,500			
12	Expense	1		960		
13	Land	2		2,000		
16	Withdrawal	2		2,000		
21	A/R	2	80			
24	Expense	2		480		
28	Expense	2		164		
30	Expense	2		40	11,136	

Accounts Receivable — Acct. No. 104

Date 1988	Description	Ref	Dr	Cr	Balance Dr	Balance Cr
June 11	Sales	GJ-1	400			
21	Collections	GJ-2		80	320	

Inventory—Food — Acct. No. 115

Date 1988	Description	Ref	Dr	Cr	Balance Dr	Balance Cr
June 4	Purchases	GJ-1	1,800			
11	Sales	1		400		
18	Withdrawal	2		50	1,350	

Prepaid Expenses — Acct. No. 125

Date 1988	Description	Ref	Dr	Cr	Balance Dr	Balance Cr
June 12	Insurance purchased	GJ-1	960		960	

Land — Acct. No. 135

Date 1988	Description	Ref	Dr	Cr	Balance Dr	Balance Cr
June 13	Purchase	GJ-2	10,000		10,000	

Accounts Payable — Acct. No. 201

Date 1988	Description	Ref	Dr	Cr	Balance Dr	Balance Cr
June 22	Electricity invoice	GJ-2		164		
28	Payment	GJ-2	164			—

Notes Payable — Acct. No. 205

Date 1988	Description	Ref	Dr	Cr	Balance Dr	Balance Cr
June 18	Bank loan	GJ-1		10,000		10,000

Mortgages Payable — Acct. No. 209

Date 1988	Description	Ref	Dr	Cr	Balance Dr	Balance Cr
June 13	Land purchased	GJ-2		8,000		8,000

Montcalm's Capital						Acct. No. 301
Date 1988	Description	Ref	Dr	Cr	Balance Dr	Balance Cr
June 1	Investment	GJ-1		2,500		2,500

Montcalm's Withdrawals						Acct. No. 302
Date 1988	Description	Ref	Dr	Cr	Balance Dr	Balance Cr
June 16	Withdrawal		1,000			
18	Withdrawal		50		1,050	

Ricardo's Capital						Acct. No. 306
Date 1988	Description	Ref	Dr	Cr	Balance Dr	Balance Cr
June 1	Investment	GJ-1		2,500		2,500

Ricardo's Withdrawals						Acct. No. 307
Date 1988	Description	Ref	Dr	Cr	Balance Dr	Balance Cr
June 14	Withdrawal		1,000		1,000	

Sales						Acct. No. 401
Date 1988	Description	Ref	Dr	Cr	Balance Dr	Balance Cr
June 11	Week's sales	GJ-1		4,900		4,900

Cost of Goods Sold						Acct. No. 501
Date 1988	Description	Ref	Dr	Cr	Balance Dr	Balance Cr
June 11	Week's sales	GJ-1	400		400	

Payroll Expense						Acct. No. 606
Date 1988	Description	Ref	Dr	Cr	Balance Dr	Balance Cr
June 24	Cook's wages	GJ-2	480		480	

Utilities Expense						Acct. No. 611
Date 1988	Description	Ref	Dr	Cr	Balance Dr	Balance Cr
June 22	Electric invoice	GJ-2	164			
30	Water invoice	2	40		204	

Rent Expense						Acct. No. 616
Date 1988	Description	Ref	Dr	Cr	Balance Dr	Balance Cr
June 3	First month's rent	GJ-1	1,000		1,000	

Figure 6.7. Montric Restaurant—general ledger accounts in ledger page format. The reader should correlate and compare these with the "T" account format in Figure 6.6.

MONTRIC RESTAURANT
Trial Balance
June 30, 1988

No.	Account Name	Dr	Cr
101	Cash	$11,136	
104	Accounts receivable	320	
115	Inventory—food	1,350	
125	Prepaid expenses	960	
135	Land	10,000	
205	Notes payable		$10,000
209	Mortgages payable		8,000
301	Montcalm's capital		2,500
302	Montcalm's withdrawals	1,050	
306	Ricardo's capital		2,500
307	Ricardo's withdrawals	1,000	
401	Sales		4,900
501	Cost of food sold	400	
606	Payroll expense	480	
611	Utilities expense	204	
616	Rent expense	1,000	
	Totals	$27,900	$27,900

Figure 6.8. Montric Restaurant—trial balance.

If the trial balance does not balance, that is, the total of the debit general ledger account balances does not equal the total of the credit balances, this indicates one or more of four types of errors or omissions:

1. The journalizing or posting of one or more unequal debits or credits has been omitted.
2. One or more unequal debit or credit amounts have been journalized or posted twice.
3. A debit entry has been journalized or posted as a credit entry or vice versa.
4. An error in addition or subtraction has been made.

Next are listed the steps to follow in determining the source of an error or omission detected when taking a trial balance:

1. Repeat the addition of the trial balance columns.

2. If there is a difference, determine the amount. If the difference can be evenly divided by 9 then there is a high probability that either
   (a) you moved a decimal point to the left, i.e., $10,000 was written as $1,000 or $100; or
   (b) you transposed two numbers by reversing their order, i.e., $480 was written as $840, $7,136 was written as $7,316, etc.
   When these two mistakes occur, the difference between the totals of the Dr and Cr columns of the trial balance is divisible by 9 without any remainder. Go back and verify that you transferred the appropriate general ledger account balances to your trial balance.
3. Divide the difference between the total of the Dr column and the total of the Cr column in half and look for the amount in the trial balance. If it appears, then most likely you have entered a debit amount as a credit amount or vice versa.
4. If this reveals no error, recalculate the balances in the individual general ledger accounts.
5. Retrace your postings from the general journal to the general ledger accounts.
6. Verify that your initial journal entries, as entered in the general journal, are in balance.

This process may appear simple when dealing with elementary textbook problems. In actuality there may be several errors to find and many more transactions than those in our examples. Finding an error can become a very lengthy and time-consuming process. The best and most economical procedure is, therefore, to avoid errors by exercising care when performing accounting functions.

Two ways of reducing the probability of committing an error are

1. Do not enter zeros in the cents columns of the general journal or general ledger—use a dash instead. This helps to unclutter the columns and to avoid confusing a zero with a six.
2. Do not use dollar signs in journals or ledgers. They add clutter and may be confused with numerals.

THE COMPUTERIZED GENERAL LEDGER

The format of the general ledger may vary according to the type of accounting system being used. Currently two broad categories of accounting system predominate: manual systems, used mainly by very small hospitality entities, and computerized systems, used by virtually everyone else. Accounting books in manual systems are usually looseleaf, and an entire page is dedicated to each general ledger account so that new pages may be added if space runs out on the preceding pages. In a computerized system the computer prints the general ledger accounts in a continuous fashion, occupying only the portion of a page that it needs to print out each account. The original printout is discarded and a new one is prepared every time additional entries are posted to the computerized ledger. Figure 6.9 gives examples of both systems. Despite the differences in format, the basic elements of a general ledger account are the same.

GENERAL LEDGER

Account: Cash — Account No.: 101

Date 1988		Ref	Dr	Cr	Balance Dr	Balance Cr
Jun 1	Brought Forward				1468 00	
2	Sale	GJ-1	500 00		1968 00	
3	Expense	GJ-1		172 00	1796 00	

Account: Accounts Receivable — Account No.: 105

Date 1988		Ref	Dr	Cr	Balance Dr	Balance Cr
Jun 1	Brought Forward				4792 00	
3		GJ-1	750 00		5542 00	
4		GJ-1	500 00		6042 00	
9		GJ-2		1362 00	4680 00	

Account: Inventory — Account No.: 108

Date 1988		Ref	Dr	Cr	Balance Dr	Balance Cr
Jun 1	Brought Forward				6666 00	
2	Cost of Sales	GJ-1		180 00	6486 00	
3	Cost of Sales	GJ-1		280 00	6206 00	
4	Cost of Sales	GJ-1		200 00	6006 00	
12	Purchased Inventory	GJ-2	1349 00		7355 00	

```
                        GENERAL LEDGER                      PAGE 1
                        --------------                 JUNE 30, 1988
        ACCOUNT
   NO.  DESCRIPTION          DATE      REF     CURRENT     BALANCES
   ---------------------------------------------------------------------
   101  CASH                                               1,468.00
        SALE              06/02/88  001 GJ     500.00
        EXPENSE           06/03/88  001 GJ    -172.00
                                               328.00      1,796.00
   ---------------------------------------------------------------------
   105  ACCOUNTS RECEIVABLE                                4,792.00
        SALE              06/03/88  001 GJ     750.00
        SALE              06/04/88  001 GJ     500.00
        COLLECTION        06/09/88  002 GJ  -1,362.00
                                              -112.00      4,680.00
   ---------------------------------------------------------------------
   108  INVENTORY                                          6,666.00
        COST OF SALES     06/02/88  001 GJ    -180.00
        COST OF SALES     06/03/88  001 GJ    -280.00
        COST OF SALES     06/04/88  001 GJ    -200.00
        PURCHASED INVENTORY 06/12/88 002 GJ  1,349.00
                                               689.00      7,355.00
   ---------------------------------------------------------------------
```

Figure 6.9. Manual and computerized general ledger accounts.

QUESTIONS

1. What is a trial balance?
2. Why is the general journal called a book of original entry?
3. May a journal entry have more credits than debits? Explain.
4. In what order are accounts listed on the chart of accounts?
5. In what sequence are journal entries entered in a journal?
6. What is posting?
7. What is the function of the general ledger?
8. What is a "T" account?
9. If the trial balance of the general ledger is in balance can we be assured that there were no errors or omissions in our work? Explain.
10. What is a chart of accounts and why is it a useful device?

EXERCISES

1. (a) Analyze the following transactions of the Rustic Hotel in terms of values exchanged and debits and credits.
   (b) Prepare a general journal on a sheet of paper and journalize these transactions.
      Feb. 15 The Rustic Hotel purchases $4,561 worth of food and beverages on account.
           18 The hotel's sales for the week amount to $6,457, of which $2,344 are on open account.
           20 The hotel collects $3,789 on open accounts.
           21 The hotel pays its creditors $3,672.
           25 The hotel buys an oven for $5,600. It pays $1,600 in cash plus two notes payable of $2,000 each. One is due at the current year end, the other at the following year end.
   (c) Is there sufficient information to determine the balance in accounts receivable and accounts payable? If not, what information is lacking? Are the accounts receivable and accounts payable of the hotel increasing or decreasing?
2. (a) Create a chart of accounts and "T" accounts for the following accounts of Roger Jones' Restaurant: Roger Jones' capital, inventory—food, cash, equipment, rent expense, sales, cost of food sold, prepaid expenses, accounts payable, utilities expense.
   (b) Analyze the following transactions and post them directly to the above "T" accounts.
      (1) Roger Jones, a sole proprietor, invested $4,000 worth of food and $20,000 cash in his new restaurant.
      (2) The restaurant purchased equipment worth $5,000.
      (3) The restaurant paid the current month's rent ($1,000) and the final month's rent ($1,000) on a one-year lease at the beginning of the month.
      (4) The restaurant recorded the week's cash sales amounting to $6,338. It used $2,446 worth of food and beverages in making these sales.
      (5) The restaurant received an electricity invoice in the amount of $1,432.
   (c) What step of the accounting cycle has been omitted? When is it useful to post in this fashion?
3. Prepare a chart of accounts for the following accounts:

Accounts payable	Land	Sales
Accounts receivable	Mortgages payable	Utilities expense
Buildings	Notes payable	Withdrawals
Cash—Rotunda Bank	Bob Gray's capital	Cost of sales
Cash—Wilmont Bank	Payroll expense	Equipment
Prepaid expenses	Inventory	Rent expense

4. (a) Draw a general ledger page using the example presented in Figure 6.4 and transfer the information from the following "T" account to the general ledger page you have drawn.

	Accounts Payable		No. 202
6/4	2,341	Beginning bal.	10,051
6/7	3,688	6/10	6,780
6/15	6,889	6/18	1,444
6/23	4,567	6/26	8,661

(b) What can be said about the company on the basis of the above transactions?

5. (a) Prepare a chart of accounts and a trial balance of the following "T" accounts.

(b) Determine the balance in the accounts receivable account.

Accounts Payable		Accounts Receivable		Cash	
	5,347			8,972	

Inventories		Property Under Construction		Building	
3,446		12,691		30,000	

Partner A's Capital		Partner B's Capital		Prepaid Expenses	
	30,000		30,000	1,277	

Withdrawals Partner A		Withdrawals Partner B		Sales	
1,000		1,000			15,000

Rent Expense		Payroll Expense		Utilities Expense	
2,000		4,370		1,454	

Land		Notes Payable		Equipment	
10,000			10,000	5,000	

Cost of Food Sold	
5,431	

Note: The balance of the accounts receivable "T" account was omitted from the above presentation.

PROBLEMS

1. The Wholey Donut Company is opening a new take-out donut shop in partnership with a local resident, John Smith, in June of 1985. The following transactions took place before you were hired. You are told to establish an accounting system and record these transactions. The partnership is called the Wholey-Smith partnership.

June 1   John Smith and the Wholey Donut Company each deposited $30,000 in the Wholey Donut partnership's bank account as their initial investment.

2   The partnership signed a $480,000 mortgage note payable to the Wholey Donut Company. It is payable $24,000 per year plus 10% interest. This note covers the purchase of the land and building to be used by the partnership. Similar land in that location recently sold for $50,000.

4   The partnership purchased kitchen supplies for cash in the amount of $2,352.

5   Donuts and beverages were purchased on credit from the Wholey Donut Company for $21,876.

8   A deposit of $600 was given to the power company and of $100 to the water company.

16   Sales for the period amounted to $25,368. They are all cash sales.

16   The cost of food and beverages used in making these sales is $9,237.

17   Salaries were paid in the amount of $6,328.

18   The water and electricity invoices were received, amounting to $96 and $772, respectively.

19   $896 was paid by the partnership to its creditors.

21   A full year's insurance policy was purchased for $4,800 cash.

23   Newspaper publicity was paid for in the amount of $2,000 for the month of June.

28   Each partner withdrew $2,500 from the partnership.

30   A monthly mortgage payment of $2,000 was made against the principal of the mortgage. One month's interest on the mortgage note was also paid.

Instructions:
(a) Journalize the above transactions.
(b) Using the chart of accounts in Table 6.2 as a guide, prepare a new chart of accounts. Add any new accounts you require and omit those that are not needed.
(c) Prepare the necessary "T" accounts and post the transactions. Be sure to number the "T" accounts according to the chart of accounts.
(d) Prepare a trial balance as of June 30, 1985.

2. The Lockwood Motel Corporation was organized on October 1, 1985 with the objective of buying some land and an unused building to be converted into a motel. The following transactions took place during the first month, October 1985:

Oct. 1   The Lockwood Motel Corporation sold shares of $500 par common stock to Mr. Lockwood for $250,000 cash.

2   The corporation borrowed $50,000 from a bank against a note payable at 12% interest (APR).

3   The corporation purchased land and a building at a total cost of $500,000. Similar land was selling for $150,000. Of this amount $100,000 was paid

in cash and a $400,000 mortgage note payable bearing 12% interest was signed for the balance.

6 The cost of remodeling the building for motel use was $105,000. Of this amount $65,000 was paid in cash. The balance of the remodeling services was received on account.

8 $1,000 was paid for advertising in the month of October.

10 A $4,800 insurance policy was purchased to provide coverage for the entire year.

12 Lodging accommodations were provided for the employees of a corporation who attended a local convention. The corporation was invoiced $6,000.

15 Cash room sales were $25,000.

16 Salaries were paid in the amount of $2,000.

18 A $300 water invoice was received and paid.

20 A $1,000 principal payment was made on the mortgage note payable and a $5,000 principal payment was made on the bank note payable. Interest on the bank note was $590 and the mortgage note was $2,236. The interest amounts were paid in addition to the principal payments.

25 The electricity invoice of $1,300 was received.

27 A full year's property taxes were paid in advance. They amounted to $3,600.

31 Cash sales for the second half of the month were $30,000.

Instructions:

(a) Journalize the above transactions.

(b) Using Table 6.2 as a guide, prepare a new chart of accounts. Add any new accounts you require and omit those that are not needed.

(c) Prepare the necessary "T" accounts and post these transactions. Be sure to number the "T" accounts according to the chart of accounts.

(d) Prepare a trial balance as of October 31, 1985.

3. Alouette Restaurant was organized by Luis Debayle Pallais in Miami, Florida.

He formed a corporation to protect himself against personal liability. The following transactions took place during the corporation's first month in existence, the month of August, 1985.

Aug. 1 The Alouette Restaurant sold 200 shares of $1,000 par common stock to Luis for $200,000.

2 The corporation borrowed $100,000 from a bank in the form of a note payable.

5 A one-year lease contract was signed for a locale. Rent is $2,000 per month. First and final months' rent were paid upon signing.

8 Equipment was purchased for $160,000; $100,000 was paid in cash and a $60,000 note payable was signed for the balance.

10 $15,000 worth of food and beverages was purchased, half on account and half for cash.

15 Salaries were paid in the amount of $3,000.

17 $2,000 was paid for advertising during the month of August.

19 $6,000 of accounts payable were paid.

22 $9,000 was invoiced to a local business for catering services rendered.

22 Food and beverages consumed in the above catering services amounted to $4,500.

24 A water invoice for $100 was received and paid.

25 An electricity invoice for $1,200 was received but not paid.

27 $6,000 was collected on accounts receivable.

28 $2,400 was paid for insurance coverage throughout the entire fiscal year, beginning August 1, 1985.

31 Cash sales for the month amounted to $27,000.

31 $9,000 worth of food and beverages was consumed in making the month's cash sales.

Instructions:

(a) Journalize the above transactions.

(b) Using Table 6.2 as a guide, prepare a new chart of accounts. Add any new accounts you require and omit those that are not needed.

(c) Prepare the necessary "T" accounts and post these transactions. Be sure to number the "T" accounts according to the chart of accounts.

(d) Prepare a trial balance as of August 31, 1985.

4. The accountant of the One Way Travel Agency is having trouble balancing the first month's trial balance. He brings the agency's trial balance and general ledger (shown below) to you, the manager of the travel agency, and requests your help. Point out to your accountant the errors he has made and indicate how to correct them.

ONE WAY TRAVEL AGENCY
Trial Balance
At January 31, 1985

	Dr	Cr
Cash	15,153.13	
Accounts receivable	21,777.29	
Commissions receivable	1,089.17	
Equipment	1,341.00	
Utility deposits	1,000.00	
Accounts payable—trade		1,374.24
Accounts payable—airlines		15,100.26
Notes payable		5,000.00
Owners' equity		20,000.00
Commission revenue		1,847.21
Payroll expense	500.00	
Supplies expense	142.12	
Advertising		265.13
Rent	800.00	
Telephone	18.70	
Utilities expense	362.17	
Totals	43,183.58	43,586.84

General Ledger

Cash

1/1	20,000.00	1/3	1,000.00
1/12	5,000.00	1/14	265.13
1/16	15,100.26	1/19	21,777.29
1/29	758.04	1/24	81.05
		1/25	1,341.00
		1/29	500.00
Totals	40,858.30		24,964.47
Bal.	15,893.83		

Accounts Receivable

1/19	21,777.29	
Totals	21,777.29	
Bal.	21,777.29	

Commissions Receivable

1/18	758.04	1/29	758.04
1/22	1,089.17		
Totals	1,847.21		758.04
Bal.	1,089.17		

Equipment

1/25	1,341.00	
Totals	1,341.00	
Bal.	1,341.00	

Utility Deposits

1/3	1,000	
Totals	1,000	
Bal.	1,000	

Accounts Payable—Trade

	1/10	61.07
	1/27	326.17
	1/28	800.00
	1/31	187.00
	Totals	1,374.24
	Bal.	1,374.24

Accounts Payable—Airlines

	1/16	15,100.26
	Totals	15,100.26
	Bal.	15,100.26

Notes Payable

	1/12	5,000.00
	Totals	5,000.00
	Bal.	5,000.00

Owners' Equity

	1/1	20,000.00
	Totals	20,000.00
	Bal.	20,000.00

Commission Revenue

	1/18	758.04
	1/22	1,089.17
	Totals	1,847.21
	Bal.	1,847.21

Payroll Expense

1/29	500.00	
Totals	500.00	
Bal.	500.00	

Supplies Expense

1/24	81.05	
1/10	61.07	
Totals	142.12	
Bal.	142.12	

Advertising

	1/14	265.13
	Totals	265.13
	Bal.	265.13

Rent

1/28	800.00	
Totals	800.00	
Bal.	800.00	

Telephone

1/31	187.00	
Totals	187.00	
Bal.	187.00	

Utilities Expense

1/27	326.17	
Totals	326.17	
Bal.	326.17	

5. The Restin Inn Motel, a sole proprietorship owned by Mr. Restin, has been operation for a month. Mr. Restin has kept track of his transactions and wishe know whether or not he earned a profit.

(a) Record and summarize the transactions below in a way that will enable Restin to know what the financial position of Restin Inn is at month (March 31, 1985), and also to know the results of its operations during M;

(b) Using the summarized information from (a), prepare a balance sheet March 31, 1985 and an income statement for the month ending Marc 1985.

Mar. 1	Mr. Restin deposited $100,000 in Restin Inn's bank account as his initial investment.
2	Purchased land and building by giving a $20,000 down payment and signing a $180,000 mortgage note for the balance. The land was appraised at $30,000. The note is payable monthly over 20 years and 12% annual interest (APR) must be paid on the outstanding balance monthly.
4	Purchased equipment for $10,000 and furniture in the amount of $15,000, giving $5,000 cash and signing two notes payable of $10,000 each, payable at the end of the current year and the end of the following year.
6	Purchased cleaning supplies in the amount of $100 on account.
8	Purchased $200 worth of office supplies for cash.
10	Paid $500 for the required licenses and taxes.
15	Deposited $5,600 for cash room rentals and recorded $1,200 in rentals on open account.
15	Paid employees $1,300.
18	Paid $681 cash for water system repairs.
23	Purchased 1-year insurance coverage for $3,600 cash.
25	Ran ad in newspaper. Cost $653 on credit.
27	Paid $500 to vendors on invoices due.
28	Collected $600 of amounts due to Restin Inn.
31	Received telephone invoice for $438.
31	Received and paid utility invoices in the total amount of $361.
31	Deposited $4,374 in cash receipts for room rentals and $341 in collections on account.
31	Paid employees $1,300.
31	Withdrew $2,500 for personal use.
31	Paid monthly mortgage installment: $750 for principal and $1,800 for interest.

7

Adjusting the Trial Balance: The Financial Statement Worksheet

The first four steps of the accounting cycle were explained in Chapters 5 and 6. Thus, up to this point we have learned how to (1) identify and (2) record the inputs of the accounting system (the business transactions), (3) how to summarize their effect on the various general ledger accounts, and (4) how to verify the accuracy of these accounts by taking a trial balance of the general ledger and proving the equality of debit and credit balances.

After the business transactions have been journalized and posted and a trial balance prepared, the next step of the accounting cycle is to adjust the trial balance in order to update certain account balances.

Business transactions were recorded during the accounting period as they took place, and thus several accounts will require adjustment to reflect the passage of time. This will be needed in order to prepare financial statements in conformity with the accrual basis of accounting (proper matching of expenses against revenues during each accounting period). Many of the amounts listed on the trial balance will be included in the financial statements without change. The balance of cash, for instance, is usually transferred without modification to the financial statements. Conversely, other accounts will have to be adjusted to show their proper balance on the financial statements.

It is important to understand that typical adjusting entries are not caused by errors and will not be triggered by the issuing of source documents. Instead, they result from the analysis of the trial balance accounts, and in many cases judgment is involved in deciding on the particular adjusting entry to be recorded.

Ordinarily, an adjusting entry affects a balance sheet and an income statement account. Hence, failure to record the adjustment will result in an overstatement or understatement of revenues and/or expenses. Correspondingly, the results of operations reported by the hospitality firm and its financial condition will also be misreported.

Adjusting entries are prepared on the last day of the accounting period. They are journalized and posted in the same manner as original entries. After the adjusting entries have been recorded, an adjusted trial balance is taken to check on the accuracy of the ledger accounts before preparing the financial statements. Generally, most hospitality firms will use a financial statement worksheet as an orderly way of presenting all the pertinent information for the preparation of financial statements.

In this chapter we commence with an analysis of the need for and purposes of adjusting entries. In our discussion we emphasize the significance of the proper application of the accrual concept of accounting in the adjustment process. Next, we divide the adjusting entries into five main types: prepayments, accruals (accrued expenses and accrued revenues), utilization of assets, unearned revenues, and bad debts.

Finally, we review the use of the financial statement worksheet as a tool for facilitating the preparation of formal financial statements. An extended illustration of a financial statement worksheet of a hospitality entity is examined using a step-by-step approach.

ADJUSTING ENTRIES: NEED AND PURPOSES

Accounting derives the proper amounts to be reported on the financial statements as the basis on which to make sound business decisions. In accomplishing this objective, we record and summarize the business transactions during each accounting period and take the trial balance of the general ledger to ascertain the equality of the value exchanges inherent to all business transactions. Yet, the analysis of the trial balance amounts might reveal that some accounts need to be adjusted so that they properly reflect the assets, liabilities, owners' equity, revenue, and expenses of the hospitality business as they should appear on the formal financial statements. Accordingly, the prime objective of adjusting entries is to update the trial balance accounts before the financial statements are prepared to reflect the passage of time from the day the transactions were first recorded to the last day of the accounting period.

Assume that a hotel maid earning $40 per day is paid for her five-day week each Friday. If the last day of the accounting period falls on a Tuesday, the appropriate expense for the preceding Monday and Tuesday would not be recognized as an expense of the current accounting period inasmuch as there was no evidence that a business transaction took place. Hence, an adjustment that records wage expenses of $80 is necessary in order to update the information to be reported on the financial statements. Likewise, the entry will also affect a balance sheet account, salaries payable (also referred to as accrued expenses), reflecting the hotel's liability for those wages.

We have already seen that the proper determination of net income on the income statement requires the consistent application of the accrual concept of accounting. That is, revenues are recognized when earned while expenses are recognized when incurred, regardless of when cash is received or paid out. Therefore, adjustments are needed when a transaction is recorded in one accounting period, but its recognition as revenue or expense, according to the accrual concept, belongs in another accounting period. The above example of unrecorded wage expenses clearly illustrates this point. Specifically, the recognition of the wage expense incurred belongs in the current accounting period even though the wage payment will be recorded in the subsequent period.

As previously noted, adjusting entries are journalized on the last day of the accounting period in the same way as are original journal entries. After adjusting entries are posted to the general ledger, the accounts will be ready for use in the preparation of financial statements. There are five basic types of adjustments:

1. Expenses paid in advance: prepayments.
2. Unrecorded revenues and expenses: accruals.
3. Utilization of assets: depreciation and inventory adjustments.

4. Unearned revenue.
5. Bad debts.

PREPAYMENTS

Prepayments are items paid in advance that will benefit one or more accounting periods. As a result of acquiring a future value at the time of the payment an asset is created that will be consumed in the operations of the hospitality business and hence become an expense.

The purpose of the prepaid adjustment is to recognize the expense by debiting the expired or used portion of the payment to the appropriate expense account while recording the decrease in the asset with a credit to the asset prepaid expenses. In this manner, the expense is recognized in the period of incurrence rather than in the period of payment.

The prepaid adjustment will result in the proper presentation of both the asset (prepaid expenses) and the expense on the financial statements. Specifically, the prepaid expense account will reflect the unexpired portion of the prepayment as of the last day of the accounting period, whereas the expense account will show the amount of the prepayment that was actually consumed (incurred) during the period.

Examples of prepayment adjustments are prepaid insurance, prepaid rent, and prepaid licenses. Let us consider the following example: On October 1, 1986, Benji's Place made a premium payment of $2,400 on a policy providing for two-year insurance coverage. When the premium is paid, an asset is created since the restaurant is acquiring future benefits in the form of insurance protection.

The general journal (GJ) entry to be recorded on the books of Benji's Place is as follows:

1986			
Oct. 1	Prepaid Insurance	2,400	
	Cash		2,400

In this entry we debited the asset account (prepaid insurance) in order to record the purchase of an item having a future value to the restaurant, namely insurance coverage for a two-year period commencing October 1, 1986.

Assuming that Benji's Place completes its recording process on December 31, 1986, the following information will appear in the prepaid insurance account resulting from the above transaction:

Prepaid Insurance

Oct. 1	2,400	
Bal. Dec. 31	2,400	

Thus, the unadjusted trial balance of Benji's Place for the year ended December 31, 1986 will show a debit balance of $2,400 in the account prepaid insurance. However, this balance is not correct, because it does not reflect the reduction of the prepayment arising from the consumption of insurance during the current accounting period. For this reason, an adjustment is required.

The adjusting entry will consist of recording the expired or used portion of the prepayment as an expense, $300 (2,400 ÷ 24 months = 100/month × 3 months = 300), while reducing the original prepayment of $2,400 to its proper future value of $2,100 (2400 − 300) as of December 31, 1986. The required adjusting entry in general journal form follows:

```
1986
————
Dec. 31    Insurance Expense       300
              Prepaid Insurance              300
```

After posting the above adjusting entry to the appropriate accounts, the adjusted balances would be:

Prepaid Insurance				Insurance Expense		
Oct. 1	2,400	Adj.	300	Adj.	300	
Bal. Dec. 31	2,100			Bal. Dec. 31	300	

We can see how the adjusted balances of prepaid insurance and insurance expense will now reflect the proper values to be reported on the financial statements for the year 1986. Prepaid insurance will reflect the unexpired (or unused) portion of the prepayment on the balance sheet of Benji's Place as of December 31, 1986, that is, $2,100 (21 months' future value of the prepayment for the period beginning January 1, 1987 and ending September 30, 1988). Likewise, the insurance expense to be reported on the income statement for the year ending December 31, 1986 will represent the portion of the insurance premium consumed during the current period, $300 (3 months commencing October 1, 1986 and ending December 31, 1986).

Although the above illustration represents the most commonly used method of recording the prepaid transaction and its corresponding adjustment, some hospitality organizations follow a different procedure in recording prepayments. They record the original prepayment as an expense rather than as an asset account. In that case, the following original entry would be recorded at the time of purchase, using the same data for Benji's Place described before:

```
1986
————
Oct. 1    Insurance Expense    2,400
             Cash                        2,400
```

In this instance, the unadjusted balance of prepaid insurance would be zero. Thus, we must adjust the accounts by transferring the total future value of the insurance premium as of December 31, 1986 or $2,100 from the insurance expense account to the asset account (prepaid insurance). In journal form, the required adjusting entry would then be

```
1986
————
Dec. 31    Prepaid Insurance       2,100
              Insurance Expense              2,100
```

Although this alternative results in a different adjusting entry, the end result is the same as if we had used the procedure first illustrated for Benji's Place. The adjusted balances for prepaid insurance and insurance expense would have identical balances to those shown before as can be seen by reviewing the following general ledger "T" accounts:

Prepaid Insurance				Insurance Expense		
Adj.	2,100			Oct. 1	2,400	Adj.	2,100
Bal. Dec. 31	2,100			Bal. Dec. 31	300	

As noted before, the adjusted balances of prepaid insurance and insurance expense are the same for the case when the prepayment was recorded as an asset. The future value of the prepayment of $2,100 will be included on the balance sheet as an asset (prepaid insurance), whereas the expired portion of the insurance premium ($300) will be one of the expenses appearing on the income statement prepared for the period ending December 31, 1986.

It follows from the foregoing illustration that the way prepaid adjustments are to be recorded will always depend upon the alternative used in recording the original transaction. In any event, the ultimate result will be identical. The asset (prepaid expenses) will reflect the future value of the prepayment on the balance sheet prepared as of the last day of the period, while the corresponding expense reported on the income statement will show the past value of the prepayment applicable to the current accounting period.

ACCRUALS

To give proper recognition to certain revenues earned or expenses incurred during the period, accrual adjustments may be required. The term accrual will denote the increase in a revenue or expense account during the accounting period not properly recognized in the normal recording process. There are two kinds of accruals: accrued expenses (unrecorded expenses) and accrued revenues (unrecorded revenues).

Accrued Expenses

Accrued expenses are expenses incurred during the current accounting period and not yet recorded, because they are generally not due to be paid until a future period. In the accrual basis of accounting, all expenses consumed during the period must be recognized in the period of incurrence. This is accomplished by recording the accrued expense adjustment, debiting the appropriate expense account and crediting the related liability account, reflecting the obligation to pay for the item(s) consumed.

Common examples of accrued expenses are accrued salaries and accrued interest. Also, some expenses incurred for which invoices have not yet been received are often recorded as accrued expenses by estimating the applicable expenses (for example, telephone, electricity, and water). The earlier case of the unrecorded wages of a hotel maid is an example of accrued salaries and wages. We shall now consider the following illustration of accrued interest.

On November 1, 1986, Tastee Restaurant borrowed $100,000 from the Third National Bank and signed a 90-day note bearing interest at the rate of 12% APR. The following entry would be recorded on November 1 for this transaction:

1986			
Nov. 1	Cash	100,000	
	Notes Payable		100,000

Assuming this was the only note on the books of the restaurant, the following balances would appear on the unadjusted trial balance for the calendar year ending December 31, 1986:

	Dr	Cr
Notes Payable		$100,000
Interest Expense	0	

That is, the account interest expense would not reflect the cost of using the $100,000 for the months of November and December, 1986, since no payment was made during that period. Obviously, this is not correct inasmuch as interest expense accrues day by day and thus must be recognized as an expense regardless of payment. We shall record the cost incurred in using the $100,000 during the months of November and December 1986 by debiting interest expense in the amount of $2,000 (100,000 × 1% monthly interest = 1,000; 2 months × 1,000 = 2,000). We then credit the corresponding liability account, accrued interest payable (or a similarly named account, such as interest payable or accrued expenses), to recognize the amount owed for interest on the note payable, which shall be paid in the near future. The adjusting entry to be recorded is

1986			
Dec. 31	Interest Expense	2,000	
	Accrued Interest Payable		2,000

After posting the above adjusting entry to the appropriate accounts, the following information will be reflected in the general ledger:

Accrued Interest Payable			Interest Expense		
	Adj.	2,000	Adj.	2,000	
	Bal. Dec. 31	2,000	Bal. Dec. 31	2,000	

In this manner, the interest expense account would show the actual expense incurred during the current period. This amount ($2,000) would be reported as an expense on the income statement, representing the cost incurred during the year ending December 31, 1986. Likewise, the accrued interest payable balance of $2,000 would appear as a liability on the balance sheet, reflecting the restaurant's obligation for the interest incurred on the note as of the last day of the period (December 31, 1986).

Accrued Revenues

Accrued revenues are revenues earned in the current accounting period and not yet recorded. We have noted before that revenues are to be recognized at the time they are earned. Thus, an adjusting entry will be required in which we record the revenues earned and the related receivable, an asset account normally called accrued income receivable (or some other similar name selected by the company). The entry is made by debiting the accrued receivable account and crediting the revenue account.

Examples of accrued revenue are not so common as those of accrued expenses. In the hospitality industry we can cite accrued interest on a note receivable, or other asset investment (for example, savings accounts), and unrecorded rent revenue. Let us consider the following illustration of accrued interest on a note receivable.

Assume that XYZ Hotel loans $10,000 to ABC Company on March 1, 1986 by signing a 60-day note bearing interest at 12% APR. This transaction would originally be recorded as follows:

```
1986
─────
March 1    Notes Receivable    10,000
               Cash                        10,000
```

If XYZ Hotel closes its books on March 31, 1986, the interest earned during the month of March would not be reflected in the accounts to be reported on the financial statements. Thus, an adjusting entry is required on March 31, 1986 to record the interest earned during March in the amount of $100 (10,000 × 12% = 1200, 1200 ÷ 12 months = 100), as follows:

```
1986
─────
March 31    Accrued Interest Receivable    100
                Interest Income                      100
```

The effect of this entry on the accounts is

Accrued Interest Receivable			**Interest Income**	
Adj.	100		Adj.	100
Bal. Dec. 31	100		Bal. Dec. 31	100

Thus, the accrued interest receivable will show an adjusted balance of $100. This will appear on the balance sheet as an asset since it reflects the revenue earned but not yet collected. At the same time, the interest income balance of $100 will appear on the income statement for the month ending March 31, 1986, representing the interest earned by XYZ Hotel during that period.

UTILIZATION OF ASSETS

Two main types of adjustments deal with the utilization or exhaustion of assets during the accounting period: depreciation or amortization of property and equipment, and inventory adjustments.

Depreciation and Amortization

With the exception of land, property and equipment (for example, buildings, auto, furniture, and equipment) have a limited useful life. Therefore, the future service potential of these assets will decline as they are used in the operations of the business. That is, the asset (property and equipment), through use, will become an expense that will be referred to as depreciation (in cases where the asset is not legally owned by the business we shall use the term amortization).

Depreciation entails the allocation of the cost of the asset to each accounting period it is expected to benefit. In this manner, depreciation will encompass the portion of the property and equipment that has expired during the accounting period and thus has become an expense used by the hospitality business in the production of revenues.

The depreciation adjusting entry will be made by debiting depreciation expense using an estimated value of the asset's expired cost during the current period. Instead of reflecting the decrease in the asset value by crediting the property and equipment, we shall credit a separate account called accumulated depreciation. This account will be considered a contra-asset account since it will be shown on the balance sheet as a reduction of the asset account property and equipment. Let us consider the following example as an illustration of depreciation adjustments.

On September 1, 1985, Best Hotel Corporation purchased furniture and equipment with an estimated useful life of 10 years for $61,000 cash. It is expected that the furniture and equipment will be worth $1,000 at the end of its 10-year estimated useful life (known as salvage or residual value). The following entry is made to record the original transaction:

1985			
Sept. 1	Property and Equipment	61,000	
	Cash		61,000

Assuming that Best Hotel Corporation closes its books on December 31, 1985, we shall have to make an adjustment to record the periodic decrease of the property and equipment during the four months ending December 31, 1985. There are several methods of estimating the amount of depreciation. We shall use the simplest method (straight-line) in recording the required depreciation adjustment. (A detailed treatment of other depreciation methods is given in Chapter 14.)

Using the straight-line method of depreciation, the adjusting entry will be

1985			
Dec. 31	Depreciation Expense	2,000	
	Accumulated Depreciation—		
	Furniture & Equipment		2,000

We estimate the amount of depreciation by spreading equally the cost of the asset (net of salvage value) over its estimated useful life. In other words, the annual depreciation expense is given by

$$\frac{\text{cost} - \text{salvage value}}{\text{estimated useful life in years}} = \frac{61,000 - 1,000}{10 \text{ years}} = 6,000$$

Since we are recording the expense applicable to the four-month period ending December 31, 1985, we use monthly depreciation of $500 (6000 ÷ 12 months), multiplied by four months: $4 \times 500 = \$2,000$:

Depreciation Expense		Accumulated Depreciation— Furniture and Equipment	
Adj. 2,000			Adj. 2,000
Bal. Dec. 31 2,000			Bal. Dec. 31 2,000

As can be seen, the depreciation expense account shows an adjusted balance of $2,000. This expense, which represents the consumption of the asset property and equipment during the current period, will be reported on the income statement. Similarly, the contra-asset account, accumulated depreciation—furniture and equipment, will appear on the balance sheet as a deduction from the asset property and equipment, as follows:

Property and equipment	$61,000
Less: Accumulated depreciation—	
furniture & equipment	2,000
	$59,000

In this manner, the original cost of the asset ($61,000) remains in the asset account reported on the balance sheet. The resulting figure of $59,000 (net of accumulated depreciation) is better known as net book value of the property and equipment.

The above procedure for recording depreciation is similarly followed in making amortization adjustments related to improvements on leased property. We shall cover this topic in Chapter 14.

Inventory Adjustments

There are two classes of inventories in a typical hospitality organization: (1) inventories held for sale (for example, food inventory), and (2) inventories used in the regular course of business (for example, housekeeping supplies inventory).

Inventories Held for Sale. The balance of the food (or beverage) inventory accounts appearing in the trial balance of a hospitality firm includes the beginning inventory plus the purchases made during the period (known as items available for sale). Obviously, inventory items are used in making the sale. Nevertheless, the cost of these sales is normally not accounted for during the period. This will be done at the end of the period by making an adjusting entry encompassing the transfer of the cost of the inventory sold from the asset account (inventory) to an expense account (cost of sales).

For example, Simplicity Restaurants showed a $31,000 balance in its general ledger food inventory account on December 31, 1986:

Food Inventory

Bal. Jan.	1	2,000	
Feb.	3	4,000	
Apr.	15	5,000	
June	30	3,000	
Sept.	10	10,000	
Dec.	4	7,000	
Bal. Dec.	31	31,000	

The $31,000 balance represents a combination of the beginning inventory of $2,000 and five purchases of food inventory items made by the restaurant during the year (total $29,000). On December 31, 1986, the last day of the accounting period, a physical count of inventory items revealed that there was $4,000 of inventory in stock. Accordingly, an adjusting entry is required to record the utilization of inventory items in making the sales during the year 1986. In journal form the entry is

```
1986
_____

Dec. 31    Cost of Food Sold       27,000
               Food Inventory                    27,000
```

We can see that the cost of inventory items used in making the 1986 food sales amounted to $27,000 (31,000 − 4,000) or the difference between the balance shown in the general ledger account and the actual inventory count on December 31. In other words, cost of food sold represents the following:

$$\underset{\text{of food sold}}{\text{cost}} = \underset{\text{food inventory}}{\text{beginning}} + \underset{\text{purchases}}{\text{food}} - \underset{\text{food inventory}}{\text{ending}}$$

$$27,000 \quad = \quad 2,000 \quad + \quad 29,000 \quad - \quad 4,000$$

At the same time, the food inventory account at the end of the period will show an adjusted balance of $4,000 that will appear on the balance sheet as an asset since it reflects the inventory items actually on hand on that date (as determined by the physical count). The topic of accounting for inventories held for sale will be covered in depth in Chapter 15.

Supplies Inventory.   As we already know, when supplies (for example, housekeeping supplies, office supplies) are purchased, their cost increases the asset account supplies, resulting in a debit to supplies inventory. As supplies are used in the normal course of business they become expenses. Nevertheless, the consumption of supplies during the period is not accounted for since it does not represent an original transaction. An adjustment recording the supplies used during the period (supplies expense) while reducing the supplies inventory account will be necessary on the last day of the accounting period.

For instance, Heath Travel Services, Incorporated purchased office supplies in the amount of $300 on May 1, 1985. This purchase will be recorded as follows:

```
1985
_____

May 1      Office Supplies Inventory    300
               Cash                                   300
```

If an additional purchase of $500 worth of office supplies is made on July 10 on account, a similar entry to record this transaction will be

```
1985
_____

July 10    Office Supplies Inventory    500
               Accounts Payable                    500
```

At the end of the six-month period ending October 31, 1985, the account office supplies inventory shows:

Office Supplies Inventory

May 1	300	
July 10	500	
Bal. Oct. 31	800	

If a count of office supplies on October 31, 1985 reveals that the total amount of supplies on hand is $200, an adjustment to record the consumption of $600 (800 − 200) of office supplies during the period is required. The adjustment will be

1985
_____

Oct. 31   Office Supplies Expense   600
               Office Supplies Inventory   600

After posting this adjusting entry to the appropriate general ledger accounts, the office supplies inventory account will show an adjusted balance of $200 to be shown as an asset on the balance sheet of Heath Travel Services, Incorporated as of October 31, 1985. This amount represents the future value of the office supplies inventory on the very last day of the accounting period. Similarly, the office supplies expense has an adjusted balance of $600 to be reported on the income statement for the six-month period ending October 31, 1985, reflecting the consumption of office supplies during that period.

BAD DEBTS

When services are sold on credit, experience has shown that not all of the amount due from the customers (accounts receivable) will be collected. In this manner, a portion of the claims against the customers will prove to be uncollectible. The loss, or expense, resulting from the failure to collect all credit sales is known as bad debts expenses. Following the conservatism concept of accounting, the carrying value of an asset should be reduced when there is evidence that cost cannot be recovered. Thus, the net carrying value of the asset accounts receivable will be decreased through the recognition of bad debts expense. This adjustment will involve the use of an estimate, such as a percentage of total sales or total accounts receivable, to be determined based on previous experience and other pertinent factors.

To illustrate, let us assume that the trial balance of Fabulous Inn at December 31, 1985 includes accounts receivable in the amount of $100,000. It is estimated that 3% of these accounts are uncollectible. An adjusting entry debiting bad debts expense $3,000 (3% of $100,000) and crediting a contra-asset account called allowance for doubtful accounts is made, as follows:

1985
_____

Dec. 31   Bad Debts Expense   3,000
               Allowance for Doubtful Accounts   3,000

This adjusting entry will result in the proper matching of bad debts expense with 1985 revenues. To this end, estimated uncollectible accounts arising from 1985 credit sales are recognized as expenses in that year. At the same time, the net carrying value of the asset, accounts receivable, is reduced by deducting an allowance for doubtful accounts from accounts receivable in the asset section of the balance sheet in the following manner:

Accounts Receivable $100,000
Less: Allowance for doubtful accounts   3,000
                                                                $ 97,000

We shall discuss accounts receivable and bad debts in greater depth in Chapter 16.

UNEARNED REVENUE

An unearned revenue (or deferred income) results when payment is received by the hospitality firm for services prior to the time they are earned. The payment does not represent revenue based on the realization principle since it has not been earned as of yet. Instead, the acceptance of the advance payment increases cash and gives rise to a liability, known as unearned revenue, resulting from the hospitality company's obligation to render the specified services at some future time.

Let us assume, for instance, that on October 10, 1985, Rx Inn received $10,000 of customers' deposits to be used against future hotel reservations. The original entry to record this transaction is

1985			
Oct. 10	Cash	10,000	
	Customers' Deposits		10,000

Customers' deposits is a liability that reflects the obligation of Rx Inn to provide room services to the specific customers at a stipulated future date. Let us further assume that $6,000 of the customers' deposits recorded on October 10, 1985 were applied to December reservations. We must then record the following adjusting entry on December 31, 1985 (the last day of the accounting period) in order to transfer the $6,000 deposit from the unearned revenue liability to the revenue earned account (room sales):

1985			
Dec. 31	Customers' Deposits	6,000	
	Room Sales		6,000

Consequently, the earned portion of the customers' deposits for the year ended December 31, 1985 ($6,000) will be included as part of the room sales account on the 1985 income statement of Rx Inn. Similarly, the adjusted balance of the customers' deposit account shown below ($4,000), will appear on the liability section of the balance sheet prepared by Rx Inn as of December 31, 1985:

Customers' Deposits

Adj.	6,000	Oct. 10	10,000
		Bal. Dec. 31	4,000

The $4,000 adjusted balance indicates the unearned portion of the customers' deposits that were received on October 10 as of the balance sheet date (December 31, 1985). When earned at some future time, the customers' deposits will be recognized as revenue.

THE ADJUSTED TRIAL BALANCE

After adjustments are recorded in the journal and posted to the general ledger, we take another trial balance of the general ledger, which is termed an adjusted trial balance. The adjusted trial balance can be used as the basis to prepare formal financial statements since it contains the proper amounts of

MERMAID HOTEL
Adjusted Trial Balance
December 31, 1986
(Thousands of Dollars)

	Debit	Credit
Cash	$120	
Accounts receivable	30	
Allowance for doubtful accounts		$ 5
Prepaid expenses	15	
Land	50	
Furniture and equipment	200	
Accumulated depreciation		60
Accounts payable		10
Notes payable		30
Mortgages payable		100
Accrued expenses		20
Customers' deposits		10
Ms. Mermaid, capital		100
Ms. Mermaid, withdrawals	10	
Room sales		200
Other income		20
Salaries and wages	60	
Utilities expense	30	
Depreciation expense	10	
Interest expense	10	
Other expenses	20	
	$555	$555

Figure 7.1. Adjusted trial balance—Mermaid Hotel.

assets, liabilities, revenue, and expenses to be reported on the balance sheet and the income statement.

Refer to Figure 7.1, which shows the adjusted trial balance of Mermaid Hotel for the year ended December 31, 1986. As stated before, financial statements can be prepared from the adjusted trial balance shown in Figure 7.1. If this is done, the income statement is ordinarily prepared first, since the net income figure (revenue less expenses) is needed to complete the balance sheet's owners' equity section. An income statement for the year ended December 31, 1986 and a balance sheet as of December 31, 1986, prepared from the adjusted

MERMAID HOTEL
Income Statement
For the Year Ended December 31, 1986
(Thousands of Dollars)

Revenues		
Room sales		$200
Other income		20
Total revenues		220
Expenses		
Salaries and wages	$60	
Utilities expense	30	
Depreciation expense	10	
Interest expense	10	
Other expenses	20	
Total expenses		130
Net income		$ 90

Figure 7.2. Income statement—Mermaid Hotel.

MERMAID HOTEL
Balance Sheet
December 31, 1986
(Thousands of Dollars)

Assets			Liabilities & Owners' Equity	
Cash		$120	Liabilities	
Accounts receivable	$ 30		Accounts payable	$ 10
Less: Allowance for doubtful accounts	5	25	Notes payable	30
Prepaid expenses		15	Mortgages payable	100
Land		50	Accrued expenses	20
Furniture and equipment	200		Customers' deposits	10
Less: Accumulated depreciation	60	140	Total liabilities	170
			Owners' Equity	
			Ms. Mermaid, capital, beginning balance	100
			Add: net income for the year 1986	90
				190
			Less: withdrawals	10
			Total owners' equity	180
Total assets		$350	Total liabilities and owners' equity	$350

Figure 7.3. Balance Sheet—Mermaid Hotel.

trial balance of the Mermaid Hotel (Figure 7.1) are presented in Figures 7.2 and 7.3. As we can see, the adjusted trial balance (Figure 7.1) has served as a basis for preparing the balance sheet and income statement of Mermaid Hotel as of December 31, 1986 and for the year then ended (Figures 7.2 and 7.3).

We shall now illustrate the use of the financial statement worksheet as a tool that will further facilitate the preparation of formal financial statements as well as the adjusting and closing entries (step 7 of the accounting cycle; to be discussed in Chapter 8).

THE FINANCIAL STATEMENT WORKSHEET

As already indicated, the financial statement worksheet does not replace the formal financial statements or journalizing and posting of adjusting and closing entries, but it is indeed an excellent device that brings together all the information necessary in the preparation of financial statements, resulting in a more timely completion of this task. It also serves as a point of reference to management in the decision-making process.

After the financial statement worksheet and the formal financial statements are completed, adjusting entries like the ones described earlier in this chapter must still be recorded in the general journal and posted to the general ledger, since the latter are the actual accounting records of the hospitality firm. The financial statement worksheet provides a convenient means of arranging the adjustment data and acts as a link between the accounting records and the formal statements while showing the net income or net loss for the period before formal financial statements are prepared.

The Worksheet Approach

The financial statement worksheet consists of a columnar sheet of paper that normally includes the following:

(1) Heading (name of company, the term *worksheet,* and the period covered).
(2) Trial balance (unadjusted) columns.
(3) Adjustment columns.
(4) Adjusted trial balance columns.
(5) Income statement columns.
(6) Balance sheet columns.

Figure 7.4 is a blank financial statement worksheet, noting the various parts (numbered as above).

NAME OF COMPANY[1]
Financial Statement Worksheet
Period Covered

Account no.	Account name	Trial balance[2]		Adjustments[3]		Adjusted trial balance[4]		Income statement[5]		Balance sheet[6]	
		Dr	Cr	Dr	Cr	Dr	Cr	Dr	Cr	Dr	Cr

Figure 7.4. Blank sheet of financial statement worksheet. (1) Heading, (2) trial balance columns, (3) adjustments columns, (4) adjusted trial balance columns, (5) income statement columns, (6) balance sheet columns.

Preparing the Financial Statement Worksheet

There are six steps in preparing a worksheet for a hospitality firm:

1. Enter the heading on the worksheet and the headings for each of the five pairs of columns: trial balance, adjustments, adjusted trial balance, income statement, and balance sheet.
2. Place the unadjusted trial balance figures in the trial balance columns.
3. Enter the necessary adjusting entries in the adjustments columns.
4. Combine the unadjusted trial balance and the adjustments to produce the adjusted trial balance.
5. Extend all the amounts in the adjusted trial balance to the income statement or balance sheet columns.
6. Determine the net income or net loss for the period as the balancing figure in both financial statement columns. Enter the net income or net loss on the worksheet, total the financial statement columns, and double underline.

NEAT RESTAURANT
Financial Statement Worksheet
Step 1 ──────────→ **For the Year Ended July 31, 1985**
(in Round Dollars)

Account title	Acct. no.	Trial balance Debit	Trial balance Credit	Adjustments Debit	Adjustments Credit	Adjusted trial balance Debit	Adjusted trial balance Credit	Income statement Debit	Income statement Credit	Balance sheet Debit	Balance sheet Credit
Cash	101	100									
Accounts receivable	104	200									
Notes receivable	105	300									
Food inventory	120	110									
Prepaid insurance	130	12									
Furniture & equipment	160	220									
Accumulated depreciation	165		88								
Accounts payable	201		150								
Notes payable	202		100								
Amy Neat, capital	301		502								
Amy Neat, withdrawals	310	50									
Sales	401		300								
Other income	403		20								
Salaries & wages	503	100									
Interest expense	510	20									
Other operating expenses	515	48									
		1,160	1,160								

Step 2

Figure 7.5. Steps 1 and 2 of the financial statement worksheet for the Neat Restaurant.

Illustrative Worksheet—Neat Restaurant

A step-by-step description of the worksheet of the Neat Restaurant follows.

Steps 1 and 2: Headings and Unadjusted Trial Balance. The worksheet for Neat Restaurant shown as Figure 7.5 includes the proper headings (step 1) and the trial balance before adjustments for the year ended July 31, 1985 (step 2).

Note that the information for the trial balance columns of the worksheet is obtained from the general ledger (step 4 of the accounting cycle). After placing the initial trial balance on the worksheet and ascertaining the equality of debit and credit balances in the general ledger, these totals are double-underlined as shown in Figure 7.5.

Steps 3 and 4: Adjustments and Adjusted Trial Balance. Adjustment information is entered in the adjustment columns on the worksheet (see Figure 7.6). An identification key letter is used to cross-reference the debit and the credit adjustments as they are entered in the adjustments columns.

The adjustments for Neat Restaurant are listed below:

(a) To adjust for expired insurance, $7 (debit insurance expense, credit prepaid insurance).

(b) To adjust for the cost of inventory used in making the sales during the period, $89 (debit cost of food sold, credit food inventory).

(c) To adjust for annual depreciation of furniture and equipment, $22 (debit depreciation expense, credit accumulated depreciation).

(d) To adjust for the accrued interest expense $5 (debit interest expense, credit accrued interest payable).

NEAT RESTAURANT
Financial Statement Worksheet
Step 1 ——————————→ **For the Year Ended July 31, 1985**
(in Round Dollars)

Account title	Acct. no.	Trial balance Debit	Trial balance Credit	Adjustments Debit	Adjustments Credit	Adjusted trial balance Debit	Adjusted trial balance Credit	Income statement Debit	Income statement Credit	Balance sheet Debit	Balance sheet Credit
Cash	101	100				100					
Accounts receivable	104	200				200					
Notes receivable	105	300				300					
Food inventory	120	110			(b) 89	21					
Prepaid insurance	130	12			(a) 7	5					
Furniture & equipment	160	220				220					
Accumulated depreciation	165		88		(c) 22		110				
Accounts payable	201		150				150				
Notes payable	202		100				100				
Amy Neat, capital	301		502				502				
Amy Neat, withdrawals	310	50				50					
Sales	401		300				300				
Other income	403		20				20				
Salaries & wages	503	100		(e) 7		107					
Interest expense	510	20		(d) 5		25					
Other operating expenses	515	48				48					
		1,160	1,160								
		Step 2									
Insurance expense	505			(a) 7		7					
Cost of food sold	500			(b) 89		89					
Depreciation expense	506			(c) 22		22					
Accrued interest	208				(d) 5		5				
Accrued salaries	209				(e) 7		7				
Interest income	402				(f) 18		18				
Accrued interest receivable	110			(f) 18		18					
				148	148	1,212	1,212				
				Step 3		**Step 4**					

Figure 7.6. Steps 3 and 4 of the financial statement worksheet for the Neat Restaurant.

(e) To adjust for accrued salaries, $7 (debit salaries and wage expense, credit accrued salaries payable).

(f) To adjust for accrued interest income, $18 (debit accrued interest receivable, credit interest income).

These adjustments are recorded in the adjustments columns of the worksheet (step 3) in the same manner as they will be (or were) journalized. In the event that the accounts to be debited or credited are not listed in the beginning trial balance, additional accounts, as needed, are added at the bottom of the worksheet.

Next, the information in the trial balance and adjustments columns of the worksheet is combined for each account in order to determine the adjusted trial balance figures (step 4). In those accounts not affected by adjusting entries, the same balance appearing in the initial trial balance is transferred to the adjusted trial balance columns. If the account in the trial balance has a debit balance, the debit adjustments are added and the credit adjustments are subtracted in calculating its adjusted balance. Similarly, if the account in the trial balance has a credit balance, credit adjustments are added and debit adjustments are deducted in determining the proper adjusted balance.

After the adjusted trial balance is completed, we must once more ascertain the equality of value exchanges (debit balances = credit balances). When this is done, we double-underline the debit and credit columns of the adjusted trial balance. At this time, these balances reflect the proper amounts that will appear on the financial statements.

Steps 5 and 6: Completion of the Worksheet. As noted earlier, the adjusted trial balance contains all the information needed to prepare the financial statements. The next step in the preparation of the worksheet is to extend all the adjusted balance figures to either the income statement or the balance sheet columns.

As shown in Figure 7.7, each item on the adjusted trial balance of Neat Restaurant is transferred to the appropriate financial statement column. Assets, liabilities, and owners' equity accounts are transferred to the balance sheet columns, whereas revenue and expense accounts are transferred to the

NEAT RESTAURANT
Financial Statement Worksheet
Step 1 ──────────→For the Year Ended July 31, 1985 ┌──Step 5──┐
(in Round Dollars)

Account title	Acct. no.	Trial balance Debit	Trial balance Credit	Adjustments Debit	Adjustments Credit	Adjusted trial balance Debit	Adjusted trial balance Credit	Income statement Debit	Income statement Credit	Balance sheet Debit	Balance sheet Credit
Cash	101	100				100				100	
Accounts receivable	104	200				200				200	
Notes receivable	105	300				300				300	
Food inventory	120	110			(b) 89	21				21	
Prepaid insurance	130	12			(a) 7	5				5	
Furniture & equipment	160	220				220				220	
Accumulated depreciation	165		88		(c) 22		110				110
Accounts payable	201		150				150				150
Notes payable	202		100				100				100
Amy Neat, capital	301		502				502				502
Amy Neat, withdrawals	310	50				50				50	
Sales	401		300				300		300		
Other income	403		20				20		20		
Salaries & wages	503	100		(e) 7		107		107			
Interest expense	510	20		(d) 5		25		25			
Other operating expenses	515	48				48		48			
		1,160	1,160								
		Step 2									
Insurance expense	505			(a) 7		7		7			
Cost of food sold	500			(b) 89		89		89			
Depreciation expense	506			(c) 22		22		22			
Accrued interest	208				(d) 5		5				5
Accrued salaries	209				(e) 7		7				7
Interest income	402				(f) 18		18		18		
Accrued interest Receivable	110			(f) 18		18				18	
				148	148	1,212	1,212	298	338	914	874
				Step 3		**Step 4**					
Net income								40			40
								338	338	914	914

↑
Step 6

Figure 7.7. Steps 5 and 6 of the financial statement worksheet for the Neat Restaurant.

income statement columns of the worksheet. For instance, the cash (asset) debit balance of $100 is extended to the debit column of the balance sheet; the salaries and wages expense debit balance of $107 is extended to the debit column of the income statement. Notice that accumulated depreciation is extended to the balance sheet credit column since it is a contra-asset account. To avoid making errors by overlooking accounts, it is best to extend the accounts line by line without skipping around, beginning with cash, which is normally the first account listed.

Once all accounts from the adjusted trial balance are extended to the appropriate financial statement columns, the worksheet can be completed by determining the net income or net loss for the period (step 6). The difference between the totals of the two income statement columns and the two balance sheet columns will represent the net income or net loss for the period. A net income is indicated if the sum of the income statement credit column (or revenues) is greater than the sum of the income statement debit column (or expenses). On the other hand, if the sum of the income statement debit column (or expenses) exceeds the sum of the income statement credit column (or revenues) a net loss has been incurred for the period. The net income or net loss is then entered in the column with the smaller totals. That is, net income will be added to the total of the income statement debit column and to the total of the balance sheet credit column. Conversely, a net loss will appear as an addition to the income statement credit column and to the balance sheet debit column totals.

Note that the financial statement worksheet of Neat Restaurant reports net income of $40 for the year ended July 31, 1985 in Figure 7.7. This amount was found by obtaining the difference between the totals of the debit and credit columns of the income statement and balance sheet. (Income statement difference: credit column $338 − debit column $298 = $40; balance sheet difference: debit column $914 − credit column $874 = $40.) As previously noted, net income is added to the debit column of the income statement and to the credit column of the balance sheet. Since the net income is a balancing figure, the totals of the debits and credits of the last four columns of the worksheet should be double-underlined as an indication that the completed worksheet is in balance.

Advantages of the Financial Statement Worksheet Approach

In sum, the advantages of the financial statement worksheet approach to the preparation of financial statements of a hospitality organization are

- It provides a check on the arithmetic accuracy of the overall accounting process.
- It can be used as a point of reference by record-keeping personnel.
- It eliminates the need for separate trial balances (both adjusted and unadjusted).
- It serves as a basis for the preparation of adjusting and closing entries (closing entries will be covered in Chapter 8).
- It may be used as a management tool in assessing a company's performance prior to the actual preparation of financial statements.
- It facilitates and speeds up the preparation of formal financial statements.

It is evident that the financial statement worksheet is an excellent aid to financial statement preparation. Once the worksheet is completed, all the information necessary to prepare formal financial statements is readily available. It will be rather simple, indeed, to prepare formal financial statements by referring to a completed worksheet in view of the fact that all the account balances have been sorted into income statement and balance sheet classifications. All that will be needed is to recast the worksheet information into more formal balance sheet and income statement formats. This will be illustrated in the following chapter.

QUESTIONS

1. Why are adjusting entries needed at the end of the accounting period?
2. Explain how adjusting entries affect the determination of the net income for the accounting period.
3. Describe the five types of adjusting entries.
4. What are prepayments? What original entry is made when expenses are paid in advance? What adjusting entry is needed at the end of the accounting period?
5. What is meant by unearned revenue? Give two examples of unearned revenue applicable to a hospitality firm.
6. What effect would the failure to make an adjusting entry for accrued interest expense have on the net income for the period?
7. What is depreciation? Why are depreciation adjustments necessary?
8. Explain the purpose of using the accumulated depreciation account in recording depreciation adjustments. In what financial statement will this account appear?
9. What is the purpose of the financial statement worksheet?
10. Describe four advantages of the financial statement worksheet approach.
11. Does the financial statement worksheet eliminate the need for formal financial statements?
12. What is bad debt expense? Why does the conservatism principle require a bad debt adjustment?
13. Accumulated depreciation in the balance sheet credit column of the financial statement worksheet of Great Escape Inn is $4,000 larger than depreciation expense in the income statement debit column of the same worksheet. Explain how this is possible.
14. What is the purpose of using key letters in recording adjusting entries in the adjustments columns of a financial statement worksheet?
15. Is it possible to prepare adjusting and closing entries and complete financial statements without preparing a financial statement worksheet? Explain.

EXERCISES

1. An examination of the prepaid insurance account of Tank Restaurants shows a balance of $9,600 as of October 31, 1986 (the end of the fiscal year) before adjustment. Prepare the required adjusting entries in the general journal under each of the following assumptions:
   (a) An examination of insurance policies reveals insurance that cost $4,000 has expired during the period.
   (b) An examination of insurance policies shows unexpired insurance of $6,400 as of October 31, 1986.
2. Travel Consultant, Inc., borrows $100,000 on October 31, 1986, from Haven National Bank for 90 days with interest payable at the time of repayment of the note at 12% APR. Prepare the required adjusting entry on December 31, 1986.

3. The balances of the following accounts, taken from the Adjusted Trial Balance columns of the financial statement worksheet of RJ Motel for the year ending December 31, 1986, are presented in random order:

(a)	Cash	$ 10	(i)	Furniture and equipment	$90
(b)	Cost of food sold	28	(j)	Room sales	85
(c)	Prepaid insurance	12	(k)	Food sales	40
(d)	Rent expense	7	(l)	Accounts receivable	22
(e)	Depreciation expense	10	(m)	Insurance expense	16
(f)	Salaries and wages	30	(n)	RJ, withdrawals	12
(g)	RJ, capital	100	(o)	Other expenses	20
(h)	Accumulated depreciation	20	(p)	Accounts payable	12

Required: Indicate to which column of the financial statement worksheet each account balance would be extended.

4. Using the information from Exercise 3, calculate the following:
   (a) Total assets
   (b) Total revenues
   (c) Total expenses
   (d) Net income for the year 1986
   (e) Total owners' equity, December 31, 1986.

5. Prepare adjusting entries in the general journal from the following information pertaining to the accounts of Perfect Place Inn as of November 30, 1986 (the end of its fiscal year):
   (a) The prepaid insurance account shows a balance of $120 representing the May 31, 1986 premium payment for one-year fire insurance coverage.
   (b) Furniture and equipment ($1,000) is being depreciated using the straight-line method and an estimated useful life of five years. (No salvage value.) Annual depreciation has not been recorded.
   (c) Salaries and wages earned by employees for November 28, 29, and 30, have not been recorded. Weekly wages (five days) amount to $800.
   (d) Interest earned on a note receivable not yet collected is $50.
   (e) The customers' deposit account has a balance of $800 before adjustments. Of these deposits, $300 were earned during November 1986.
   (f) The food inventory account reveals an unadjusted balance of $80. The correct amount of food inventory on hand is $30 on November 30, 1986.

6. Data pertaining to the accounts of Revelation Inn for period ending February 28, 1986 follow:
   (1) A two-year fire insurance premium of $660 had been paid on December 1, 1985.
   (2) A customer paid a $40 deposit on January 1, 1986 to be applied against a March 1986 reservation.
   (3) The total daily payroll is $400 and employees are paid each Friday for all work done during the preceding week. February 28 falls on a Wednesday.
   (4) The motel has furniture and equipment that cost $5,000 and has an estimated life of 10 years (no salvage value). The monthly depreciation has not been recorded.
   (5) Rent of $2,800 for the month of February 1986 will be paid on March 1, 1986.
   (6) Included in the room sales account are advance payments of $450 for services to be rendered in March 1986.
   (7) The office supplies inventory account has an unadjusted balance of $1,300. Office supplies on hand were $1,120 on February 28, 1986.
   (8) The balance of the notes payable account ($10,000) represents a 14% interest-bearing note dated January 1, 1986 and due July 1, 1986.
   Required:
   (a) Prepare adjusting entries in the general journal on February 28, 1986.
   (b) Explain the effect on net income of not making each adjusting entry.

PROBLEMS

1. Selected account balances were taken from the trial balance of Glowing Inn (before adjustments) for the year ended August 31, 1986.

Prepaid insurance	$ 240
Accumulated depreciation, building	50
Accumulated depreciation, furniture and equipment	10
Salaries and wages expense	102
Interest expense	60
Customers' deposits	20
Housekeeping supplies inventory	70
Building	1500
Notes payable	200
Furniture and equipment	500

Required:

(a) Record the necessary adjusting entries as of August 31, 1986 in the general journal using the following information:

  (1) The balance of prepaid insurance represents a two-year insurance policy purchased on June 1, 1986.

  (2) An inventory of housekeeping supplies revealed $10 on hand on August 31, 1986.

  (3) Depreciation on the building is calculated using the straight-line method and an estimated useful life of 30 years (no salvage value).

  (4) Depreciation on the furniture and equipment is calculated using the straight-line method and an estimated useful life of 10 years (no salvage value).

  (5) Customers' deposits represent advance payments received in July 1986 for August and September 1986 reservations. Of the deposits, $9 were used during August 1986.

  (6) Interest on the $200 note issued on June 1, 1986 has not been recorded. The annual interest rate is 15%.

(b) Determine the adjusted balances of the following accounts: prepaid insurance; customers' deposits; accumulated depreciation, building; interest expense; salaries and wages expense; and housekeeping supplies inventory.

2. The following transactions were engaged in by Dolphin Travel Services (a proprietorship) during its first month of operation in 1985:

Oct. 1 Mr. David Dolphin invested $150,000 to start a new business under the name Dolphin Travel Services.

   2 Borrowed $100,000 from the Fourth National Bank to be repaid in 90 days (12% APR).

   5 October office rent is paid, $1,000.

   6 Purchased furniture and equipment on account, $50,000.

   8 Paid cash for supplies, $800.

  10 Sales commissions received in cash, $20,000.

  15 Paid salaries and wages, $2,000.

  20 Paid $1,200 for a one-year general insurance coverage.

  21 Paid $20,000 toward the furniture and equipment purchase of October 6.

  24 Paid salaries and wages, $2,500.

  28 Sales commissions: $25,000 in cash, $28,000 on account.

Required:

(a) Enter the October transactions in the general journal.

(b) Post the journal entries to general ledger "T" accounts and determine account balances.

(c) Set up a 10-column financial statement worksheet.

(d) Take a trial balance of the general ledger using the first two money columns of the worksheet.

(e) Complete the adjustments columns of the financial statement worksheet using the following adjustment information:

   (1) Salaries and wages incurred, but not yet paid, as of October 31, 1985: $400.

   (2) Record the expired insurance for the month of October 1985.

   (3) Record accrued interest for the month of October.

   (4) Use straight-line depreciation and a 10-year estimated useful life in recording depreciation.

   (5) Commissions earned, not yet recorded, $5,000.

   (6) Supplies inventory on hand at October 31, 1985, $200.

(f) Complete the financial statement worksheet, determining the amount of net income or net loss of Dolphin Travel Services for the month of October, 1985.

(g) Prepare an income statement of Dolphin Travel Services for the month ended October 31, 1985, and a balance sheet as of October 31, 1985.

3. The account balances (in thousands of dollars) in the general ledger of On Board Travel Agency on July 31, 1985 (the end of its fiscal year), *before adjustments,* were as follows:

Debit balances		**Credit balances**	
Cash	$ 30	Accumulated depreciation	$ 80
Accounts receivable	158	Notes payable	100
Notes receivable	20	Accounts payable	120
Furniture and fixtures	300	Aly Seat—capital	100
Inventories	20	Sales	382
Prepaid insurance	14	Other income	20
Salaries expense	120		
Interest expense	60		
Other expenses	80		
	$802		$802

The data for the adjustments are as follows:

   (1) The prepaid insurance balance represents an entry made on May 31, 1985 for the cost of a one-year policy expiring on May 31, 1986.

   (2) Interest on the $100,000 note payable issued on June 30, 1985 is due to be paid on September 30, 1985 at a 12% annual rate of interest.

   (3) Inventories at July 31, 1985, $7,000.

   (4) Furniture and fixtures are being depreciated using the straight-line method and an estimated useful life of five years (salvage value = 0). Annual depreciation has not been recorded.

   (5) Salaries for the last two days of the period ended July 31, 1985 have not been recorded, $1,000.

Required:

(a) Record adjusting entries in the general journal.

(b) Post adjusting entries, adding other "T" accounts as necessary.

(c) Prepare an adjusted trial balance as of July 31, 1985.

(d) Prepare in good form a balance sheet as of July 31, 1985, a statement of owners' capital, and an income statement for the year ended July 31, 1985.

4. The general ledger of Jolly Restaurant on December 31, 1986, shows the following accounts and balances (presented in random order):

Cash	$ 5,000
Accounts receivable	2,000
Furniture and equipment	14,000
Accumulated depreciation	2,000
Accounts payable	4,000

Prepaid insurance	1,200
JJ, capital	8,000
JJ, withdrawals	2,000
Salaries and wages expense	6,000
Sales	20,000
Notes payable	4,000
Advertising expense	1,500
Other operating expenses	4,000
Housekeeping supplies inventory	1,800
Interest expense	500

The adjustment data for the year 1986 are

1. The balance in the prepaid insurance account represents a one-year insurance policy purchased on September 1, 1986.
2. An inventory of housekeeping supplies showed $1,100 worth of supplies used during the year.
3. The furniture and equipment is depreciated using the straight-line method and a five-year estimated useful life (salvage value $500).
4. Interest on a six-month note ($4,000) dated August 1, 1986 and bearing interest at the rate of 15% per year, has not been recorded.
5. Salaries and wages for the five-day week ended Friday, January 2, 1987, $200, will be paid on that day.

Required:

(a) Prepare a complete financial statement worksheet for the year ended December 31, 1986, entering the adjustments directly on the worksheet.

(b) Prepare a balance sheet, income statement and statement of owners' equity as of and for the year ending December 31, 1986.

5. The following account balances in random order have been extracted from the general ledger of FRB Inn as of December 31, 1986.

Account title	Acct. no.	Trial balance Debit	Trial balance Credit	Adjustments Debit	Adjustments Credit	Adjusted trial balance Debit	Adjusted trial balance Credit	Income statement Debit	Income statement Credit	Balance sheet Debit	Balance sheet Credit
Accounts payable	201		1,000								
Accounts receivable	110	3,000									
Accumulated depreciation	175		200								
Accrued interest payable	215										
Cash in bank	103	1,000									
Common stock	301		1,000								
Depreciation expense	598										
Insurance expense	595										
Interest expense	596										
Furniture and fixtures	170	1,000									
Prepaid insurance	132	600									
Notes payable	202		1,000								
Sundry expenses	572	100									
Salaries expense	500	400									
Room sales	400		2,000								
Other income	402		400								
Utilities expense	580	200									
Supplies expense	515										
Supplies inventory	120	300									
Retained earnings	305		1,000								
		6,600	6,600								

Required:

(a) Use the data provided on the next page to adjust the trial balance for the year ended December 31, 1986.

(b) Complete the financial statement worksheet determining the net income or (loss) for the year 1986.

Adjustment data:

(1) Supplies inventory physical count at December 31, 1986, $200.

(2) Note payable was issued on October 1, 1986, bearing interest at 12% APR, due January 2, 1987.

(3) Furniture and fixtures are depreciated using the straight-line method over a 10-year estimated useful life.

(4) Prepaid insurance represents the premium, paid June 1, 1986, for one-year coverage.

8

Completing the Accounting Cycle

In Chapter 7 it was explained how the financial statement worksheet helps organize the accounting data needed to produce the output (or end product) of the accounting system—information to management in the form of financial statements. Usually, the remaining steps in the accounting cycle can be completed in a timely fashion using the financial statement worksheet as a point of reference. The completed worksheet will provide the information required to prepare the formal income statement and balance sheet. These statements will then be used by management and other financial statement users in appraising the past performance of the hospitality business and in making economic decisions regarding the future of the firm. Moreover, the financial statement worksheet will also be used to complete the final step of the accounting cycle—closing the books. This last step is needed to make the accounting records ready for the next accounting period by transferring the net income (or net loss) of the period to the owner(s) of the hospitality firm.

In this chapter we first illustrate the use of the financial statement worksheet in the preparation of formal financial statements—step 6 of the accounting cycle. The financial statement worksheet of Neat Restaurant (see Figures 7.5–7.7) is used as the basis to prepare the balance sheet, statement of owners' equity, and income statement of the restaurant as of and for the year ended July 31, 1985.

Next, the seventh and last step of the accounting cycle, closing the books, is reviewed. In this regard, we explain the need and purposes of closing entries, setting forth the main differences between nominal and real accounts. An in-depth coverage of each of the four closing entries will be presented. Also, a postclosing trial balance is prepared as a means to check, one more time, the accuracy of the general ledger.

Once closing procedures are completed we consider an optional additional procedure known as reversing entries. These entries are journalized at the beginning of each accounting period in order to facilitate the recording of certain income and expense transactions taking place during the period.

Then, the main differences and similarities between certain procedures used by proprietorships (and partnerships) and those applicable to corporations are highlighted. Finally, a flowchart of all the steps in the accounting cycle is included for review purposes.

PREPARATION OF FINANCIAL STATEMENTS: STEP 6 OF THE ACCOUNTING CYCLE

As noted earlier, after the financial statement worksheet is completed, all of the information needed to prepare the financial statements is readily available. Nonetheless, the data must be rearranged into a more formal financial statement presentation.

Two basic financial statements are prepared using the financial statement columns of the worksheet: (1) the income statement and (2) the balance sheet. In addition, many hospitality firms prepare a separate statement of owners' equity or capital (statement of retained earnings for a corporation) using data from the worksheet. Figure 7.7, the worksheet of Neat Restaurant for the year ended July 31, 1985, is used as the basis to prepare formal financial statements for the restaurant.

Income Statement Preparation

The income statement for the period is normally prepared first. All of the information needed to prepare the income statement of Neat Restaurant for the year ended July 31, 1985 is found in the income statement columns of the completed worksheet (Figure 7.7). The credit column lists the individual revenue accounts, totaling $338, whereas the debit column contains the individual expenses, a total amount of $298.

The income statement for Neat Restaurant for the year ended July 31, 1985 is given in Figure 8.1.

NEAT RESTAURANT[1]
Income Statement
For the Year Ended July 31, 1985

Revenues[2]		
Sales		$300
Other income		20
Interest income		18
Total revenues		338
Expenses[3]		
Salaries and wages expense	$107	
Insurance expense	7	
Cost of food sold	89	
Interest expense	25	
Depreciation expense	22	
Other operating expenses	48	
Total expenses		298
Net income[4]		$ 40

Figure 8.1. Neat Restaurant income statement. (1) Statement heading (name of company, name of statement, and period covered); (2) revenue section; (3) expense section; (4) net income (or net loss) amount.

This simple format income statement consists of four sections:

(1) Statement heading (name of company, name of statement, and period covered)
(2) Revenue section
(3) Expense section
(4) Net income (or net loss) amount

Statement of Owners' Equity

Once the income statement is done, the next statement that is normally prepared is the statement of owners' equity. It is completed by adding the net income of the period to the beginning capital, and subtracting the withdrawals for the period. The resulting amount will represent the ending capital and will also appear on the balance sheet as an indication of the owners' equity in the business on the last day of the accounting period.

The information needed for the beginning capital amount and for the withdrawals made during the period is generally found in the balance sheet columns of the financial statement worksheet. However, if additional investments were made by the owner(s) during the current accounting period, it becomes necessary to refer to the owners' capital account in the general ledger to determine the actual amounts invested, which must be added to the beginning capital in preparing the statement of owners' equity.

The net income for the period is the balancing number on the income statement and balance sheet columns of the worksheet, and it is also the bottom figure on the first basic financial statement (the income statement). As noted before, we add the net income to the beginning balance of owners' capital on the statement of owners' equity. Conversely, we deduct a net loss from the beginning capital balance, if applicable.

The formal statement of owner's equity of Neat Restaurant for the year ended July 31, 1985 is given in Figure 8.2.

NEAT RESTAURANT
Statement of Owners' Equity
For the Year Ended July 31, 1985

Beginning balance	$502
Add: Net income for the year	40
	542
Less: Withdrawals	50
Ending balance	$492

Figure 8.2. Neat Restaurant statement of owner's capital.

Balance Sheet Preparation

The information necessary to prepare the balance sheet is found in the balance sheet columns of the worksheet. The balance sheet debit column contains all the asset accounts to be included on the balance sheet. Similarly, the balance sheet credit column contains the liabilities of the company and the owners' equity accounts. It also includes the contra-asset accounts (e.g., accumulated depreciation) to be deducted from the corresponding assets on the formal balance sheet.

A simple form of the balance sheet usually consists of

- statement heading (name of company, name of statement, and statement date)
- asset section
- liability section
- owners' equity (owners' capital ending balance)

As previously indicated, the balance sheet is based on the fundamental accounting equation and thus follows the premise of equality inherent in the double-entry accounting system, namely, that assets are equal to liabilities plus owners' equity.

The balance sheet of Neat Restaurant as of July 31, 1985, is shown in Figure 8.3. We can see that the financial statement worksheet debit column

NEAT RESTAURANT
Balance Sheet
July 31, 1985

Assets		
Cash		$100
Accounts receivable		200
Notes receivable		300
Accrued interest receivable		18
Food inventory		21
Prepaid insurance		5
Furniture and equipment	$220	
Less: Accumulated depreciation	110	110
Total assets		$754
Liabilities & Owner's Equity		
Liabilities		
Accounts payable		$150
Notes payable		100
Accrued interest		5
Accrued salaries		7
Total liabilities		262
Owner's Equity		492
Total liabilities & owner's equity		$754

Figure 8.3. Neat Restaurant balance sheet.

total of $914 (Figure 7.7) does not agree with the total assets on the formal balance sheet ($754). The worksheet debit column includes the withdrawals account ($50), which is not an asset account. Furthermore, the accumulated depreciation (shown in the credit column of the worksheet) was deducted from the asset account furniture and equipment ($110) on the balance sheet. The reconciliation of the total amount in the debit column of the worksheet and the total assets on the balance sheet follows:

Balance sheet worksheet debit column		$914
Less: Withdrawals	50	
Accumulated depreciation	110	160
Total assets on balance sheet		$754

The above illustrations of the financial statements of Neat Restaurant are examples of simple format financial statements. As we progress, we shall see that there are several alternatives of presenting financial and operating data on the financial statements. Chapters 11, 12, and 13 will include an in-depth coverage of the presentation of financial statements in the hospitality industry.

CLOSING THE BOOKS: STEP 7 OF THE ACCOUNTING CYCLE

After the financial statements are completed, the last step of the accounting cycle is the closing procedures needed to prepare the general ledger for the next accounting period.

As stated in Chapter 2, revenues belong to the owner(s) whereas expenses must be absorbed by the owner(s). The closing process will credit the owners with their share of revenues while debiting the owners with the expenses they must absorb, thereby increasing owners' equity with the revenues of the period and decreasing owners' equity with the expenses of the period.

Based on the foregoing, we shall call revenues and expenses temporary (or nominal) accounts. Their balances will be closed or cleared at the end of each accounting period inasmuch as revenue and expenses are established as subdivisions of owners' equity during each accounting period in order to determine the periodic net income (or net loss). However, once the output of the accounting system has been produced (financial statements) these temporary accounts have served their purpose and will be closed by reducing them to zero. In this manner, revenues and expenses will have a fresh start at the beginning of each new accounting period.

Balance sheet accounts, on the other hand, are referred to as permanent (or real) accounts. They will not be closed at the end of the period. Rather, the ending balances of assets, liabilities, owners' equity, and contra-asset accounts (such as accumulated depreciation) will be carried forward to the next accounting period.

The three main objectives of closing the books can be summarized as follows:

1. to close temporary accounts, reducing their balance to zero.
2. to transfer the net income (or net loss) to the appropriate owners' equity account.
3. to make the general ledger ready for the next accounting period.

CLOSING PROCESS

As a practical matter, after the financial statements are prepared, the adjusting entries which are shown on the worksheet are posted to the general ledger in order to bring it into agreement with the financial statements. Once the general ledger accounts reflect the proper adjusted balances, we are ready to close the revenue and expense accounts, transferring the net income (or net loss) of the period to the owner(s) of the hospitality organization. The closing entries are first recorded in the general journal and then posted to the general ledger.

In lieu of transferring each revenue and expense account directly to the owners' capital account, the income summary account is created as a means of simplifying the closing procedures. This account will, in turn, be closed by transferring its balance to the appropriate owners' equity account. We shall again refer to the completed financial statement worksheet as a basis to complete the closing process. The actual procedures for closing the books consist of four entries:

1. Close all revenue accounts to income summary.
2. Close all expense accounts to income summary.
3. Close the income summary account to the appropriate owner(s) equity account.
4. Close the withdrawals(s) account to the capital(s) account (only applicable to proprietorships and partnerships).

The closing entries will be reviewed using the Neat Restaurant worksheet for the year ended July 31, 1985 (Figure 7.7) as a point of reference.

Entry No. 1:   Closing the Revenue Accounts

Since all the revenue accounts have a normal credit balance, we need to debit all revenue accounts appearing in the income statement credit column of the financial statement worksheet to bring their balance to zero. At the same time, we credit the income summary account for the total of all revenue account balances as reflected in the income statement credit column of the worksheet.

The first closing entry for Neat Restaurant is shown below:

1985			
July 31	Sales	300	
	Interest Income	18	
	Other Income	20	
	Income Summary		338
	To close revenue accounts.		

After posting the above entry to the general ledger, the accounts will show the following:

Sales					**Other Income**			
Closing 1	300	Bal. July 31	300		Closing 1	20	Bal. July 31	20

Interest Income					**Income Summary**			
Closing 1	18	Bal. July 31	18				Closing 1	338

Note that the double-ruled lines in the revenue accounts indicate that the debits and credits are equal and the account has a zero balance. Also note that the amount of the period's revenue ($338) has been transferred to the credit side of the income summary account.

Entry No. 2:   Closing the Expense Accounts

The second closing entry will reduce all expense accounts to a zero balance by transferring them to the income summary account. Since the expense accounts all have debit balances, they will have to be credited to obtain a zero balance. The income summary account is debited for the total of all the expenses.

The information for closing expenses is found in the debit column of the worksheet. The expense accounts are closed in the order in which they appear on the worksheet. After transferring the total of all the expense accounts to income summary, the debit side of this account will include all expenses.

The second closing entry for Neat Restaurant is:

1985			
July 31	Income Summary	298	
	Salaries and wages		107
	Interest expense		25
	Other operating expense		48
	Insurance expense		7
	Cost of food sold		89
	Depreciation expense		22
	To close the expense accounts		

After posting the first two closing entries to the general ledger, the balance of income summary will represent the net income (or net loss) of the period inasmuch as its credit side includes the total revenues (closing entry no. 1) and the debit side includes the total expenses (closing entry no. 2). We have already seen that the excess of revenues over expenses is the net income of the period.

The income summary account for Neat Restaurant appears below:

Income Summary

Closing 2	298	Closing 1	338

Thus, the income summary account has a credit balance of $40 (338 − 298), which is the net income of Neat Restaurant for the year ended July 31, 1985.

Entry No. 3:   Closing the Income Summary Account

After the first two closing entries are recorded and posted to the general ledger, all the revenue and expense accounts have zero balances, and the income summary account has a balance equal to the net income or loss for the accounting period.

The third closing entry will transfer the balance of the income summary account to the appropriate owner's equity account. As a result of this, the capital account will increase with the net income of the period or decrease with a net loss. After revenues and expenses are closed, the income summary has served its purpose and is closed to the capital account. The third closing entry for Neat Restaurant follows:

1985			
July 31	Income Summary	40	
	Amy Neat, capital		40
	To close the income summary account		

In "T" account form, the income summary and the capital account of Neat Restaurant will reflect the following:

Income Summary

Closing 2	298	Closing 1	338
Closing 3	40		
	338		338

Amy Neat, Capital

		July 31 Bal.	502
		Closing 3	40

Note that after the first three closing entries are recorded and posted, the capital account shows an increase of $40, resulting from the transfer of net income from the income summary account to Amy Neat, capital. Similarly, the income summary account has no balance.

Entry No. 4:   Closing the Owner's Withdrawals

The last closing entry completes the closing process by transferring the owner's withdrawals account balance to the capital account. The withdrawals account is considered a nominal account, and thus it is temporary in nature. It remains open during each period in order to account for the amounts withdrawn by the owner(s). The withdrawals account, however, is closed at the end of the period by crediting it (since it has a normal debit balance) and debiting the owner's capital account. The last closing entry for Neat Restaurant is

1985
―――

July 31	Amy Neat, Capital	50	
	Amy Neat, Withdrawals		50
	To close the withdrawals account		

The effects of the above entry in the capital and withdrawals accounts are shown below:

Amy Neat, Capital

Closing 4	50	Bal. July 31	502
		Closing 3	40
	50		542
		Bal.	492

Amy Neat, Withdrawals

| Bal. July 31 | 50 | Closing 4 | 50 |

After all closing entries are recorded and posted, the balance of the capital account will be in agreement with the owner's equity balance shown on the balance sheet (see Figure 8.3). The balance will include the amount of capital at the beginning of the period plus additional investments (if applicable) made during the period, net income addition or net loss deduction, and withdrawal deductions. To facilitate review of the closing process, Figure 8.4 summarizes the four closing entries described in the preceding pages.

THE POSTCLOSING TRIAL BALANCE

After the closing process has been completed, a new trial balance is prepared in order to check the equality of the debit and credit balances found in the general ledger.

The postclosing trial balance will only include real accounts (balance sheet accounts) since only those will remain open at the end of the closing process. The nominal (or temporary) accounts would have no balance and thus would not appear on the postclosing trial balance. The postclosing trial balance will therefore serve as a final check on the equality of the accounts, and it will ascertain that the ledger is in balance to begin a new accounting period.

The postclosing trial balance of Neat Restaurant as of July 31, 1985 is presented in Figure 8.5. Note that no revenue or expense accounts are listed and that the Amy Neat, capital account has been increased by the periodic net income as a result of the closing process.

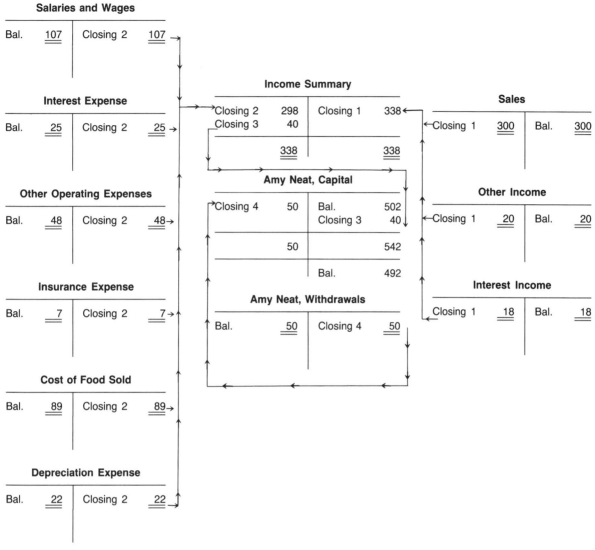

Figure 8.4. Neat Restaurant closing procedures for the year ended July 31, 1985.

NEAT RESTAURANT
Postclosing Trial Balance
July 31, 1985

	Dr	Cr
Cash	$100	
Accounts receivable	200	
Notes receivable	300	
Accrued interest receivable	18	
Food inventory	21	
Prepaid insurance	5	
Furniture and equipment	220	
Accumulated depreciation		$110
Accrued interest		5
Accrued salaries		7
Notes payable		100
Accounts payable		150
Amy Neat, capital		492
	$864	$864

Figure 8.5. Neat Restaurant postclosing trial balance.

151

REVERSING ENTRIES: AN OPTIONAL PROCEDURE

An optional procedure often used in practice is to record reversing entries of accrual adjustments on the first day of each accounting period. The main purpose of reversing entries is to simplify the recording of payments and receipts of accruals by allowing these transactions to be entered on the books in a routine fashion. In recording reversing entries, we reverse the debits and credits used in the accrual adjusting entries.

To illustrate, we refer to a two-year note payable of $1,000 (issued on July 1, 1985, bearing annual interest at the rate of 12%) on the books of TCI Hotel. The interest is payable annually on June 30. On December 31, 1985, the following adjusting entry was recorded to accrue interest from July 1 to December 31, 1985 ($12\% \times 1,000 = 120 \div 2 = 60$).

1985			
Dec. 31	Interest expense	60	
	Accrued interest payable		60
	To record six-months' interest		

On January 1, 1986 (the first day of the new accounting period) we record the following entry in the GJ:

1986			
Jan. 1	Accrued interest payable	60	
	Interest expense		60
	To reverse accrual		

The June 1986 interest payment will then be recorded in a routine manner as follows:

1986			
June 30	Interest expense	120	
	Cash		120
	To record payment of 12% interest		

After posting the above entries to the general ledger, the interest expense would reflect the actual expense for the period commencing January 1, 1986 and ending June 30, 1986, as follows:

Accrued Interest Payable				Interest Expense			
Jan. 1 Reversing	60	Bal.	60	June 30	120	Jan. 1 Reversing	60
				Bal.	60		

PROCEDURES APPLICABLE TO A CORPORATION

The accounting process for a corporation is basically the same as for a single proprietorship (or partnership), which has been the subject of our in-depth review in the last few chapters. Nonetheless, there are some differences:

- Corporations will have one additional accrual adjustment, namely, the accrual of income taxes. This will result from the fact that corporations are subject to taxation upon their income, whereas partnerships and proprietorships do not pay a separate income tax. The accrual will entail a debit to income taxes expense and a credit to income taxes payable.
- Corporations do not have withdrawal accounts since shareholders are normally not allowed to take money and/or property out of the business for personal use. However, a comparable transaction for a corporation would be the recording of dividends paid to shareholders, which are debited to dividends and credited to cash. Dividends will be considered a contra-equity account (in the same manner as withdrawals) and will be closed to the appropriate equity account during the closing process (i.e., retained earnings).
- The closing process of corporations is very much the same as has been illustrated in this chapter for Neat Restaurant (a proprietorship), but the retained earnings account is used to transfer net income to owners' equity in the case of corporations.

We consider the following closing entries of Dynasty Hotels on October 31, 1986 (the end of its fiscal year) to illustrate the closing procedures applicable to corporations.

Entry No. 1

1986

Oct. 31	Room sales	80,000	
	Food sales	35,000	
	Beverage sales	18,000	
	Other income	5,000	
	Income Summary		138,000
	To close revenue accounts		

Entry No. 2

1986

Oct. 31	Income Summary	121,000	
	Salaries and wages		55,000
	Cost of sales		25,000
	Supplies expense		15,000
	Depreciation expense		8,000
	Other expenses		3,000
	Income tax expense		15,000
	To close expense accounts		

Entry No. 3

1986

Oct. 31	Income Summary	17,000	
	Retained Earnings		17,000
	To close the income summary account		

Entry No. 4

	1986			
Oct. 31	Retained Earnings		4,000	
	Dividends			4,000
	To close the dividends account			

The effect of the above entries on the general ledger accounts is presented below:

Income Summary

Closing 2	121,000	Closing 1	138,000
Closing 3	17,000		
	138,000		138,000

Retained Earnings

Closing 4	4,000	Bal.	3,000
			17,000
	4,000		20,000
		Bal.	16,000

Dividends

Bal.	4,000	Closing 4	4,000

It is apparent that the closing of revenue and expense accounts is exactly the same for corporations, partnerships, and proprietorships (closing entries no. 1 and no. 2). The transfer of net income to owners' equity is essentially the same for corporations (closing entry no. 3), except for the use of the retained earnings account. As far as closing entry no. 4 is concerned, some corporations will omit this entry altogether by recording the dividends as a direct reduction of retained earnings, as we shall describe in Chapter 17.

THE ACCOUNTING CYCLE: FLOWCHART

In this chapter and the three preceding ones, the accounting cycle has been subjected to an in-depth review. We conclude this chapter with a flowchart showing all the steps of the accounting cycle (Figure 8.6).

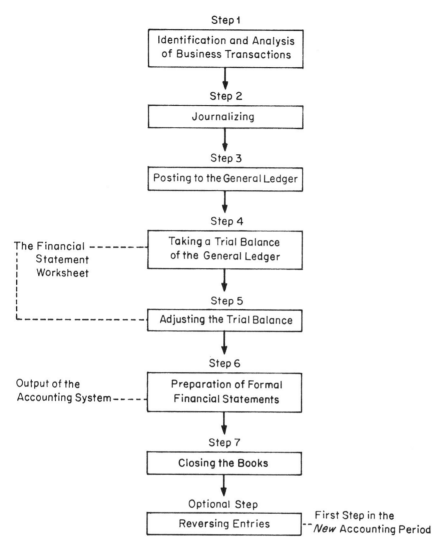

Figure 8.6. Accounting cycle flowchart.

QUESTIONS

1. How is the financial statement worksheet used in the preparation of formal financial statements? *ORGANIZING IT REV+EXP find net NET INCOME OR LOSS*

2. What is the primary objective of an income statement? List the main sections of a simple-form income statement.

3. Is the financial statement worksheet a substitute for formal financial statements? Discuss. *NO*

4. What are the main elements of a statement of owners' equity? *CORP - share capital*

5. What are the principal reconciling items between the balance sheet debit column of the financial statement worksheet and the total assets on the balance sheet? *- bring up to date* *- less accumulated depreciation + withdrawals* *CONTRA ASSET ACCOUNT*

6. Distinguish between adjusting and closing entries. *- close out temporary accts.*

7. What are the major objectives of closing entries? *- clear your acc start pretty new year accounts*

8. What are real accounts? What are nominal accounts? List three examples of each. *balance sheet account* *temporary accounts* *3 - Rev + exp*

9. Describe the four steps needed to complete closing procedures. What is the purpose of the income summary account? *— accumulate all our exp + rev*

10. What is the purpose of a postclosing trial balance? *— no temporary accounts*

11. Which of the following accounts will not have a balance in a postclosing trial balance?

    (a) Withdrawals N
    (b) Prepaid rent Y
    (c) Land Y
    (d) Accounts receivable Y
    (e) Room sales N
    (f) Customers' deposits Y
    (g) Accrued interest payable Y
    (h) Cash Y
    (i) Common stock Y
    (j) Accumulated depreciation Y
    (k) Interest expense N
    (l) Cost of food sold N

— simplify payment receipts at annual year end date

12. What is the purpose of reversing entries? What type of adjusting entries are normally reversed?

13. Distinguish between closing procedures for partnerships and corporations. *pg 153*

14. List all the steps in the accounting cycle. *SEE CHART pg 155*

closing procedures for proprietorship

EXERCISES

1. Indicate the effect on net income of extending the following accounts on a financial statement worksheet:
    (a) Prepaid rent to the income statement credit column.
    (b) Accumulated depreciation to the income statement credit column.
    (c) Insurance expense to the balance sheet debit column.
    (d) Accrued salaries payable to the income statement credit column.
    (e) Common stock to the balance sheet credit column.

2. The R Hotel Corporation uses the following accounts for its accounting system. For each item, indicate whether the account appears on the balance sheet or the income statement, and also indicate the accounts that would be closed at the end of the accounting period:

    (a) Rooms salaries
    (b) Accrued interest payable
    (c) Cash
    (d) Mortgages payable
    (e) Accounts receivable
    (f) Interest income
    (g) Common stock
    (h) Depreciation expense
    (i) Income tax expense
    (j) Food sales
    (k) Income tax payable
    (l) Accrued interest receivable
    (m) Unearned revenue
    (n) Prepaid expenses

3. Consider the following data for A Hotel Corporation:

Accounts receivable	$ 2,000
Cash	1,000
Retained earnings, end of period	20,000
Total liabilities	118,000
Room sales	100,000
Total expenses	140,000
Common stock	150,000
Property and equipment, at cost	300,000
Food sales	50,000
Other income	5,000
Prepaid expenses	2,000
Short-term investments	3,000
Accumulated depreciation	50,000
Inventories	10,000
Long-term investments	20,000

(a) Compute the following amounts:
   (1) Total assets
   (2) Total shareholders' equity
   (3) Net income for the period
   (4) Retained earnings, beginning of period (assume no dividends were declared during the period)
(b) Using the above data prepare a postclosing trial balance as of the end of the period.

4. Consider the following data included in the adjusted trial balance of Proven Travel Company on November 30, 1987.

	Dr	Cr
Salaries expense	30,000	
Accrued salaries payable		1,000

Required:
(a) Record the appropriate reversing entry in the general journal on December 1, 1987.
(b) Record payment of $5,000 salaries in the general journal on December 4, 1987.

PROBLEMS

1. Consider the following account balances from the income statement columns of the financial statement worksheet of M&B Restaurant for the year ended December 31, 1988.

	Dr	Cr
Food sales		100,000
Beverage sales		40,500
Other income		1,000
Rent expense	10,000	
Salaries and wages	65,000	
Supplies expense	10,000	
Insurance expense	10,500	
Depreciation and amortization	5,000	
Other operating expenses	2,500	
Interest expense	2,500	
	105,500	141,500

(a) Prepare the income statement of M&B Restaurant for the year ended December 31, 1988.

(b) Record closing entries in the general journal.

2. Following are the financial statement columns of the October 1987 worksheet of Aquarius Place.

	Income statement		Balance sheet	
	Dr	Cr	Dr	Cr
Cash			6,000	
Accounts receivable			5,000	
Accrued interest receivable			1,000	
Inventories			6,000	
Land			50,000	
Building			100,000	
Furniture and equipment			30,000	
Accumulated depreciation				50,000
Prepaid expenses			2,000	
Accounts payable				10,000
Notes payable				20,000
Mortgages payable				60,000
Accrued expenses				8,000
A. Aquarius, capital				10,000
Sales		150,000		
Other income		10,000		
Salaries and wages	60,000			
Interest expense	3,000			
Depreciation and amortization	5,000			
Other expenses	50,000			
	118,000	160,000	200,000	158,000

Required:

(a) Prepare an income statement for the month of October 1987.

(b) Prepare a statement of owner's equity for the month ended October 31, 1987 (additional investments by Mr. Aquarius during October 1987 amounted to $4,000).

(c) Prepare a balance sheet as of October 31, 1987.

(d) Prepare closing entries in general journal form.

(e) Prepare a postclosing trial balance as of October 31, 1987.

(f) What balances for the following accounts will be carried forward to November 1, 1987?

    (1) Building

    (2) Accrued expenses

    (3) Sales

    (4) Salaries and wages

    (5) Accrued interest receivable

    (6) Mortgages payable

    (7) A. Aquarius, capital

3. The income statement and balance sheet columns of the financial statement worksheet of An Important Restaurant Corp., for the period ended July 31, 1988, are shown at the top of the next page.

	Income statement		Balance sheet	
	Dr	Cr	Dr	Cr
Cash			3,000	
Accounts receivable			5,000	
Accounts payable				1,000
Income taxes payable				650
Interest expense	200			
Salaries and wages	1,300			
Property and equipment			10,000	
Accumulated depreciation				2,000
Common stock				5,700
Retained earnings				8,000
Income tax expense	650			
Other expenses	500			
Sales		3,000		
Other income		300		
	2,650	3,300	18,000	17,350

(a) Prepare an income statement, a statement of retained earnings, and a balance sheet as of July 31, 1988 and for the period then ended.
(b) Record closing entries in the general journal.
(c) Open "T" accounts for each account listed on the financial statement worksheet. Post closing entries to the "T" accounts.
(d) Prepare a postclosing trial balance.
4. The account balances in the ledger of Lively Inn on February 28, 1988 (the end of its fiscal year), were as follows:

Debit balances		Credit balances	
Cash	$ 300	Accumulated depreciation	$ 55
Accounts receivable	225	Notes payable	100
Food inventory	140	Accounts payable	120
Furniture and fixtures	200	Common stock	200
Supplies inventory	10	Retained earnings 2/28/87	300
Prepaid insurance	50	Room sales	200
Salaries expense	100	Food sales	130
Interest expense	50		
Payroll tax expense	10		
Other expenses	20		
	$1105		$1105

The data for the adjustments are as follows:
(1) Cost of food sold, $100.
(2) Interest accrued on notes payable, $20.
(3) Supplies inventory February 28, $5.
(4) Salaries incurred during February, but not paid to employees, $20.
(5) Expired insurance not recorded, $10.
(6) Depreciation for the year, $20.
Required:
(a) Set up simple "T" accounts with the balances given above.
(b) Record adjusting entries in the general journal.
(c) Post adjusting entries, adding other "T" accounts as necessary.

(d) Prepare a balance sheet and an income statement sheet as of and for the period ended February 28, 1988.

(e) Journalize closing entries.

(f) Post closing entries to the general ledger "T" accounts.

(g) Prepare a postclosing trial balance as of February 28, 1988.

(h) Record reversing entries in the general journal on March 1, 1988.

9

Special-Purpose Journals and Subsidiary Ledgers

In previous chapters, we saw that the general journal is the accounting book of original entry used to record transactions initially in the accounting system. However, it is practical to use the general journal as the sole book of original entry only when there are few transactions to record, as in the case of the sample problems included in a book of this nature. When the number of transactions increases to the level encountered in even a small hospitality entity, introducing and processing transactions in the accounting system through the general journal becomes both cumbersome and unnecessarily time consuming.

To facilitate the introduction and processing of numerous transactions, other journals, called special-purpose journals, should be used. These journals are designed to accelerate steps 2 and 3 of the accounting cycle—journalizing and posting.

Another accounting tool that enables a business to save time, and also to enhance the usefulness of its accounting information, is the subsidiary ledger. Subsidiary ledgers give a manager the detailed composition of a general ledger account balance.

This chapter first explains the advantages and use of special-purpose journals and subsidiary ledgers. Subsequently, the sales journal, the cash receipts journal, purchases journal, and cash disbursements journals are discussed individually. The format of each special-purpose journal is presented, accompanied by a detailed explanation of its use. The format and use of the accounts receivable and accounts payable subsidiary ledgers are also explained, along with the general ledger control account and the preparation of subsidiary ledger schedules. Next, some additional hotel accounting records and journals are presented and their functions are briefly explained, followed by an overview of the night auditor's duties. Finally, the chapter will include a discussion of automated accounting systems and their potential impact on the accounting process.

A hotel will be used as an example in this chapter, since hotels usually have several departments, thus enabling us to explain this stage of the accounting process in a more comprehensive manner.

THE ADVANTAGES OF SPECIAL-PURPOSE JOURNALS

As explained in Chapter 6, at least six steps are required to record a simple journal entry in the general journal. A complex journal entry, such as shown in Figure 9.1, would require more than twice as many steps. What renders this

General Journal   Page 6

Date 1986	Description	Dr	Cr
March 29	Accounts receivable	6,000	
	Room sales		4,000
	Food & beverage sales		900
	Tennis club sales		500
	Telephone department sales		600
	Sales to Milton Corp		

Figure 9.1. Example of a complex general journal entry.

process so cumbersome is the fact that the name of each account being debited or credited must be repeated for each entry. Furthermore each debit and credit entry must then be posted individually to its corresponding general ledger account.

Not only is it excessively time consuming to record such an entry through the general journal but it would occupy six lines (five for the entries and one for the explanation) in the general journal and five lines in the general ledger. In addition, there is the possibility for error every time a debit or credit entry is posted individually to the general ledger. When we consider that companies make hundreds or even thousands of such journal entries daily, the benefits to be derived from a more efficient system of recording and posting transactions become apparent. Special-purpose journals provide such an efficient system for journalizing and posting.

The advantages of special-purpose journals may be summarized as follows:

1. Time is saved in journalizing because account titles do not have to be repeated for each entry.
2. Time is saved in posting because, as we shall learn, entries are posted cumulatively to the general ledger.
3. The possibility for error diminishes as a result of making fewer posting entries.
4. Information is more readily accessible since it is recorded in more compact form, both in the special-purpose journals and the general ledger.
5. The separation of duties accelerates the accounting process by allowing employees to become specialized in recording one type of transaction.
6. The separation of duties provides greater control, since various employees will work on different stages of a single transaction, allowing multiple verification of their work.

THE USE OF SPECIAL-PURPOSE JOURNALS

Special-purpose journals are designed for the specific purpose of recording only one type of frequently recurring business transaction, whence the name special-purpose journal. More than 95% of all business transactions are either sales, cash receipts, purchases, cash disbursements, or payroll transactions. Since these types of transactions tend to recur so frequently, they provide a natural basis for grouping accounts in the different types of special-purpose journals. The following is a list of the most commonly used special-purpose journals and their abbreviations:

- Sales journal (SJ)
- Cash receipts journal (CR)
- Purchases journal (PJ)
- Cash disbursements journal (CD)
- Payroll journal (PRJ)
- General journal (GJ)

The sales journal is used to record sales transactions exclusively. Although sales may be made on a cash basis or on credit terms, the sales journal that we shall use in this text records all sales transactions, both cash and credit as a debit to accounts receivable. In the case of cash sales, a credit entry is also made to the accounts receivable account through the cash receipts journal. This allows all sales transactions to be recorded in the sales journal and all cash transactions to be recorded in the cash receipts journal. Without such a procedure, credit sales would have to be recorded in the sales journal and cash sales in the cash receipts journal, thereby eliminating one of the advantages of the special-purpose journals, namely, the compact recording of accounting information. The sales journal allows the manager to have a comprehensive record of the company's sales and related information in one journal.

The cash receipts journal is used to record all cash receipts, be they from cash sales, from collections on previous credit sales, from additional cash investments by the owners, from the sale of property and equipment, or from loan proceeds.

The purchases journal is used to record all purchases on account. This includes purchases of both assets and services.

The cash disbursements journal is used to record all cash payments and discounts for prompt payment. Payments for cash purchases, payments on account, and loan repayments are all recorded in the cash disbursements journal.

The payroll journal is used to record payroll information. It is discussed fully in Chapter 10.

The general journal is used to record transactions not recorded in any of the other journals. It is also used to record adjusting entries, closing entries, and correcting entries. Since entries of these types affect various accounts and are infrequently made, the flexibility provided by the general journal is ideal for this purpose.

PURPOSE OF SUBSIDIARY LEDGERS

In order to make informed decisions, a manager must not only know the total balance in general ledger accounts payable and accounts receivable accounts, but also how much is owed each individual supplier and how much is owed by each client. The manager also needs to know the detailed composition of certain asset accounts containing numerous items (such as the inventory account). Such detail is provided by subsidiary ledgers.

Specifically, the accounts receivable subsidiary ledger allows a manager to determine:

- Each client's balance due.
- The age of each client's balance due.
- The frequency and amount of each client's purchases.

This information enables a manager to adjust current collection procedures and future credit policies with regard to each client. Similar information is required concerning each supplier. A manager scheduling the company's payments and purchases should know

- The amount owed to each supplier.
- The due date of the next payment.
- The volume of purchases from each supplier (they may wish to negotiate a volume purchase discount).

A breakdown of the information contained in the accounts payable general ledger account is provided by the accounts payable subsidiary ledger.

A subsidiary ledger may consist of individual ledger pages, individual ledger cards, or a continuous computer printout. When a subsidiary ledger exists, entries made in the corresponding special-purpose journal are repeated in the appropriate subsidiary ledger accounts. Sales entered in the sales journal and collections entered in the cash receipts journal are also entered in each client's subsidiary ledger account.

Similarly, purchases and payments on account are entered in the purchases and cash disbursements journals, and also in the suppliers' individual accounts payable subsidiary ledger accounts.

Posting to the subsidiary ledger should occur as soon as possible after the journalizing step, so that the manager can know the current balance in each client's or supplier's account.

In addition to the accounts receivable and accounts payable subsidiary ledgers, a business may have other subsidiary ledgers, such as individual employee payroll ledger and inventory subsidiary ledger. These are discussed in Chapters 10 and 15, respectively.

THE SALES JOURNAL

Up to now we have been recording credit sales by making the following simple entry:

```
Accounts receivable          1,000
        Sales                              1,000
        To record a $1,000 sale
```

(A cash sale, of course, would have involved a debit to cash.) In the hospitality industry, however, there are many types of sales. There may be room sales, food and beverage sales, tennis club sales, telephone sales, etc. In many states there is also a sales tax. The sales journal, therefore, must not only provide an easy manner of debiting accounts receivable, but also of crediting the various sales accounts and the sales tax payable account.

The page from the sales journal of the Fairview Hotel shown in Figure 9.2 includes entries for sales made from March 29 to March 31. The total for

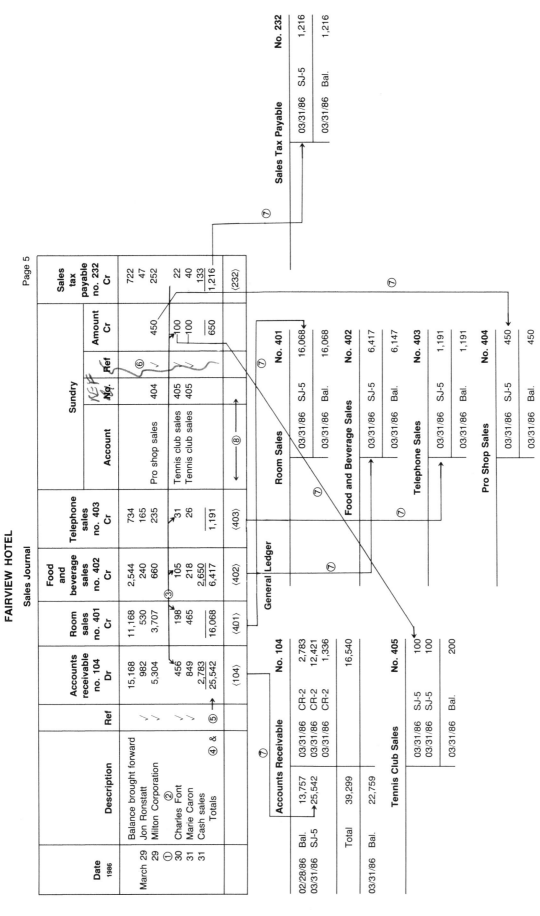

Figure 9.2. Fairview Hotel sales journal and partial general ledger. The three credits to the accounts receivable general ledger account correspond to cash sales and collections on credit sales posted from page 2 of the cash receipts journal (not shown).

entries made up to March 29 is brought forward from the previous journal page and appears on line 1 of page 5 of this journal alongside the description "balance brought forward." (This term is always used to describe the cumulative total balance from a previous journal or ledger page.)

The leftmost column of the sales journal is used to record the date of the transaction. The description column is used to enter the name of the client and/or invoice number. It is followed by the Ref column, in which a check is entered as each transaction is posted to the subsidiary ledger, the procedure for which will be explained later. The next column is the accounts receivable column, which is used to record the debit to accounts receivable for every sale. As noted before, even cash sales should be recorded as debits to accounts receivable in the sales journal. Finally, to the right of the accounts receivable debit column are the columns for entering credits in various sales accounts. The Sundry columns are for recording infrequent sales in the smaller hotel departments, such as tennis club memberships. The last column to the right is used to record the sales tax charged to clients and payable to the state.

Journalizing Credit Sales in the Sales Journal

The following steps are required to record a credit sale in the sales journal and post it to the appropriate subsidiary ledger (indicated by encircled numbers in Figure 9.2):

1. Enter the date of the transaction in the date column, the year should be entered in small digits under the word "date," and the month and day of the first transaction on the same line as the transaction. For subsequent transactions on the same page, only the day's date need be entered.
2. Enter the name of the client and/or invoice number in the description column.
3. Enter the debit to accounts receivable in the accounts receivable column and the credits to the sales and sales tax payable accounts in their corresponding credit columns. For infrequent sales, the name of the sales account is written in the sundry account column, the account number in the sundry no. column and the amount of the credit in the sundry amount column. The sundry Ref column is given a check when the amount is posted to the general ledger.

Journalizing Cash Sales in the Sales Journal

Cash sales from the various hotel departments are recorded in a manner similar to credit sales, as outlined in steps 1–3, except that the phrase "cash sales" is entered in the description column and no posting is made to the accounts receivable subsidiary ledger. The total cash sales of each department are journalized daily in a single entry, based on information provided by each department.

Posting to the General Ledger

After all the entries for an accounting period have been made in the sales journal, the accounting process continues as follows:

4. Total the various columns in the sales journal.
5. Add the totals across (cross-foot) to determine that the total in the ac-

counts receivable debit column equals the sum of the credit column totals, thereby verifying that all journal entries are in balance.

6. Post the individual amounts in the sundry column to the appropriate
general ledger account and make a check in the sundry Ref column
beside each posted amount. Be sure to enter SJ, symbol for the sales
journal, and the journal page number after the date in the general ledger
"T" account.

7. Post the column totals to their general ledger accounts and calculate the
new account balances. (Here, also, enter the symbol SJ and the page
number.)

8. Below each sales journal account column total write the number of the
general ledger account to which it was posted.

The reader is urged to trace these journalizing and posting steps in Figure
9.2.

THE CASH RECEIPTS JOURNAL

The cash receipts journal is used to record all cash that is received by the
hospitality entity. The usual sources are cash sales, collections on credit sales,
receipts of loan proceeds, and the sale of property and equipment. A cash
receipts journal with its corresponding general ledger accounts is shown in
Figure 9.3. This journal contains the Fairview Hotel's cash receipts entries for
the first two days of April 1986.

The cash receipts journal has the usual date, description, and Ref columns.
After the Ref column come the cash in bank column, for recording debits to the
cash account, three accounts receivable columns, and a sundry column. The
first accounts receivable column is used to record credits to accounts receivable
for cash sales. The other two are used to record credits to accounts receivable
for payments made by transient clients and city ledger clients.

Hotels classify their clients according to the credit privileges they receive.
Transient clients enjoy limited credit privileges at the hotel. They are billed
periodically (usually weekly) when staying at the hotel and must pay their
invoice when checking out of the hotel. City ledger clients either enjoy extended credit privileges directly from the hotel or pay with a credit card. Their
accounts remain open on the hotel's books until payment is received subsequent to their checking out. Hotels may maintain two separate subsidiary
ledgers, called the guest (transient) ledger and the city ledger, for recording
sales to these two categories of clients. They may also record their payments
by these two client categories in separate columns of the cash receipts journal.
The $456 credit in the city ledger column of the cash receipts journal shown in
Figure 9.3 corresponds to a payment made by Charles Font for services rendered to him in March and recorded in the sales journal shown in Figure 9.2.

The sundry columns are used to record receipts of an infrequent nature,
such as those from loan proceeds, refunds, or the sale of property and equipment.

Journalizing in the Cash Receipts Journal

The following steps are required to record a journal entry in the cash receipts journal (indicated by encircled numbers in Figure 9.3):

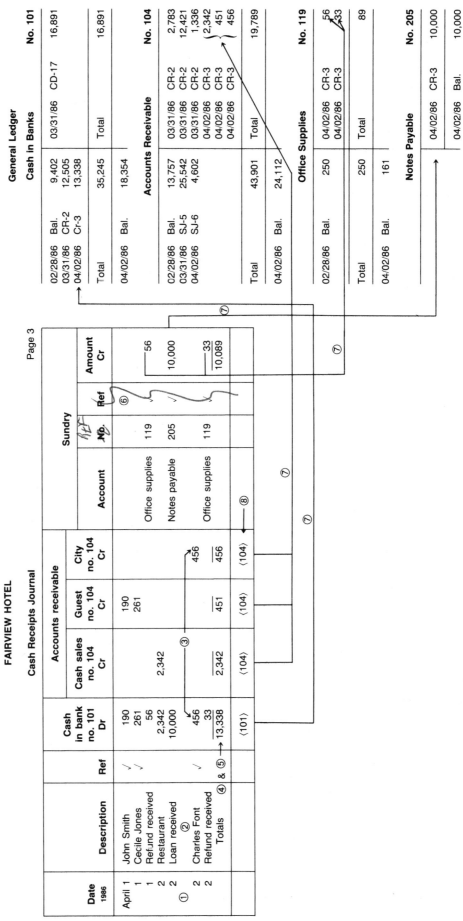

Figure 9.3. Fairview Hotel cash receipts journal.

1. Enter the date of the transaction in the date column using the same procedure described in the sales journal.
2. Enter a brief annotation to identify the cash source. In the case of client payments, the client's name and/or account number is entered in this column. Cash receipts from restaurant sales are identified as such. Sundry receipts are identified by their source.
3. Enter the debit in the cash column and the credits in the appropriate credit columns. Payments by transient guests are recorded in the guest column and payments by guests enjoying extended credit privileges are recorded in the city column. Use the sundry column to record receipts from sources other than sales and collections, following the same procedure detailed in journalizing step 3 of the sales journal.

Posting to the General Ledger

After all the entries for an accounting period have been made in the cash receipts journal, the general ledger accounts are posted by following the same steps listed for posting to the general ledger from the sales journal (of course, substituting the symbol CR for SJ where necessary). These steps are identified by the numbers 4–8 in Figure 9.3.

The reader should trace all of the journalizing and posting steps in Figure 9.3.

THE ACCOUNTS RECEIVABLE SUBSIDIARY LEDGER

To enable a manager to know the balance in each client's account, all sales charges and payment credits from the sales journal and cash receipts journal are also posted to the individual client subsidiary ledger accounts. Accordingly, the total of all the subsidiary ledger account balances should equal the balance in the accounts receivable account in the general ledger. The general ledger account that corresponds to a specific subsidiary ledger is called that subsidiary ledger's "control account." The procedure of comparing the total of the balances in all the subsidiary ledger accounts to the balance in the corresponding control account is called "making a schedule of the subsidiary ledger."

In the case of the hospitality industry, the general ledger accounts receivable account may serve as the control account for two subsidiary ledgers—the guest ledger and the city ledger. Both of these subsidiary ledgers must be totaled in order to balance with the accounts receivable control account. The city subsidiary ledger of the Fairview Hotel, along with the sales journal, the cash receipts journal and the accounts receivable control account are shown in Figure 9.4.

FAIRVIEW HOTEL

Sales Journal

Date 1986	Description	Ref	Accounts receivable no. 104 Dr	Room sales no. 401 Cr	Food and beverage sales no. 402 Cr	Telephone sales no. 403 Cr	Sundry Account	No.	Ref	Amount Cr	Sales tax payable no. 232 Cr
	Balance brought forward		15,168	11,168	2,544	734					722
March 29	Jon Ronstatt	✓	982	530	240	165					47
30	Milton Corporation	✓	5,304	3,707	660	235	Pro shop sales	404	✓	450	252
31	Charles Font	✓	456	198	105	31	Tennis club sales	405	✓	-100	22
31	Marie Caron	✓	849	465	218	26	Tennis club sales	405	✓	100	40
31	Cash sales		2,783		2,650						133
	Totals		25,542	16,068	6,417	1,191				650	1,216
			⟨104⟩	⟨401⟩	⟨402⟩	⟨403⟩					⟨232⟩

Accounts Receivable   No. 104

02/28/86	Bal.	13,757		03/31/86	CR-2	2,783*
03/31/86	SJ-5	25,542		03/31/86	CR-2	12,421*
04/02/86	SJ-6	4,602		03/31/86	CR-2	1,336*
				04/02/86	CR-3	2,342
				04/02/86	CR-3	451
				04/02/86	CR-3	456
	Total	43,901			Total	19,789
04/02/86	Bal.	24,112				

Cash Receipts Journal

Date 1986	Description	Ref	Cash in bank no. 101 Dr	Cash sales no. 104 Cr	Guest no. 104 Cr	City no. 104 Cr	Sundry Account	No.	Ref	Amount Cr
April 1	John Smith	✓	190		190					
1	Cecile Jones	✓	261		261					
1	Refund received		56				Office supplies	119	✓	56
2	Restaurant		2,342	2,342						
2	Loan received		10,000				Notes payable	205	✓	10,000
2	Charles Font	✓	456			456				
2	Refund received		33				Office supplies	119	✓	33
	Totals		13,338	2,342	451	456				10,089
			⟨101⟩	⟨104⟩	⟨104⟩	⟨104⟩				

City Ledger

FAIRVIEW HOTEL — Page 2 — City Ledger

Jon Ronstatt
21 Maple Rd.
Miami, FL — Credit terms 30 days
Account No. 2472

(A) (B) (C) (D) (E) (F) (G)

02/28/86	Balance	2,321	Dr
03/29/86	Room	530	Dr
03/29/86	Food & beverage	240	Dr
03/29/86	Telephone	165	Dr
03/29/86	Sales tax	47	Dr
04/02/86	Bal. forward	3,303	Dr

FAIRVIEW HOTEL — Page 2 — City Ledger

Linda Farr
15 NW 30 Ave.
Westwood, IL — Credit terms 30 days
Account No. 2481

| 02/28/86 | Bal. | 3,472 | Dr |
| 04/02/86 | Bal. forward | 3,472 | Dr |

FAIRVIEW HOTEL — Page 1 — City Ledger

Charles Font
1213 E. Bentwood Dr.
Carlton, VA — Credit terms 30 days
Account No. 2499

03/30/86	Room	198	Dr
03/30/86	Food & beverages	105	Dr
03/30/86	Telephone	31	Dr
03/30/86	Tennis club	100	Dr
03/30/86	Sales tax	22	Dr
03/30/86	Balance	456	Dr
04/02/86	Payment	456	Cr
04/02/86	Bal. forward	0	

FAIRVIEW HOTEL — Page 2 — City Ledger

Milton Corporation
451 West Paddock St.
Carlton, VA — Credit terms 30 days
Account No. 2691

03/29/86	Room	3,707	Dr
03/29/86	Food & beverage	660	Dr
03/29/86	Telephone	235	Dr
03/29/86	Pro shop	450	Dr
03/29/86	Sales tax	252	Dr
04/02/86	Bal. forward	5,304	Dr

FAIRVIEW HOTEL — Page 1 — City Ledger

Marie Caron
444 Eastview Blvd.
Wayward, MO — Credit terms 30 days
Account No. 2788

03/31/86	Room	465	Dr
03/31/86	Food & beverages	218	Dr
03/31/86	Telephone	26	Dr
03/31/86	Tennis club	100	Dr
03/31/86	Sales tax	40	Dr
04/02/86	Bal. forward	849	Dr

*These three credits to the accounts receivable general ledger account correspond to cash sales and collections on credit sales posted from page 2 of the cash receipts journal (not shown).

Figure 9.4. Fairview Hotel sales journal, cash receipts journal, accounts receivable control account, and city ledger. The first three credits to the accounts receivable general ledger account are as in Figure 9.3.

Description of an Accounts Receivable Subsidiary Ledger Account

An accounts receivable subsidiary ledger account consists of the seven parts listed below. They are identified by encircled letters on the first subsidiary ledger account shown in Figure 9.4, that of Jon Ronstatt. They are also shown on the hotel's accounts receivable subsidiary ledger account in Figure 9.5.

(A) The name and address of the client.
(B) The client's account number.
(C) The subsidiary ledger page number, if the client's ledger has more than one page.
(D) The authorized credit terms.
(E) A column for the transaction date.
(F) A description column for indicating the type of sale (for example, room, or food and beverage).
(G) One or more columns for entering the
    (1) balance brought forward (if any)

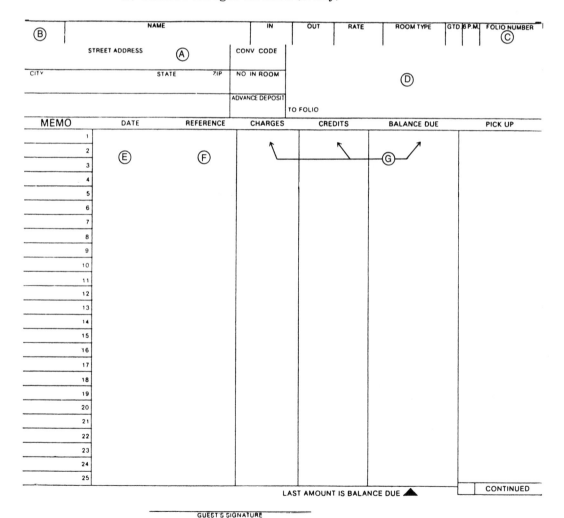

Figure 9.5. Hotel accounts receivable subsidiary ledger account.

(2) debits for sales
(3) credits for collections or allowances
(4) new account balance.

Posting to the Accounts Receivable Subsidiary Ledger and Preparing a Subsidiary Ledger Schedule

The steps for posting to a subsidiary ledger from the sales journal and cash receipts journal, and for preparing a subsidiary ledger schedule, are listed below, and may be traced in Figure 9.4.

1. Enter the date and type of sale first; then post the charge (debit) corresponding to each type of sale from the accounts receivable column of the sales journal to the subsidiary ledger charges (debit) column. Calculate the new balance in the account.
2. Make a check in the Ref column of the sales journal on the same line as the posted entry.
3. Enter the date of the payment, and then post the credits from the cash receipts journal accounts receivable column to the subsidiary ledger credit column. Calculate the new balance.
4. Make a check in the Ref column of the cash receipts journal on the same line as the posted entry.
5. Take a total of the balances in all the city subsidiary ledger accounts and all the guest subsidiary ledger accounts to verify that it equals the balance in the accounts receivable control account.

Figure 9.6 shows both the guest ledger and city ledger schedules for the Fairview Hotel. The sum of the totals of these schedules ($24,112) is equal to the balance in the accounts receivable control account in Figure 9.4, indicating that the subsidiary ledgers are in balance with their control account.

FAIRVIEW HOTEL

Guest Ledger		City Ledger	
Rogers Enterprises Inc	$ 3,456	Jon Ronstatt	$ 3,303
Daniel Fult	289	Linda Farr	3,472
James Watson	1,156	Milton Corporation	5,304
Denise Karmel	4,467	Marie Caron	849
Judy Flanigan	1,816	Total	$12,928
Total	$11,184		

Figure 9.6. Fairview Hotel guest ledger and city ledger schedules at 04/02/86.

THE PURCHASES JOURNAL

The purchases journal serves to record all purchases on account. A purchases journal is shown in Figure 9.7 along with some related general ledger accounts. After the usual date, description, and Ref columns, there is a column for recording credits to accounts payable. To the right of the accounts payable column, there are columns for recording debits to the most frequently used expense and purchase accounts, followed by a sundry column for recording transactions in the less frequently used accounts.

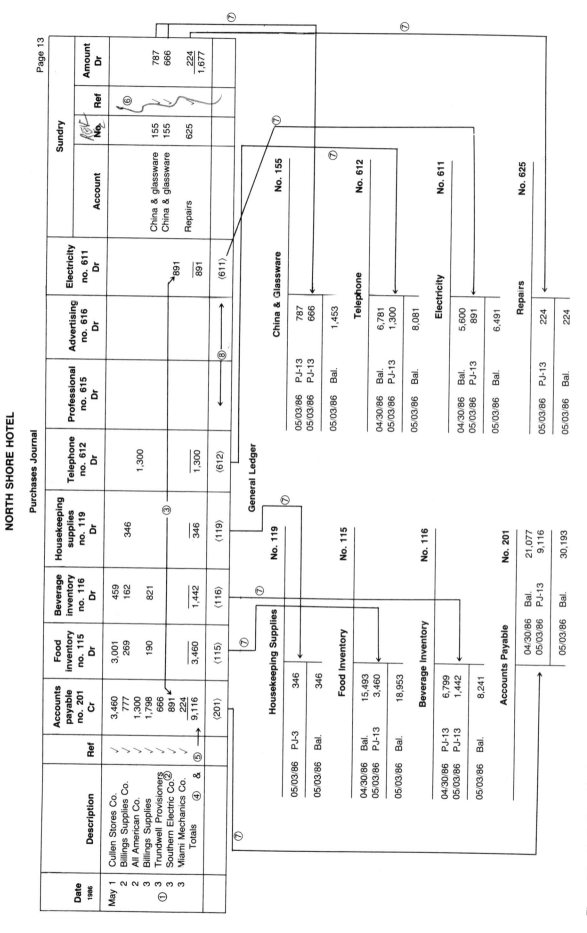

Figure 9.7. North Shore Hotel purchases journal and partial general ledger.

Journalizing in the Purchases Journal

The following steps are required to record entries in the purchases journal (indicated by encircled numbers in Figure 9.7):

1. Enter the date of the transaction in the date column of the purchases journal in the usual manner.
2. Enter the name of the supplier and invoice number or account number in the description column.
3. Enter the credit to accounts payable in the accounts payable column and the corresponding debits in the appropriate expense or purchase account columns. Use the sundry column to record entries in the less frequently used accounts, following the same procedure specified in step 3 for journalizing in the sales journal.

Posting to the General Ledger

After all entries for the accounting period have been made in the purchases journal, the general ledger accounts are posted by following the steps previously explained for posting to the general ledger from the sales journal (substituting purchases journal for sales journal). The reader should track the journalizing and posting steps as shown in Figure 9.7.

THE CASH DISBURSEMENTS JOURNAL

The cash disbursements journal is used to record all cash payments. Since payments are usually made by check, it is often called the check register. Included in this journal are payments on account, cash purchases, and loan repayments. A cash disbursements journal is shown in Figure 9.8. The first two columns of the journal are the usual date and description columns. The third column is for listing the number of the check by which payment is made. The next column is the cash in bank column for entering credits to the cash account. There is a second credit column in the cash disbursements journal called purchase discounts. This column is used to record discounts offered by suppliers for payment of their invoices within a specified period of time. For instance, if the original invoice amount is $1,000 and the purchaser is entitled to a 2% discount, then the check amount of $980 is entered in the cash in bank column, the $20 discount is entered in the discount column, and a debit for $1,000 is entered in the accounts payable column. Credit terms are expressed in abbreviated form as follows: 2/10, net 30, which means that a 2% discount will be granted by the supplier if payment is made within 10 days, and if payment is made after 10 days no discount will be granted but the account will be delinquent if payment is not made within 30 days.

To the right of the discount column is the usual Ref column. The accounts payable column serves to record debits to the accounts payable account. Further to the right are columns for recording debits to the most frequently used purchase and expense accounts, and to the far right are the usual sundry columns for recording debits to infrequently used accounts.

Journalizing in the Cash Disbursement Journal

The steps required to record entries in the cash disbursements journal are listed at the top of p. 178. The reader should be sufficiently familiar with these steps by now to be able to identify them in Figure 9.8 without the numerical

NORTH SHORE HOTEL

Cash Disbursements Journal

Date 1986	Description	Check number	Cash in bank no. 101 Cr	Purchase discounts no. 503 Cr	Ref	Accounts payable no. 201 Dr	Food inventory no. 115 Dr	Beverage inventory no. 116 Dr	Office supplies no. 120 Dr	Laundry no. 614 Dr	Sundry Account	No.	Ref	Amount Dr
	Balance brought forward		10,111	145		8,407	1,160	368	116	205				
May 11	Cullen Stores Co.	2347	3,391*	69	✓	3,460								
12	Billings Supplies Co.	2348	761*	16	✓	777								
12	White-All Cleaners	2349	198							198				
12	Universal Office Supplies	2350	99						99					
12	Exterminal Co.	2351	250								Prepaid fumigation	126	✓	250
13	Billings Supplies Co.	2352	1,762*	36	✓	1,798								
13	Trundwell Provisioners	2353	653*	13	✓	666								
13	Collings Bank	2354	2,000								Cash in savings account	102	✓	2,000
13	Exterminal Co.	2355	250								Prepaid fumigation	126	✓	250
	Totals		19,475	279		15,108	1,160	368	215	403				2,500
			⟨101⟩	⟨503⟩		⟨201⟩	⟨115⟩	⟨116⟩	⟨120⟩	⟨614⟩				

176

General Ledger

Cash in Bank — No. 101

Date	Ref.	Debit	Date	Ref.	Credit
05/10/86	Bal.	22,461	05/13/86	CD-15	19,475
05/13/86	CR-12	18,388			
	Total	40,849		Total	19,475
05/13/86	Bal.	21,374			

Cash in Savings Account — No. 102

Date	Ref.	Debit
05/10/86	Bal.	6,000
05/13/86	CD-15	2,000
05/13/86	Bal.	8,000

Food Inventory — No. 115

Date	Ref.	Debit	Date	Ref.	Credit
05/10/86	Bal.	26,891	05/13/86	GJ-5	10,722
05/13/86	CD-15	1,160			
	Total	28,051		Total	10,722
05/13/86	Bal.	17,329			

Beverage Inventory — No. 116

Date	Ref.	Debit	Date	Ref.	Credit
05/10/86	Bal.	16,999	05/13/86	GJ-5	7,444
05/13/86	CD-15	368			
	Total	17,367		Total	7,444
05/13/86	Bal.	9,923			

Office Supplies — No. 120

Date	Ref.	Debit	Date	Ref.	Credit
05/10/86	Bal.	1,489	05/13/86	GJ-5	781
05/13/86	CD-15	215			
	Total	1,704		Total	781
05/13/86	Bal.	923			

Prepaid Fumigation — No. 126

Date	Ref.	Debit
05/10/86	Bal.	1,500
05/13/86	CD-15	500
05/13/86	Bal.	2,000

Accounts Payable — No. 201

Date	Ref.	Debit	Date	Ref.	Credit
05/13/86	CD-15	15,108	04/30/86	Bal.	8,407
			05/03/86	PJ-13	9,116
			05/13/86	PJ-14	2,942
	Total	15,108		Total	20,465
			05/13/86	Bal.	5,357

Purchase Discounts — No. 503

Date	Ref.	Credit
05/10/86	Bal.	1,689
05/13/86	CD-15	279
05/13/86	Bal.	1,968

Laundry — No. 614

Date	Ref.	Debit
05/10/86	Bal.	981
05/13/86	CD-15	403
05/13/86	Bal.	1,384

Figure 9.8. North Shore Hotel cash disbursements journal and partial general ledger. The starred purchases appear in the purchases journal of Figure 9.7. A 2% discount is taken because they were made on credit terms of 2% 10 days, net 30 days, and were paid within 10 days.

references provided for the other special-purpose journals:

1. Enter the date of the transaction in the date column of the cash disbursements journal in the usual manner.
2. Enter the name of the check payee (recipient) in the description column. The supplier's account number might be entered for payments on account, as well as the invoice number.
3. Enter the number of the check in the check number column.
4. Enter the credit to the cash account for the amount of the check.
5. If paying on account and entitled to a discount, then enter the amount of the discount in the discount column.
6. If paying on account, enter a debit in the accounts payable column for the full invoice amount. For any other type of payment, enter debits in the appropriate account columns. Use the sundry columns to record entries in the less frequently used accounts, using the procedure described in step 3 for journalizing in the sales journal.

Posting to the General Ledger

After all entries for the accounting period have been made in the cash disbursements journal, the general ledger accounts are posted by following the same steps previously described for posting to the general ledger from the sales journal (substituting cash disbursements journal for sales journal).

THE ACCOUNTS PAYABLE SUBSIDIARY LEDGER

The accounts payable subsidiary ledger contains a detailed breakdown of the accounts payable account in the general ledger and informs the manager how much is owed to each supplier. In order to accomplish this, credits for purchases recorded in the purchases journal and debits for payments recorded in the cash disbursements journal are also posted to the individual supplier ledger accounts. Therefore, the total of all the individual subsidiary ledger account balances should equal the balance in the accounts payable control account in the general ledger.

Description of an Accounts Payable Subsidiary Ledger Account

An accounts payable subsidiary ledger account consists of the seven parts listed below and identified by encircled letters on the first subsidiary ledger account shown in Figure 9.9, that of Cullen Stores Co.:

(A) The name and address of the supplier
(B) The supplier's account number
(C) The subsidiary ledger page number, if the ledger has more than one page
(D) The credit terms authorized by the supplier
(E) A column for the transaction date
(F) A description column for entering the supplier's invoice number or the payment check number

(G) One or more columns for entering:
  (1) Balance brought forward (if any)
  (2) Credits for purchases
  (3) Debits for payments
  (4) Debits for discounts
  (5) New account balances.

The procedure for posting to the accounts payable subsidiary ledger and preparing a subsidiary ledger schedule is the same as that explained for the accounts receivable subsidiary ledger. One potential difference is that usually there is only one subsidiary ledger schedule for suppliers instead of the two subsidiary ledgers that a hotel maintains for accounts receivable. The total of the supplier account balances in this subsidiary ledger schedule should equal the balance in the accounts payable control account. Figure 9.10 shows a subsidiary ledger schedule for the accounts payable subsidiary ledger shown in Figure 9.9. A comparison of the total of this subsidiary ledger with the balance in the accounts payable control account indicates that they are equal and the subsidiary ledger is in balance with its control account.

THE CASHIER'S DAILY REPORT AND OTHER FREQUENTLY USED JOURNALS

So far in this chapter we have explained the basic journals used by a hospitality entity. However, each entity tends to have its own version of these journals and its own procedures for collecting and transferring data from the different departments to the general ledger and subsidiary ledgers. To that end, the additional accounting records shown in Figure 9.11 (p. 183) are frequently used in the hospitality industry. Of particular importance is the cashier's daily report, a record of daily receipts used by the various department cashiers in a hospitality entity to (1) reconcile sales with receipts and (2) provide the necessary cash sales information for recording in the cash receipts journal. For example, the $2,342 in cash sales receipts shown on the cashier's daily report in Figure 9.11 are recorded in the cash receipts journal shown in Figure 9.3.

Because such a large percentage of the accounting activity of a hotel is related to the rooms department, in many hotels the front office has a separate cash receipts and cash disbursements journal, such as the one shown in Figure 9.11, called the front office cash receipts and cash disbursements journal. Figure 9.12 shows one way cash receipts information may flow to the general ledger and accounts receivable subsidiary ledger when such a journal is used in addition to the summary cash receipts journal.

Notice that the accounts receivable subsidiary ledger must be posted directly from the front office cash receipts and cash disbursements journal, when one exists, because it is used to record receipts on an individual client basis. The summary cash receipts journal will only contain column totals transferred to it from the front office cash receipts and cash disbursements journal.

The right half of the front office cash receipts and cash disbursements journal is used to record cash advances or disbursements such as COD deliveries made on behalf of guests. In Figure 9.11 we see that John Allan received a $100 cash advance.

Column totals are transcribed in the usual manner to the summary cash

NORTH SHORE HOTEL

Purchases Journal

Date 1986	Description	Ref	Accounts payable no. 201 Cr	Food inventory no. 115 Dr	Beverage inventory no. 116 Dr	Housekeeping supplies no. 119 Dr	Telephone no. 612 Dr	Professional fees no. 615 Dr	Advertising no. 616 Dr	Electricity No. 611 Dr	Sundry Account	Sundry No.	Sundry Ref	Sundry Amount Dr
May 1	Cullen Stores Co.	✓	3,460	3,001	459									
2	Billings Supplies Co.	✓	777	269	162	346								
2	All American Co.	✓	1,300				1,300							
3	Billings Supplies Co.	✓	1,798	190	821						China & glassware	155	✓	787
3	Trundwell Provisioners	✓	666								China & glassware	155	✓	666
3	Southern Electric	✓	891							891				
3	Miami Mechanics Co.	✓	224								Repairs	625	✓	224
	Totals		9,116	3,460	1,442	346	1,300			891				1,677
			⟨201⟩	⟨115⟩	⟨116⟩	⟨119⟩	⟨612⟩			⟨611⟩				

Accounts Payable No. 201

			Dr				Cr
05/13/86	CD-15		15,108	04/30/86	Bal.		8,407
				05/03/86	PJ-13		9,116
				05/13/86	PJ-14		2,942
	Total		15,108		Total		20,465
				05/13/86	Bal.		5,357

Cash Disbursements Journal

Date 1986	Description	Check number	Cash in bank no. 101 Cr	Purchase discounts no. 503 Cr	Ref	Accounts payable no. 201 Dr	Food inventory no. 115 Dr	Beverage inventory no. 116 Dr	Office supplies no. 120 Dr	Laundry no. 614 Dr	Sundry Account	Sundry No.	Sundry Ref	Sundry Amount Dr
May 11	Balance brought forward		10,111			8,407	1,160	368	116	205				
12	Cullen Stores Co.	2347	3,391	145	✓	3,460								
12	Billings Supplies Co.	2348	761	69	✓	777								
12	White-All Cleaners	2349	198	16						198				
12	Universal Office Supplies	2350	99						99					
12	Exterminal Co.	2351	250								Prepaid fumigation	126	✓	250
13	Billings Supplies Co.	2352	1,762	36	✓	1,798								
13	Trundwell Provisioners	2353	653	13	✓	666								
13	Cullings Bank	2354	2,000								Cash in savings account	102	✓	2,000
13	Exterminal Co.	2355	250								Prepaid fumigation	126	✓	250
	Totals		19,475	279		15,108	1,160	368	215	403				2,500
			⟨101⟩	⟨503⟩		⟨201⟩	⟨115⟩	⟨116⟩	⟨120⟩	⟨614⟩				

Accounts Payable Subsidiary Ledger

(A) (B)

Supplier: Cullen Stores Co.
1250 Ponciana Way
Miami, FL

Page 3

Credit terms: 2/10, net 30

Account No. 113

(E) (F) (G)

		Check	Discount		
05/01/86	Invoice no. 34168			3,460	Cr
05/11/86	Check #2347	3,391	69	3,460	Dr
05/11/86	Bal. forward			0	

(C) (D)

Supplier: Billings Supplies Co.
400 W. 46 Street
Miami, FL

Page 2

Credit terms: 2/10, net 30

Account No. 115

		Check	Discount		
05/02/86	Invoice #467-B			777	Cr
05/03/86	Invoice #589-B			1,798	Cr
05/12/86	Check #2348	761	16	777	Dr
05/13/86	Check #2352	1,762	36	1,798	Dr
05/13/86	Bal. forward			0	

Supplier: Trundwell Provisioners
566 Weather Lane
Miami, FL

Page 3

Credit terms: 2/10, net 30

Account No. 121

		Check	Discount		
05/03/86	Invoice #111069			666	Cr
05/10/86	Invoice #111382			1,120	Cr
05/13/86	Check #2353	653	13	666	Dr
05/13/86	Bal. forward			1,120	Cr

Supplier: Miami Mechanics Co.
111 Federal Highway
Miami, FL

Page 2

Credit terms: 5/60, net 90

Account No. 123

		Check	Discount		
05/03/86	Invoice #3336-A10			224	Cr
05/13/86	Bal. forward			224	Cr

Supplier: All American Co.
440 Telephone Way
Miami, FL

Page 4

Credit terms: net 30

Account No. 127

		Check	Discount		
05/02/86	Invoice #7-04123			1,300	Cr
05/11/86	Invoice #7-04978			1,822	Cr
05/13/86	Bal. forward			3,122	Cr

Supplier: Southern Electric Co.
999 Powerhouse Road
Miami, FL

Page 4

Credit terms: net 30

Account No. 135

		Check	Discount		
05/03/86	Invoice #247-469			891	Cr
05/13/86	Bal. forward			891	Cr

Figure 9.9. North Shore Hotel purchases journal, cash disbursements journal, accounts payable control account, and accounts payable subsidiary ledger.

NORTH SHORE HOTEL

Trundwell Provisioners	$1,120
Miami Mechanics Co.	224
All American Co.	3,122
Southern Electric Co.	891
Total	$5,357

Figure 9.10. North Shore Hotel. Accounts payable subsidiary ledger schedule for the subsidiary ledger of Figure 9.9.

receipts journal for subsequent transfer to the general ledger accounts receivable control account in the general ledger. Since this journal is submitted to the accounting office daily, the entire page is dated rather than each line.

The city journal is used by the front desk to record charges that will subsequently be transferred to individual city ledger cards. It is used in those cases when the city ledger is maintained by the central accounting office or when there is no time at the front desk for posting charges to individual city ledger accounts. It is also submitted to the accounting office daily, and so the entire sheet is dated, rather than each line.

The transfer journal (shown in Figure 9.11) is used to record transfers of charges between two guests or to transfer guests from the guest ledger to the city ledger and vice versa. It is also used to transfer a guest to other ledgers that may be in use, such as the delinquent ledger for overdue accounts. This journal helps the night auditor verify that all transfers have been made on the subsidiary ledger.

THE NIGHT AUDITOR'S DUTIES

The primary duty of the night auditor is to verify that all guest charges and payments are posted to clients' accounts, i.e., the accounts receivable subsidiary ledger. To do this, the night auditor prepares a special schedule called the daily transcript, an example of which is presented in Figure 9.13.

Before preparing the daily transcript the night auditor takes the following steps:

1. Reconciles the total guest charge sales and credit card sales, as reported on the departmental cashiers' daily reports, with the total of the guest charge vouchers and credit card vouchers received from each department.
2. Verifies that all vouchers have been posted to the appropriate clients' accounts receivable subsidiary ledgers.
3. Posts the appropriate daily room charge to each client's subsidiary ledger account based on the daily room reports shown in Figure 9.14.

After the above preliminary verification, the night auditor is ready to prepare the daily transcript using information posted to each individual subsidiary ledger account. In the first two columns the room number and the guest's account number are entered. The previous day's balance on each individual ledger account is then entered in the balance brought forward column, and all of the current day's charges from the various departments in the appropriate columns to the right. Any cash advance given to the client is entered in the cash advances column. Charges transferred to the client from another account

FAIRVIEW HOTEL

Front Office Cash Receipts and Cash Disbursements Journal

				Cashier: Mary James			Watch: 4:00 PM–12:00 PM		Date: 4/1/86		
				Receipts			**Disbursements**				
					Accounts receivable			**Accounts receivable**			
Acct no.	Room no.	Guest	Ref	Cash 101 Dr	Guest 104 Cr	City 104 Cr	Cash 101 Cr	Paid for:		Guest 104 Dr	City 104 Dr
3231	42	John Allan					100	Cash advance			100
3232	101	Bill Tenor		292	292						
3231	42	John Allan		406		406					
		Totals		698	292	406	100				100

Cashier's Daily Report	
Department: Restaurant	**Cashier:** F. Williams
Date: 4/2/86	**Time:** 1:00 AM to 12:00 PM

Sales
Guest vouchers	$ 560
Credit cards	320
Cash	2,342
Total sales receipts	$3,222
Currency	1,361
Checks	981
Guest vouchers	560
Credit card vouchers	320
Total enclosed	$3,222
(over) under	0
Total	$3,222

City Journal

Description	Room no.	Rooms	Restaurant	Other		Advances
				Description	Amount	
Mary Penin	361	160	53	Tennis club	150	200

Transfer Journal

Name and address	Room	Guest acct.	Guest ledger		City ledger		Delinquent ledger	
			Dr	Cr	Dr	Cr	Dr	Cr
John Mobely	346	36912		1,248	1,248			
Sandra Potts						469	469	

Figure 9.11. Fairview Hotel. Cashier's daily report, and other frequently used journals.

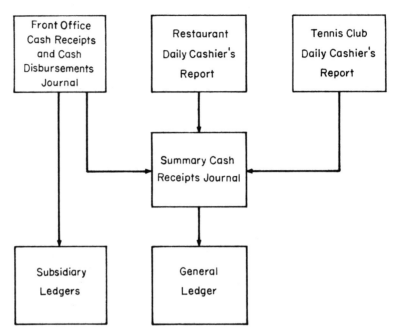

Figure 9.12. Flow of hotel cash receipts information when more than one cash receipts journal is used.

are entered in the first transfers column. The total of departmental charges, advances, and transfers-in is thus entered in the total charges column. Client payments, allowances, and charges transferred out of the client's account are entered in the appropriate credit columns. The new account balance is then calculated by subtracting the credits from the total charges, and it is entered in the balance forward column on the far right.

Toward the bottom of the transcript is a line entitled city. This line is used to record all entries from the city journal when one is in use. Since these charges have not been transcribed to individual city ledger accounts, they must be recorded as totals directly from the current day's city journal.

As final verification that all charges and credits have been posted to clients' accounts, the night auditor totals all the columns of the transcript. The totals for each department column must equal the total of vouchers sent by that department according to the cashier's daily report. Also, the total in the balance forward column must equal the total of all the individual subsidiary ledger accounts balances. The verification is completed by cross-footing (adding across) the column totals to determine that the balance brought forward column total, plus the day's charge totals, less the day's credit totals, equals the balance forward column total on the daily transcript.

After preparing the daily transcript, the night auditor sends the following items to the central accounting office:

- the daily transcript
- the rooms report and housekeeper's report
- the transfer journal
- the city journal (if central accounting is responsible for posting the city ledger)
- departmental cashier's reports, with all vouchers and cash register tapes; and a summary of the front office cash receipts and cash disbursements journal
- all accounts of guests who have checked out and paid

SAMPLE HOTEL

Daily Transcript

Date: August 5, 1988

Room no.	Guest acct.	Bal. brought forward	Room	Restaurant	Bar	Snack bar	Cash advances	Transfers in	Total charges	Credits		Bal. forward
										Cash	Allowances	Transfers out	
48	3468	1,234	120	58	35				313	500	20		1,027
77	3469	361	80			8	100		88	120			329
65	3471	2,671	180	127	160	15	200		667	1,000	100		2,238
91	3473	98	80		10				105				203
100	3474	667	80	25	15				120				787
Subtotal		5,031	540	210	220	23	300		1,293	1,620	120		4,584
City		12,432	1,347	326	279	162	500		2,614	1,273	312		13,461
Totals		17,463	1,887	536	499	185	800		3,907	2,893	432		18,045

Figure 9.13. Sample hotel daily transcript.

Daily Rooms Report Date: _____									
Room no.	Guest acct. no.	Number of occupants	Room rate	Sales tax	Room no.	Guest acct. no.	Number of occupants	Room rate	Sales tax
101					161				
102					162				
103					163				
104					164				
105					165				
106					166				
107					167				
108					168				

Housekeeper's Report Date: _____					
Room no.	Status	Room no.	Status	Room no.	Status
101		131		161	
102		132		162	
103		133		163	
104		134		164	
105		135		165	
106		136		166	
107		137		167	

Figure 9.14. Room reports used by the night auditor. The daily rooms report is prepared by the night desk clerk and the housekeeper prepares the housekeeper's report. After updating the daily rooms report for late arrivals, the night auditor compares the daily report with the housekeeper's report to verify that every room reported as occupied is included in the daily rooms report. He or she then posts the room rate and sales tax shown on the daily rooms report to each client's ledger.

Aside from preparing the daily transcript, the night auditor may have other duties:

- Preparing the daily report of operations—a summary sheet of all the hotels sales and receipts of the month to date, including the calculation of statistics such as average room rate or percentage occupancy
- Posting all charges from the city journal to the city ledger
- Helping the front desk clerk catch up with any reports that have not been prepared
- Preparing new account cards for guests that have been at the hotel seven days
- Notifying the credit department of unpaid balances overdue more than a certain number of days, any unusually large charges, or accounts with balances in excess of a specified limit

AUTOMATED ACCOUNTING SYSTEMS

Recent advances in automation have considerably accelerated the accounting process and brought the convenience offered by a computer within the reach of even small hospitality entities.

In the earlier stages of the automation process mechanical posting machines such as the cash register or NCR 4200 helped accelerate the accounting process by

- posting mechanically (faster than manual posting)
- accumulating various totals automatically as the posting occurs
- cross-footing these totals automatically (verifying that debit and credit totals balance)

With the introduction of computers, the accounting process has been accelerated further. Today even microcomputers (personal computers) can post journal entries, checks, sales invoices, or other source documents to their respective accounts, update the journals of original entry, post to the general ledger, and prepare up-to-date financial statements in little more time than it takes the computer to print out the financial statements. Such microcomputers with all the necessary peripherals now cost in the thousands of dollars, instead of the tens of thousands they used to cost. Larger computers can, of course, process more data faster and can provide more varied types of reports.

While requiring information to be entered only once, computers can prepare all the journals mentioned in this chapter. This not only accelerates the process of preparing the journals, but also eliminates the need for some of them, such as the city journal. It is just as easy for the front desk to enter an amount in the computer as it is to enter it in the city journal, and the computer will then enter it automatically in the individual ledger account as well as the general ledger control account. Computer systems that begin recording sales transactions at the point of sale are known as point-of-sale systems. The computers at airline ticket counters or travel agencies and computerized cash registers are part of point-of-sales systems. The sales information is immediately used to update all accounting records.

Although the use of a computer is a great aid in the accounting process, the basic accounting records remain the same. Sales journals, general ledgers, and other accounting records contain the same information, whether generated by hand or by computer. Therefore, by learning the process of manual accounting a basis is formed that facilitates the understanding of computerized accounting systems.

There are three stages in a computer system (see Figure 9.15): (1) input, (2) processing, and (3) output. These stages can be subdivided into five steps as follows:

Input
1. Instructions must be entered initially, telling the computer what to do with the data that it will process.
2. Any previously processed data (e.g., the previous month's general ledger) that are going to be modified by new data (checks, invoices, or journal entries) must be entered in the computer.
3. New data (checks, invoices, or journal entries) must be entered.
Processing
4. The computer must merge the new data with the previous data and process it as instructed.
Output
5. The computer must generate the processed data.

The instructions that tell the computer what to do are called the program. Programs are generally known as software; the physical computer equipment

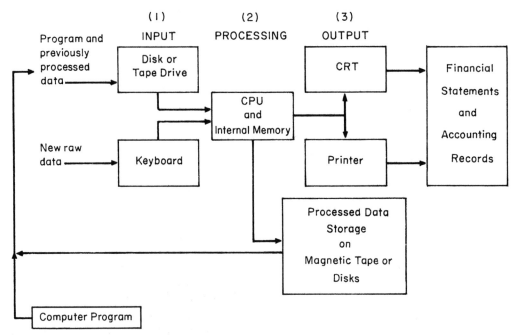

Figure 9.15. The basic elements of a computer system.

itself is known as hardware. Since program instructions can be voluminous, it would be impractical to type them in every time. Prewritten programs are usually entered automatically from magnetic tape or disk using a tape drive or disk drive, which reads information into a computer thousands of times faster than it can be typed in by hand. Since previously processed data are also stored on tape or disks, they are also entered again via magnetic tape or disks. New data, however, must be entered by typing them into the computer, although progress is being made in developing technology that will allow the computer to receive voice commands (many already use a device that can read a previously typed page).

Once all the necessary information has been entered, the computer must process the data. This takes place in the central processing unit (CPU), which consists of a control unit that interprets the program and tells the arithmetic unit in what order and with what numbers to perform the specified arithmetic functions, and an arithmetic unit for making arithmetic and logical calculations. The CPU is accompanied by an internal memory, which enables the computer to hold the program it is executing, the data being processed, and the results of the processing in the form of ending balances or other arithmetic output.

Finally, the processed information must be communicated. This is done in the output stage. The processed information may be shown temporarily on a CRT (a TV-like screen) or a printer may reproduce the information on paper (hard copy) for more permanent use. In addition to these two forms of output the processed information may also be stored on magnetic disk or tape, ready for subsequent automatic input into the CPU and internal memory for further processing.

Because of its processing speed a computerized accounting system provides financial statements and other accounting reports on a more timely basis for use in the managerial decision-making process.

QUESTIONS

1. Why are special-purpose journals used in accounting?
2. Besides the general journal, what are the five most commonly used special-purpose journals and why are they divided into these five types?
3. Which journal is used to record purchases on credit? cash purchases?
4. What is another name for the cash disbursements journal? Explain.
5. When special-purpose journals are used, what is the general journal used for?
6. In what journal would the proceeds of a loan be recorded? the proceeds from the sale of property or equipment? the proceeds from the sale of services for cash?
7. What is the purpose of the sundry columns in the special-purpose journals?
8. What is a control account? What is a subsidiary ledger schedule?
9. What is the function of the two Ref columns in the special-purpose journals?
10. What is the function of subsidiary ledgers in general? the accounts receivable subsidiary ledger? the accounts payable subsidiary ledger?
11. What is the function of the cashier's daily report?
12. Who prepares the daily transcript? Why is the daily transcript prepared?
13. What reports are used to post room charges to clients' accounts?
14. What are the advantages of automatic machine posting?
15. What are the three stages in a computer system? Describe them.

EXERCISES

1. State in which journal(s) each of the following transactions would be recorded.
   (a) Purchased a grill costing $1,000 on 60 days credit.
   (b) Paid wages of $789 to an employee.
   (c) Recorded a closing entry.
   (d) Made a $500 credit sale.
   (e) Made an $800 cash sale.
   (f) Collected $350 on account.
   (g) Accrued $250 of electricity expense.
   (h) Purchased $2,000 worth of inventory for cash.
   (i) Paid a $670 supplier's invoice that was due.
   (j) Received the proceeds of a $5,000 loan from the bank.
2. Below are presented one page each from the Rigor Restaurant's sales journal and cash receipts journal. Prepare the necessary general ledger and subsidiary ledger accounts using the "T" account format. Number the subsidiary ledger accounts in numerical sequence beginning with 1. Then post from the sales journal and cash receipts journal to the general ledger and accounts receivable subsidiary ledger accounts performing all required posting steps.

Sales Journal   Page 2

Date 1987	Description	Ref	Accounts receivable no. 104	Food sales no. 401	Beverage sales no. 402	Sundry			
						Account	No.	Ref	Amount
Jan. 2	Joe Rosol		754	260	454	Souvenirs	403		40
2	Mary Brown		152	97	55				
2	Williams, Inc.		1,589	889	433	Souvenirs	403		267
2	Cash sales		8,247	6,121	1,746	Candy machines	404		380
5	Cash sales		6,322	4,810	1,512				

Cash Receipts Journal   Page 3

Date 1987	Description	Ref	Cash in bank no. 101	Cash sales no. 104	Credit sales no. 104	Account	No.	Ref	Amount
Jan. 2	Sold oven		1,000			Equipment	142		1,000
2	Bank loan		30,000			Notes payable	205		30,000
2	Cash sales		8,247	8,247					
5	Payment—Joe Rosol		200		200				
5	Payment—Williams, Inc.		1,000		1,000				
5	Cash sales		6,322	6,322					

3. Answer the following questions based on the cash disbursements journal below:
   (a) Describe each of the transactions recorded in the journal.
   (b) What do the amounts recorded on the line described as "balance brought forward" represent?
   (c) What do the checks in the first Ref column signify? What do the checks in the sundry Ref column signify?
   (d) What do the numbers in brackets beneath each column total signify?

Cash Disbursements Journal   Page 3

Date 1986	Description	Check no.	Cash no. 101	Purchase discounts no. 502	Ref	Accounts payable no. 201	Account	No.	Ref	Amount
Dec. 31	Balance brought forward		112,302	3,672	√	108,403				7,571
31	Brown's suppliers	363	883	18	√	901				
31	Local National Bank	364	10,000				Notes payable	205	√	10,000
31	Laurel Food Purveyors	365	2,381	49	√	2,430				
31	Kill-All Fumigators	366	622		√	622				
31	National Electric Equipment	367	2,446				Equipment	142	√	2,446
31	Powerful Electric Co.	368	1,089		√	1,089				
31	City of Miami	369	362				Licenses	612	√	362
	Totals		130,085	3,739		113,445				20,379
			⟨101⟩	⟨502⟩		⟨201⟩				

(e) What is the most likely reason that separate columns were not provided for the notes payable account, the equipment account, and the licenses account?

(f) How would you cross-foot this journal? What is the purpose of cross-footing a journal?

4. (a) From the following transactions select those that should be posted to the general ledger accounts payable and purchase discount accounts in the general ledger and its subsidiary ledger accounts. Prepare general ledger and subsidiary ledger "T" accounts, post them directly and calculate the balance for each account. Do *not* journalize them.

June 1	Purchased $1,000 worth of food on 2/10, net 30 credit terms from Brown's Suppliers.
2	Purchased a refrigerator for $2,500 cash from All-Electronics, Inc.
3	Purchased $562 worth of office supplies from Pencil Worth Office Supplies on account. Terms are 5/15, net 60.
4	Purchased $1,824 worth of beverages from Bubbling Brook Beverage purveyors on 2/20, net 45 credit terms.
10	Paid the appropriate amount to settle the outstanding balance due Brown's Suppliers for the June 1 purchase, taking the discount into consideration.
16	Received invoice for $85 from the Kleen-Kline Garbage Pick-up Company, terms are net 15 days.
20	Paid the appropriate amount to reduce the balance due Bubbling Brook Beverage purveyors to one-half the current balance. (Take the discount into consideration.)
21	Paid $300 to Pencil Worth Office Supplies on account.
25	Paid $50 for a part-time secretary who worked today on a contract basis.

(b) Prepare a subsidiary ledger schedule. What is the control account for the accounts payable subsidiary ledger? Does your subsidiary ledger schedule balance with its control account?

5. Answer the following questions concerning the daily transcript presented on the next page:

(a) Describe the function of each column in the daily transcript.

(b) What is the function of the line labeled city?

(c) What is the purpose of the daily transcript?

PROBLEMS

1. The Tranquil Inn Motel had the following sales and receipts during the month of April 1986. (Add 5% sales tax to all sales and round sales tax amounts to the nearest dollar.)

April 4	John Brown spent three days at the motel and paid $240 for his room, $120 for food, $40 for beverages. He also spent $40 at the souvenir shop (record souvenir shop sales in the sundry columns).
6	Marilyn Roberts enjoyed extended credit privileges and left the following open balance in her account: $580 for her room, $324 for food, and $77 for beverages. She also brought some tennis balls at the pro shop (record in sundry columns) for $15.
7	Cash sales for the week were food $1,892, beverages $767, souvenir shop $387, and pro shop $124.
8	The proceeds of a $10,000 loan were received.
10	Jim Konklin paid his bill at the hotel as follows: room $341, food $161, and beverages $65.
11	The Walton Co. enjoyed extended credit privileges at the motel and

Daily Transcript

April 3, 1987

Room no.	Guest account	Balance brought forward	Room	Restaurant	Cash advances	Transfers in	Total charges	Credits			Balance forward
								Cash	Allowances	Transfers out	
61	489	235	120	44	100	10	274				509
44	492	462	60				60	50			472
102	493	581	90	23			113	70		10	614
38	510	329	60				60				389
Subtotal		1,607	330	67	100	10	507	120		10	1,984
City		1,340	540	252	50		842	300			1,882
Total		2,947	870	319	150	10	1,349	420		10	3,866

held a small convention there. It accumulated the following balance in its account: rooms $2,640, food $1980, and beverages $992.

14 Cash sales for the week were food $2,361, beverages $1,824, souvenir shop $823, and pro shop $361.

17 Robert Magnuson incurred the following charges at the motel and paid with a credit card: room $340, food $121, and beverages $66.

18–27—The motel was closed.

28 Marilyn Roberts paid $300 on account.

29 The credit card company paid Robert Magnuson's bill. The card company does not charge the establishment for its services, and so the full amount of the bill was collected by the motel.

30 Cash sales for the last week in April were food $873, beverages $431, souvenir shop $162, and pro shop $91.

30 William Joseph has been at the hotel seven days, will pay cash upon departure, and has incurred the following charges: room $560, food $310, and beverages $112. It is hotel policy to invoice guests who do not enjoy extended credit privileges every seven days.

   (a) Prepare a sales journal and cash receipts journal similar to those in Figures 9.2 and 9.3 and journalize these transactions. Be sure to include sundry columns when preparing your journals.

   (b) Assign account numbers to your accounts using the chart of accounts in Chapter 6 as a guide.

   (c) Prepare the required general ledger and subsidiary ledger accounts in "T" account format. Assume beginning account balances are zero.

   (d) Post from the journals to the general ledger and subsidiary ledger accounts, performing all required posting steps. Number the subsidiary ledger accounts in numerical sequence beginning with 1.

   (e) Prepare an accounts receivable subsidiary ledger schedule and verify that it balances.

2. The Fun-and-Sun Tour Bus Line made the following purchases and payments during the month of November:

Nov. 1 Purchased food worth $1,348 on 2/10, net 30 credit terms from Trusting Food, Inc.

   5 Purchased beverages worth $894 on 2/30, net 60 credit terms from the Drink-All Corporation.

   8 Purchased cleaning supplies for $779 cash, from the Quick-Kleen Company.

   10 Paid the appropriate amount due for food purchases made November 1 from Trusting Food, Inc.

   15 Purchased a freezer for $2,361 cash from U-Kool-It Company.

   18 Paid November rent of $2,000 to Solid State Real Estate Company.

   19 Received water invoice for $400 from the Eversweet Water Co. but did not pay it immediately. The invoice covers the period from the November 1 to November 15.

   21 Received and paid the fuel invoice for $1,872 from Growler Gas Company.

   25 Purchased kitchen equipment worth $1,312 on 2/10, net 45 terms from the Havital Company (record in sundry columns).

   28 Paid the appropriate amount to reduce the outstanding balance with the Drink-All Corporation to half the current balance. Take discount into consideration.

   (a) Prepare a purchases journal and cash disbursements journal similar to those in Figures 9.7 and 9.8 and journalize these transactions. Be sure to include sundry columns.

(b) Assign account numbers to your accounts using the chart of accounts in Chapter 6 as a guide.

(c) Prepare the required general ledger and subsidiary ledger accounts in "T" account format. Assume beginning account balances are zero.

(d) Post from the journals to the general ledger and subsidiary ledger accounts, performing all required posting steps. Number the subsidiary ledger accounts in numerical sequence beginning with 1.

(e) Prepare an accounts payable subsidiary ledger schedule and verify that it balances.

3. The Lofty Pines Hotel (located next to a lake) had the following sales and cash receipts during the month of July. (Add 5% sales tax to all sales and round sales tax amounts to the nearest dollar.)

July 5   Peter Gordner spent five days at the hotel. He enjoyed extended credit privileges, and so he charged the following to his account: room $750, food $342, and beverages $134.

7   Cash sales at the hotel for the week were food $6,671, beverages $3,642, candy machines $1,012, and boat rentals $892 (record candy machines and boat rentals in the sundry columns).

9   John Karstens stayed at the hotel four days and paid for the following upon departure: room $500, food $205, and beverages $106.

11   The hotel sold an old piece of kitchen equipment for $1,000 cash.

12   Peter Gordner paid $500 on his account.

14   Cash sales for the week were room $5,581, food $2,877, beverages $1,431, candy machines $984, and boat rentals $651.

18   Barbara Rushmont stayed at the hotel and incurred the following charges: room $640, food $112, and beverages $55. She paid with a credit card.

20   The hotel borrowed $10,000, for which it signed a note payable to the bank.

21   Charles McMoor enjoyed extended credit privileges at the hotel and left the following charges open on his account when he departed: room $1,340, food $742, and beverages $464.

28   Cash sales for the week were food $3,456, beverages $1,448, candy machines $631, and boat rentals $346.

30   Charles McMoor paid $1,000 on his account.

30   It is hotel policy to invoice every seven days those guests who do not enjoy extended credit privileges. Joanne Barlot, a transient guest, was invoiced for the following, since it was her seventh day at the hotel: room $1,050, food $544, and beverages $378.

(a) Prepare a sales journal and cash receipts journal similar to those in Figures 9.2 and 9.3 and journalize these transactions. Be sure to include sundry columns.

(b) Assign account numbers to your accounts using the chart of accounts in Chapter 6 as a guide.

(c) Prepare the required general ledger and subsidiary ledger accounts in "T" account format. Assume beginning account balances are zero.

(d) Post from the journals to the general ledger and subsidiary ledger accounts, performing all required posting steps. Number the subsidiary ledger accounts in numerical sequence beginning with 1.

(e) Prepare an accounts receivable subsidiary ledger schedule and verify that it balances.

4. The Wait-less Fast Food Diet Restaurant made the following purchases and payments during the month of May:

May 4   Purchased food worth $2,560 on 5/10, net 45 credit terms from Fed-Up Foods Co.

6   Purchased cleaning supplies from Sanitary Mary, Inc. for $560 cash.

10 Purchased some tables from the All-Restaurant Co. for $1,200 cash (record in sundry columns).

14 Paid the appropriate amount to reduce the balance due Fed-Up Foods Co. by half. Take the discount into consideration.

15 Paid $5,000 of notes payable that were due to First Bank (record in sundry columns).

17 Received and paid the electricity invoice for the first 15 days of May to All-Electric Co. It amounted to $996.

18 Purchased $1,450 worth of food and $560 worth of beverages from the International Food Supply, Co. on 2/10, net 30 credit terms.

20 Paid the appropriate amount to reduce the remaining balance in the Fed-Up Foods Co. account by half. No discount may be taken since the discount period has expired.

25 Received the water invoices for the first 20 days of the month from the City Water Co. but did not pay it. The amount is $344.

28 Paid the appropriate amount to reduce the balance in the International Food Supply Co. by half. Remember you are paying within the discount period.

(a) Prepare a purchases journal and cash disbursements journal similar to those in Figures 9.7 and 9.8 and journalize these transactions. Be sure to include sundry columns.

(b) Assign account numbers to your accounts using the chart of accounts in Chapter 6 as a guide.

(c) Prepare the required general ledger and subsidiary ledger accounts in "T" account format. Assume all beginning account balances are zero, except for the notes payable account, which has a beginning balance of $10,000.

(d) Post from the journals to the general ledger and subsidiary ledger accounts, performing all required posting steps. Number the subsidiary ledger accounts in numerical sequence beginning with 1.

(e) Prepare an accounts payable subsidiary ledger schedule and verify that it balances.

5. Using the format presented in Figure 9.13, prepare a daily transcript for a 10-room hotel, the Overnite Inn, on September 5, 1987, based on the information in the daily rooms report and housekeeper's report below. All guests are transient (do not enjoy extended credit privileges).

Daily Rooms Report				Date: September 5, 1987
Room no.	Guest account	Number of occupants	Room rate	Sales tax
1		0		
2	3467	1	$50	$2.50
3		0		
4		0		
5	3469	2	$70*	$3.50
6	3471	1	$50	$2.50
7	3470	1	$40	$2.00
8		0		
9		0		
10	3468	1	$40	$2.00

*Double occupancy rate.

Housekeeper's Report			Date: September 5, 1987
Room	Status	Room	Status
1	Unoccupied	6	Occupied
2	Occupied	7	Occupied
3	Unoccupied	8	Unoccupied
4	Unoccupied	9	Unoccupied
5	Occupied	10	Occupied

The night auditor received the following signed guest vouchers with the cashier's report from the restaurant and bar:

Restaurant	
Date: 9/5/87	
Lunch	$15.00
Tax	.75
	$15.75
ROOM #7	
Frank Murphie	

Restaurant	
Date: 9/5/87	
Breakfast	12.00
Tax	.60
	$12.60
ROOM #5	
Ronald Carter	

Restaurant	
Date: 9/5/87	
Lunch	$18.00
Tax	.90
	$18.90
ROOM #10	
M. Pizzaio	

Restaurant	
Date: 9/5/87	
Lunch	$30.00
Tax	1.50
	$31.50
ROOM #5	
Ronald Carter	

Bar	
Date: 9/5/87	
2 Manhattans	5.00
Tax	.25
	$ 5.25
ROOM #6	
B. Garden	

Bar	
Date: 9/5/87	
3 Martinis	$9.50
Tax	.45
	$ 9.95
ROOM #2	
J. Phipps	

Cash Advance
Date: 9/5/87
I, J. Phipps, received $20.00 cash advance from Overnite Inn.
signed: *J. Phipps*

In addition to the above, you are given the following information:

(a)

Guest account no.	Account balance at 9/4/87
3467	0
3468	$ 89
3469	$798
3470	$115
3471	$ 65

(b) Upon reviewing his subsidiary ledger card you notice that guest number 3469 paid $700 on his account today.

(c) You also notice that yesterday a $15 bar invoice has been posted erroneously to guest account number 3469 whereas it should be posted to guest account number 3470. Use the transfer columns to make the correction.

(d) Guest number 3471 was charged a $70 room rate yesterday by mistake. The current room rate is $50. Use the allowances column to make the correction.

(e) Mr. J. Phipps' account is number 3467.

Payroll Accounting

The sale of services, a labor-intensive endeavor, is the major source of revenue in the hospitality industry. It is only logical, therefore, that payroll and related expenses be the major expense category in the typical hospitality entity. Figure 10.1 shows, as is to be expected, that in 1981 fully 33.9% of every dollar of revenue was spent by the hospitality industry on payroll and related expenses in the United States, far exceeding any other expense category in the industry. Knowledge of payroll accounting and control methods is consequently of primary importance in the industry.

In this chapter, first basic concepts and terms relating to payrolls are explained. This is followed by a discussion of the various types of payroll deductions and employer payroll taxes. The employer's obligations for reporting and paying payroll taxes to the federal and state governments are discussed next, followed by an explanation of the use of the payroll journal and employee subsidiary ledgers. The last three sections of the chapter include a summary of the wage-hour law's impact on the hospitality industry, a brief explanation of IRS tip reporting requirements, and a discussion of some procedures for controlling salaries and wages.

BASIC PAYROLL ACCOUNTING CONCEPTS

We have previously learned that salaries and wages are recorded by an entry such as the following:

	Dr	Cr
Salaries and Wages	350	
Cash		350
To record a $350 payroll payment		

This simple form of recording salaries and wages does not take into account the fact that deductions must be made from an employee's pay in compliance with federal, and sometimes state, regulations. Additional deductions may also be made, at the employee's request, for such purposes as funding savings accounts and paying union dues. Furthermore, the employer must pay certain payroll-related taxes levied on him by the federal and state governments, which are not deductible from an employee's pay.

In discussing these aspects of payroll accounting such terms as wages, salaries, overtime, gross earnings, and net pay will be used. Wages are a form of remuneration calculated at an hourly rate, which is agreed upon when an employee is hired. A salary is calculated on a monthly or annual basis. Usually administrative personnel are paid on a salaried basis.

Overtime is a term born of the Fair Labor Standards Act, which applies to

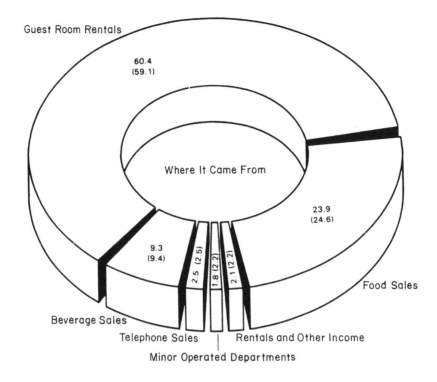

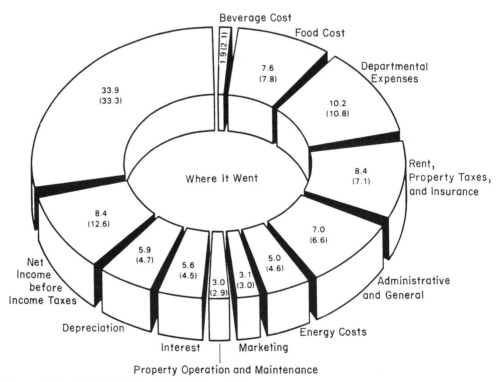

Figure 10.1.   The U.S. lodging industry dollar, 1981.

Reprinted with permission from *U.S. Lodging Industry 1982*, a publication of the national accounting firm of Laventhol & Horwath.

all businesses engaged in interstate commerce and specifies that the normal work week consists of 40 hours. It further specifies that certain employees who work more than 40 hours per week must be paid for hours worked in excess of 40 during a week, at a rate no less than one and one half times the normal hourly rate. Since employers may pay voluntarily more than this rate, the overtime rate is established at the time the employee is hired.

Gross earnings and net pay are related to deductions from an employee's pay. An employer is required to act as a collection agent of the federal and, in some cases, the local governments by deducting tax amounts from an employee's pay. The employer must remit these amounts to the federal, state, and/or city governments. These employee taxes are calculated on the basis of the employee's gross earnings—the total amount of wages or salaries earned. An employee may also request that other deductions be made from gross earnings. The actual amount of pay the employee receives after making these deductions is called net pay. The net pay of an employee who earned $2,000, with a required tax deduction of $300 and an additional voluntary deduction of $100 for investment in a savings plan would be calculated as follows:

Gross earnings	$2,000
Less:	
Deduction for taxes	300
Savings plan deduction	100
Net Pay:	$1,600

DEDUCTIONS FROM GROSS SALARIES AND WAGES

The three principal categories of payroll deductions are

1. Amounts withheld from employees to cover their federal and, where applicable, state and city income tax liability.
2. Amounts withheld to pay the federal social security tax (FICA tax).
3. Any other amount an employee may authorize to be deducted to meet personal financial planning objectives.

Withheld Income Taxes

The Current Tax Payments Act of 1943, which is part of the Internal Revenue Code (IRC) requires employers to withhold from an employee's gross salaries and wages an amount to be applied against that employee's potential income tax liability at the end of the year. This deduction is called withheld income tax and the amount is obtained from tables published by the Internal Revenue Service (IRS) in Circular E, "Employer's Withholding Tax Guide." Since the income tax payable by an employee depends on the employee's total annual gross salaries and wages, the employee's marital status, and the number of withholding allowances claimed, several tables are included in Circular E to cover these various conditions. One withholding allowance can be claimed for each dependent plus one for the husband and one for the wife. Figure 10.2 shows an example of the table for married employees who are paid weekly (1982–1983 rates).

In order for the employer to find the proper withholding amount in the tax tables, an employee must submit a signed IRS Form W-4 to inform the employer concerning marital status, number of dependents claimed, and any additional amounts desired to be withheld to cover any tax liability.

MARRIED Persons—WEEKLY Payroll Period

(For Wages Paid After June 1982 and Before July 1983)

And the wages are—		And the number of withholding allowances claimed is—										
At least	But less than	0	1	2	3	4	5	6	7	8	9	10 or more
		The amount of income tax to be withheld shall be—										
$0	$47	$0	$0	$0	$0	$0	$0	$0	$0	$0	$0	$0
47	48	.20	0	0	0	0	0	0	0	0	0	0
48	49	.30	0	0	0	0	0	0	0	0	0	0
49	50	.40	0	0	0	0	0	0	0	0	0	0
50	51	.50	0	0	0	0	0	0	0	0	0	0
51	52	.60	0	0	0	0	0	0	0	0	0	0
52	53	.80	0	0	0	0	0	0	0	0	0	0
53	54	.90	0	0	0	0	0	0	0	0	0	0
54	55	1.00	0	0	0	0	0	0	0	0	0	0
55	56	1.10	0	0	0	0	0	0	0	0	0	0
56	57	1.20	0	0	0	0	0	0	0	0	0	0
57	58	1.40	0	0	0	0	0	0	0	0	0	0
58	59	1.50	0	0	0	0	0	0	0	0	0	0
59	60	1.60	0	0	0	0	0	0	0	0	0	0
60	62	1.80	0	0	0	0	0	0	0	0	0	0
62	64	2.00	0	0	0	0	0	0	0	0	0	0
64	66	2.30	0	0	0	0	0	0	0	0	0	0
66	68	2.50	.20	0	0	0	0	0	0	0	0	0
68	70	2.70	.40	0	0	0	0	0	0	0	0	0
70	72	3.00	.70	0	0	0	0	0	0	0	0	0
72	74	3.20	.90	0	0	0	0	0	0	0	0	0
74	76	3.50	1.20	0	0	0	0	0	0	0	0	0
76	78	3.70	1.40	0	0	0	0	0	0	0	0	0
78	80	3.90	1.60	0	0	0	0	0	0	0	0	0
80	82	4.20	1.90	0	0	0	0	0	0	0	0	0
82	84	4.40	2.10	0	0	0	0	0	0	0	0	0
84	86	4.70	2.40	0	0	0	0	0	0	0	0	0
86	88	4.90	2.60	.30	0	0	0	0	0	0	0	0
88	90	5.10	2.80	.50	0	0	0	0	0	0	0	0
90	92	5.40	3.10	.80	0	0	0	0	0	0	0	0
92	94	5.60	3.30	1.00	0	0	0	0	0	0	0	0
94	96	5.90	3.60	1.20	0	0	0	0	0	0	0	0
96	98	6.10	3.80	1.50	0	0	0	0	0	0	0	0
98	100	6.30	4.00	1.70	0	0	0	0	0	0	0	0
100	105	6.80	4.50	2.10	0	0	0	0	0	0	0	0
105	110	7.40	5.10	2.70	.40	0	0	0	0	0	0	0
110	115	8.00	5.70	3.30	1.00	0	0	0	0	0	0	0
115	120	8.60	6.30	3.90	1.60	0	0	0	0	0	0	0
120	125	9.40	6.90	4.50	2.20	0	0	0	0	0	0	0
125	130	10.20	7.50	5.10	2.80	.50	0	0	0	0	0	0
130	135	11.00	8.10	5.70	3.40	1.10	0	0	0	0	0	0
135	140	11.80	8.70	6.30	4.00	1.70	0	0	0	0	0	0
140	145	12.60	9.50	6.90	4.60	2.30	0	0	0	0	0	0
145	150	13.40	10.30	7.50	5.20	2.90	.60	0	0	0	0	0
150	160	14.60	11.50	8.40	6.10	3.80	1.50	0	0	0	0	0
160	170	16.20	13.10	10.00	7.30	5.00	2.70	.40	0	0	0	0
170	180	17.80	14.70	11.60	8.60	6.20	3.90	1.60	0	0	0	0
180	190	19.40	16.30	13.20	10.20	7.40	5.10	2.80	.50	0	0	0
190	200	21.00	17.90	14.80	11.80	8.70	6.30	4.00	1.70	0	0	0
200	210	22.60	19.50	16.40	13.40	10.30	7.50	5.20	2.90	.60	0	0
210	220	24.20	21.10	18.00	15.00	11.90	8.80	6.40	4.10	1.80	0	0
220	230	25.80	22.70	19.60	16.60	13.50	10.40	7.60	5.30	3.00	.70	0
230	240	27.50	24.30	21.20	18.20	15.10	12.00	8.90	6.50	4.20	1.90	0
240	250	29.40	25.90	22.80	19.80	16.70	13.60	10.50	7.70	5.40	3.10	.80
250	260	31.30	27.70	24.40	21.40	18.30	15.20	12.10	9.10	6.60	4.30	2.00
260	270	33.20	29.60	26.00	23.00	19.90	16.80	13.70	10.70	7.80	5.50	3.20
270	280	35.10	31.50	27.80	24.60	21.50	18.40	15.30	12.30	9.20	6.70	4.40
280	290	37.00	33.40	29.70	26.20	23.10	20.00	16.90	13.90	10.80	7.90	5.60
290	300	38.90	35.30	31.60	28.00	24 70	21.60	18.50	15.50	12.40	9.30	6.80
300	310	40.80	37.20	33.50	29.90	26.30	23.20	20.10	17.10	14.00	10.90	8.00

Figure 10.2. Sample page from IRS Circular E.

In those states with a personal income tax, the state income tax withholding amount, usually a fixed percentage, must be determined. State income taxes are much lower than federal income taxes.

Social Security Tax

The Federal Insurance Contributions Act (FICA) of 1935 provides for workers to receive monthly pension payments upon reaching the designated retirement age. In 1965, the Medicare Program, providing certain medical insurance coverage, was added to the benefits receivable by retirees. Both of these programs are funded by taxes collected under FICA.

To fund these benefits, as of 1983, employers must withhold 6.7% of an employee's gross salaries and wages up to maximum salaries and wages of $35,700 in any one year. The maximum salaries and wages subject to the FICA tax and the percentage deduction rate have been steadily increasing, as is evident from Table 10.1, and are expected to increase even further in the future.

Other Deductions

In addition to the deductions required by federal and local governments, employees may authorize their employer to deduct other amounts from gross salary or wages to meet their own personal needs. Some of the most typical of these voluntary deductions are listed below:

- Savings plan
- Pension fund and retirement income plans
- Medical insurance plan
- Union dues
- Loan repayments
- Charitable contributions

Authorization to deduct specific amounts for the above purposes is given in writing by the employee to the employer.

TABLE 10.1. FICA rates and Base Amounts[a]

| Year | Rate (%) | Base amount | Maximum tax | |
			Employer	Employee
1978	6.05	$17,700	$1,071	$1,071
1979	6.13	22,900	1,404	1,404
1980	6.13	25,900	1,588	1,588
1981	6.65	29,700	1,975	1,975
1982	6.70	32,400	2,171	2,171
1983	6.70	35,700	2,392	2,392
1984	7.00[b]	37,800	2,646	2,533

Source: Prentice-Hall, Inc., "Federal Taxes," Vol. 1 (Dec. 15, 1983), Par. 3145.

[a]As of this writing, FICA rate increases for 1985 through 1990 are expected to be as follows:

1985	7.05%
1986–1987	7.15%
1988–1989	7.51%
1990	7.65%

[b]The employee's rate for 1984 was 6.7%.

JOURNALIZING SALARIES AND WAGES

Since amounts deducted from an employee's pay must be remitted by the employer to the federal and local governments and to the organizations administering the various voluntary deduction amounts, all payroll deductions are recorded as liabilities of the employer. The employer is merely acting as collection agent for the various organizations and has no right to keep the funds. An example of a payroll journal entry to record the salary of a hypothetical employee, John Adams, and the assumptions upon which it is based, is given in Figure 10.3.

Assumptions

John Adams:
  is married
  has five allowances
  is paid weekly and requested $10 union dues withheld
  received gross wages of $300
  has earned $35,600 in gross wages to date in the current year
  (1983)

Journal Entry

	Dr	Cr
Salaries & wages expense	$300.00	
Withheld income tax payable		$ 23.20
FICA tax payable (6.7% × 100.00)		6.70
Union dues payable		10.00
Cash		260.10
To record John Adam's weekly salary		

Figure 10.3. Example of payroll journal entry for hypothetical employee. John must pay FICA tax on $100 of this week's earnings subject to the FICA tax. The FICA tax payable is calculated according to Table 10.1.

EMPLOYER TAXES AND WORKERS' COMPENSATION INSURANCE

In addition to the taxes levied on employees and deducted from their pay, the employer is responsible for certain payroll-related federal and state taxes and insurance payments, which constitute an additional expense for the employer. These additional employer expenses may be divided into three categories:

1. Social security (FICA) taxes
2. Federal and state unemployment taxes
3. Workers' compensation insurance

The employer is required to pay a FICA tax equal in amount to that paid by the employee, 6.7% of gross salaries and wages in 1983. The one exception to this—tip income—is discussed later in this chapter.

Additionally, the Federal Unemployment Tax Act (FUTA) imposed a tax on the employer to fund the establishment and administration of employment offices throughout the United States. In 1983, the tax rate was 3.5% of gross salaries and wages up to maximum wages of $7,000. Since all states have a similar unemployment tax, the federal government allows part of the state tax

TABLE 10.2. Calculation of Federal and State Unemployment
Taxes

	Employee turnover		
	Low	Average	High
Gross salaries and wages	$10,000	$10,000	$10,000
State unemployment tax rate	1%	2.7%	4.5%
State unemployment tax	$100	$270	$450
Federal unemployment tax rate (3.5% less 2.7%)	0.8%	0.8%	0.8%
Federal unemployment tax	$80	$80	$80
Total unemployment tax	$180	$350	$530

to be applied as a credit against the federal unemployment tax. This results in a lower effective rate of federal unemployment tax, as will be explained when we discuss the state unemployment tax. Since the federal unemployment tax is an employer expense, no payroll deduction is made for it.

As of this writing, all states have levied an unemployment tax on employers (Alabama, Alaska, California, New Jersey, and Rhode Island also levy it on employees), the proceeds of which are used to pay a weekly subsidy (unemployment compensation benefits) to employees who have lost their jobs. The rates for this tax vary. The initial rate assigned to a company by all states is 2.7% of gross salaries and wages. Companies with good employment histories will have the rate reduced and companies with high employee turnover will have it raised. In Florida the maximum gross salary or wages subject to this tax in 1983 was $7,000, the same as for the FUTA tax. In 1983 the unemployment tax rate in Florida varied from 1% for employers with low employee turnover to 4.5% for employees with high employee turnover.

The federal government allows a maximum credit of 2.7% to be taken against the FUTA tax of 3.5%. Thus, an employer who has lower employee turnover and receives a state unemployment tax rate of less than 2.7% will pay less total unemployment taxes, and an employer with high turnover and a state tax rate above 2.7% will pay more total unemployment taxes. This can be seen more clearly in Table 10.2.

Every state requires employers to carry some form of workers' compensation insurance. In some cases the state administers the fund and in others private insurance companies sell the coverage. The purpose of this insurance is to reimburse workers for injury or death incurred while at work. This insurance constitutes an employer expense. The premium is usually paid at the beginning of the year and is adjusted by an additional payment or a refund at year end depending on the employer's experience factor. The amount paid varies from state to state and is based on gross salaries and wages, subject to an upper limit and to the degree of risk in each employment category. Since payment is made before the coverage is actually used, workers' compensation payments are usually debited to a prepaid workers' compensation account.

Journalizing Employer's Payroll Taxes and Workers' Compensation Insurance

The employer's portion of the FICA tax as well as the federal and state unemployment taxes and workers' compensation insurance are charged to their individual expense accounts. The corresponding credit entries are made

---

Assumptions

John Adams:
  is paid weekly
  received gross wages of $300
  has earned $6,800 in gross wages to date in the current
    year
  the amount of workers' compensation insurance expired
    is $6
  state unemployment tax rate is 2.7%

Journal Entry

	Dr	Cr
FICA tax expense (6.7%)	$20.10	
FUTA tax expense (0.8% × $200)	1.60	
State unemployment compensation		
(0.027 × $200)	5.40	
Workers' compensation insurance		
Expense	6.00	
FICA payable		$20.10
FUTA payable		1.60
State unemployment tax payable		5.40
Prepaid workers' compensation		6.00
To record payroll taxes incurred by John Adams' employer		

Figure 10.4. Journal entry to record John Adam's employer's payroll tax expense. The employer must pay only FUTA and state unemployment taxes on $200 of John Adam's gross wages this week since the other $100 are in excess of the $7,000 maximum earnings subject to these taxes.

to their respective current liability account and prepaid workers' compensation account. Figure 10.4 indicates the required journal entry to record John Adam's employer's payroll tax expense. The employer's payroll tax entries are usually made in the general journal.

INDEPENDENT CONTRACTOR

Sometimes it is necessary to hire personnel on an independent contract basis. Such personnel work for several business entities without becoming the exclusive employee of any one of them. Examples of this type of worker are temporary help, musicians or entertainers, and cleaning people. The employer is not responsible for deducting employee payroll taxes and does not incur liability for employer's payroll taxes when hiring workers on an independent contract basis. Certain strict requirements of the IRS must be complied with in order to classify a worker as an independent contractor.

EMPLOYER REPORTING REQUIREMENTS

Both the federal and state governments require the employer to report and pay payroll taxes and withheld income taxes periodically. Each employer must obtain an employee identification number by filing form SS-4 with the IRS. This employer identification number must be entered in all reports sent to the IRS. Sole proprietorships, partnerships, and corporations must all obtain employer identification numbers whether or not they have any employees, since the number is also used to relate income tax information to a business entity.

IRS form 941 is used to report payroll taxes due to the federal government.

TABLE 10.3. Timetable for Depositary Payments

Amount of employer's and employees' FICA tax due plus employee withheld income taxes	Payment due dates
$500 or more but less than $3000 at the end of any month	Must deposit in a depository bank by the fifteenth of the following month
$3000 or more at any of following dates: 3, 7, 11, 15, 19, 22, 25, or last day of month	Must deposit within three banking days (excluding Saturdays, Sundays, and holidays) after the specified date

It must be submitted by the employer to the IRS no later than one month after the end of each calendar quarter, i.e., by April 30, July 31, October 31, and January 31.

The actual payment of the taxes is subject to a different timetable, which depends on the amount of tax due. If the amount due is less than $500, it may be mailed to the nearest IRS Center along with form 941 by the last day of the month following the end of the quarter. If the amount due is $500 or more, then it must be deposited in a depository bank (most banks are so designated by the IRS), along with a depository receipt by the due date shown in Table 10.3.

Federal unemployment taxes need not be paid until the total amount due exceeds $100 in any of the four calendar quarters. When this amount is reached the taxes must be deposited in a depository bank along with a depository receipt by the last day of the month following the end of the quarter. If FUTA taxes due for the year do not exceed $100 until the last quarter of the year they may be mailed to the nearest IRS center by January 31,[1] along with IRS form 940, used for reporting the annual FUTA tax liability.

At year end the employer is responsible for reporting to each individual employee the total amount of earnings, FICA tax withheld, and federal and local income taxes withheld. This is done by providing each employee with a W-2 form, which must be distributed to employees by January 31 of the following year. The employer must also send a copy of each W-2 to the Social Security Administration along with form W-3, which contains a total for each of the categories reported on the W-2 tax forms. Form W-3 is due on the last day of February.

States have different reporting and payment requirements for the unemployment compensation tax. Florida requires, for example, form UCT-6 to be filed on a quarterly basis, on the last day of the month following each calendar quarter. The amount of state unemployment tax payable must be remitted by the employer with the report.

PAYROLL RECORDING PROCEDURES

An effective payroll recording system consists of the following three elements:

1. Adequate source documents containing the basic information needed to calculate salaries and wages due.

---

[1]Form 940 may be mailed by February 11 if tax payments have been made on a timely basis during the year.

Overtime Authorization
Employee name: _____
Date overtime to be worked: _____
_____ _____
Date signed   Supervisor

Figure 10.5. Employee overtime record form.

2. A payroll journal to record payroll information compactly and efficiently.
3. Employee subsidiary ledgers to provide detailed payroll data concerning each employee.

Every employer should have an employee file, which should contain, as a minimum, the employee's application, employment contract and any amendments thereto, any voluntary payroll deduction authorizations, and W-4 form.

The contract should specify the employee's salary, if salaried, or hourly wage rate. It should also specify the overtime pay rate, number of days sick leave allowed, holidays allowed, and employee benefits such as pension and insurance plans.

Additionally, for wage-earning employees, a record of hours worked and, in the case of overtime hours, an authorization slip (see Figure 10.5) is recommended. A supervisor's authorization is important to control overtime hours, which are paid at a higher rate. The record of hours worked may be maintained manually by a supervisor, but a commonly used record of time worked is the clock punch time card. This card, plus any overtime authorization slip, is turned in to the accounting department weekly and serves as the basis for determining the weekly gross wage amount.

The Payroll Journal

After the employee's gross earnings have been determined, the necessary payroll information is recorded in the payroll journal, also called the payroll register. The payroll journal is a special-purpose journal designed to:

- Facilitate the process of recording and posting payroll information
- Accumulate information for preparing payroll tax reports
- Record all payroll information compactly in one journal

A sample payroll journal is shown in Figure 10.6 along with its related general ledger accounts.

The journal includes a date column, a column for the name of the employee being paid, and the usual Ref column, where a check is made to indicate that the appropriate employee's individual subsidiary ledger account has been updated with the current payroll information.

The expense distribution columns are used to record the employee's gross pay as an expense (debit) of the department where he or she works. There is a sundry column for recording the salaries and wages of employees in minor departments. After the expense distribution columns come the deductions columns for recording payroll tax deductions and other employee-authorized deductions. Since these must be paid by the the employer to third parties, they

Payroll Journal

Date 1986	Employee	Ref	Expense distribution — Rooms No. 606 Dr	Food and beverage No. 607 Dr	Administrative and general No. 608 Dr	Sundry — Account	Sundry — No.	Sundry — Ref	Sundry — Amount Dr	Deductions — Withheld federal income tax No. 230 Cr	Deductions — FICA tax withheld No. 231 Cr	Deductions — Savings plan No. 235 Cr	Deductions — Medical insurance No. 236 Cr	Net pay No. 101 Cr
Oct 14	Michelle Brandon	✓		200						16	13		10	161
14	Michael Carver	✓	700							80	67	100	20	733
14	Robert Delane	✓	200							65	47	50	30	508
14	Barbara Norden	✓			1,000					23	13		10	154
14	William Peterson	✓			2,000					120	134	150	30	1,566
14	Paul Rand	✓		300						50	34		20	396
14	Frank Ward	✓								41	20		10	219
14	Susan Young	✓	300			Pool	609	✓	500	26	20	10	20	234
	Totals		1,200	500	3,000				500	421	348	310	150	3,971
			<606>	<607>	<608>					<230>	<231>	<235>	<236>	<101>

Partial General Ledger

Cash No. 101

10/13/86 Bal.	10,000	10/13/86 PRJ-11 3,971
10/14/86 Bal.	6,029	

Withheld Federal Income Tax Payable No. 230

		10/13/86 Bal. 8,750
		10/14/86 PRJ-11 421
		10/14/86 Bal. 9,171

FICA Tax Payable No. 231

		10/13/86 Bal. 15,500
		10/14/86 PRJ-11 348
		10/14/86 Bal. 15,848

Due to Savings Plan Fund No. 235

		10/13/86 Bal. 2,550
		10/14/86 PRJ-11 310
		10/14/86 Bal. 2,860

Medical Insurance Payable No. 236

		10/13/86 Bal. 3,000
		10/14/86 PRJ-11 150
		10/14/86 Bal. 3,150

Rooms, Salaries, and Wages No. 606

10/13/86 Bal.	30,000	
10/14/86 PRJ-11	1,200	
10/14/86 Bal.	31,200	

Food & Beverage Salaries & Wages No. 607

10/13/86 Bal.	13,000	
10/14/86 PRJ-11	500	
10/14/86 Bal.	13,500	

Administrative and General Salaries and Wages No. 608

10/13/86 Bal.	62,000	
10/14/86 PRJ-11	3,000	
10/14/86 Bal.	65,000	

Pool Salaries and Wages No. 609

10/13/86 Bal.	11,000	
10/14/86 PRJ-11	500	
10/14/86 Bal.	11,500	

Figure 10.6. Sample payroll journal. This journal does not include a column for state income tax withholding. In those states where such a tax exists, an additional withholding column is required for this purpose.

are recorded as liabilities (credits) on the employer's balance sheet. Finally, to the far right is the net pay column for recording the amount of pay actually received by the employee.

The payroll shown in Figure 10.6 was paid in cash. A check was drawn for the total amount in the net pay column and each employee's net pay amount was placed in an envelope along with a pay slip. The pay slip contains all the necessary information to enable an employee to verify that the net pay has been properly calculated.

When a payroll is paid by check, an additional column is added to the payroll journal for entering the check number. In this case, the pay slip is usually an integral part of the payroll check.

Employee Subsidiary Ledger

The employee subsidiary ledger contains a detailed breakdown per employee of all information contained in the general ledger payroll expense accounts and payroll-related liability accounts. This detailed information

- Helps management verify that it has followed correct payroll procedures
- Provides employee information during the year if requested, and at year-end on form W-2
- Helps management prepare payroll tax reports to the IRS and the local governments

A sample employee subsidiary ledger is shown in Figure 10.7. A subsidiary ledger contains all required information for calculating employee's pay. It also contains a detailed record of an employee's payment dates, gross salary or wages, payroll deductions and net pay. If the employee were paid by check it would also contain a record of the paycheck numbers.

Each employee subsidiary ledger is usually totaled quarterly. A subsidiary ledger schedule (a total of all the individual subsidiary ledger balances) is then prepared to verify the balances in the general ledger departmental salaries and wages accounts as well as other information to be presented on the quar-

Name: Michelle Brandon
1417 S.W. 90th Street
Miami, FL 33111

Social Security No. 999-99-9999
Birthdate: March 10, 1960
Other deductions: Med. ins. $10/week

Marital status: Married
Regular rate: $5.00

Number of Exemptions: 2
Overtime rate: $7.50

Payroll date	Hours worked		Gross earnings	Withheld federal income tax	FICA tax withheld	Other deductions		Net pay
	Regular	Overtime				Savings plan	Medical insurance	
10-07-86	40	2	215	18	14	—	10	173
10-14-86	40	—	200	16	13	—	10	161

Figure 10.7. Sample employee subsidiary ledger. There are no entries prior to October 7, 1986, nor totals for the previous quarters because the October 7, 1986 pay period was this employee's first with the company.

terly payroll tax reports to the local and federal governments. Having quarterly totals also facilitates the preparation of W-2 forms at year end, since only four amounts need be added to verify annual totals.

Journalizing a Payroll and Posting to the Employee Subsidiary Ledger

The steps for recording a payroll are as follows:

1. Enter the date on which the payroll period ends in the date column.
2. Enter the name of the employee in the Employee column.
3. Enter the amount of the employee's gross salary or wages in the column for the department to which it will be charged. If it is to be charged to a department with few employees it should be entered in the sundry columns by entering the name of the account, the account number, and the amount.
4. The amount of withheld federal income tax to be deducted is obtained from IRS Circular E based on the employee's W-4 information and is entered in the column marked accordingly.
5. The FICA tax to be deducted is calculated on the employee's gross salary or wage amount and is entered in the FICA tax column.
6. Any voluntary deductions, such as those listed earlier in the chapter, would be entered in their appropriate columns. In this example two voluntary deductions are available—a savings plan and medical insurance.
7. All of the deduction amounts are subtracted from the employee's gross salary or wages, and the net pay amount is entered in the net pay column.
8. Enter the above information on each employee's subsidiary ledger (which will be discussed subsequently) and make a check in the Ref column appearing immediately after the employee's name.

Posting to the General Ledger

After the payroll is complete, the information is posted to the general ledger as follows:

1. Total the various columns in the payroll journal.
2. Add the totals across (cross-foot) to determine that the total of all the debit columns equals the total of all the credit columns.
3. Post the column totals to their general ledger accounts, except for the sundry column.
4. Below each account column total in the payroll journal enter the number of the general ledger account to which it was posted.
5. Post each amount in the sundry column to its general ledger account individually and make a check in the sundry Ref column next to each posted amount.

PAYROLL ACCRUAL

When a firm's accounting period cut-off date does not coincide with the end of a payroll period, an accrual entry must be made to record the partial pay period that falls within the current accounting period.

This accrual entry must not include accruals for withheld taxes nor amounts

Assumptions

Department	Rooms
Payroll period ends	January 2
Accounting period ends	December 31
Days in work week	7 days
Payroll amount	$700.00
Withheld income tax for pay period	70.00
FICA tax for pay period	46.90
Savings plan deduction for pay period	35.00
Federal unemployment tax for pay period	14.00
State unemployment tax for pay period	8.40

Accrual Entry

	Dr	Cr
Employee's salaries		
Room's salaries and wages	$500.00	
Accrued salaries and wages payable		$500.00
Employer's payroll taxes		
FICA tax expense	33.50	
Federal unemployment tax expense	10.00	
State unemployment tax expense	6.00	
Fica tax payable		33.50
Federal unemployment taxes payable		10.00
State unemployment taxes payable		6.00
To accrue five-sevenths of the seven-day pay period ending January 2		

Figure 10.8.   Sample accrual entry.

corresponding to voluntary employee deductions since these do not become a liability of the firm until the payroll is actually paid. A sample accrual entry, along with the assumptions upon which it is based, is presented in Figure 10.8.

RECORDING PAYROLL EXPENSES UNDER THE UNIFORM SYSTEM OF ACCOUNTS

Under the Uniform System of Accounts for Hotels, all salaries and wages are charged to the salaries and wages expense account. This account is divided into subsidiary accounts for each department, from which charges are distributed to the various departmental income and expense statements. Payroll taxes and employee benefits are charged to the payroll taxes and employee benefits account, shown in Figure 10.9. They too are subsequently distributed to the various departments, some of which are listed in the bottom section of Figure 10.9. Notice that some salaries and wages are distributed to the payroll taxes and employee benefits account. These charges correspond to the salaries and wages of employees in the personnel department. A diagram showing the flow of all payroll-related accounting information to some typical hotel departments is shown in Figure 10.10.

ONE-WRITE OR PEGBOARD PAYROLL SYSTEMS AND COMPUTERIZED PAYROLL SYSTEMS

Accounting systems known as one-write or pegboard systems are available that save time and eliminate some copying errors. These systems enable an employee simultaneously

Payroll Taxes and Employee Benefits

	Current period
Payroll taxes	
Federal retirement	$
Federal unemployment	
State unemployment	———
Total payroll taxes	———
Social insurance	
Nonunion insurance	
Nonunion pension	
State health insurance	
Union insurance	
Union pension	
Workmen's compensation insurance	———
Total social insurance	———
Personnel department	
Salaries and wages	
Employee benefits	
Total payroll and related expenses	———
Employee relations	
Medical expenses	
Miscellaneous	———
Total other expenses	———
Total payroll taxes and employee benefits	
Charged to	———
Rooms	$
Food and beverage	
Casino	
Telephone	
Garage–parking	
Golf course	
Golf pro shop	
Guest laundry	
Swimming pool–cabanas–baths	
Tennis	
Other operated departments	
Administrative and general expense	
Marketing	
Guest entertainment	
Property operation, maintenance, and energy costs	
House laundry	
Print shop	———
Total	———

Figure 10.9. Payroll taxes and employee benefits account.

Source: Hotel Association of New York City. "Uniform System of Accounts for Hotels," Seventh Revised Edition, p. 89 (Oct. 1976).

- Write the payroll check
- Make the entry in the payroll journal
- Post the employee's subsidiary ledger

This is done by designing the check, the payroll journal, and the subsidiary ledgers so that their information columns all coincide. The check, the ledger, and the journal have holes on their left-hand margin and are aligned by inserting these holes into the pegs of a pegboard supplied with the system. Carbon paper or NCR paper is used to transfer information written on the check to the employee ledger and from the ledger to the payroll journal.

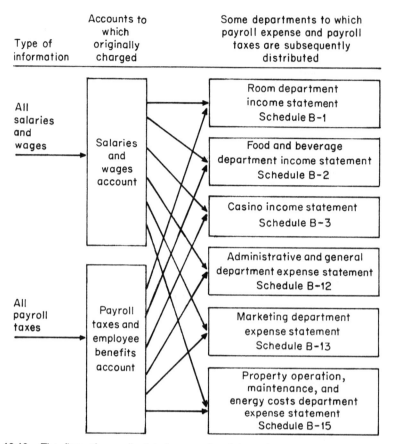

Figure 10.10. The flow of payroll-related accounting information under the uniform system of accounts.

This represents a considerable saving of an employee's time, which would otherwise be spent in copying the information twice. It also eliminates the errors that might be committed in these two copying steps. A typical pegboard system is pictured in Figure 10.11.

A computerized payroll system makes all payroll calculations, prints out employees' checks, prints payroll tax checks to the government, and updates the general ledger and employees' subsidiary ledgers automatically. It also prints out all required government reporting forms. It can do this because it contains the following information in its memory:

- A list of salaried employees and their salary amounts
- The hourly rate and overtime rate of wage earning employees
- All required and voluntary deductions
- Employee payroll tax rates
- The department to which each employee's salary is to be charged

Only the hours worked by each employee and any changes in employee salaries, wages, or deductions need to be entered in the computer before it prints out all required payroll documents.

Some computerized payroll systems, called after-the-fact payroll systems, are not programmed to print checks or to calculate deductions and net pay amount. All payroll information must be calculated manually and entered into the computer. The computer system will then prepare a payroll journal and

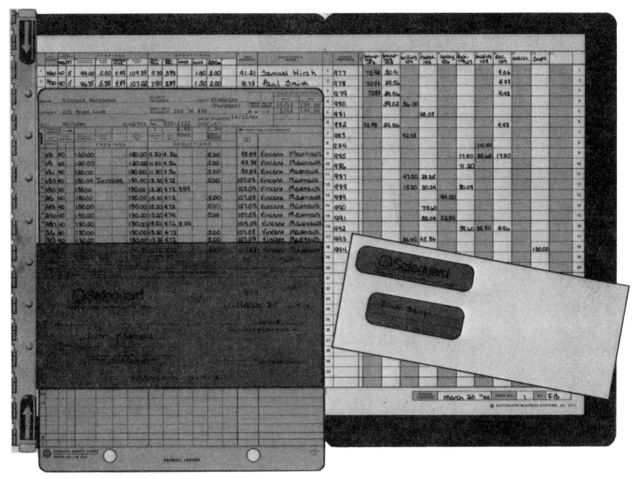

Figure 10.11. Pegboard payroll system.

individual employee subsidiary ledgers and will print out the necessary information for preparing government payroll tax reports. Some after-the-fact systems will also print out all government reports in the proper format and will print W-2 and W-3 forms at year end.

IMPACT OF THE WAGE–HOUR LAW ON PAYROLL ACCOUNTING

Commonly known as the wage–hour law, the Fair Labor Standard Act was passed by Congress in 1938. It was not made applicable to hotels and restaurants until 1967, when food and beverage establishments having sales of at least $250,000 were brought under the Act. Effective December 31, 1981, this limit has been increased to $362,000.

The wage–hour law is a complicated and intricate act including more than 20 amendments or additions. Its impact on the hospitality industry is felt mainly through the following provisions:

- It establishes the tip credit
- It establishes a minimum hourly wage
- It establishes (as of this writing) the minimum overtime pay rate as one

and one half times the basic hourly rate and specifies that any hours over 40 worked during a week or over 8 during any day must be paid at the overtime rate. It also provides tests to determine which employees are exempt from the minimum wage and minimum overtime rate
- It defines employer recordkeeping requirements

We have already discussed the effect of overtime and overtime rates on payroll accounting. In this section we explain the tip credit and its relationship to the minimum wage, and briefly review how properly maintained payroll records aid in complying with the recordkeeping requirements of the Act.

The Tip Credit

The tip credit, which has great impact on the hospitality industry because of its large number of tip earning employees, was instituted by The Fair Labor Standard Act on January 1, 1980. As of this writing this provision of the Act allows an employer to consider, as part of the employee's minimum wage, tips received and kept by an employee, up to an amount equal to 40% of the minimum hourly wage, which the Act establishes at \$3.35/hour. Thus, an employer may apply up to \$1.34/hour (40% $\times$ \$3.35) of an employee's tip income against the employer's minimum wage payment requirement. Employees may be paid an hourly wage as low as \$2.01 (3.35 − \$1.34) if they actually earn and keep tips equivalent to at least \$1.34/hour. The total of tips plus 60% of wages earned must never be less than the minimum wage. Tips used by an employer to meet minimum wage payment requirements are called "tips deemed wages."

Although the tip credit provision is quite clear in its intent, it has secondary implications with regard to payroll accounting procedures and related recordkeeping requirements. These requirements of the wage–hour law are rather far ranging. The most pertinent requirements for a hospitality firm are that records in the following areas be maintained accurately for each employee and preserved by an employer for at least two years (and in some cases three years):

- Actual time worked
- Overtime paid
- Employees compensated with board, lodging, or other facility
- Employees exempt from the law
- Tipped employees

In order to avoid violating tip credit provisions, separate records of wages, tips deemed wages, and tips must also be maintained. This separation is made most easily on the payroll journal and employee subsidiary ledgers by adding additional columns for tips and tips deemed wages, thus allowing ready verification of the fact that the minimum wage requirement has been met. The separate recording in the payroll journal and employee subsidiary ledgers of wages, tips deemed wages, and tips also facilitates compliance with payroll tax reporting requirements for tips, which, as we shall see in the following section, are different than those for salaries and wages.

REPORTING TIP INCOME

Not only do tips constitute a significant form of remuneration in the hospitality industry, but they also entail more complex IRS reporting requirements.

Form **4070** (Rev. March 1975) Department of the Treasury Internal Revenue Service	**Employee's Report of Tips to Employer**	**Social Security Number**
Employee's name and address		Tips received directly from customers . $
Employer's name and address		Tips received on charge receipts . . $
Month or shorter period in which tips were received from , 19 , to , 19		Total tips . $
Signature		Date

Figure 10.12. IRS Form 4070—Employee's Report of Tips to Employer.

Employee's Daily Record of Tips

Employer's name

Month		Year

Date	Tips received directly from customers	Tips received on charge receipts
1	$	$
2		
3		
4		
5		
6		
7		
8		
9		
10		
11		
12		
13		
14		
15		
16		
Sub- totals	$	$

(Continued on back) Form **4070A**   (Rev. 3–75)

Figure 10.13 Form 4070A—Employee's Daily Record of Tips.

These requirements have been complicated even more by the Tax Equity and Fiscal Responsibility Act (TEFRA) of 1982.

All employees who earn $20 or more per month in tips while working for one employer must report these tips to their employer by the tenth day of the following month on IRS form 4070—Employee's Report of Tips to Employer—shown in Figure 10.12. A subsidiary form, 4070A, is used by an employee to record daily tip income, but is not submitted to the employer (Figure 10.13).

Employers must know the amount of tips earned by each employee because they are required by the IRS to deduct the employee's FICA tax and income tax withholding for these tips from the employee's wages. If the employee's gross wages are insufficient to cover all required tax deductions, the employer must report this undeducted amount to the IRS at year end. The employer is not liable for FICA tax on these tips unless they are also deemed wages and the employer is given credit for these tips as part of the minimum wage. The employer must deduct both the employee's and employer's FICA tax and the employee's income tax withholding from tips deemed wages. This apparently complex situation is clarified by the following:

	Reported tips deemed wages	Reported tips not deemed wages
Employee FICA tax and withheld income tax deduction required	Yes	Yes
Employer liable for FICA tax	Yes	No

The employee's FICA tax must be deducted from an employee's pay up to the point when the total of wages plus tips deemed wages and tips not deemed wages reaches the maximum earnings limit subject to the FICA tax during a year ($39,600 in 1985). An employer is liable for its FICA tax until the employee's wages plus tips deemed wages (excluding tips not deemed wages) reaches the maximum earnings limit subject to the FICA tax.

As suggested previously, separate records must be maintained for wages, tips deemed wages, and tips not deemed wages in order to determine when each of these earnings limits is reached.

New Tip-Reporting Requirement in TEFRA

An additional tip-reporting requirement incorporated in TEFRA applies to establishments that serve food or beverage, employ 10 or more employees, and are not fast-food or carry-out establishments. Every employer falling under the Act and whose employees, as a group, are not reporting tips equivalent to at least 8% of the establishment's gross receipts must allocate additional tip income to its employees in order to achieve this required 8% level.

These allocated tips are called imputed tips. Allocation may be made by negotiation with each employee, according to hours worked, or by a direct method such as the server's name on checks or receipts. No withheld income tax or FICA tax must be deducted from an employee's wages for imputed tips, nor is an employer liable for its FICA tax on imputed tips—the employer must merely report them to the IRS at year end. Employees, of course, must include these imputed tips as part of their earnings on their personal income tax return at year end.

A certain amount of relief from the 8% requirement may be available on an individual establishment basis if an employer believes that tips actually received are less than 8% of gross sales. In this case, the employer may request from the IRS a reduction to the actual percentage, but never less than 5%. The merits of each individual request determine whether or not it is granted.

Since tip-earning employees will now pay higher taxes, they will in turn bring pressure to bear on their employers for higher wages. This will tend to raise personnel costs in the hospitality industry as a whole.

CONTROLLING SALARIES AND WAGES EXPENSE

Because salaries and wages are such a significant part of hospitality industry expenses it is of primary importance to control them effectively. A twofold approach to this problem is the most effective and consists of (1) adequate planning and (2) implementation of certain measures, called internal control procedures, to minimize the possibility of willful or involuntary errors in executing payroll functions.

Adequate planning of personnel needs is important because it avoids waste through overstaffing. This is accomplished by defining job tasks and employee productivity, and by preparing estimates of future sales.

Internal control procedures involve the separation of responsibility for the following payroll functions:

- Control of personnel files
- Preparation of the payroll
- Paying employees
- Recording payroll information
- Reconciling the payroll bank account

By dividing responsibility for these functions among different employees, the probability of discovering errors or fraud increases since the employees involved in the payroll function will be reviewing each other's work. Also, certain established procedures may be used to increase internal control:

- Require two signatures on important documents such as checks or when making changes in personnel file documents
- Use card punch time clocks to help assure that the correct time is entered on the card
- Rotate payroll personnel. Rotated personnel have a better chance to discover errors previously undetected
- Require a supervisor's written authorization of overtime hours

In addition, properly designed management reports enable management to detect unusual changes in a payroll-related account. Showing payroll-related accounts in as much detail as possible facilitates the detection of small changes in accounting balances. Similarly, showing the percentage relationship of the various payroll expenses to sales or to some other logical standard of reference facilitates detection of small changes in amounts. Showing comparison amounts for previous periods also makes unusual variations stand out.

However, even the most elaborately designed internal control system can be overcome with time if there is collusion among employees. Frequent management review of payroll functions is therefore necessary. This review should not only determine that current internal control procedures are being carried out effectively but should also include a review of the procedures themselves in case changes in the accounting system may have made some procedures obsolete.

QUESTIONS

1. On the average, what percentage of every revenue dollar was used to pay salaries and wages and related expenses in the hospitality industry during 1981?
2. What are three types of deductions an employer may make from employees' earnings?
3. What taxes must an employer pay on the earnings of its employees? Exclude workers' compensation insurance.
4. How are deductions from an employee's pay recorded on the books of the employer? How are the employer's payroll taxes recorded on the employer's books?
5. What is the difference between an employee and an independent contractor? Describe the differences in the procedure involved in paying each.
6. What is the function of the following IRS forms?
   (a) W-4
   (b) W-2 and W-3
   (c) 941
   (d) 940
7. How often must an employer file form 941? form 940? How often must an employer pay FICA taxes and withheld income taxes to the federal government? federal unemployment taxes?
8. What payroll functions should not be performed by the same person in order to maximize internal control?
9. Besides internal control procedures, what other procedures are there for controlling payroll and related expenses?
10. When should payroll and related expenses be accrued? When and why should the accrual entry be reversed?
11. What is the tip credit? What is the maximum amount of the tip credit?
12. What law governs overtime hours, the overtime rate, and the tip credit?
13. What are imputed tips? What type of employers must report imputed tips?
14. What act requires an employer to report imputed tips and how is the amount of imputed tips determined?
15. Must an employer pay FICA tax on reported tips that are not deemed wages? on imputed tips? on tips deemed wages?

EXERCISES

1. The Welcome Home Hotel paid John Wilson for the week ended August 10, 1983, as follows:
   - Gross salary, $1,500.
   - Federal income tax withheld, $403.
   - State income tax withheld, $75.
   - Weekly deduction for savings account, $60.
   - Deduction for medical insurance with Helpful Medical Co., $50.
   - Cumulative gross earnings as of August 3, 1983, $35,000.
   - FICA rate for 1983 on maximum earnings (see Table 10.1), 6.7%.
   - State unemployment tax base rate on maximum earnings of $7,000, 2.7%.
   - Federal unemployment tax rate is 3.5%, less the state unemployment tax base rate.
   - Ignore workers' compensation insurance.
   (a) Based on the specific deduction amounts and payroll tax rates indicated above, as well as any additional information given, show the journal entry or entries required to record John Wilson's pay and the hotel's payroll tax obligations. Round amounts to nearest dollar.

(b) What payroll record would indicate to the hotel the amount of John Wilson's cumulative earnings to date?

2. The Gosipol Restaurant, an elegant table restaurant, has more than 10 tip-earning employees. It pays its servers more than the minimum wage and in addition allows them to keep all reported tips. B. Crawford's payroll information as well as all pertinent tax rate information is provided below:
   - Gross weekly wage, $300.
   - Reported tips for September 1983, $1,000. Assume no tips are deemed wages. If you were to look up the required withheld income tax for B. Crawford's gross pay and exemptions in the appropriate IRS withholding table, you would find that the additional amount to be withheld on $1,000 of remuneration, if taxable, is $68.
   - B. Crawford is married and has three dependents. Obtain withheld income tax amount from Figure 10.2.
   - Authorized weekly deduction for health insurance with the Helpful Medical Insurance Co., $25.
   - State income tax withholding rate, 5%. Tips are subject to state income tax.
   - Cumulative gross earnings to August 31, 1983, including wages and reported tips, $40,000.
   - Cumulative gross wages only, earned to October 2, 1983, $12,000.
   - FICA tax rate and maximum taxable earnings for 1983 may be obtained from Table 10.1.
   - State unemployment tax base rate, 2.7% on maximum earnings of $7,000.
   - Federal unemployment tax rate is 3.5%, less the state unemployment tax base rate.
   - Ignore workers' compensation insurance.

   (a) Prepare the journal entry that the employer must make to record B. Crawford's pay and the employer's payroll tax liabilities for the week ended October 9, 1983. Round amounts to nearest dollar.

   (b) What payroll record would indicate to the restaurant the amount of B. Crawford's cumulative earnings to date?

   (c) What is the minimum amount of tips that the restaurant must report to the IRS at year end if gross restaurant sales are $3,000,000?

3. The Stamfort Hotel pays its bellhops less than the minimum wage, whenever reported tips are sufficient to allow it to do so. The following wage and tip information is provided concerning John Willing, a hotel bellhop, for the week ended November 21, 1983: Round amounts to nearest dollar.
   - Hours worked during the week, 40 hours (did not work more than 8 hours on any day).
   - Tips earned and reported during the week, $120.
   - Weekly wages paid by his employer correspond to the minimum required by The Fair Labor Standards Act, taking into account tips earned.
   - Tips not deemed wages as per the data stated above.
   - John Willing's cumulative gross earnings (wages plus tips) through November 14, 1983, $30,000
   - FICA tax rate, 6.7% on maximum earnings, per Table 10.1.
   - Withheld income taxes per Figure 10.2. John Willing is married and has two dependents.
   - State unemployment tax base rate is 2.7% on maximum earnings of $7,000.
   - Federal unemployment tax rate is 3.5%, less an exemption for the state unemployment tax base rate.
   - Ignore workers' compensation insurance.

   (a) Calculate John Willing's hourly tip earnings. How much does the Stamfort hotel have to pay him in order to comply with the Fair Labor Standard Act based on John Willing's hourly tip earnings?

   (b) Show the journal entry to record John Willing's wages, tips deemed wages, and payroll taxes, as well as his employer's payroll tax liabilities.

4. The following information is given concerning Cirila Mathews, an airline stewardess apprentice (round amounts to nearest dollar):
   - Hours worked, 60 hours (worked no less than 8 hours on any day).
   - Hourly wage, $4.00.
   - No special agreement was made with her employer concerning her overtime rate.
   - Authorized weekly deduction for union dues, $5.
   - Cumulative earnings to February 7, 1983, $6,000.
   - Withheld income tax information should be obtained from Figure 10.2. Cirila is married and has two dependents.
   - FICA tax rate for 1983 is 6.7% on maximum earnings, per Table 10.1.
   - State unemployment tax base rate on maximum earnings of $7,000, 2.7%.
   - The airline's state unemployment tax experience rate, 2%.
   - Federal unemployment tax rate is 3.5%, less the state unemployment tax base rate.
   - Ignore workers' compensation insurance.
   (a) Calculate the journal entry or entries required to record her pay for the week ended February 14, 1983.
   (b) What payroll record would indicate to her employer the amount of Cirila Mathews' cumulative earnings to date?
5. The Funway Travel Agency's fiscal year ends September 30, 1983, a Friday. The company's payroll cut-off date is Wednesday, September 28, 1983, in order to give the company time to prepare the payroll by Friday, the company's payday. The following information is available concerning the Funway Travel Agency.
   - Average daily gross payroll, $700.
   - Average daily withheld income taxes, $100.
   - FICA tax for 1983 on maximum earnings per Table 10.1, 6.7%.
   - State unemployment tax base rate on maximum earnings of $7,000, 2.7%.
   - Funway Travel Agency's state unemployment tax experience rate, 4%.
   - Federal unemployment tax rate is 3.5%, less the state unemployment tax base rate.
   - No employee had cumulative gross earnings in excess of $6,000.
   - Ignore workers' compensation insurance.
   - Round amounts to nearest dollar.
   (a) Does the Funway Travel Agency need to accrue any payroll or payroll taxes before closing its books on September 30?
   (b) If so, prepare the accrual entry.
   (c) If you feel an accrual entry is necessary, do you also feel a reversing entry is necessary? Explain.

PROBLEMS

1. Based on the following information for the Sleepy Hollow Hotel, perform the following steps. Round amounts to nearest dollar.

Employee	Motel department	Pay rate	Hours worked[a]	Cumulative earnings through Oct. 8, 1983	Married	Dependents	Deductions Save-it-plan	Deductions Safety Medical Co.
C. Gilon	Rooms	$300/wk	40	$35,500	Yes	3	$20	$20
R. Furm	Coffee Shop	4/hr	50	6,820	Yes	1	10	10
A. Bruyere	Coffee Shop	5/hr	45	5,000	Yes	2	10	15

[a]Worked no less than 8 hours on any day.

(a) Prepare and journalize a payroll journal for the week ended October 15, 1983. Use Figure 10.2 to obtain correct withheld income tax amounts. No special agreement concerning the overtime rate was reached with the employees.

The company pays by check and the last payroll check number used was 3672. FICA tax is 6.7% in 1983. See Table 10.1 for maximum earnings subject to FICA tax on 1983.

(b) Prepare subsidiary ledgers for each employee and post to them from the payroll journal, using all required posting steps.

(c) Prepare a general journal and record any payroll-related entries that should be recorded in this journal. The state unemployment tax base rate is 2.7% on maximum earnings of $7,000; the company's state unemployment tax experience rate is 4%; the federal unemployment tax rate is 3.5%, less the state unemployment tax base rate.

(d) Prepare general ledger "T" accounts and post to them from the payroll journal and general journal. Assume beginning balances are zero.

2. Use the following information from the Princely Palate Restaurant to execute the instructions listed below (round amounts to nearest dollar):

Employee	Restaurant department	Pay rate	Hours worked[a]	Cumulative earnings through Nov. 21, 1983	Married	Dependents	Deductions		
							Save-it-plan	Union dues	State income tax
I. Rong	Restaurant	$300/wk	40	$40,600	Yes	5	$25	$0	$15
U. Fine	Kitchen	5/hr.	50	25,000	Yes	4	15	0	15
S. Tate	Kitchen	4/hr.	45	6,800	Yes	2	10	5	9
M. Wether	Restaurant	4/hr.	50	6,500	Yes	2	10	5	10
B. Short	Bar	5/hr.	40	12,000	Yes	3	20	5	10

[a]Worked no less than 8 hours on any day.

(a) Prepare and journalize a payroll journal for the week ended November 28, 1983. Use Figure 10.2 to obtain the correct withheld income tax amounts. No special agreement regarding overtime rates was reached with the employees. The company pays its payroll in cash. FICA tax is 6.7% in 1983. See Table 10.1 for maximum earnings subject to FICA tax in 1983.

(b) Prepare subsidiary ledgers for the first three employees and post to them from the payroll journal using all required posting steps.

(c) Prepare a general journal and record any payroll related entries that should be recorded in this journal. The state unemployment tax base rate is 2.7% on maximum earnings of $7,000. The company's state unemployment tax experience rate is 2%. The federal unemployment tax rate is 3.5%, less the state unemployment tax base rate.

(d) Prepare general ledger "T" accounts and post to them from the payroll journal and general journal. Assume beginning balances are zero.

3. Based on the following information for the week ended October 15, 1983, execute the instructions (a) – (c). Assume that no employee worked less than 8 hours on any day. (Use 1983 FICA tax information from Table 10.1 and income tax withholding information from Figure 10.2.)

Employee's name	William Galt	John Western	Mary Riddle
Department	Rooms	Coffee shop	Coffee Shop
Total hours worked	50	45	40
Hourly rate	$5.00	$6.00	$4.00
Married	Yes	Yes	Yes
Withholding allowances	3	4	2
Union dues	$10.00	$15.00	—
Savings plan	$10.00	$5.00	$5.00
Cumulative year-to-date earnings (1983)	$35,600	$20,000	$6,900
State unemployment tax rate	2.7%	2.7%	2.7%
Federal unemployment tax rate (3.5%−2.7%)	0.8%	0.8%	0.8%

Note: Assume maximum wages subject to FUTA and SUTA are $7,000.

(a) Prepare a weekly payroll journal for the company. The information is for the week ended October 15, 1983. The company pays in cash.

(b) Prepare the journal entry to record salaries and wages expense. In what journal is this entry made?

(c) Prepare the journal entry to record payroll tax expense. In what journal is this entry made?

4. Answer the following questions based on the information given. (Use the 6.7% FICA tax rate and assume none of the employees will have earned the maximum subject to the FICA tax unless otherwise noted.) Round amounts to nearest cents:

(a) John Smith worked 40 regular hours in one week and reported average weekly tips of $50. What is the minimum hourly wage his employer must pay him?

(b) William Martin worked 30 regular hours in a week and reported average weekly tips of $100. What is the minimum hourly wage his employer must pay him?

(c) Mary Zufa worked 30 regular hours in a week. She was paid wages of $75 and reported tips of $80. What amount does her employer have to withhold in employee FICA tax and how much employer's FICA tax is the employer liable for?

(d) Karl Rogan worked 40 regular hours in a week. He earned $80.40 in wages and reported $115.00 in average weekly tips. His employer also imputed tips amounting to $20 (under a negotiated agreement) because reported tips did not amount to 8% of the food and beverage establishment's gross sales. The establishment had more than 10 tip-earning employees and was considered an elegant restaurant. What amount does his employer have to withhold in employee FICA tax and how much employer's FICA tax must the employer pay?

(e) Paul Walters has earned $35,700 in wages and tips not deemed wages (see Table 10.1) in 1983. His employer has paid him $20,100 in wages. If Paul Walters is paid $200 this week for 40 hours of work and reports $180 in tips, how much FICA tax must his employer withhold from Paul's wages and reported tips? Must the employer withhold income tax from Paul's wages and reported tips? How much FICA tax is the employer liable for?

(f) Marlene Johnston has earned $35,700 in wages, tips deemed wages, and tips not deemed wages (see Table 10.1) in 1983. Her employer has paid her $15,000 in wages and she has earned $6,000 in tips deemed wages during the current year. Her employer paid Marlene $85 in wages and she reported $160 in tips during the current week in which she worked 25 hours. How much FICA tax must the employer withhold from Marlene's wages, tips deemed wages, and tips not deemed wages? Must the employer withhold income taxes from Marlene's wages, tips deemed wages, and tips not deemed wages? How much FICA tax is the employer liable for?

(g) Myrtle Fox has earned $6,900 in 1983. She was paid $300 in weekly wages during the current week. Her employer has a state unemployment tax base rate of 2.7% and an experience rate of 4%, payable on the first $7,000 of wages paid. The federal unemployment tax rate is 3.5%, also payable on the first $7,000 of wages paid, less any necessary adjustment for the appropriate state unemployment tax rate. How much state unemployment tax must her employer pay? How much federal unemployment tax? How much unemployment tax must Myrtle pay?

III

Financial Statements

11

The Balance Sheet

Financial statements and other accounting reports are the end-product of the accounting system. As a final product, the financial statements communicate information to hospitality management and to other users, which will serve as a basis upon which to make rational decisions concerning the future of the hospitality firm.

Hospitality management, as well as creditors, investors, and other users of accounting information, are primarily concerned with the analysis and interpretation of the data included in the financial statements. However, before they are ready to understand and use the accounting information effectively, they must be armed with a good understanding of how financial statements are prepared. In achieving this basic accounting understanding, in Part II an in-depth review of how hospitality business transactions are processed through the accounting system was made. This involved identifying the value exchanges, recording them, transferring the recorded entries to a book of final entry (the general ledger), adjusting the account balances at the end of the period by using the financial statement worksheet, and finally preparing the financial statements with the completed worksheet serving as a point of reference.

In Part II we also learned to prepare simple form financial statements. Starting with this chapter, we discuss in greater depth the preparation of formal financial statements. In this chapter we will emphasize the review of the balance sheet. In Chapter 12 we examine the income statement based on the Uniform System of Accounts the Hotels presentation.[1] Finally, Chapter 13 will include an actual set of financial statements from the annual report of La Quinta Motor Inns, Inc. a publicly held company in the hospitality industry.

In addition to the balance sheet and the income statement, a third basic financial statement is required for a complete financial statement presentation: the statement of changes in financial position. We shall explain the basic objectives of this third basic financial statement in Chapter 13, but we do not include an in-depth coverage of it because it is befitting to discuss this topic in more advanced textbooks.

This chapter first explains the main objectives for preparing a formal balance sheet, and then describes the scope and content of a properly classified balance sheet. In doing so, an analysis of the major categories of accounts included in a hospitality industry balance sheet is made. We also explain the statement of retained earnings as a supporting statement to the balance sheet.

The two balance sheet formats, the account form and the report form balance sheets, are then discussed, illustrating the main differences in arranging balance sheet items. The chapter concludes with an illustrative balance sheet as presented in "Uniform System of Accounts for Hotels."[2]

---

[1] Hotel Association of New York City, "Uniform System of Accounts for Hotels," Seventh Revised Edition (Oct. 1976).

[2] *Ibid.*

THE BALANCE SHEET: SCOPE AND OBJECTIVES

The balance sheet is a status report, that is, it reflects the financial position of a company at a point in time. That is why it is sometimes called "statement of financial position." The balance sheet tells the readers what resources are owned by the hospitality firm and where these resources came from. The financial position of the hospitality firm is shown by listing the assets (resources owned by the business), its liabilities (creditors' claims), and the equity of the owners of the firm as of a specific date known as the "balance sheet date."

We have seen how the balance sheet is an expanded version of the fundamental accounting equation, and thus expresses the dual-aspect concept of accounting. It follows that the sum of assets shown on the balance sheet must always equal the sum of liabilities plus owners' equity. Up to this point, we have learned to prepare a simple form balance sheet. This format was acceptable for obtaining a good understanding of a balance sheet, its relationship to the income statement, and the duality aspect of how business transactions always affect the different elements of the balance sheet (i.e., every transaction can be expressed in terms of its balance sheet effect).

However, the main objective for preparing a balance sheet is to provide users with useful and reliable information concerning the financial position of the hospitality firm as of the balance sheet date. In achieving this prime objective, the assets, liabilities, and owners' equity are classified into account categories.

THE CLASSIFIED BALANCE SHEET

There is, indeed, a certain degree of flexibility in classifying assets, liabilities, and owners' equity accounts. Thus, not every hotel, restaurant, airline, or travel agency will make the same balance sheet classifications. Nonetheless, we shall examine an acceptable version of a classified balance sheet for a hospitality firm, keeping in mind that other classifications are equally acceptable. A detailed review of the individual balance sheet categories will be included. (Refer to Figure 11.1 to aid in understanding the following discussion material.)

ASSETS

Assets are resources or properties owned by the hospitality organization and represent future values owned by the business. A more formal definition of assets is included in a fairly recent pronouncement of the Financial Accounting Standards Board (FASB): "Assets are probable future economic benefits obtained or controlled by a particular entity as a result of past transactions or events."[3] The key points included in this definition are

- Probable future economic benefits
- Controlled by the organization
- Resulting from past transactions or events

[3]Financial Accounting Standards Board, *Statement of Financial Accounting Concepts No. 3*, "Elements of Financial Statements of Business Enterprises" (Dec. 1980), Par. 19.

HOSPITALITY SAMPLE FORM CO., INC.
Balance Sheet
December 31, 1987
(in thousands of dollars)

Assets
Current assets
  Cash $ 4,080
  Marketable securites   600
  Accounts receivable, less allowance for
    doubtful accounts of $200   2,060
  Inventories   2,200
  Prepaid expenses   1,300
    Total current assets   10,240
Property and equipment
  Land   16,800
  Buildings   73,000
  Furniture, fixtures, and equipment   20,100
    Total property and equipment   109,900
  Less accumulated depreciation   14,100
    Net property and equipment   95,800
Other assets
  Deferred charges   2,250
  Investments and advances to affiliates   10,200
  Other   600
    Total other assets   13,050

    Total assets $119,090

Liabilities & Shareholders' Equity
Current liabilities
  Current portion of long-term debt $ 3,000
  Accounts payable   1,400
  Income taxes payable   200
  Accrued expenses   1,800
    Total current liabilities   6,400
Long-term liabilities
  Long-term debt, less current installment in-   88,000
    cluded above
  Notes payable due 1990   12,000
    Total long-term liabilities   100,000
Deferred taxes   4,800
Shareholders' equity
  Common stock (par value $0.10 per share)   1,650
  Additional paid-in capital   4,100
  Retained earnings   2,140
    Total shareholders' equity   7,890
    Total liabilities & shareholders' equity $119,090

Figure 11.1. Balance sheet for Hospitality Sample Form Co., Inc.

The first key point of this definition (probably future economic benefits) addresses the issue of reasonable expectation. That is, based on the available evidence we can expect a future benefit to the organization that should eventually result in an increase in cash inflows. The second key element of an asset (control feature) relates to the ability of the firm to obtain the future economic benefit as well as give others access to it. The third key element of an asset (past transactions or events) refers to the fact that the transactions giving rise to the future benefit controlled by the firm have already occurred.

Cost is the proper basis to account for assets on the balance sheet, except when there is convincing evidence that cost cannot be recovered, in which case we use the lower of cost or market (replacement value) following the conservatism concept of accounting.

Classification of Assets

For balance sheet purposes, assets are customarily classified into three general categories: current assets, property and equipment, and other assets. However, we already indicated that there is a high degree of flexibility in practice, both in terms of terminology and presentation of specific asset items, especially in the property and equipment and other assets classifications. We shall examine several acceptable alternative presentations throughout this book.

The asset classifications are listed on the balance sheet in their order of liquidity or expected conversion into cash. Thus, current assets are always listed first since they include the most liquid assets.

CURRENT ASSETS

Current assets consist of cash and other assets that are reasonably expected to be converted into cash or consumed by the hospitality firm within one year from the balance sheet date, the normal operating cycle of the business. The typical current assets of a hospitality firm include cash, marketable securities, receivables (notes and accounts receivable), inventories, and prepaid expenses.

Cash

Since cash is the ultimate measure of liquidity, it is always the first current asset listed on the balance sheet. Cash includes actual currency as well as any type of negotiable instruments that are readily convertible into money. Hence, cash items for an ordinary hotel or restaurant include checking accounts in banks, savings accounts, certificates of deposit, sales drafts signed by credit card customers, and cash on hand (house banks, for example). In all cases we are referring to unrestricted funds, which are funds that can be used at the firm's discretion at any time.

Marketable Securities

Marketable securities are temporary investments that can readily be resold whenever cash is needed by the hospitality organization. Since these short-term investments are intended as a ready source of cash, they are highly liquid, and thus marketable securities are listed on the balance sheet following cash.

Marketable securities include stock investments in other corporations as well as bond investments. FASB Statement No. 12 (1975) requires that marketable securities be shown on the balance sheet at the lower of total cost or total market value. This method of valuation gives recognition to the substantial declines in market value of many equity securities during the early 1970s. Prior to 1975, marketable securities were valued at cost. At the present time, when marketable securities are valued at cost, the market value would also be disclosed in the balance sheet parenthetically, in order to provide relevant information to users of financial statements in evaluating the financial position of the hospitality enterprise.

Accounts Receivable

Accounts receivable represent amounts due from customers of the hospitality organization for services rendered on credit. These accounts are expected to be realized in cash within one year from the balance sheet date, and thus are listed on the balance sheet as current assets.

In a hotel operation there are two principal sets of accounts receivable maintained by the organization: the guest ledger and the city ledger. The guest ledger covers accounts from customers currently registered at the hotel, while the city ledger reflects credit charges by authorized persons or companies who are not registered guests. Both city and guest ledger amounts are combined in the presentation of accounts receivable on the balance sheet.

The amount of accounts receivable is largely dependent on the credit policies of the hospitality firm. It is important to recognize that the faster accounts receivable are converted into cash, the better the financial condition of a company. Moreover, older accounts receivable represent a very difficult management problem. It follows that the establishment of a proper policy covering the extension of credit and the collection of accounts is of utmost importance to a hospitality service company.

Notes Receivable

Short-term notes receivable represent amounts due to the hospitality organization evidenced by a formal written promise to pay the specified amount of money within the normal operating cycle of one year. These notes are usually interest bearing.

Allowance for Doubtful Accounts

Experience has shown that not all notes receivable and accounts receivable can be collected in full. Consequently, we must provide for possible losses on notes receivable and accounts receivable in order to conform to GAAP. Such provision is included as a direct reduction of the receivables on the balance sheet using the account "allowance for doubtful accounts" (see Figure 11.1).

The allowance for doubtful accounts is a contra-asset account since it is shown as a direct reduction of an asset account, notes receivable or accounts receivable.

The amount of the provision for doubtful accounts is based upon historical experience, industry averages, specific appraisal of individual accounts, or other accepted methods. It should represent the portion of accounts and notes receivable estimated to be uncollectible.

Inventories

Inventories consist of merchandise and supplies essential to the conduct of the business. In the hospitality service industry, inventories usually consist of food, beverages, and supplies. As a rule, the hospitality service companies are not inventory intensive, that is, inventories represent a very small fraction of the total assets of the enterprise. Nevertheless, proper inventory control management is an extremely important consideration to many segments of the hospitality industry, especially the food service business, due to the perishable nature of food inventory.

Disclosure of the basis for valuing inventories must be stated either on the face of the balance sheet or in an appended footnote. Following GAAP, inventories are valued at the lower of cost or market. A detailed coverage of methods of determining inventory cost is given in Chapter 15.

Prepaid Expenses

Prepaid expenses represent advance payments made by the hospitality firm for benefits expected to be received within one year from the balance sheet date. Typical expenses subject to prepayment in the hospitality industry include insurance, licenses, property taxes, and rent.

Prepaid expenses are included under current assets because they are expected to be consumed by the business within one year from the balance sheet date. They will not be converted into cash but "if not paid in advance, they would require the use of current assets during the operating cycle."[4] Therefore, prepaid expenses will become expenses when consumed during the next accounting period.

PROPERTY AND EQUIPMENT

Property and equipment comprise long-lived assets (with a useful life in excess of one year) used in the production of revenue. Some common items included under property and equipment in a hospitality company balance sheet are land, building and building improvements, furniture, fixtures, equipment, motor vehicles, and improvements to leased property (leasehold improvements). These assets are usually listed on the balance sheet according to their degree of permanence. However, there is no uniformity in the way hospitality companies do this.

All property and equipment, with the exception of land, have a limited useful life, and thus we allocate the cost of these assets over their estimated useful life in accordance with GAAP. (We have already noted that this allocation process is referred to as depreciation.) The property and equipment are then shown on the balance sheet at net book value, which is cost less accumulated depreciation.

ACCUMULATED DEPRECIATION

The accumulated depreciation represents the total amount of the property and equipment that have been depreciated from the time of purchase to the balance sheet date. It is a contra-asset account, appearing as a deduction of the total cost of the property and equipment on the balance sheet.

OTHER ASSETS

Other items having a probable future economic benefit to the hospitality firm that do not fit the criteria of current assets or property and equipment

[4]American Institute of Certified Public Accountants Committee on Accounting Procedure, Accounting Research and Terminology Bulletins, *Accounting Research Bulletin No. 43,* Final Edition (Sept. 1961), p. 20.

should either be listed separately or grouped under the general category "other assets."

Some examples of other assets in the hospitality industry are deferred charges, cash surrender value of officers' life insurance, long-term investments, long-term receivables, and intangible assets (goodwill, patents, trademarks, franchises).

There is no uniform way to present other assets on the balance sheet. Some hospitality firms may show, for example, investments and advances to affiliates and others as a separate heading following total current assets. (Refer to Figure 11.3, which appears later in the chapter.) Conversely, other firms may include these long-term investments under other assets or as a separate category following property and equipment.

Long-Term Investments

Long-term investments comprise investments in securities of other corporations, which are either (1) not readily marketable, or (2) not intended as a ready source of cash, and include investments in affiliated companies made for control purposes. In such cases, any amounts due from these affiliates for cash advances are combined with the corresponding investment account on the balance sheet.

A common type of long-term investment for control purposes is the establishment of a parent–subsidiary relationship whereby the parent company has the ability to exert influence or legal control over the subsidiary by virtue of owning more than 50% of the outstanding shares of stock of the subsidiary company.

Deferred Charges

Deferred charges (also referred to as deferred expenses) represent long-term prepayments for expenditures that are expected to benefit several future periods. In the hospitality industry we find such items as preopening expenses, organization costs, prepaid financing costs, and prepaid advertising included under deferred charges.

Preopening expenses are those expenditures made prior to the opening of a new hotel, restaurant, or travel agency, and include payroll costs, supplies, and other costs incurred in order to get the facility ready for opening its doors to the public. Since no revenue is earned at such time, all expenditures are capitalized (charged to an asset account). After operations commence, these expenditures will become expenses through the write-off of the asset account (preopening expenses) over its estimated useful life.

Cash Surrender Value of Officers' Life Insurance

The cash surrender value of officers' life insurance refers to the cash value accumulated up to the balance sheet date on the life insurance policies covering the lives of certain officers and other key members of the hospitality organization. Since it is not the company's intention to cancel or surrender the insurance policy in the normal course of business, this long-term future value is shown under other assets on the balance sheet.

Intangible Assets

Intangible assets are assets with no physical existence, possessing rights that are of future value to the hospitality firm. All intangible assets are charged to operations (expensed) through the process of amortization, which involves the systematic recording of periodic charges to operations over the estimated useful life of the respective asset, not to exceed 40 years.[5] Consequently, intangible assets are shown on the balance sheet net of accumulated amortization.

Goodwill, franchises, trademarks, and patents are some examples of intangible assets. Goodwill relates to the excess of the purchase price over the appraised value of net assets (other than goodwill) of a purchased company. Goodwill can be purchased, not built into a business, and thus it can be recorded only in connection with the acquisition of a business. It reflects the combination of intangible factors such as location, management expertise, and reputation, relating to the purchased firm's ability to realize high returns to its owners in the future.

Franchises refer to the legal right granted by an organization to render or produce specific services or products. This right is normally stated in a franchise agreement that defines the geographical area as well as other terms of the franchise relationship. Examples of hospitality businesses that operate as franchises are McDonalds, Burger King, Wendy's, Holiday Inn, and Dunkin Donuts. The cost of obtaining the franchise is shown on the balance sheet net of amortization over the duration of the franchise.

LIABILITIES

Liabilities are outsiders' claims against the company's resources (assets). They represent obligations to creditors of the firm. More formally: "Liabilities are probable future sacrifices of economic benefits arising from present obligations of a particular entity to transfer assets or provide services to other entities in the future as a result of past transactions or events."[6] Three key points are included in the preceding definition:

1. Current duty or responsibility to other entities to be settled through the probable future transfer of assets or providing services.
2. Obligation or future sacrifice of economic benefits.
3. Arising from transactions that have already occurred.

It is evident that the existence of a legally enforceable claim is not a prerequisite for an obligation to be included as a liability as long as the transfer of assets or services is otherwise probable.

Classification of Liabilities

Liabilities are customarily classified into two categories: current liabilities and long-term liabilities. In theory, liabilities should be listed in their probable order of liquidation, that is, those that are expected to be paid first are

[5]American Institute of Certified Public Accountants, *Opinions of the Accounting Principles Board Opinion No. 17,* "Intangible Assets" (Aug. 1970), Par. 29.

[6]Financial Accounting Standards Board, *Statement of Financial Accounting Concepts No. 3,* "Elements of Financial Statements of Business Enterprises" (Dec. 1980), Par. 28.

shown first, those expected to be paid next are shown next, and so on. As a practical matter, however, in many instances there is no particular sequence in which individual current liability and long-term liability items appear in the balance sheet. In all cases current liabilities are shown first.

CURRENT LIABILITIES

"Current liabilities are obligations that are expected to be paid, or settled otherwise, within one year from the balance sheet date, the normal operating cycle. Such obligations normally require the use of current assets or the creation of other current liabilities."[7] Some common current liabilities in the hospitality industry are accounts payable, short-term notes payable, current portion of long-term debt, income taxes payable, accrued expenses, and unearned revenue.

Short-Term Notes Payable

Short-term notes payable are formal written promises made by the hospitality firm to pay money to creditors within one year from the balance sheet date. A note payable may be given to secure an extension of time in which to pay an accounts payable or may arise when the company borrows money from a bank or other financial institution for business use.

Normally, in a bank loan, the bank collects interest when the loan is repaid. However the interest due as of the balance sheet is not shown under notes payable, only the principal due on the note. The interest due, if any, will be shown on a separate line under accrued interest or will be combined with other accrued expenses.

Current Portion of Long-Term Debt

The current portion of long-term debt is the portion of a mortgage or other long-term obligations due to be paid within one year from the balance sheet date. Since it represents an amount owed within one year from the balance sheet date, it is deducted from the total long-term debt and shown as a current liability.

Income Taxes Payable

Income taxes payable comprise the amount of federal and state income taxes still owed to the government as of the balance sheet date.

Accrued Expenses

Accrued expenses represent expenses incurred during the accounting period, but not yet paid or recorded. The typical expenses that are subject to accrual include salaries, interest, and payroll taxes.

Unearned Revenue

Unearned revenue reflects revenues received or billed in advance of the performance of the service. In this case a future service is owed the customer

---

[7]American Institute of Certified Public Accountants, *Accounting Principles Board Statement No. 4,* "Basic Concepts and Accounting Principles Underlying Financial Statements of Business Enterprises" (Oct. 1970), Par. 198.

instead of cash, and thus the hospitality firm is indicating that such services are forthcoming.

Customer deposits received by a hotel as deposits on room reservations represent unearned revenue since the hotel will not recognize these amounts as revenue until actually earned, when the customers receive the service. Similarly, the unearned portion of rentals received or charged to guests will be included with unearned revenue or listed under a separate listing as a current liability.

LONG-TERM LIABILITIES

Long-term liabilities are those obligations due after one year from the balance sheet date. Typical long-term liabilities in the hospitality industry are mortgages payable, bonds payable, and notes payable.

Mortgages Payable

Mortgages payable represent promissory notes secured by a claim against real property, normally land and buildings. It has been a major source of cash traditionally used in financing several segments of the hospitality industry, especially hotels and motels.

As previously stated, any portion of the mortgage due within one year from the balance sheet will be shown as a current liability. Furthermore, additional disclosures of interest rate, maturity date, etc., will be included as a note to the financial statements.

Bonds Payable

Bonds are long-term obligations that normally require seminannual interest payments and that can be issued or sold at par, at a discount (below par), or at a premium (above par) subject to all conditions stated on a bond indenture.

According to APB opinion No. 21, when bonds are sold at a premium, the current carrying value of bonds payable shown on the balance sheet will include the amount of the premium. Likewise, if bonds are sold at a discount, the amount of the discount will be subtracted from bonds payable on the balance sheet. The amount of the bond discount or bond premium will then be amortized (written off) over the life of the bond. The amortization of bond discount will result in an increase of interest expense, whereas the amortization of bond premium will reduce interest expense.

Long-Term Notes Payable

Notes payable included under long-term liabilities represent promissory notes due to be paid over periods extending beyond one year from the balance sheet date.

OTHER LIABILITIES

There are some items that do not clearly fit the criteria to be considered either current or long-term liabilities. Since they typically represent long-term obligations of the hospitality firm arising from the operation of the business, many firms show them on a separate line right after long-term liabilities. Examples of those items, at times referred to as other liabilities, include deferred income taxes, minority interest, and pension obligations.

Deferred taxes represent the timing difference caused by using different accounting methods for tax- and financial-reporting purposes. The most significant timing difference to a hospitality firm relates to the use of an accelerated method of depreciation for tax purposes while using straight-line depreciation for financial statement reporting purposes. This will cause tax expense on the income statement to be higher than taxes actually payable as stated on the tax return form. The difference is called deferred tax. (Deferred taxes will be discussed further in Chapter 14.) Other timing differences include those arising from capitalized interest during the construction period and preopening costs.

A discussion of minority interest and pension obligations is not included in this book, inasmuch as these are topics more befitting advanced texts.

OWNERS' EQUITY

As discussed in Chapter 4, the title used in referring to the owners' equity on the balance sheet depends on the particular legal form of organization used by the hospitality firm. In all cases, however, the owners' equity section of the balance sheet will represent the difference between the total assets and the total liabilities, reflecting the equity interest of the owner(s) of the organization.

We shall focus our attention on the corporate form of legal organization, the predominant legal form of organization in the United States. Hence, we shall review the main items of the shareholders' equity (or stockholders' equity), the term used in referring to the owners' equity of a corporation. Additional coverage of corporation accounting is included in Chapter 17.

Shareholders' equity is the "residual ownership interest in the assets of an entity that remains after deducting its liabilities."[8] It is divided into two basic parts: (1) contributed capital and (2) retained earnings.

CONTRIBUTED-CAPITAL ACCOUNTS

The contributed-capital accounts reflect the shareholders' contributions to the firm through the issuance of capital stock. The contributed-capital accounts include common stock, preferred stock, and additional paid-in capital.

Common Stock

Common stock represents the ownership rights given by a corporation and formalized by the issuance of shares of common stock. If only one type of capital stock is authorized by the corporate charter, it is common stock. Therefore, common shareholders are considered the sole owners of the corporation.

The amount shown on the corporate balance sheet for common stock represents either the par value or the stated value of the issued shares of common stock.

---

[8]Financial Accounting Standards Board, *Statement of Financial Accounting Concepts No. 3,* "Elements of Financial Statements of Business Enterprises" (Dec. 1980), Par. 43.

Preferred Stock

Preferred stock is a special type of stock that some corporations have been given authorization to issue by their board of directors. Preferred shareholders have priority over common shareholders in distribution of assets in the event of liquidation, dividends, and other specified areas.

Additional Paid-In Capital

Additional paid-in capital reflects the amount received from shareholders in excess of the par value or stated value of the issued shares of both common and preferred stock. Traditionally, paid-in additional capital was referred to as capital surplus. But, the use of this term has been discontinued as a result of the misleading implications of the word "surplus."

RETAINED EARNINGS

The amount of retained earnings represents the cumulative net income of the hospitality firm since its formation, net of any amounts paid out to shareholders in the form of dividends. Retained earnings should not be confused with cash or any other asset. The earnings retained by the business may have been invested into the business for many different purposes, including the purchase of new kitchen equipment, expansion (opening new restaurants or hotels), and renovation of hotel rooms.

The importance to users of financial statements of understanding the changes in retained earnings between two balance sheet dates is the major reason why the amount of retained earnings that appears on the balance sheet is usually supplemented by a separate statement of changes in retained earnings.

STATEMENT OF RETAINED EARNINGS

The statement of retained earnings includes the detail of the changes occurring in the retained earnings balance from the beginning to the end of the period. There are two main elements that explain the changes in retained earnings between two balance sheet dates: (1) net income or net loss, and (2) dividends.

The net income or net loss for the period, as shown on the income statement, is added to/or deducted from the beginning balance of retained earnings. From this total, dividends declared during the period are deducted, resulting in the

ABC INNS
Statement of Retained Earnings
For the Year Ended December 31, 1988

Balance, December 31, 1987	$10,000
Add: Net income for the year	6,000
Total	16,000
Less: Dividends	2,000
Balance, December 31, 1988	$14,000

Figure 11.2. Statement of retained earnings for ABC Inns.

ending balance of retained earnings to be shown on the shareholders' equity section of the corporate balance sheet.

From the foregoing it is apparent that retained earnings is the link between the balance sheet and the income statement in that the net income from the income statement is added to the beginning balance of retained earnings in the determination of the ending balance of retained earnings. The resulting amount is shown on the balance sheet net of dividends. An illustrative statement of retained earnings is given in Figure 11.2.

BALANCE SHEET FORMATS

As previously stated, there is a great degree of flexibility in the presentation of individual items on the balance sheet. Yet, at all times the balance sheet is seen as an expression of the fundamental accounting equation (assets = liabilities + owners' equity).

There are two basic balance sheet formats: the account form and the report form. In the account form, the assets are listed on the left-hand side, and the equities (liabilities and owners' equity) are listed on the right-hand side. The illustrative balance sheet included in the Uniform System of Accounts for Hotels (see Figure 11.3) serves as an example of the account form.

The report form of the balance sheet, on the other hand, lists assets at the top of the page and equities below assets. This format is widely used for external reporting purposes. An example of the report form was the balance sheet included as Figure 11.1.

ILLUSTRATIVE BALANCE SHEET: UNIFORM SYSTEM OF ACCOUNTS FOR HOTELS

We now examine the balance sheet presentation based on the seventh revised edition of the Uniform System of Accounts for Hotels, (see Figure 11.3). It is important, however, to recognize that not all hotels or motels need to adhere to this format; on the contrary, each operation's balance sheet should be modified to meet individual requirements. Moreover, the balance sheet of a hotel (or motel) will not differ materially from that of other companies inside or outside the hospitality industry, enabling restaurants, airline companies, and other hospitality organizations to refer to this format in the preparation of their balance sheets.

The following comments will serve to review important items, thereby facilitating the understanding of this balance sheet format in light of what this chapter has covered:

1. There are two comparative balance sheets in this format: the current year and the preceding year balance sheets. The latter is included for comparative purposes.
2 Assets are classified into four general categories: current assets, investments and advances, property and equipment, and other assets.
3. Cash items specifically listed are house banks, demand deposits, time deposits, and certificates of deposit. House banks refers to cash on hand required for normal operations. They are principally cash in cash registers and other change-making funds, better known as "floats."
4. Receivables are gathered under three headings: (a) trade accounts re-

Balance Sheet

Assets

Current Assets	Date	
	19____	19____
Cash	$	$
House banks		
Demand deposits		
Time deposits and certificates of deposit		
Marketable securities		
Receivables		
Accounts receivable—trade		
Notes receivable		
Other		
Total receivables		
Less allowance for doubtful accounts		
Inventories		
Prepaid expenses		
Other current assets		
Total current assets		
Investments and advances		
Affiliates		
Others		
Property and Equipment, at cost		
Land		
Buildings		
Leasehold and leasehold improvements		
Construction in progress		
Furniture and equipment		
Less accumulated depreciation and amortization		
China, glassware, silver, linen, and uniforms		
Other assets		
Security deposits		
Cash surrender value of life insurance, net		
Deferred expenses		
Preopening expenses		
Other		
Total assets	$	$

Liabilities & Shareholders' Equity

Current Liabilities	Date	
	19____	19____
Notes payable	$	$
Accounts payable		
Current maturities on long-term debt		
Unearned income		
Federal and state income taxes		
Accrued liabilities		
Salaries and wages		
Interest		
Taxes other than income		
Other current liabilities		
Total current liabilities		
Long-term debt, less current portion		
Other noncurrent liabilities		
Deferred income taxes		
Minority interest		
Shareholders' equity		
Preferred stock, par value $____		
Authorized ____ shares		
Issued ____ shares		
Common stock, par value $____		
Authorized ____ shares		
Issued ____ shares		
Additional paid-in capital		
Retained earnings		
Less common stock in treasury, at cost		
____ shares 19 ; ____ shares 19		
Total shareholders' equity		
Commitments and contingencies		
Total liabilities and shareholders' equity	$	$

Figure 11.3. Sample balance sheet based on USAH.

Source: Hotel Association of New York, "Uniform System of Accounts for Hotels," Seventh Revised Edition (Oct. 1976), pp. 2–3.

ceivable, (b) notes receivable, and (c) other. Receivables due from officers and employees of the firm are shown separately as other receivables.

5. Investments and advances include a separate listing of (a) investments and amounts due from affiliated or associated companies, and (b) other investments in securities purchased for long-term purposes, along with amounts due that are not currently collectible. The basis for valuation of all investments and advances should be disclosed.

6. Property and equipment items include leasehold and leasehold improvements, construction in progress, and china, glassware, silver, linen, and uniforms. Except for land, all property and equipment is subject to depreciation, amortization, or a special write-off procedure in the case of china, glassware, silver, linen, and uniforms. A detailed review of depreciation, amortization, and the special write-off procedure is included in Chapter 14.

7. Other assets listed separately are security deposits made for telephone, electricity, or other similar services, cash surrender value of life insurance policies (net of loans), and deferred expenses relating to long-term prepayments that will benefit future periods. Because preopening expenses are fairly common deferred expenses incurred prior to opening a hotel or restaurant, a separate listing is provided.

   Intangible assets such as goodwill and franchise fees paid for a hotel or fast-food franchise are also listed under other assets and are amortized over their respective useful lives by writing them off as expenses.

8. Current liabilities consist of accrued expenses, unearned income, current portion of long-term debt, and other payables. Other current liabilities include credit balances in accounts receivable and deposits for reservations received in advance.

9. Long-term liabilities, referred to as long-term debt, represent the portion of the long-term obligations due after one year from the balance sheet date. As noted earlier, the principal forms of long-term debt in the hospitality industry are mortgages, bonds, and notes payable. An appropriate description of the type of long-term debt, the interest rate, maturity date, and other pertinent data is normally disclosed in a note to the financial statements.

10. As indicated earlier in this chapter, other obligations are normally listed separately before shareholders' equity. In this presentation they are minority interest and deferred income taxes arising from timing differences in the recognition of income tax expense for financial statement and tax purposes.

11. Shareholders' equity incorporates the two types of capital stock described before: preferred stock and common stock. Although a separate heading is not included for contributed capital accounts (preferred stock, common stock, and additional paid-in capital), they are all listed before retained earnings.

12. An additional item, treasury stock (common stock in treasury), was deducted from the shareholders' equity section for it represents a contra-equity account. Treasury stock consists of shares of capital stock reacquired by the corporation, but not formally canceled. Further discussion of treasury stock appears in Chapter 17.

13. Commitments and contingencies give recognition to items not included on the balance sheet that are disclosed in the notes to the financial

statements in order to conform to accounting pronouncements, which will be explained in Chapter 19.

QUESTIONS

1. What is the primary purpose of a balance sheet?
2. What is a classified balance sheet? Discuss the significance of account classifications in the preparation of a balance sheet.
3. Explain how the account form of a balance sheet differs from the report form.
4. What are the common categories of assets?
5. What are current assets? Give three examples.
6. What are current liabilities? Give three examples.
7. What is a contra-asset account? How should such accounts be shown on the balance sheet? Give two examples.
8. Distinguish between current and long-term liabilities.
9. What are non-current assets? Give two examples.
10. What is property and equipment? Give four examples.
11. What are intangible assets? Give three examples.
12. Distinguish between common stock and retained earnings.
13. Review the main differences between the owners' equity section of a sole proprietorship and that of a corporation.
14. What are deferred income taxes? Discuss.

EXERCISES

1. Classify the items listed below, using the following classification scheme:

(a) Current assets (CA)	(e) Long-term liabilities (LTL)
(b) Property and equipment (PE)	(f) Owners' equity (OE)
(c) Other assets (OA)	(g) Revenues (R)
(d) Current liabilities (CL)	(h) Expenses (E)

(1) Note payable in three years	(10) Accrued rent
(2) Prepaid licenses	(11) Cash
(3) Beverage inventory	(12) Accounts receivable
(4) Franchise fee revenue	(13) Interest paid
(5) Rent paid	(14) Building
(6) Accumulated depreciation	(15) Goodwill
(7) J.R., capital	(16) Taxes paid
(8) J.R., withdrawals	(17) Rent collected
(9) Salaries payable	(18) Customers' deposits

2. Consider the following account balances of Magnum Inn, as of December 31, 1988:

Accounts payable	$ 2,000	Income taxes payable	$ 100
Accounts receivable	4,000	Food inventory	1,000
Accrued interest payable	200	Furniture and equipment	3,000
Accrued wages	100	Land	5,000
Accumulated depreciation—building	1,000	Mortgages payable (current portion)	100
Accumulated depreciation—furniture and equipment	100	Mortgages payable	14,000
Allowance for doubtful accounts	10	Prepaid Insurance	100
Building	20,000	Retained earnings	?
Cash	1,000	Security deposits	200
Common stock	15,000	Treasury stock	100
Deferred charges	200	Unearned revenue	200

Required:

(a) Determine total current assets.

(b) Determine total current liabilities.

(c) Determine total assets.

(d) Determine the net book value of property and equipment.

(e) Determine total shareholders' equity.

3. Indicate the classification of each of the accounts in column 1 by inserting the correct letter from column 2.

Column 1
(1) Certificates of deposit
(2) Notes receivable
(3) Construction in progress
(4) Preopening expenses
(5) Paid-in additional capital
(6) Preferred stock
(7) Cash surrender value of life insurance
(8) Land
(9) Accumulated depreciation
(10) Bonds payable
(11) Accrued interest payable
(12) Beverage inventory
(13) Interest receivable
(14) Franchise fee
(15) Rent paid in advance
(16) Unearned rent
(17) Allowance for doubtful accounts

Column 2
(a) Property and equipment
(b) Intangible assets
(c) Current assets
(d) Contra-assets
(e) Contributed capital
(f) Current liabilities
(g) Long-term liabilities
(h) Other assets

4. Based on the balance sheet format shown in Figure 11.3, classify the following items as current assets (CA), investments (I), property and equipment (PE), other assets (OA), current liabilities (CL), long-term liabilities (LTL), shareholders' equity (SE), and other (O):

(a) Land
(b) Leasehold improvements
(c) Additional paid-in capital
(d) Preferred stock
(e) Unearned income
(f) Current maturities on long-term debt
(g) Federal income taxes payable
(h) Prepaid expenses
(i) Minority interest
(j) Accrued payroll taxes
(k) Marketable securities
(l) Investments in subsidiaries
(m) Preopening expenses
(n) China, glassware, silver, linen, and uniforms
(o) Accounts payable
(p) Cash
(q) Deferred charges
(r) Inventories

PROBLEMS

1. Prepare a properly classified balance sheet of Baker's Heaven Restaurant, Inc., as of December 31, 1988 using the data given below:

Cash	$ 22,600	Furniture and equipment	$ 30,000
Accounts receivable	25,500	Goodwill	10,000
Marketable securities	20,500	Accumulated depreciation	35,000
Accounts payable	30,000	Allowance for doubtful	
Food inventory	7,500	accounts	1,000
Additional paid-in capital	20,000	Common stock	100,000
Beverage inventory	9,200	Retained earnings, 12/31/87	23,200
Income taxes payable	5,200	Accrued salaries	3,000
Prepaid expenses	5,100	Notes payable (due in 1995)	80,000
Land	50,000	Net income for the year 1988	10,200
Building	120,000	Dividends declared in 1988	7,200

2. Using the balance sheet format of Figure 11.3 and the information provided below, prepare the balance sheet of Bayview Hotels, Inc., as of November 30, 1988, and a statement of retained earnings for the year then ended.

BAYVIEW HOTELS, INC.
Adjusted Trial Balance
November 30, 1988

Debit balances		Credit balances	
Cash	$ 6,000	Accumulated depreciation	$ 6,000
Short-term investments	10,000	Notes payable	
Notes receivable		(short-term)	20,000
(due 1/2/89)	13,000	Accounts payable	8,000
Accounts receivable	4,000	Allowance for doubtful	
Inventories	6,000	accounts	2,000
Prepaid expenses	2,000	Customers' deposits	1,000
Furniture and equipment	40,000	Common stock	30,000
China, glassware, and uniforms	2,000	Additional paid-in capital	2,000
Franchises	6,000	Retained earnings	15,000
Preopening expenses	8,000	Sales	120,000
Treasury stock	9,000		
Departmental expenses	40,000		
General and administrative expenses	56,000		
Interest expense	2,000		
	$204,000		$204,000

Additional Information?
(a) Income taxes for the year ended November 30, 1988 have not been recorded. Income tax rate, 50%.
(b) Dividends declared during the fiscal year 1988 were $5,000. They were already deducted from retained earnings.

3. Selected data on Speedy Air Lines, Inc., for the year ended October 31, 1987, appear below:

Dividends	$ 24,000	Maintenance and operating	
Current maturities of long-term debt	15,300	supplies inventories	$38,000
Accounts payable	160,000	Cash	10,000
Accounts receivable	280,000	Short-term investments	28,000
Deferred income taxes	330,000	Long-term investments	30,000
Long-term debt	157,000	Accrued expenses	60,000
Flight equipment	2,300,000	Unearned transportation revenues	20,000
Ground property and equipment	370,000	Income taxes payable	3,300
Accumulated depreciation	1,200,000	Notes payable (short-term)	80,000
Prepaid expenses	10,500	Additional paid-in capital	90,000
Common stock	60,000	Retained earnings	?
Preferred stock	10,000	Allowance for doubtful accounts	8,000

Required:
(a) Prepare a properly classified balance sheet as of October 31, 1987.
(b) Prepare a statement of retained earnings for the year ended October 31, 1987 (retained earnings balance October 31, 1986, $829,200).

12

The Statement of Income

The statement of income—the second basic financial statement—is a statement of flow, reflecting the results of operations of the hospitality firm for a particular period of time (a month, a quarter, or a year).

The statement of income (also known as the income statement or statement of operations) indicates whether management has achieved its primary objective of securing an acceptable level of earnings for the owners of the hospitality organization. This is done by showing the revenues earned by the firm during a specific accounting period, the expenses associated with earning these revenues, and the resulting net income or net loss for the period reported.

The information concerning profit-oriented activities is of utmost importance to all parties interested in the hospitality firm. Yet, different kinds of information are needed for internal and external purposes. Internally, hospitality management requires the determination of income or loss by department or segment of the business in addition to the performance of the company as a whole. External users, on the other hand, do not require the same amount of detail concerning revenues and expenses, and thus the income statement will not be as elaborate as the report prepared for internal purposes.

As stated in previous chapters, the balance sheet presentation for a hotel, restaurant, club, or any other segment of the hospitality service industries will not differ materially from that of other commercial firms, whether the statement is prepared for internal or external use. However, the income statement presentation involves a different approach, especially if it is prepared for management purposes. For instance, the operations of a hotel might include room rentals, sales of food and beverages, casinos, and entertainment, and therefore it tends to be highly departmentalized. As a result, hotel management must be apprised of the individual performance of all major revenue-producing departments or activities in order to conduct an effective operational analysis as the basis for making intelligent decisions concerning the future of the business. Through the development of the Uniform System of Accounts for Hotels (USAH), this specific need for information has been effectively addressed.

In this chapter we first give a general overview of the statement of income by describing its major components. Moreover, the relationship between the balance sheet and the income statement is reviewed. A clear contrast between a hospitality income statement and that of manufacturing and merchandising firms is also presented.

Then, the chapter examines the USAH, the most comprehensive hospitality industry system. This examination follows a step-by-step approach in discussing the various sections of the long-form income statement based on the seventh revised edition of USAH approved by the American Hotel and Motel

Association and currently considered the acceptable accounting manual for the lodging industry.

A discussion of the USAH short-form income statement, used for external reporting purposes, is also included. This presentation serves as an illustration of an alternative way of reporting the detail of retained earnings on the financial statements, in view of the fact that the income statement is combined with the retained earnings data in the presentation of the statement of income and retained earnings. The remainder of the chapter deals with the accounting treatment and presentation of special items in the income statement.

THE STATEMENT OF INCOME

As already indicated, the statement of income shows the results of hospitality business operations over a period of time. Revenues and expense accounts are set up to describe the various aspects of the firms' operations, with the difference in these accounts representing either net income or net loss.

The heading of an income statement should include the following:

- Name of the hospitality firm
- The title of the statement (statement of income, income statement, or statement of operations)
- Time period covered by the statement

It is important to recognize that the issue date of the statement, e.g., December 31, 1988, is not sufficient, we must also indicate its time period, i.e., whether the statement refers to the month ended December 31, 1988 or the year ended December 31, 1988. A properly headed income statement might include the information "For the Month Ended December 31, 1988."

There are two general formats for income statements: (1) single-step and (2) multistep. With the single-step format, all revenues and gains (such as other income) are first totaled; total expenses and costs are then deducted from total revenues to arrive at the income before income taxes. Finally, income taxes are deducted in determining the amount of net income for the period. In this manner, we arrive at net income in one step. By contrast, the multistep income statement arrives at net income in various steps, providing for more detailed information about operations. Figure 12.1 gives an example of a single-step income statement, normally used for external reporting purposes. Note that income taxes is always the last expense appearing on the income statement because it is based on the amount of income before income taxes.

INCOME STATEMENT COMPONENTS: REVENUES, EXPENSES, GAINS AND LOSSES

The basic components of an income statement are revenues, expenses, gains, and losses. All these elements can be combined in different ways to obtain several measures of enterprise performance. While the resulting net income (or net loss) is the final measure of operating performance, several intermediate components can be utilized to evaluate operating results. Intermediate components in a hotel income statement include such items as operated departmental income and income before fixed charges. Other operations

MONIQUE TRAVEL AGENCY
Income Statement
For the Month Ended December 31, 1987

Revenues		
Commissions		$25,000
Other income		5,000
		30,000
Expenses		
Salaries and wages	$5,000	
Supplies	2,000	
General and administrative	3,500	
Advertising and promotion	1,500	
Interest	1,000	
Depreciation	2,000	
Other	1,000	
		16,000
Income before income taxes		14,000
Income taxes		7,000
Net income		$ 7,000

gains + losses [handwritten annotation]

Figure 12.1. Income statement for Monique Travel Agency.

in the hospitality industry might include gross profit (or gross margin), operating income, income before rent, or occupation costs.

Revenues

Revenues have been defined as the inflows of cash or other properties in exchange for goods and services. A more formal definition of revenues is incorporated in Statement of Financial Accounting Concepts No. 3: "Revenues are inflows or other enhancements of assets of an entity or settlements of its liabilities (or a combination of both) during a period from delivering or producing goods, rendering services, or other activities that constitute the entity's ongoing major or central operations."[1]

Revenue results in an increase in equity attributable to the normal operations of the organization. Generally, revenues encompass all income-producing activities of the hospitality firm resulting from sales of products, services, or commissions. In a restaurant, for example, the major sources of revenue are food and beverage sales. A hotel organization has room sales, food and beverage sales, and casino sales. Other sources of revenue that may apply to segments of the hospitality industry include interest income, franchise fees, management fees, and dividend income.

Recognition of revenue is an area of major concern inasmuch as early recognition of revenue not only has a major effect on the determination of net income, but also produces a corresponding increase in equity. In accordance with the realization concept of accounting (see Chapter 3), revenue is to be recognized at the time it is earned, which generally occurs when goods are sold or services are rendered. Revenue is to be measured by the cash received plus the fair market value of any other asset or assets received.

---

[1]Financial Accounting Standards Board, *Statement of Financial Accounting Concepts No. 3*, "Elements of Financial Statements of Business Enterprises" (Dec. 1980), Par. 63.

Expenses

Expenses are goods or services consumed in the regular operations of a business by virtue of the process of earning revenues. In Statement No. 3, expenses are defined in the following manner: "Expenses are outflows or other using up of assets or incurrences of liabilities (or a combination of both) during a period from delivering or producing goods, rendering services, or carrying out other activities that constitute the entity's ongoing major or central operations."[2]

As we have already seen, the proper matching of expenses against revenues during each accounting period is a crucial objective in the preparation of an income statement. In recognizing expenses, what is important is when the expense is incurred, not when payment is made. We recognize salaries and wages expenses, for instance, in the period the employees actually work for the organization, regardless of when the cash is paid out. The transactions and events that give rise to expenses can take many different forms: cost of goods sold, salaries and wages, rent, interest, depreciation, and so on.

Gains and Losses

Gains are defined in Statement No. 3 as follows: "Gains are increases in equity (net assets) from peripheral or incidental transactions of an entity and from all other transactions and other events and circumstances affecting the entity during a period except those that result from revenues or investments by owners."[3] Losses, on the other hand, "are decreases in equity (net assets) from peripheral or incidental transactions of an entity and from all other transactions and other events and circumstances affecting the entity during a period except those that result from expenses or distributions to owners."[4] Simply stated, gains and losses are increases (or decreases) in equity resulting from transactions not related to the entity's main operations. They are thus considered secondary activities. Examples are gains resulting from changes in foreign exchange rates and losses related to assessments of fines or damages by courts.

RELATIONSHIP OF THE INCOME STATEMENT TO THE BALANCE SHEET

There is a clear relationship between the first two basic financial statements that must be recognized throughout our income statement review. As discussed in Chapter 11, the amount of net income (or net loss) reported on the income statement is added to (or subtracted from) the beginning balance of retained earnings in determining the ending balance of retained earnings shown in the equity section of the balance sheet, net of earnings distributions in the form of dividends. Consequently, the net income reported on the income statement, together with the dividends declared during the period, generally serves to explain the change in retained earnings between balance sheets prepared at the beginning and at the end of the accounting period. To illustrate this relationship, we review the example shown as Figure 12.2. As can be seen from Figure 12.2, the earnings for the year 1987 ($6,000), together with

[2]*Ibid.*, Par. 65.
[3]*Ibid.*, Par. 67.
[4]*Ibid.*, Par. 68.

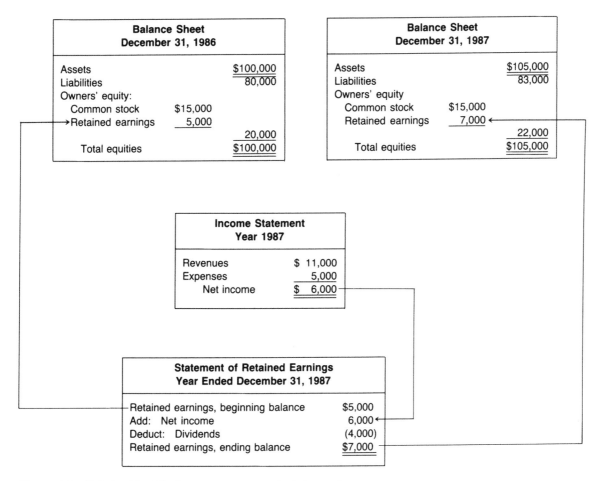

Figure 12.2. Relationship of the income statement to the balance sheet.

the dividends declared during that year ($4,000), explain the change in retained earnings between the beginning (1986) and ending (1987) balance sheets, establishing a clear link between the balance sheet and the income statement.

CONTRAST OF A HOSPITALITY INCOME STATEMENT WITH OTHER COMMERCIAL ENTERPRISES INCOME STATEMENTS

A typical hospitality firm earns revenue by offering various services to the public. A hotel or motel offers accommodation services; a country club offers its members the use of its pool, tennis courts, and other facilities; a restaurant offers its customers a dining experience.

Alternatively, a merchandising or manufacturing firm earns revenue by selling goods. If these firms are unable to sell the goods, they can be inventoried and marketed in the future. Consequently, the most significant expense a typical commercial company incurs is the cost of the merchandise it sells (cost of goods sold or manufactured). Traditionally, the cost of goods sold has been directly deducted from revenue in arriving at the gross profit from sales (often called gross margin).

A summarized format of an income statement for a commercial firm is as follows:

Sales	$xx
Less: Cost of sales	xx
Gross profit	xx
Less: Operating expenses	xx
Income before income taxes	xx
Income taxes	xx
Net income	$xx

This format clearly focuses on the importance of gross profit from sales in the evaluation of the overall profitability of a manufacturing or merchandising firm.

By contrast, hospitality firms' operations are largely departmentalized, denoting the significance of the various services provided to customers. This unique feature of a great number of hospitality firms requires the classification of both revenue and expenses on the income statement according to the different activities of the business. As a result, relating expenses attributable to specific revenue-producing activities becomes an effective management tool in the evaluation of departmental performance. While other commercial firms rely on gross profit from sales as a basic measure of profitability, hospitality companies emphasize the determination of departmental income in the evaluation of operating performance. The basic structure of a hospitality firm income statement is summarized below:

Departmental revenues	$xx
Less: Departmental expenses	xx
Departmental Income	xx
Less: Indirect expenses	xx
Income before income taxes	xx
Income taxes	xx
Net income	$xx

This format places emphasis on the determination of departmental income, from which indirect expenses are deducted to arrive at income before income taxes. The term "indirect expenses "implies that these are expenses not directly related to specific revenue-producing activities or departments. Indirect expenses include both operating and nonoperating items.

Another unique feature of hospitality industry income statements is the great significance of labor costs to the industry. While the cost of sales is normally the major expense for manufacturing and merchandising companies, payroll costs represents the principal expense category for hospitality firms as a result of the labor-intensive nature of the industry. In fact, for many hospitality firms payroll costs are well over one-third of total revenues.

Moreover, fixed expenses (e.g., depreciation and interest) are also considered very important in the evaluation of a hospitality firm's operating results, denoting the capital-intensive nature of the industry. These fixed costs do not vary in direct proportion with changes in sales and are treated as indirect expenses in the formal income statement.

All of the aforementioned operating characteristics of hospitality industry companies have been taken into account in the development of USAH, an all-inclusive format that embraces nearly all the major sources of hospitality service revenues.

THE UNIFORM SYSTEM
OF ACCOUNTS FOR HOTELS:
DEVELOPMENT AND MAIN PURPOSES

The Uniform System of Accounts for Hotels (USAH) was developed in 1923 by the Hotel Association of New York City with the prime objective of providing a uniform classification, organization, and presentation of financial information, thereby creating a "common language" in the reporting of financial statements within the lodging industry. The USAH was approved by the American Motel and Hotel Association and has been updated on several occasions in order to keep it current. The latest revision (seventh edition), published in 1977, included a number of changes needed for the financial statements to conform to new pronouncements of the AICPA and the FASB.

The USAH has served as the guiding light in the formulation of other uniform systems in the hospitality service industries. These systems include, among others, the Uniform System of Accounts for Restaurants, supported by the National Restaurant Association, and the Uniform System of Accounts for Clubs, sponsored by the Club Managers Association. We have selected the USAH for an in-depth review since it incorporates most revenue-producing activities included in all the other systems.

Through the development of a uniform presentation of financial statements, the following objectives are achieved by using a uniform system of accounts:

- Facilitates comparability between financial statements of hospitality firms. It is possible to compare a firm's current performance not only with that of previous years but also with similar operations of the same segment of the industry.
- Enables the efficient flow of managerial information by showing the operating results of each major revenue-producing unit or department, thereby providing a basis for analyzing and evaluating departmental performance.
- Recognizes the need for and importance of a proper system of responsibility accounting. The specific grouping of revenue and expense items permits the evaluation of the individual(s) responsible for a particular unit. (Detailed coverage of responsibility accounting is given in Chapter 18.)
- Provides a convenient and effective accounting system, which can be used by any operation within the applicable segment of the hospitality industry. This includes a standardized format of organizing, classifying, and preparing financial statements.
- Simplifies the development of regional, national, and even worldwide industry statistics in the hospitality industry. These can be utilized as a measure of operating performance by individual firms searching for operational problem areas in need of managerial attention. Currently, two firms, Laventhol and Horwath (L&H) and Pannell, Kerr, Forster & Co. (PKF) prepare annual reports consisting of current statistics of the U.S. lodging industry. The presentation of both firms' industry studies is based on the seventh revised edition of the USAH.

In addition to the industry studies cited above, other annual studies by L&H include "Restaurant Industry Operations Reports," and "Worldwide Lodging Industry Studies."

In sum, the USAH provides a convenient and efficient method of presenting the results of operations of specific segments of the industry. As indicated before, the USAH has become the generally accepted manual for reporting lodging industry operating results. This system is, indeed, an excellent tool that gives high priority to management's need for information upon which to base operating judgments. Further, the USAH is fairly flexible and can be easily adapted to suit the needs of individual operations. It is important to recognize, however, that the USAH is not mandatory.

We now discuss the long-form income statement presentation of the USAH, a format that is best suited for managerial purposes.

CONTENTS OF THE LONG-FORM INCOME STATEMENT—USAH

As previously stated, the long-form income statement based on the USAH is designed for internal management use, in line with the major objectives discussed earlier. It summarizes the results of operations of the hotel in more detail than is contained in the traditional short-form income statement prepared for external purposes. The arrangement of revenue and expense items reported on this format makes possible the effective measurement of all major revenue-producing activities of the hotel operation.

The basic structure of the long-form income statement is shown in Figure 12.3. Section I contains all revenue-producing activities of the hotel. Expenses directly attributable to these revenue-producing departments are charged against the appropriate unit. The determination of departmental income is then made by deducting departmental expenses from departmental revenues. The departmental income serves as a basis on which to evaluate departmental performance.

In Section II undistributed operating expenses are deducted from total departmental income in determining "income before fixed charges," a measure of the overall efficiency of the entire operation. The undistributed operating expenses are incurred for the benefit of the whole organization and therefore are not allocated to specific departments. For instance, the salary of the general manager is assumed to be incurred for the benefit of the entire organization, and not for the benefit of a particular department.

Section III consists of fixed charges deducted in arriving at income before income taxes. These fixed expenses are the capital costs of the hotel inasmuch as they are a function of the cost of the property and thus are beyond the

Section I:	Operated departments	
	Departmental revenue	$xx
	Less: Departmental expenses	xx
	Operated departmental income	xx
Section II:	Less: Undistributed operating expenses	xx
	Income before fixed charges	xx
Section III:	Less: Fixed charges	xx
	Income before income taxes	xx
	Less: Income taxes	xx
	Net income	$xx

Figure 12.3. Basic structure of the long-form income statement.

control of operating management. As a result, fixed expenses are not taken into account in the evaluation of the overall operating performance, which is measured by income before fixed charges. Finally, income taxes are deducted from income before income taxes in determining the net income (or net loss) for the period, commonly referred to as the "bottom line" figure.

Theoretically, many of the indirect costs (undistributed operating expenses and fixed expenses) could be allocated to operated departments. For instance, marketing expenses can be allocated on the basis of departmental revenues. Likewise, heat, light, and power could be apportioned on the basis of space occupied or meter readings. Other basis of apportioning indirect costs to operated departments might be total departmental payroll, number of persons employed in each department, and total department earnings.

Nevertheless, allocation of indirect expenses is not considered a reliable and precise procedure because it is not possible to assign costs to the various operating departments on a logical and accurate basis at all times. As a result, departmental earnings may vary depending on the particular basis of allocation used. Hence, a large number of hotel operations do not allocate indirect costs to operated departments. Instead, they take the position that indirect expenses are incurred on behalf of the business as a whole.

The in-depth review of the long-form income statement following USAH focuses on the analysis of the three major sections and the individual captions of the statement (a complete blank statement is given in Figure 12.4). Also, selected supporting schedules, containing detailed information of various captions summarized on the statement, are examined. Reference to these supporting schedules appears opposite each applicable caption on the long-form income statement.

Section I: Operated Departments

The prime objective of Section I is to segregate all revenues and expenses applicable to each revenue-producing activity of the hotel in order to determine the departmental income (or loss). (This should also serve as a basis for evaluating each department head's performance.) While each major revenue-producing department (or activity) of the operation will be shown on a separate line on the statement, minor revenue-producing departments and other miscellaneous sources are combined into one heading.

In order to facilitate the determination of departmental income, the USAH format has five working columns: (1) net revenue, (2) cost of sales, (3) payroll and related expenses, (4) other expenses, and (5) income or loss.

The net revenue column (1) includes the total revenues derived by each individual unit from sales, net of allowances for rebates and overcharge adjustments. Columns (2), (3), and (4) consist of three summarized expense categories charged to specific departments of the company. Column (5) then represents the resulting departmental income (or loss). Thus, the determination of each department's income (or loss) becomes a fairly simple mechanical calculation, as follows:

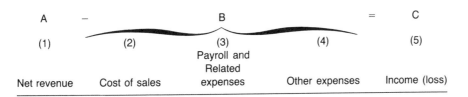

Long Form Statement of Income

Schedule B

		Current period			
	Schedules	Net revenue	Cost of sales	Payroll and related expenses	Other expenses	Income (loss)
Operated departments						
Rooms	B-1	$	$	$	$	$
Food and beverage	B-2					
Casino	B-3					
Telephone	B-4					
Garage–Parking lot	B-5					
Golf course	B-6					
Golf pro shop	B-7					
Guest laundry	B-8					
Swimming pool–cabanas–baths	B-9					
Tennis	B-10					
Other operated departments	B-					
Rentals and other income	B-11	___	___	___	___	___
Total operated departments		$	$	$	$	
Undistributed operating expenses						
Administrative and general expenses	B-12					
Marketing	B-13					
Guest entertainment	B-14					
Property operation, maintenance, and energy costs	B-15					
Total undistributed operating expenses				$	$	
Income before fixed charges	B-16					
Rent, property taxes, and insurance						
Interest	B-16					
Depreciation and amortization						
Income before income taxes and gain or loss on sale of property						
Gain or loss on sale of property	B-16					
Income before income taxes						
Income taxes	B-16					$
Net income						$

Figure 12.4. Schedule B, long form statement of income.

Source: Hotel Association of New York, "Uniform System of Accounts for Hotels," Seventh Revised Edition (Oct. 1976), pp. 16–17.

In other words, departmental income (5) is the excess of departmental revenues (1) over departmental expenses (2, 3, and 4). If departmental expenses exceed departmental revenues, the resulting figure will be a departmental loss. The above relationships can be expressed (as illustrated above) using the equation

$$C = A - B$$

where C is departmental income, B the departmental expenses (cost of sales, payroll and related expenses, and other expenses), and A the departmental net revenue. In the case of a departmental loss (that is, for B greater than A)

$$D = B - A$$

where D is departmental loss (indicated by brackets in the statement).

We now discuss some of the individual units included under operated departments, commencing with the rooms department. Reference is made to the long-form income statement (Figure 12.4) throughout our discussion.

Rooms Department. Rooms revenue is generally the major source of income for a lodging operation, and so it is listed first on the long-form income statement. Schedule B-1 contains additional information concerning the composition of the rooms department heading, which is summarized on the formal statement.

Rooms revenue is classified into transient and permanent, depending on whether or not the guest has established residency in the hotel for an extended period. The net revenue of the rooms department consists of total rooms revenue less allowances given in the form of adjustments for rebates and overcharges.

The expenses directly attributable to the rooms department are broken down in the income statement into two categories: (1) payroll and related expenses and (2) other expenses. Cost of sales does not apply to the rooms department, since room rentals do not involve the sale of goods, only of services. Therefore, the determination of rooms departmental income or loss consists of:

$$\underset{(1)}{\underset{\text{net revenue}}{\text{rooms}}} - \underset{(3 \text{ and } 4)}{\underset{\text{departmental expenses}}{\text{rooms}}} = \underset{(5)}{\underset{\text{departmental income}}{\text{rooms}}}$$

If rooms departmental expenses exceed net revenue, there will be a departmental loss:

$$\underset{(3 \text{ and } 4)}{\underset{\text{departmental expenses}}{\text{rooms}}} - \underset{(1)}{\underset{\text{net revenue}}{\text{rooms}}} = \underset{(5)}{\underset{\text{departmental (loss)}}{\text{rooms}}}$$

Because the rooms department is mainly concerned with service activity, payroll and related expenses representing the cost of staffing the rooms department of the hotel is the major expense category. Not only are salaries and wages included here, but also payroll taxes and employee benefits applicable to employees of the rooms department such as the front office manager, room clerks, maids, housekeepers, doormen, and porters.

Other expenses attributable to the rooms department are grouped together in the income statement and are itemized on departmental schedule B-1. These expenses relate primarily to the materials used in making up the rooms (laundry and cleaning supplies, linen, guest supplies, etc.), travel agent commissions for obtaining room business, and the cost of reservation service.

Food and Beverage Department.   As a result of the close ties between the food and beverage departments, which are generally under the responsibility of one department head, the seventh edition of the USAH recommended one combined heading for food and beverage operations on the income statement. Nonetheless, the food and beverage departmental schedule B-2 (see Figure 12.5) provides the necessary information with respect to revenue and expense categories of each of these departments.

The calculation of food and beverage departmental income entails the deduction of three expense categories (cost of sales, payroll and related expenses, and other expenses) from the net departmental revenue:

$$\begin{array}{ccc} \text{food and beverage} & \text{food and beverage} & \text{food and beverage} \\ \text{departmental income} = & \text{net revenue} & - \text{departmental expenses} \\ (5) & (1) & (2, 3, \text{and } 4) \end{array}$$

Schedule B-2: Food and Beverage

	Current period
Revenue	
Food	$
Beverage	
Total	
Allowances	
Net revenue	
Other income	
Total	
Cost of sales	
Cost of food consumed	
Less: Cost of employees' meals	
Net cost of food sold	
Cost of beverage sold	
Net cost of sales	
Gross profit	
Expenses	
Salaries and wages	
Employee benefits	
Total payroll and related expenses	
Other expenses	
China, glassware, silver, and linen	
Contract cleaning	
Kitchen fuel	
Laundry and dry cleaning	
Licenses	
Music and entertainment	
Operating supplies	
Other operating expenses	
Uniforms	
Total other expenses	
Total expenses	
Departmental income (loss)	$

Figure 12.5.   Schedule B-2, Food and beverage.

Source: Hotel Association of New York, "Uniform System of Accounts," Seventh Revised Edition (Oct. 1976), p. 23.

A departmental loss occurs when food and beverage expenses exceed net revenue.

A major cost in the food and beverage department is cost of sales, representing the raw materials used in the preparation of meals and drinks. As shown by departmental schedule B-2 (Figure 12.5), the calculation of net cost of food sold first requires the deduction of the cost of employee meals from the total cost of food consumed by guests and employees. The cost of employee meals will in turn be charged against the respective departments whose employees are served (it is included as a payroll and related expense).

The combined cost of food and beverage sold is deducted from the total food and beverage net revenue in arriving at the gross profit from the sale of food and beverage (also referred to as gross margin), which is considered an important measure of profitability, insofar as it reflects the earnings available to cover all the other operating costs of the department.

Another significant expense category in the food and beverage department is the payroll and related expenses, that is, the cost of staffing the food and beverage operation: salaries and wages, payroll taxes, and employee benefits provided to cooks, chefs, bartenders, dishwashers, waiters, cashiers, and so on.

Other operating expenses applicable to the food and beverage operation are the cost of items used in serving the guests (china, glassware, silver and linen) and the cost of utility items (cleaning supplies, paper supplies, kitchen fuel, and guest supplies).

Casino Department. Acknowledging the significance of casino operations, one of the fastest growing segments of the lodging industry, the seventh edition of the USAH incorporated a separate line for a casino department on its long-form income statement format.

The calculation of casino departmental income involves the deduction of departmental expenses (payroll and related expenses, and other expenses) from net departmental revenues.

Payroll and related expenses, the major cost of the casino operation, are the salaries and wages, payroll taxes, and employee benefits attributable to employees exclusively engaged in the generation of casino revenues, such as managers, floormen, casino cashiers, hosts, and runners.

A second major group of costs in the casino department (listed under other expenses) relates to complimentary travel, rooms, and food and beverage provided to casino patrons. Other casino operating costs are cleaning expenses, licenses and taxes, commissions, and uniforms.

Telephone Department. Even though the telephone department is listed on the income statement as an income-producing activity, this department has traditionally operated at a loss. The departmental loss results primarily from the very high cost of telephone equipment, which is not compensated by the commissions charged by the hotel for calls made through the switchboard. However as a result of the deregulation of the telephone industry this trend is being reversed. The calculation of the telephone departmental income or loss is made as follows:

$$\begin{matrix} \text{telephone} & & \text{telephone} & & \text{telephone} \\ \text{departmental (loss)} & = & \text{departmental expenses} & - & \text{departmental net revenue} \\ \text{(5)} & & \text{(2, 3, and 4)} & & \text{(1)} \end{matrix}$$

The main source of telephone departmental revenue is derived from the charges made by the hotel for the use of the telephone facilities by guests for local and long distance calls, including commissions and service charges, net of allowances granted for overcharges and rebates.

The telephone cost of sales is also known as cost of calls. The determination of gross profit (loss) from telephone sales entails the deduction of cost of calls from telephone net revenue on departmental schedule B-4. The cost of calls includes amounts paid by the hotel for local and long distance calls, along with the cost of renting or owning the telephone equipment. With the recent trend toward ownership, the amount of depreciation of telephone equipment should become a very significant cost of operating the telephone department.

The remaining categories of telephone operating costs are payroll and related expenses, and other expenses. Payroll and related expenses include the salaries and wages, the payroll taxes, and the benefits of telephone operators, supervisors, and messengers. Other expenses include the cost of uniforms for employees of the telephone department and the cost of printing telephone vouchers and message envelopes.

Other Operated Departments. As stated earlier, the long-form income statement format of the USAH is rather flexible and can be adapted to meet the reporting needs of individual hotel and motel companies. In this regard, other major revenue-producing departments of the operation are listed separately on the income statement, when applicable and refer to departments operated by the hotel, as opposed to similar services operated by others under rental or concession arrangements, for example, garage/parking lot, guest laundry, tennis, barbershop, cigar and newsstand, and gift shop departments.

Other operated departments are treated in the same way as the major departments. The departmental income or loss is determined by deducting the pertinent departmental expenses (cost of sales, payroll and related expenses, and other expenses) from the departmental net revenue. A separate departmental schedule should be prepared for each operated unit or department.

Rentals and Other Income. One of the changes incorporated in the seventh revised edition of the USAH is the expansion of the store rentals heading (not considered in the determination of departmental income in the past) into "rentals and other income." As a result, rentals and other income includes all revenue-producing activities of the hotel not listed as part of a specific operated department: rental income, interest income, dividend income, and the like.

Since rentals and other income is part of the operated-departments section of the long-form income statement, it is taken into consideration in the calculation of total departmental income or loss, but because these revenue sources do not constitute an actual operated department, any related expenses are treated as a direct reduction from the revenue generated. Consequently, the net rentals and other income figure, shown in column 1 of the statement, is carried over to the departmental income column (5), as shown in the following example:

	(1) Net revenue	(2)	(3)	(4)	(5) Income (loss)
Rentals and other income	10,000		no amounts		10,000

Supporting schedule B-11 (see Figure 12.6) shows the major sources of revenue reported as rentals and other income, including rental income received for hotel space used for stores, offices, clubs, and the like (rental commissions and

Schedule B-11:   Rentals and Other Income

	Current period
Space rentals	
Stores	$ _____
Offices	_____
Clubs	_____
Others	_____
Total rentals	_____
Concessions	
Barbershop	_____
Beauty shop	_____
Checkrooms and washrooms	_____
Cigar and newsstand	_____
Fountain and gift shop	_____
Guest laundry	_____
Public stenographer	_____
Restaurant	_____
Swimming pool–cabanas–baths	_____
Transportation	_____
Valet	_____
Total concessions	_____
Commissions	
Auto rentals	_____
Flowers	_____
Garage–parking lot	_____
Photography	_____
Radio and television	_____
Sundries	_____
Taxicabs	_____
Telegraph	_____
Total commissions	_____
Interest income	_____
Vending machines	_____
Cash discounts earned	_____
Salvage	_____
Miscellaneous	_____
Total rentals and other income	$ _____

Figure 12.6. Schedule B-11, rentals and other income.
Source: Hotel Association of New York, "Uniform System of Accounts," Seventh Revised Edition (Oct. 1976), p. 57.

other related expenses are deducted from these captions), and net revenue received from the barbershop, guest laundry, restaurant, and other concessions, for the right granted to outside parties to operate departments that might otherwise be operated by the hotel.

Other items contained under rentals and other income are commissions received from auto rentals, taxicabs, telegraph, and so on; interest income; vending machine income (net of applicable cost of sales); and cash discounts earned for early payment made to vendors.

It is important to recognize that some of the items listed under rentals and other income might not clearly fit the description of operating income. A typical example is interest income, normally included after operating income on income statements prepared for most commercial entities. Though the USAH recommends the inclusion of interest earned on bank deposits, notes receivables, and other sources under rentals and other income, it further recognizes that in certain situations where contractual agreements state that interest income should not be included in operating income "it would be appropriate to report interest income separately, as a line item below Income before fixed charges and income taxes."[5]

Departmental Income (Loss). We have already seen that departmental income or loss is determined by deducting from total departmental net revenue the sum of departmental expenses (cost of sales, payroll and related expenses, and other expenses).

The operated-department income reflects the total income generated by all revenue-producing departments and activities of the operation. The overall profitability of the operation will depend on whether the total contribution of the operated departments covers all other operating costs as well as the fixed expenses of the organization. We shall now examine the second section of the long-form income statement, the undistributed operating expenses.

Section II: Undistributed Operating Expenses

The undistributed operating expenses are considered the overhead expenses of a hotel; that is, they are incurred for the benefit of the overall organization and hence are not allocated to any specific department, since it is not possible or practical to do so.

The undistributed operating expenses include four groupings of expenses: (1) general and administrative, (2) marketing, (3) guest entertainment, and (4) property operation, maintenance, and energy costs. Since all these items represent operating expenses, no amounts will appear under the columns "net revenue" or "cost of sales" on the income statement based on the USAH.

General and Administrative Expenses. General and administrative expenses (schedule B-12) include costs of a general nature that relate to all departments in such a way that they are not assigned to any one department. That is, general and administrative expenses benefit the entire operation and are broken down into two categories on the income statement: "payroll and related expenses" and "other expenses."

Salaries and wages, payroll taxes, and employee benefits associated with the employment of the general manager, accounting office personnel, data processing personnel, and other administrative employees are part of general and administrative payroll and related expenses inasmuch as these expenses provide general benefit to all units. Likewise, departmental schedule B-12 includes detailed information concerning the composition of other expenses, which include professional fees, management fees, travel, general insurance, bad debts, printing, stationery and postage, and dues and subscriptions.

Marketing. Marketing, a new term introduced in the seventh edition of the USAH, encompasses all costs incurred by the organization with the prime objective of obtaining and retaining customers. Included here are the salaries, wages, and other payroll-related expenses associated with employees working toward the marketing effort, namely, sales managers, advertising managers and staff, research analysts, and public relations managers and staff.

On schedule B-13 (see Figure 12.7) the marketing expenses are broken down by the different activities of the marketing function: sales, advertising, merchandising, public relations and publicity, research, fees and commissions,

[5]Hotel Association of New York City, "Uniform System of Accounts for Hotels," Seventh Revised Edition (Oct. 1976), p. 59.

Schedule B-13: MARKETING

	Current period
Sales	
Salaries and wages	$
Employee benefits	
Total payroll and related expenses	
Operating supplies	
Other operating expenses	
Postage and telegrams	
Trade shows	
Travel and entertainment	
Total sales	
Advertising	
Salaries and wages	
Employee benefits	
Total payroll and related expenses	
Exchange (due bills)	
Other operating expenses	
Outdoor	
Print	
Magazines—group and travel	
Magazines—other	
Newspapers	
Production	
Radio and television	
Total advertising	
Merchandising	
Salaries and wages	
Employee benefits	
Total payroll and related expenses	
In-house graphics	
Other selling aids	
Point of sale material	
Total merchandising	
Public relations and publicity	
Salaries and wages	
Employee benefits	
Total payroll and related expenses	
Civic and community projects	
Fees for outside services	
Other operating expenses	
Photography	
Total public relations and publicity	
Research	
Salaries and wages	
Employee benefits	
Total payroll and related expenses	
Guest history	
Other operating expenses	
Outside services	
Total research	
Fees and commissions	
Advertising agency	
Franchise fees	
Hotel representatives	
Marketing fees	
Other operating expenses	
Total fees and commissions	
Other selling and promotion expenses	
Association dues	
Complimentary guests	
Credit card costs—internal	
Direct mail	
Total other selling and promotion expenses	
Total marketing	$

Figure 12.7. Schedule B-13, marketing.

Source: Hotel Association of New York, "Uniform System of Accounts," Seventh Revised Edition. (Oct. 1976), pp. 66–67.

259

and other selling and promotional expenses. In addition to payroll costs, other marketing expenses are aimed at the creation of customers' perception of hotel services. They include travel and entertainment, printing, radio and television fees, and trade show expenses.

Guest Entertainment.   Guest entertainment was added as an undistributed operating expense in the seventh edition of the USAH, recognizing the significance of these costs in the recent past.

Guest entertainment expenses are generally designed to attract business to other major departments. When this is not the case, however, they should not be included as undistributed operating expenses. Instead, the entertainment expenses are part of the food and beverage operation, which is the way these expenses were recorded prior to the completion of the seventh revision of the USAH.

Examples of guest entertainment expenses are the salaries, wages, and other payroll costs of the entertainment director, social director, sports director, and clerical staff. In addition, contract entertainment costs, complimentary rooms, food and beverage supplied to musicians and entertainers, film rentals, games, and the cost of scenery and stage props are also considered guest entertainment costs incurred with the prime objective of attracting business to other departments of the lodging establishment.

Admission charges and minimums intended to cover the cost of musicians and entertainers are normally deducted from the guest entertainment costs in arriving at the net cost of guest entertainment.

Property Operation, Maintenance, and Energy Costs.   Property operation, maintenance and energy costs are expenses associated with the operation and maintenance of the property. They include operation of the heating, refrigeration, air conditioning, and other mechanical systems in the hotel.

Like in the case of other undistributed operating costs, property, operation, maintenance, and energy costs are broken down into payroll costs and other costs. Payroll and related expenses relate to personnel such as the chief engineer and assistants, plumbers, electricians, and elevator mechanics. Other expenses include the cost of materials used in repairing buildings, furniture, fixtures and equipment, painting and decorating supplies, and heating and other utility costs.

Income before Fixed Charges.   Income before fixed charges (traditionally known as house profit), is regarded as the best measure of overall managerial efficiency inasmuch as all revenues and expenses that are under the responsibility and control of operating management are considered in its calculation. That is why bonuses are often based on the amount of income before fixed charges, considered a good way to evaluate managerial performance and operating success.

Income before fixed charges represents the amount of income after deducting the total undistributed operating expenses (sum of payroll and related expenses, and other expenses on the income statement) from total operated-department income. The remaining expenses, not yet recognized, are mainly capital costs. They are unrelated to operating performance, being a function of the cost of the property. As a result, they do not affect the determination of income before fixed charges.

Section III: Fixed Charges

Fixed charges are, in effect, the capital costs of the hospitality organization. By reason of the capital-intensive nature of the hospitality industry (especially the lodging segment), fixed charges represent a very significant expense on the income statement. Almost thirty cents of each revenue dollar is needed to cover fixed costs.

Because fixed expenses are a function of investment and financing decisions made by top management, they are considered nonoperating, noncontrollable costs (not under the direct control of operating management). Thus, they are not taken into consideration in the evaluation of operating performance, as measured by income before fixed charges.

The fixed expenses are rent, property taxes, fire insurance (a function of the value of property), depreciation, amortization, and interest expense. The amount remaining after deducting fixed expenses from income before fixed charges is called income before income taxes (and gain or loss on sale of property, if applicable).

GAIN (OR LOSS) ON SALE OF PROPERTY

When a material gain (or loss) results from the sale of property (land, buildings, or equipment) during the accounting period, a separate heading is shown on the income statement based on the USAH (following the deduction of fixed expenses). If a gain, it is reflected as an addition to income; alternatively, a loss from the sale of property (in brackets) is treated as a reduction from income.

The resulting figure, after accounting for the gain or loss from sale of property as outlined above, is referred to as income before income taxes and includes all revenues earned net of all expenses incurred, except for income taxes, during the accounting period. Finally, the provision for income taxes is calculated on the basis of income before income taxes.

INCOME TAXES

Income taxes, the last expense reported on a corporate income statement, reflects the portion of the corporate earnings paid and/or due to be paid to the government in compliance with the rules and regulations of the IRS and other government agencies responsible for the collection of income taxes. Since federal and state income tax laws have been designed with different objectives in mind than GAAP, it is not unusual that the financial statement treatment of certain transactions will differ from their tax treatment. A typical example is the difference between book and tax depreciation.

In all such cases, there is a need to account for the effects of timing differences between accounting or book income (on the financial statements) and taxable income (on the tax return). This results in deferred income tax, which simply represents the accumulated value of postponed taxes, that is, the total amount of taxes the hospitality firm defers by using tax treatments resulting in lower taxable income than the book income (income before income taxes) shown on the income statement.

In addition, there is a need to segregate on the income statement the amount of income taxes currently payable (current income tax) and the amount deferred (deferred income tax), if applicable. An expanded discussion of deferred income taxes appears in Chapter 14.

For the sake of simplicity, we shall use 50% as the corporate income tax rate in most of the examples and problems throughout this book. However, the actual tax rate as of this writing is 15% on the first $25,000 of earnings subject to taxation, 18% on the next $25,000 of earnings, 30% on the next $25,000 of earnings; 40% on the next $25,000 of earnings, and 46% on earnings in excess of $100,000.

ILLUSTRATIVE INCOME STATEMENT

Figure 12.8 is an example of the long-form income statement (based on the USAH) of Easy Inn for the year ended December 31, 1988. This illustrative statement should prove useful in reviewing the major sections of the long-form income statement outlined in the preceding pages.

Statement of Income and Retained Earnings: An Overview

The USAH short-form income statement, directed to external parties, resembles the single-step format discussed earlier in this chapter other than for the combination of the income statement and the retained earnings statements. Generally, the combination of these two statements is suited for small- and medium-sized hospitality firms. Large lodging corporations normally in-

EASY INN
Statement of Income
For the Year Ended December 31, 1988

	Net revenues	Cost of sales	Payroll and related expenses	Other expenses	Income (loss)
Operated departments					
Rooms	$3,728,168	$ —	$1,051,343	$ 410,099	$2,266,726
Food and beverage	1,423,580	373,864	821,050	153,747	74,919
Telephone	204,136	293,440	40,322	4,695	(134,321)
Rentals and other income	16,116	—	—	—	16,116
Total operated departments	5,372,000	667,304	1,912,715	568,541	2,223,440
Undistributed operating expenses					
Administrative and general expenses			162,863	164,829	
Marketing			48,348	96,696	
Property operation, maintenance and energy costs			186,553	484,947	
Total undistributed operating expenses			397,764	746,472	1,144,236
Income before fixed charges	$5,372,000	$ 667,304	$2,310,479	$1,315,013	1,079,204
Property taxes and insurance				$ 193,392	
Interest				263,020	
Depreciation and amortization				359,924	816,336
Net income					$ 262,868

Figure 12.8. Income statement for Easy Inn.

clude a separate statement of retained earnings and at times also a separate statement of shareholders' equity (to be discussed in Chapter 13).

In looking at the short-form statement of income and retained earnings in Figure 12.9, it is evident that the total revenues and expenses applicable to the major revenue-producing activities of the operation are listed separately under revenues and/or costs and expenses. Similarly, the individual expenses included as "undistributed operating expenses" (administrative and general, marketing, guest entertainment, and property operation, maintenance, and energy costs) are listed separately under the caption "costs and expenses." The same is true of "fixed expenses" (rent, property taxes and insurance, depreciation, and amortization and interest). In addition, the gain or loss on sale of property is reported in the same manner as it was on the long-form income statement, just before income taxes are deducted in the determination of net

Statement of Income and Retained Earnings

	Period Ending	
	19—	19—
Revenues		
Rooms	$	$
Food and beverage		
Casino		
Telephone		
Garage and parking		
Other operating revenues		
Rentals and other income	——	——
Total	——	——
Costs and expenses		
Rooms		
Food and beverage		
Casino		
Telephone		
Garage and parking		
Other operating costs and expenses		
Administrative and general		
Marketing		
Guest entertainment		
Property operation, maintenance, and energy costs		
Rent, property taxes and insurance		
Interest expense		
Depreciation and amortization	——	——
Total	——	——
Income before gain or loss on sale of property and income taxes	——	——
Gain or loss on sale of property		
Income before income taxes	——	——
Income taxes		
Current	——	——
Deferred	——	——
Net income		
Retained earnings at beginning of year		
Less dividends	——	——
Retained earnings at end of year	$	$

Figure 12.9. Short-form statement of income and retained earnings.

Source: Hotel Association of New York, "Uniform System of Accounts," Seventh Revised Edition (Oct. 1976), p. 11.

income. Further, when differences between tax income and book income occur, the breakdown of income taxes into current and deferred portions is shown.

The beginning balance of retained earnings is added to the net income for the period, and from the resulting figure we deduct dividends declared during the period. This figure represents the ending balance of retained earnings shown on the shareholders' equity section of the balance sheet.

Income per common share—commonly referred to as earnings per share (EPS)—is used by present and prospective investors in evaluating management's success in achieving an acceptable return for the owners of the firm. All publicly held companies are required to report the EPS figure on the face of the income statement. The calculation of EPS may be very simple if the company has a simple capital structure (net income divided by the number of common shares outstanding). However, it will be quite difficult for companies with a complex capital structure (with more than one class of stock outstanding and/or common stock equivalents such as convertible bonds, stock options, and warrants). In those cases, a number of adjustments and assumptions are required in compliance with detailed guidelines provided by APB Opinion No. 15 issued in May 1969. The complexities of calculating earnings per share are not covered in this book.

EXTRAORDINARY ITEMS

Gains and losses of an unusual and nonrecurring nature are reported near the bottom of the income statement, net of their income tax effect. In this manner, financial statement users can evaluate the company's performance without taking into consideration extraordinary items that are not expected to happen again.

APB Opinion No. 30 explains the criteria for identifying and reporting extraordinary items. According to the definition included in this opinion, treatment as an extraordinary item is restricted to very rare and unusual occurrences: "Extraordinary items are events and transactions that are distinguished by their unusual nature and by the infrequency of their occurrence."[6] Events that serve as clear examples of extraordinary items are earthquakes, hurricanes, hail storms, or other major casualties causing property damage to lodging establishments, restaurants, or travel service firms. If material, the extraordinary item (net of the corresponding income tax effect) is deducted from income before extraordinary items on the income statement. Additionally, appropriate disclosure of specific details concerning extraordinary items is required. This is normally part of the notes to the financial statements.

PRIOR-PERIOD ADJUSTMENTS

When an item is treated as a correction of earnings applicable to a prior period, an adjustment to the beginning balance of retained earnings is necessary. The prior-period adjustments frequently involve the correction of a material error associated with the financial statements of a prior period.

Prior-period adjustments, which are very rare, are excluded in the deter-

[6]American Institute of Certified Public Accountants, *Accounting Principles Board Opinion No. 30,* "Reporting the Results of Operations" (June 1973), Par. 20.

mination of the current period's net income inasmuch as they do not relate to the business activities of the current period. Instead, an adjustment to the accumulated earnings of prior periods is made through a charge or credit to the opening balance of retained earnings.

Examples of prior-period adjustments include the material understatement of the income tax provision of a prior period and settlements of significant amounts resulting from litigation or similar claims directly related to prior periods.

DISCONTINUED OPERATIONS

According to APB Opinion No. 30, gains and losses from the disposal of a segment of a hospitality business should be reported separately from continued operations on the statement of income. In addition, the results of the discontinued operations of a segment of a hospitality business that has been sold, abandoned, or otherwise disposed of (but still operating), together with the gain or loss on the sale, are shown on the income statement under discontinued operations before extraordinary items.

The phrase "a segment of a business" refers to a portion of the company that represents a major line of business or class of customer. For instance, a food distributor disposes of a division that sells food through a chain of fast-food restaurants while continuing to operate its other division, which sells food wholesale primarily to supermarket chains: "Both divisions are in the business of distribution of food. However, the nature of selling food through fast food outlets is vastly different than that of wholesaling food to supermarket chains. Thus, by having two major classes of customers, the company has two segments of its business."[7] Accordingly, the results of discontinued operations of the chain of fast-food restaurants disposed of, together with the gain or loss on the sale, are reported as a discontinued operation on the statement of income.

There are two primary reasons for segregating the results of continuing operations from those of discontinued operations:

1. To provide useful information needed for evaluating the impact of discontinued operations on the business organization.
2. To enable the financial statement users to base future projections on income from continuing operations.

QUESTIONS

1. What is the main objective of the statement of income?
2. Define (a) revenues, (b) expenses, (c) gains and losses.
3. Distinguish between the single-step format and the multistep format used in the preparation of an income statement.
4. What are the major sources of revenue for (a) a table service restaurant, (b) a fast-food operation, (c) a hotel, (d) a travel agency, (e) an airline company?
5. What is meant by revenue recognition?
6. How are gains and losses shown on the income statement? Give three examples.
7. What are the major differences between a hospitality firm income statement and that of other commercial enterprises?

[7]American Institute of Certified Public Accountants, *Accounting Principles Board Opinion No. 30*, "Accounting Interpretations" (Nov. 1973), Par. 4.

8. Describe four major goals of the Uniform System of Accounts for Hotels.
9. In an income statement based on the USAH (seventh edition), what information is reported in the operated departments section?
10. What are undistributed operating expenses? Give one example of each category of such expenses under the seventh edition of the USAH.
11. What is the significance of income before fixed charges? — *evaluate management*
12. What are fixed charges? List three examples.
13. What is gain (or loss) on sale of property?
14. What is the basic objective of the short-form income statement?
15. What are extraordinary items? Give three examples. *unusual or non recurring*
16. What is earnings per share (EPS)?
17. Describe the main items that explain the change in retained earnings between two periods. *Net income or loss, dividends*
18. Describe the proper treatment of gains and losses from the disposal of a major segment of a hospitality business.
19. What are prior-period adjustments? How do they affect (a) retained earnings *+ or - to open.* and (b) current income? Give two examples. *NO*

occur when an item is treated as a correction

EXERCISES   *applicable to a prior period*

1. Using the following information, prepare the food departmental schedule of Precious Inn for the period ended December 31, 1987:

Revenue	
Coffee shop	$ 70,000
Restaurant	120,000
Banquets	25,000
Other income	5,000
Employee meals	4,000
Cost of food consumed	80,000
Salaries, wages, and related expenses	50,000
China, glassware, silver, and linen	5,000
Licenses	1,000
Laundry and cleaning	700
Printing, stationery, and postage	800
Supplies	1,000
Other expenses	1,200

2. Consider the following operating data of the E&R Restaurant for the month of June 1987:

Food sales	$100,000
Beverage sales	60,000
Cost of food sold	38,000
Cost of beverage sold	15,000
Fire loss	5,000
Other income	3,000
Salaries and wages	40,000
Operating supplies	7,000
Taxes	20,000
Laundry and cleaning	5,000
China, glassware, and uniforms	8,000
Depreciation and amortization	25,000
Interest	12,000
Gain on sale of building	8,000

What were the restaurant's (1) total revenue, (2) total expenses, (3) gains or losses, (4) extraordinary items, and (5) net income in June?

3. Consider the partial information (not all the income statement items are in-

cluded) of IRA Inn from its 1987 income statement based on the USAH (seventh edition):

Room sales	$300,000
Rentals and other income	30,000
Net income	25,000
Income before fixed charges	80,000
Depreciation and amortization	10,000
Rent, property taxes, and insurance	20,000
Total undistributed operating expenses	75,000
Rooms—payroll and related expenses	120,000
Rooms—other expenses	90,000
Food and beverage income	50,000

Based on the foregoing information, answer the following questions:
(a) What is the rooms department income (or loss)?
(b) What is the total operated departments' income (or loss)?
(c) Assuming that the only operated department not listed above was the telephone department, what was its department income (or loss)?
(d) What is the income before income taxes? (Income tax rate is 50%.)

4. Selected accounts appearing in the income statement and balance sheet columns of the financial statement worksheet of All Travel Services for the year ending December 31, 1988 are listed in alphabetical order below:

Accumulated depreciation: building	$ 28,000
Cash	10,000
Commissions earned	230,000
Depreciation and amortization	10,000
Dividends payable (only dividend declared in 1988)	2,000
Interest expense	5,000
Inventories	6,000
Notes payable	30,000
Operating expenses	70,000
Prepaid expenses	6,000
Rental income	10,000
Retained earnings	22,000
Salaries and wages	70,000
Selling expenses	50,000

(a) Prepare a single-step income statement for the year 1988.
(b) Determine the amount of retained earnings to be reported in the balance sheet at the end of the year 1988.

PROBLEMS

1. Consider the following operating data (in thousands of dollars) given in random order for Income Motels, Inc., at November 30, 1987, the end of its fiscal year:

Room rentals	$ 59,000
Utilities	7,000
Rentals of real estate property	2,200
Maintenance and repairs	5,800
Loss on settlement of lawsuit	2,000
Food sales	20,000
Beverage sales	11,500
Direct operating expenses: motels	16,200
Direct operating expenses: restaurants	24,700
Telephone revenue	24,100
General and administrative expenses	20,000
Cost of sales: telephone	17,700

Interest expense	8,400
Depreciation and amortization	6,400
Other income	7,000
Income taxes	4,700
Licenses and taxes	2,000
Cash dividends	1,000
Gain from property disposition	3,000

(a) Prepare a short-form income statement for the year ending November 30, 1987.

(b) Prepare a statement of retained earnings for the year ending November 30, 1987. (Retained earnings balance November 30, 1986 is $25,000.)

2. The adjusted trial balance of Cherished Restaurant is shown below, with the accounts listed in alphabetical order.

CHERISHED RESTAURANT
Adjusted Trial Balance
December 31, 1988

Accounts payable		$ 23,000
Accounts receivable	$ 30,000	
Accrued interest payable		1,000
Accumulated depreciation		55,000
Administrative and general expenses	85,000	
Building	325,000	
Cash	10,000	
Common stock		150,000
Cost of sales	180,000	
Depreciation expense	15,000	
Food inventory	20,000	
Furniture and equipment	60,000	
Income taxes expense	20,000	
Income taxes payable		20,000
Insurance expense	15,000	
Land	35,000	
Long-term investments	20,000	
Miscellaneous expenses	15,000	
Mortgages payable (current portion $15,000)		160,000
Notes payable (due 1989)		20,000
Prepaid insurance	6,000	
Retained earnings		57,000
Salaries and wages	150,000	
Sales		500,000
	$986,000	$986,000

(a) Prepare a simple-form income statement for the year ended December 31, 1988.

(b) Prepare a statement of retained earnings for the year ended December 31, 1988.

(c) Prepare a classified balance sheet as of December 31, 1988.

3. The following represent the account balances of RF Inn, Inc., for the year ended December 31, 1988:

Accounts receivable—net of allowance for doubtful accounts of $5,000	$ 85,000	Interest income	$ 2,000
		Rooms—other expenses	150,000
Accounts payable	65,000	Rooms—payroll	120,000
Accrued expenses	25,000	Store rentals	3,000
Administrative and general—payroll	30,000	Guest entertainment—other	5,000
Administrative and general—other	60,000	Deferred charges	5,000
Building	800,000	Food and beverage—payroll	130,000
Accumulated depreciation	100,000	Food and beverage—other	112,000

Amortization expense	1,000	Energy costs—payroll	20,000
Common stock—par value $1.00	100,000	Repairs and maintenance—payroll	20,000
Additional paid-in capital	40,000	Mortgages payable due in installments	
Repairs and maintenance—other	10,000	to 2002, installments due in 1989	
Energy costs—other	30,000	$20,000	720,000
Depreciation expense	34,000	Land	150,000
Furniture and equipment	50,000	Income taxes payable	35,000
Cost of sales—food & beverage	200,000	Dividends payable—declared on Dec. 26, 1988	20,000
Cost of sales—telephone	14,000	(Loss) on sale of property	(10,000)
Inventories	70,000	Interest expense	15,000
Prepaid expenses	5,000	Property taxes and insurance	28,000
Food and beverage sales	490,000	Marketing—other	20,000
Cash	25,000	Marketing—payroll	25,000
Room sales	600,000	Telephone—payroll	12,000
Telephone sales	30,000	Telephone—other	9,000

Using the foregoing data, answer the following questions related to the balance sheet and the USAH income statement of RF Inn, Inc., as of and for the year ended December 31, 1988:

(a) Rooms department income (loss)—year 1988.

(b) Rentals and other income—year 1988.

(c) Total operated departments income (loss)—year 1988.

(d) Total undistributed operating expenses—year 1988.

(e) Income before fixed charges—year 1988.

(f) Income before income taxes and gain (or loss) on sale of property—year 1988.

(g) Income before income taxes—year 1988.

(h) Net income for the year 1988 (income tax rate 50%).

(i) Total current assets at December 31, 1988. [List items as they would appear on the balance sheet.]

(j) Total current liabilities as December 31, 1988. [Show individual items as they would appear on the balance sheet.]

(k) Total property and equipment at December 31, 1988.

(l) Total assets at December 31, 1988.

(m) Total retained earnings at December 31, 1988. (Retained earnings at December 31, 1987, $70,000.)

(n) Total shareholders' equity at December 31, 1988.

4. Using the following data for Topper Inn, as of January 31, 1988 (the end of its fiscal year), prepare (1) a statement of income (under USAH) for the year ended January 31, 1988 and (2) a balance sheet as of January 31, 1988.

Accounts receivable—net of		Depreciation	$ 80,000
allowance for doubtful		Prepaid insurance	6,000
accounts of $3,000	$120,000	Land	300,000
Accounts payable	155,000	Building	1,500,000
Administrative and general—payroll	50,000	Furniture and equipment	100,000
Administrative and general—other	97,000	Cash	65,000
Telephone—cost of sales	20,500	Loss on sale of land	30,000
Room sales	780,000	Income tax expense	70,000
Food and beverage sales	550,000	Fire insurance	10,000
Telephone sales	43,000	Real estate taxes	45,000
Advertising and sales promotion—other	50,000	Income taxes payable	14,000
Repairs and maintenance—payroll	40,000	Bonds payable	1,000,000
Repairs and maintenance—other	20,000	Bad debt expense	3,000
Energy costs	40,000	Accrued expenses	55,000
Accumulated depreciation	350,000	Inventories	105,000
Investments	30,000	Common stock—400,000 shares out-	
Store rentals	20,000	standing—$1 par value	400,000
Interest expense	110,000	Dividends payable (representing	
Other income	40,000	the only dividends declared	
Rooms—payroll	150,000	during the year ended	
Rooms—guest supplies	15,000	January 31, 1988)	50,000

Rooms—linen and laundry	50,000	Retained earnings—balance Feb. 1 1987	182,000
Telephone—payroll	28,000	Food and beverage—cost of sales	200,000
Telephone—other	2,500	Food and beverage—payroll	180,000
Guest entertainment—other	2,000	Food and beverage—other	70,000

5. Prepare a statement of income and expense for APB Hotel in accordance with the USAH, based on the following ledger balances for the year ended September 30, 1988.

Heat, light, and power—payroll and related expenses	$ 22,000	Fire insurance	$ 2,400
Garage/parking lot—other expenses	400	Marketing—payroll and related expenses	1,000
Telephone—net sales	31,500	Repairs and maintenance—other expenses	42,100
Repairs and maintenance—payroll and related expenses	11,300	Store rentals	18,000
Property taxes	96,500	Rooms—payroll and related expenses	214,000
Room sales	927,000	Depreciation expense	138,000
Telephone—cost of sales	43,000	Food—other expenses	44,000
Garage/parking lot—payroll and related expenses	600	Telephone—payroll and related expenses	14,000
Administrative and general—other expenses	105,000	Interest expense	67,000
Garage/parking lot—cost of sales	28,000	Beverage—payroll and related expenses	40,900
Other income	24,150	Telephone—other expenses	1,000
Food—payroll and related expenses	322,000	Marketing—other expenses	45,000
Beverage—net sales	209,200	Food sales	734,150
Heat, light, and power—other expenses	74,300	Provision for income taxes	50%
Beverage—cost of sales	64,000	Administrative and general—payroll and related expenses	117,000
Rooms—other expenses	79,000	Garage/parking lot, net sales	32,100
		Food—cost of sales	313,000
		Beverage—other expenses	9,600

13

Financial Statements of a Major Hospitality Firm

In the preceding two chapters we completed an in-depth review of two basic financial statements of hospitality entities: the balance sheet and the income statement. Throughout our discussion we emphasized the major objective of financial statements, that of communicating information to management and other interested parties on the hospitality firm's financial condition and the overall results of its activities for a period of time.

Most of the information contained in Chapters 11 and 12 centered around the presentation of fairly simple financial statements. However, the statements of major companies in the hospitality industry have many features other than those illustrated thus far. Consequently, in order to provide the readers with an insight into the financial reporting done by an actual firm in the hospitality industry, we shall examine the financial statements of La Quinta Motor Inns, Inc. (referred to as La Quinta) included in the 1983 annual report to its shareholders.

This chapter first introduces La Quinta, a major hospitality firm, by giving a description of La Quinta's activities and service concept.

We then review the 1983 financial statements of La Quinta. These statements are a part of the company's annual report, which each year is sent to its shareholders. The published annual report includes several other areas besides the financial statements, and these are examined (i.e., auditor's report, letter to shareholders, footnotes), in Chapter 19.

An in-depth look at the balance sheet and the income statement of La Quinta as of May 31, 1983 and for the year then ended is included as part of our overall financial statement review.

During the course of our review, an additional basic financial statement called the statement of changes in financial position (SCFP) is presented. Once we complete the general overview of the statement of changes in financial position, major features of La Quinta's statement of changes in financial position included in the 1983 annual report to shareholders are noted.

Finally, the statement of shareholders' equity of La Quinta included in the 1983 annual report is examined. As we shall see, changes in all the shareholders' equity accounts are explained in such a statement.

It is important to recognize that several pages of explanatory notes (usually in the form of footnotes) accompany the financial statements and are considered an integral part of these statements. They provide detailed information for certain items shown in summary form on the financial statements. A detailed presentation of this topic will appear in Chapter 19. (Reference should be made to La Quinta's notes to the 1983 financial statements in Chapter 19 as deemed appropriate.)

LA QUINTA MOTOR INNS, INC.: BACKGROUND INFORMATION

Introduction

La Quinta Motor Inns, Inc. was incorporated under the laws of Texas, and is headquartered in San Antonio, Texas. It has been among the nation's fastest growing lodging chains, with the number of rooms having roughly doubled (to over 14,000) during the five years ending May 31, 1983.

Service Concept

La Quinta is involved in the development, ownership, operation, or licensing of motor inns, mainly in the Southwest, South, and Midwest.

La Quinta caters to a particular market segment of the lodging industry—the business traveler. In fact, more than 75% of La Quinta's clientele consists of business and corporate executives, and the majority appear to be loyal repeaters.

La Quinta differentiates itself from other motor inns in terms of location, service mix, and price. Prices range between those of luxurious full-service motor inns and budget hotels. Since a company's typical motor inn provides a minimum of public areas (for example, banquet facilities and meeting rooms), La Quinta is able to offer lower rates than those charged for comparable rooms by motor inns with more extensive facilities.

The inns are located conveniently for the business traveler, on or near major traffic arteries. They are usually accessible to airports and are near heavy commercial activity, such as downtown, or office and industrial parks. As a result, the company feels that the selection of sites for its motor inns is one of the major factors in La Quinta's success.

La Quinta inns are simply designed with the intention to provide the guests with clean, quiet, and well-maintained rooms. The properties are usually smaller than those of many competitors (not bigger than 120 to 130 rooms). The efficiency and simplicity of its operations enables La Quinta to charge 15–25% less for its rooms, as mentioned earlier.

Foodservice is provided to La Quinta's customers through free-standing restaurants (operated by several national and regional chains), which are typically adjacent to La Quinta's inns. Generally, La Quinta builds the motor inns next to existing restaurants. When this is not the case, La Quinta builds the restaurant facility and leases it to a restaurant chain, which is responsible for the restaurant's operation, maintenance, taxes, and insurance costs. At May 31, 1983, La Quinta had an ownership interest in 78 such restaurants leased to and operated by third parties.

The individual motor inns are as a rule managed by retired couples, many without previous lodging experience. They attend a formal 12-week training program, including both classroom instruction and on-the-job experience, before they are assigned to their first property. The simple product concept and the streamlined operation help simplify the task of the husband and wife teams, allowing them to direct their attention to the guests.

Regional general managers support the management couples in their tasks. They are formally trained, experienced lodging professionals, who are responsible for the development of management skills of inn managers, as well as for the control of La Quinta's quality standards and earnings goals.

TABLE 13.1. Motor Inns Operated and Licensed by La Quinta on May 31, 1983

	Inns	Rooms
La Quinta Motor Inns		
Owned 100%	51	6,413
Owned 80%	2	242
Owned 61%	1	101
Owned 55%	1	168
Owned 50%	55	6,571
	110	13,495
Rodeway Inns		
Owned 100%	3	293
Owned 67%	1	128
	4	421
Ramada Inn		
Owned 100%	1	141
Total owned and operated	115	14,057
La Quinta Motor Inns licensed		
to others	14	1,832
Total	129	15,889

Source: La Quinta Motor Inns, Inc., Annual Report 1983, p. 13.

Current Property Ownership

The chart adapted from La Quinta's 1983 annual report (see Table 13.1) indicates that as of May 31, 1983, La Quinta's two most significant interests were (1) wholly owned (100% ownership) and (2) 50% owned La Quinta Motor Inns, evidencing the importance of joint ventures in its financing policies. Table 13.1 also shows that in addition to ownerhsip in La Quinta Motor Inns, the company had ownership interests in four Rodeway Inns and one Ramada Inn, and licensed 14 La Quinta Motor Inns to other parties.

FINANCIAL STATEMENTS

The financial statements from La Quinta's 1983 annual report to its shareholders are shown in Figures 13.1–13.4. We highlight major features concerning each of the financial statements in the following sections of this chapter.

Balance Sheet (Figure 13.1)

A. Observe that the financial information is presented for two years (1983 and 1982). The presentation of comparative financial statements facilitates the analysis of the financial position of La Quinta as of May 31, 1983, as compared to the previous year.

B. Note that the statements contain the designation "La Quinta Motor Inns, Inc.: Combined Balance Sheets." The term "combined" used in the title of each statement indicates that La Quinta owns other smaller corporations (subsidiaries) and unincorporated ventures (joint ventures) in which the company has an ownership interest and exercises legal, financial, and operational control.

La Quinta Motor Inns, Inc.
Combined Balance Sheets

	May 31	
	1983	1982
ASSETS		
Current assets:		
Cash	$ 871,000	1,963,000
Short-term cash investments (note 8)	44,182,000	37,210,000
Receivables:		
Trade	2,924,000	2,466,000
Other	3,209,000	3,424,000
Income taxes	2,740,000	—
Prepaid expenses and other	2,183,000	1,964,000
Total current assets	56,109,000	47,027,000
Notes receivables, excluding current installments	9,961,000	6,821,000
Investments, at cost	6,821,000	307,000
Property and equipment, at cost, substantially all pledged (note 2):		
Buildings	232,665,000	179,981,000
Furniture, fixtures and equipment	49,528,000	38,494,000
Land	36,217,000	28,621,000
Leasehold and land improvements	3,155,000	1,726,000
Total property and equipment	321,565,000	248,822,000
Less accumulated depreciation and amortization	45,082,000	34,951,000
Net property and equipment	276,483,000	213,871,000
Motor inns under development, substantially all pledged (notes 2 and 8):		
Construction in process	28,113,000	28,644,000
Short-term cash investments restricted for capital expenditures	17,772,000	20,693,000
Total motor inns under development	45,885,000	49,337,000
Deferred charges and other assets, at cost less applicable amortization	8,942,000	7,007,000
	$404,201,000	324,370,000

Figure 13.1. La Quinta Motor Inns, Inc., combined balance sheets.

C. Short-term cash investments is the most significant current asset shown on La Quinta's balance sheet. These cash investments will be used to meet future costs of specific motor inns under construction.

D. The noncurrent portion of notes receivable is listed following the total current asset section since it is due after one year from the balance sheet date.

E. As is the normal situation for most lodging chains, La Quinta has a substantial investment in land, buildings and equipment. Note the manner in which the contra-asset account accumulated depreciation and amortization is deducted from the total cost of property and equipment in determining the net property and equipment. Also note that substantially all property and equipment has been pledged as collateral for borrowings.

F. Another significant asset in the balance sheet is the motor inns under development (mostly pledged as collateral for loans), serving as evidence of the continuing expansionary trend of La Quinta.

G. In place of the general group of other assets (illustrated in Chapter 11), La Quinta has individual asset categories (notes receivable, investments, motor inns under development, and deferred charges and other assets).

H. Included in deferred charges are the issuance costs related to industrial

	May 31	
current = a year or less	1983	1982
LIABILITIES AND SHAREHOLDERS' EQUITY		
Current liabilities:		
Current installments of long-term debt (note 2)	$ 5,919,000	5,833,000
Accounts payable:		
Trade	2,296,000	2,500,000
Other	7,534,000	8,522,000
Income taxes	—	1,658,000
Accrued expenses:		
Payroll and employee benefits	2,847,000	2,592,000
Interest	2,653,000	451,000
Property taxes and other	2,284,000	2,151,000
Total current liabilities	23,533,000	23,707,000
Long-term debt, excluding current installments (note 2)	243,451,000	189,717,000
Deferred credits, principally income taxes	17,123,000	11,592,000
Partners' capital (note 3)	26,348,000	20,030,000
Shareholders' equity (notes 2 and 5):		
Common stock, par value $.10 per share. Authorized 20,000,000 shares; issued 14,400,136 shares in 1983 and 14,288,032 shares in 1982	1,440,000	1,429,000
Additional paid-in capital	49,982,000	49,027,000
Retained earnings	42,324,000	28,868,000
Total shareholders' equity	93,746,000	79,324,000
Commitments and contingencies (notes 7, 8 and 9)		
	$404,201,000	324,370,000

development revenue bonds, loan fees, and motor inn preopening costs. They are amortized over their estimated useful lives as described in note 1 to the financial statements (see Chapter 19).

I. The current liabilities section includes the portion of the long-term liabilities that is due to be paid within one year from the balance sheet date.

J. The most significant liability category is long-term debt (excluding the current portion). This is a clear indication of the high use of debt financing (known as financial leverage) in relation to equity financing. The specific types of long-term debt instruments are described in note 2.

K. The section of the balance sheet between long-term debt and shareholders' equity is rather complex. It consists of deferred credits (principally income taxes) and partners' capital.

Deferred income taxes, as mentioned in earlier chapters, result from using different accounting methods for tax and financial statement reporting purposes, generating income taxes that are not to be paid currently. Consequently, they are deferred to future periods.

Partners' capital, on the other hand, relates to La Quinta's equity in the net assets of unincorporated joint ventures included in the combined financial statements. Summary financial information on these joint ventures is included in note 3.

L. The shareholders' equity section contains three items: common stock, additional paid-in capital, and retained earnings. As previously noted, common stock together with additional paid-in capital reflect the capital contributed by La Quinta's shareholders. Retained earnings, on the other hand, are the accumulated earnings of La Quinta not distributed to its shareholders in the form of dividends. Additional information on the changes in the shareholders' equity accounts is included in the statement of changes in shareholders' equity (Figure 13.4).

M. No amounts are shown by La Quinta for commitments and contingencies. Instead, they are fully explained in notes 7, 8, and 9, which are included in Chapter 19.

Statement of Earnings (Figure 13.2)

A. The combined statement of earnings of La Quinta is also presented in comparative form for the years ended in 1983, 1982, and 1981. In contrast to the balance sheet, three years of comparative data are required.

La Quinta Motor Inns, Inc.
Combined Statements of Earnings

	Years ended May 31		
	1983	1982	1981
Revenues:			
Motor inn	$108,281,000	98,127,000	79,029,000
Restaurant rental and other	5,097,000	4,529,000	3,736,000
Total revenues	113,378,000	102,656,000	82,765,000
Operating costs and expenses:			
Motor inn direct	53,958,000	47,925,000	38,669,000
Selling, general and administrative	9,286,000	9,673,000	8,114,000
Depreciation and amortization	13,544,000	10,412,000	8,484,000
Total operating costs and expenses	76,788,000	68,010,000	55,267,000
Operating income	36,590,000	34,646,000	27,498,000
Other income (deductions):			
Interest income	10,202,000	7,479,000	2,226,000
Interest on long-term debt	(25,646,000)	(18,921,000)	(14,950,000)
Interest capitalized	4,346,000	3,228,000	2,945,000
Gain on sale of assets, principally motor inns	3,159,000	1,249,000	961,000
Partners' equity in earnings and losses (note 3)	(6,224,000)	(6,117,000)	(4,329,000)
Net other deductions	(14,163,000)	(13,082,000)	(13,147,000)
Earnings before income taxes	22,427,000	21,564,000	14,351,000
Income taxes (note 4)	8,971,000	9,273,000	5,740,000
Net earnings	$ 13,456,000	12,291,000	8,611,000
Earnings per common and common equivalent share	$ .93	.90	.69

Figure 13.2. La Quinta Motor Inns, Inc., combined statements of earnings.

B. La Quinta uses a modified single-step form of income statement. Operating costs and expenses are deducted from operating revenues in arriving at operating income.

C. As a result of concentrating on the sale of rooms, La Quinta's most significant source of revenue and expenses is from motor inns. Restaurant rental and other revenues are mainly related to the leasing of restaurants adjacent to La Quinta Motor Inns to several restaurant chains.

D. Included under operating costs and expenses is depreciation and amortization (principally on property and equipment).

E. Other income (deductions) contains all nonoperating income and costs. As a result of the extensive use of financial leverage, the interest on long-term debt is a significant amount, and shows an increasing trend over the three-year period ending May 31, 1983. Interest income is primarily related to short-term cash investments.

F. Partners' equity in earnings and losses represents the total share in earnings and losses of the unincorporated joint ventures included in the combined income statement.

G. Income taxes (provision for income taxes) represents the expense for federal and state income taxes on La Quinta's corporate income. It is normally shown as the last corporate expense on the income statement and includes both the deferred portion and the currently payable portion of income taxes. As explained in note 4, income taxes include a substantial portion of deferred taxes arising principally from timing differences between the financial reporting and the income tax reporting of depreciation, construction loan interest, preopening costs, loan fees, and gains realized on the sale of motor inns.

H. Earnings per common share is computed by dividing net earnings by the number of common shares and common share equivalents outstanding during the period. It is reported immediately below net earnings on the statement of earnings. As noted in Chapter 11, common share equivalents are outstanding securities that could result in more common shares being issued by the corporation (e.g., employee stock options, convertible debt). As a result, they are only relevant to corporations that possess a complex capital structure, such as La Quinta. For example, La Quinta has a stock option plan that provides for the granting of options to purchase common shares of the company to certain officers and key employees.

Statement of Changes in Financial Position—Overview

Before we examine the contents of La Quinta's statement of changes in financial position, a general overview of this third basic financial statement is presented. As noted earlier, the preparation of this statement is not dealt with in this book.

The statement of changes in financial position, traditionally called funds statement, is designed to provide information about the flow of financial resources during the period. APB Opinion No. 19, issued in 1971, requires that whenever financial statements are published, a statement of changes in financial position covering the same period of time as the income statement shall be included.

The statement of changes in financial position (under the working-capital approach) explains the changes in working capital (excess of current assets over current liabilities) from one accounting period to the next. The cash and working-capital resources of a business are, indeed, important indicators of financial health. Though a much larger amount of working capital is required in industries where it is necessary to carry larger inventories that do not move quickly, hospitality firms cannot operate efficiently without an adequate amount of working capital. By showing where the specific resources of the firm have been obtained (sources of working capital) and how they have been used by management (uses of working capital), the statement provides insights into the financial and investing operations of the hospitality firm, enhancing significantly the reader's understanding of what happened to the business during the year.

The statement of changes in financial position is divided into three parts: (1) sources, (2) uses, and (3) changes in working-capital components (current assets and current liabilities). The sources of working capital are listed in the first section of the statement. They represent ways in which the hospitality company has obtained funds needed to finance the operations during the period. Typical sources of working capital include:

- Working capital provided by operations
- Issuance of long-term obligations (e.g., mortgages, bonds)
- Sale of capital stock (common or preferred)
- Sale of property and equipment (buildings, land, furniture, and fixtures)
- Sale of long-term investments

Reasons accounting for decreases in working capital during the period are listed in the second section of the statement as uses of funds (or working capital). They represent different ways in which the company employed the additional funds acquired during the period. Typical uses of working capital are

- Additions to property and equipment (i.e. land, buildings, furniture, and equipment)
- Repayment (or retirement) of long-term debt
- Dividends
- Purchase of long-term investments

Working capital is treated as a residual item on the statement of changes in financial position prepared under the working-capital approach. If the sources of working capital are higher than the uses, the resulting amount is shown on the statement as an increase in working capital. In contrast, if the uses of working capital exceed the sources, this is indicated as a decrease in working capital on the statement.

The third (and last) section of the statement lists the individual changes in current assets and current liabilities (referred to as working-capital components) during the period.

In addition to the working-capital approach described in the preceding section, a statement of changes in financial position focusing on cash can also be prepared. Such a statement (referred to as a cash flow statement) would show the flow of funds defined as cash, rather than as working capital.

The working capital approach has undoubtedly been more widely used for external reporting purposes than the cash approach. Nevertheless, several proposals are currently under consideration to add a cash focus presentation of a statement of changes in financial position. For instance, the Financial Committee of the American Hotel and Motel Association has issued a proposal for the preparation of a funds statement following the cash flow approach. Additionally, the FASB is currently reviewing a proposal that would require the preparation of a statement of changes in financial position under the cash approach.

Statement of Changes in Financial Position
(Figure 13.3)—La Quinta Motor Inns, Inc.

A. As indicated before, the combined statement of changes in financial position for La Quinta provides a summary of its major financing and investing activities during the period. It was prepared using the working-capital approach, thereby focusing on the net change (increase) in working capital during the period.

B. The first major section of the statement lists the individual sources of working capital. A most important source is the working capital provided by operations, but the most significant source of working capital for La Quinta is long-term borrowings, denoting the use of substantial leverage in financing La Quinta's operations during the period.

C. Other sources of working capital included the sale of common stock, capital contributed by partners, and the sale of long-term assets.

D. The second section of the statement (uses of working capital) shows where the funds were used or invested during the period. One item accounted for most of the total uses of working capital, that is, the additions to property and equipment, and motor inns under development. This is a clear indication of the rapidly growing pace of La Quinta's expansion program.

E. No dividends were paid by La Quinta during the three years ended May 31, 1983. Accordingly, earnings are being reinvested in the company for expansion purposes.

F. Other significant uses of working capital are long-term debt reductions and increases in investments and other long-term assets (e.g., notes receivable, deferred charges).

G. Since the total sources of working capital exceeded the total uses in all three years, a net increase in working capital was reported in the statement.

H. The last section of the statement proved the change in working capital by listing the changes in the individual components of working capital (current assets and current liabilities). The sum of the changes in the individual working-capital components was equal to the net increase in working capital reported on the statement.

Statement of Shareholders' Equity (Figure 13.4)

A. La Quinta's combined statement of shareholders' equity presents the sources of changes in each category of stockholders' equity, including retained earnings. Some of these items relate to matters not covered in an introductory accounting book and are only presented to illustrate the comprehensive nature of the financial information included in actual financial statements.

B. The only item affecting retained earnings during the year ended May 31, 1983 was the addition of net earnings for the year 1983.

C. Common stock and additional paid-in capital were increased as a result of the exercise of stock options during the period. Additional coverage of equity transactions is included in Chapter 17.

La Quinta Motor Inns, Inc.
Combined Statements of Changes in Financial Position

	Years ended May 31		
	1983	1982	1981
Sources of working capital:			
Net earnings	$ 13,456,000	12,291,000	8,611,000
Items not requiring (providing) working capital:			
Depreciation and amortization:			
Property and equipment	12,407,000	9,729,000	7,927,000
Other	1,137,000	683,000	557,000
Deferred income taxes	5,604,000	2,782,000	1,722,000
Partners' equity in earnings and losses	6,224,000	6,117,000	4,329,000
Other, net	(3,000)	(12,000)	41,000
Working capital provided by operations	38,825,000	31,590,000	23,187,000
Long-term borrowings	67,901,000	58,053,000	30,940,000
Capital contributions by partners	2,719,000	2,546,000	4,442,000
Depreciated cost of assets sold or retired	3,190,000	2,196,000	2,152,000
Proceeds from sales of common stock, net of expenses	966,000	17,682,000	11,382,000
Total working capital provided	113,601,000	112,067,000	72,103,000
Uses of working capital:			
Additions to property and equipment and motor inns under development	74,757,000	78,267,000	48,906,000
Reduction of long-term debt	14,167,000	8,030,000	10,300,000
Cash distributions to partners	2,625,000	3,484,000	4,705,000
Increase in notes receivable	3,140,000	1,118,000	395,000
Increase (decrease) in investments	6,584,000	(129,000)	(54,000)
Increase in deferred charges and other assets	3,072,000	3,756,000	1,161,000
Total working capital used	104,345,000	94,526,000	65,413,000
Increase in working capital	$ 9,256,000	17,541,000	6,690,000
Changes in components of working capital:			
Increase in current assets:			
Cash and short-term cash investments	5,880,000	22,023,000	10,555,000
Receivables	243,000	2,382,000	569,000
Income taxes	2,740,000	—	—
Prepaid expenses and other current assets	219,000	92,000	13,000
	9,082,000	24,497,000	11,137,000
Increase (decrease) in current liabilities:			
Note payable to bank and current installments of long-term debt	86,000	(1,326,000)	2,420,000
Accounts payable and accrued expenses	1,398,000	8,559,000	1,021,000
Income taxes	(1,658,000)	(277,000)	1,006,000
	(174,000)	6,956,000	4,447,000
Increase in working capital	$ 9,256,000	17,541,000	6,690,000

Figure 13.3. La Quinta Motor Inns, Inc., combined statements of changes in financial position.

La Quinta Motor Inns, Inc.
Combined Statements of Shareholders' Equity

| | Common stock | | Additional paid-in | Retained | |
	Shares	Amount	capital	earnings	Total
Balances at May 31, 1980	7,011,806	$ 701,000	20,516,000	8,173,000	29,390,000
Five-for-four stock split	1,928,658	193,000	—	(193,000)	—
Cash in lieu of fractional shares	—	—	—	(14,000)	(14,000)
Issuance of common stock, net of expenses	600,000	60,000	10,422,000	—	10,482,000
Exercise of stock options	132,331	13,000	887,000	—	900,000
Net earnings	—	—	—	8,611,000	8,611,000
Balances at May 31, 1981	9,672,795	967,000	31,825,000	16,577,000	49,369,000
Four-for-three stock split	3,567,973	357,000	(357,000)	—	—
Cash in lieu of fractional shares	—	—	(18,000)	—	(18,000)
Issuance of common stock, net of expenses	1,000,000	100,000	17,005,000	—	17,105,000
Exercise of stock options	47,264	5,000	572,000	—	577,000
Net earnings	—	—	—	12,291,000	12,291,000
Balances at May 31, 1982	14,288,032	1,429,000	49,027,000	28,868,000	79,324,000
Exercise of stock options	112,104	11,000	955,000	—	966,000
Net earnings	—	—	—	13,456,000	13,456,000
Balances at May 31, 1983	14,400,136	$1,440,000	49,982,000	42,324,000	93,746,000

Figure 13.4. La Quinta Motor Inns, Inc., combined statements of shareholders' equity.

IV

Selected Topics

14

Property and Equipment

As has already been noted, the hospitality industry is predominantly service oriented. Rendering the types of services typical to hospitality firms—lodging, board, and travel—requires a large investment in costly property and equipment such as hotel buildings and airplanes. In the case of hotels, for instance, revenues are determined by

- Number of rooms (size of the hotel)
- Average room rate (class of the hotel)
- Percentage occupancy

The first two of these are directly related to the amount of investment in property and equipment. In fact, property and equipment comprise more than 80% of the total assets of the typical hospitality industry firm. This chapter explains the accounting procedures involved in acquiring, depreciating, and disposing of property and equipment.

First property and equipment are defined and the different types of property and equipment used in the hospitality industry are described. Then an explanation of the procedures for recording the acquisition of property and equipment follows. Subsequently, a description of the procedures most commonly used to depreciate and amortize property and equipment is presented. Next the procedures for disposing of property and equipment are examined. In conclusion, an example of the financial statement presentation of the property and equipment and depreciation accounts is presented.

PROPERTY AND EQUIPMENT IN THE HOSPITALITY INDUSTRY

Property and equipment includes all tangible assets: (1) acquired for use in the ordinary operation of the business and (2) having a useful life of more than one year. Leaseholds and leasehold improvements are included in this classification, even though they are intangible assets, because they give a hospitality firm the right to use tangible, physical assets. Property and equipment have sometimes been referred to as fixed assets; however, this term is falling into disuse, since it implies a permanence that these assets do not all possess.

With the exception of land, which does not wear out, and construction in progress, which includes property and equipment not yet in service, all property and equipment are subject to a decline in value resulting from the process of aging. This loss of value may be produced by the asset wearing down or merely by some effect of the passage of time (obsolescence or changing markets, for instance). As described in Chapter 7, this decline in value (cost expiration) is recorded through a procedure called depreciation. In the case of leasehold and leasehold improvements, the term amortization is used to account for this cost expiration.

PROPERTY AND EQUIPMENT CATEGORIES

The Uniform System of Accounts for Hotels (USAH) includes the following categories in the property and equipment classification:

- Land
- Building
- Leaseholds and leasehold improvements
- Construction in progress
- Furniture and equipment
- China, glassware, silver, linen, and uniforms

The property and equipment categories are normally listed in order of permanence, as shown above. Restaurants and clubs have their own uniform system of accounts, which provide for similar property and equipment categories.

The land account includes all land used by a firm directly or indirectly to generate revenues during its ordinary course of operations. Land used for golf courses and parking lots is included along with land on which buildings are constructed. In this latter case, the cost of the land must be segregated from the value of the building constructed upon it in order to allow depreciation of the buildings. As stated before, land is never depreciated.

Leasehold and leasehold improvements include expenditures made to acquire the rights to a lease or to improve property on which the hospitality firm already has leasehold rights.

Construction in progress includes all expenditures related to the construction of property or equipment. This account is charged with the cost of materials, labor, and advances on contracts involved in the construction of property and equipment. It can also be charged with any additional interest incurred due to the fact that the construction is taking place. This is an important category in the hospitality industry because hotel and restaurant chains tend to expand continually, and airlines are constantly contracting for the construction of new equipment.

Property and equipment under construction are not depreciated. When construction is completed, the asset under construction is transferred to the appropriate property and equipment account, where the process of depreciation begins.

The furniture and equipment category includes all the furniture, furnishings, and removable equipment owned by a firm. Room furniture, office furniture and equipment, kitchen equipment, and vehicles are included in this asset category.

The category of china, glassware, silver, linen, and uniforms includes all dishes, glasses, stemware, and silverware used by a restaurant or hotel. Also included are bed linen and restaurant linen as well as employee uniforms. Kitchen utensils are usually expensed when purchased, but are included in this category when it is not management policy to expense them.

The property and equipment categories mentioned above are not inflexible. For instance, a major category such as furniture and equipment may be subdivided into smaller categories such as furniture, furnishings, equipment, and vehicles. The degree to which account categories are subdivided depends upon the materiality or significance of the assets to be recorded therein. Also, subsidiary ledgers may be created to record specific data and accumulated depreciation amounts for each item of property or equipment when their value warrants it.

RECORDING CAPITAL LEASES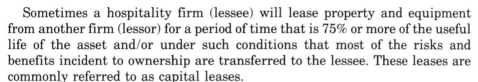

Sometimes a hospitality firm (lessee) will lease property and equipment from another firm (lessor) for a period of time that is 75% or more of the useful life of the asset and/or under such conditions that most of the risks and benefits incident to ownership are transferred to the lessee. These leases are commonly referred to as capital leases.

The conditions for capital lease treatment are specified in FASB statement No. 13. When these conditions exist it is assumed that the lease contract is an installment purchase. According to FASB Statement No. 13, the future contractual lease payments over the life of the lease are totaled and discounted using a procedure called present value. The present value of these future lease payments is recorded in the appropriate property and equipment account as if the asset had been purchased, and a corresponding liability is established for the lease obligation.

RECORDING PROPERTY AND EQUIPMENT

Property and equipment are recorded at cost. Cost includes the actual purchase price of the asset as well as any expenditures required to transport it to the place where it will be used and to prepare it for use. Some representative expenditures of this type are

- Transportation costs
- Sales taxes, legal fees, and sales commissions
- Land clearing expenses
- Installation costs

The matching concept requires that transportation and preparation expenses be added to the cost of an asset rather than be considered current period expenses. Since by definition, property and equipment benefit more than one annual accounting period (refer to the definition of an asset in Chapter 2), expenditures to make such assets operational will also benefit future accounting periods and therefore should be included as part of the cost of the asset. When an expenditure is made for goods or services that are not entirely consumed in the current accounting period and the expenditure is recorded as an asset on the balance sheet rather than an expense on the income statement, we say that the expenditure has been capitalized, or that it is a capital expenditure. It should be noted that interest paid for loans to buy equipment that is ready for use should not be capitalized. Such interest is an expense incurred for the use of money, and is not a preparation or construction cost.

Property and Equipment Improvements versus Maintenance and Repairs Expense

The need to differentiate between expenditures that should be capitalized and expenditures that should be expensed in the current accounting period goes beyond the initial purchase phase of property and equipment. Differentiation between these two types of expenditures is required in deciding whether to record later expenditures as improvements of property and equipment or as current period maintenance and repairs expenses. Expenditures related to property and equipment should be recorded as maintenance and repairs expense when they merely restore the property or equipment to its original condition. Expenditures should be added to the cost of the particular property or equipment (capitalized) when the expenditure (1) increases the capacity of the property or equipment, (2) improves its quality, or (3) extends its life beyond that expected when originally purchased. Such expenditures should be depreciated over their useful lives or the useful life of the property or equipment they affect, whichever is shorter.

Journal Entry to Record the Purchase of Property or Equipment

An example of a journal entry to record the purchase and overhaul of a used electric generator is presented in Figure 14.1. It is assumed that the generator only needed minor repairs to be operational, therefore the overhaul is a life-extending expenditure that should be capitalized.

RECORDING DEPRECIATION OF PROPERTY AND EQUIPMENT

Property and equipment represents capitalized expenditures that will benefit future accounting periods as well as the current one. Their cost must therefore be allocated to these future periods as an expense through the process of depreciation. Accounting Research Bulletin (ARB) No. 43 defines depreciation as a "system of accounting which aims to distribute the cost or other basic value of tangible capital assets, less salvage (if any), over the estimated useful life of the unit (which may be a group of assets) in a systematic and rational manner."[1]

According to this definition the three factors involved in depreciating property and equipment are

1. The estimated useful life of the property or equipment.
2. Its salvage value.
3. The depreciation method used.

Estimated Useful Life

The useful life of an asset is the period during which an asset will be of value to a firm in the firm's revenue-generating process. Since this period cannot be determined with certainty it must be estimated by management. In

[1]American Institute of Certified Public Accountants, Committee on Accounting Procedure, Accounting Research and Terminology Bulletins, *Accounting Research Bulletin No. 43*, Final Edition (Sept. 1961), p. 76.

Assumptions	
Purchase price	$5,000
Transportation costs	1,000
Overhaul cost	2,000
Installation costs	500

Journal Entry		
	Dr	Cr
Equipment	8,500	
Cash		8,500
To record the acquisition and overhaul of a used electric generator		

Figure 14.1. Journal entry to record purchase and overhaul of electric generator.

making this estimate management must take into consideration the three factors that may, singly or in combination, cause an asset to lose value for their particular firm:

1. Physical deterioration caused by wear and tear.
2. Obsolescence produced by technological developments.
3. Inadequacy arising out of growth of the firm or changes in the industry (e.g., small airplanes may be inadequate after an airline opens new and longer routes).

Salvage Value

Property and equipment that is no longer useful to one firm may still have value for another firm. The salvage value (or residual value) of property and equipment is the amount that can be obtained for it when no longer of use to the original owner. In some instances the only value that can be obtained is the asset's scrap value. Because salvage value is based on estimates and the end of an asset's useful life may be so far in the future, it is often assumed to be zero.

DEPRECIATION METHODS

The definition of depreciation given above states that the cost of property and equipment must be distributed in a "systematic and rational manner." In order to be rational, depreciation must record the expiration of an asset's value accurately over its useful life. Some property or equipment loses value at a constant rate over its useful life. In other cases it loses value in relation to the amount of use given to it. In yet other cases it loses value more rapidly in the early years of its life than in the later years. In order to allow for systematic and rational depreciation under any one of these circumstances, four depreciation methods are available:

1. straight-line method
2. units-of-output method
3. declining-balance method
4. sum-of-years'-digits method

Straight-Line Depreciation

The straight-line depreciation method is based on the assumption that the cost of a particular property or equipment will expire at a constant rate over

TABLE 14.1. Straight-Line Depreciation of Tour Bus

Year	Depreciable base		Straight-line rate		Depreciation expense	Accumulated depreciation	Net book value
1	$10,000	×	0.20	=	$2,000	$ 2,000	$10,000
2	10,000	×	0.20	=	2,000	4,000	8,000
3	10,000	×	0.20	=	2,000	6,000	6,000
4	10,000	×	0.20	=	2,000	8,000	4,000
5	10,000	×	0.20	=	2,000	10,000	2,000

its useful life. This method allocates an asset's cost, less salvage value, evenly over its useful life. When using this method cost less salvage value is the depreciable base of the asset, the amount that will actually be depreciated. The formula for calculating annual straight-line depreciation is

$$\frac{\text{cost} - \text{salvage value}}{\text{estimated useful life of asset}} = \text{annual depreciation expense}$$

Thus, a tour bus costing $12,000, with a $2,000 salvage value and a useful life of five years, would be subject to a $2,000 annual depreciation expense calculated as follows:

$$\frac{\$12,000 - \$2,000}{5} = \$2000$$

Table 14.1 shows the depreciable base, depreciation expense, accumulated depreciation, and net book value (cost less accumulated depreciation) of the tour bus over its useful life.

The straight-line depreciation rate can also be expressed in terms of percentages. Thus the annual depreciation rate for an asset with a 10-year useful life can be expressed as $\frac{1}{10}$ or 10%. The straight-line depreciation rate of our tour bus, for example, is 20% since it has a useful life of five years and $\frac{1}{5}$, or 20%, of its depreciable base is depreciated annually.

Units-of-Output Method

The units-of-output method is based on the assumption that the cost of a particular property or equipment will expire at a constant rate in proportion to the amount of use given to the asset. In the case of the tour bus, the amount of depreciation per mile traveled would have to be determined. Its annual depreciation expense would depend on the number of miles the tour bus traveled during the year. To calculate this, management must estimate the number of miles the tour bus is capable of traveling over its useful life, rather than estimating its useful life in terms of years. The formula for calculating annual depreciation under the units-of-output method is

$$\frac{\text{annual depreciation}}{\text{expense}} = \frac{\text{cost less salvage value}}{\text{estimated units of output}} \times \text{annual units of output}$$

This formula multiplies the depreciation per unit of output times the annual units of output. Assuming that the tour bus with a $12,000 cost and a

TABLE 14.2. Units-of-Output Method for Depreciating Tour Bus

Year	Depreciable base	Depreciation per mile		Miles traveled		Depreciation expense	Accumulated depreciation	Net book value
1	$10,000	$0.05	×	40,000	=	$2,000	$ 2,000	$10,000
2	10,000	0.05	×	20,000	=	1,000	3,000	9,000
3	10,000	0.05	×	60,000	=	3,000	6,000	6,000
4	10,000	0.05	×	50,000	=	2,500	8,500	3,500
5	10,000	0.05	×	30,000	=	1,500	10,000	2,000

$2,000 salvage value will travel 200,000 miles before it is worthless, the depreciation rate is

$$\frac{12,000 - 2,000}{200,000} = \$0.05/\text{mile}$$

Table 14.2 shows the depreciable base, depreciation expense, accumulated depreciation, and net book value of the tour bus under the assumption that the tour bus will travel the 200,000 miles in five years in the annual amounts indicated in the chart.

Accelerated-Depreciation Methods

In addition to the straight-line and units-of-output depreciation methods, which produce constant depreciation rates based on the asset's useful life or on its total output over its useful life, two other depreciation methods are available. These methods are called accelerated-depreciation methods because they result in higher depreciation expense during the first years of the asset's useful life than over the later years. The two most commonly used methods are the declining-balance method and the sum-of-the-years'-digits method.

Declining-Balance Method

The declining-balance method calculates annual depreciation expense based on net book value, that is, the cost of the asset less accumulated depreciation. Although salvage value is not taken into account in the formula for calculating declining-balance depreciation, an asset should never be depreciated below its salvage value. Net book value for each successive year is multiplied by the selected depreciation rate. This rate is usually double the straight-line rate, although other rates such as one-and-one-half times the straight-line rate can also be used. When double the straight-line depreciation rate is used, this method is called the double-declining-balance (DDB) method. The formula for calculating double-declining-balance depreciation is:

$$\begin{array}{c}\text{annual} \\ \text{depreciation} \\ \text{expense}\end{array} = 2 \times \begin{array}{c}\text{straight-line} \\ \text{depreciation} \\ \text{rate}\end{array} \times \begin{array}{c}\text{cost less} \\ \text{accumulated} \\ \text{depreciation}\end{array}$$

As previously explained, the annual straight-line depreciation rate is obtained by dividing the asset's useful life into 1. Our tour bus with a five-year useful life has a straight-line depreciation rate of ⅕ or 20% and a double-declining-balance rate of 40% (2 × 20%). The net book value (cost less accumu-

TABLE 14.3. Double-Declining-Balance Method for Depreciating Tour Bus

Year	Depreciable base	Depreciation expense	Accumulated depreciation	Net book value
1	$12,000	$12,000 × 0.40 = $4,800	$ 4,800	$7,200
2	12,000	7,200 × 0.40 = 2,880	7,680	4,320
3	12,000	4,320 × 0.40 = 1,728	9,408	2,592
4	12,000	592	10,000	2,000
5	12,000	-0-[a]	10,000	2,000

[a]With this method, the tour bus would have been depreciated below its $2,000 salvage value in year 4. Since an asset should never be depreciated below its salvage value, only $592 of depreciation expense should be recorded in year 4. Accordingly, no depreciation expense is recorded in year 5.

lated depreciation) for successive years is multiplied by this 40% rate to determine the annual depreciation expense.

The depreciable base, annual depreciation expense, accumulated depreciation, and net book value of the tour bus over its useful life are shown in Table 14.3.

Sum-of-the-Years'-Digits Method

The sum-of-the-years'-digits (SYD) method is another method of accelerated depreciation in the early years of an asset's useful life. It uses the depreciable cost of an asset (cost minus salvage value) as its depreciable base. The depreciable base is multiplied by a fraction the denominator of which is the sum of the years of estimated useful life of the asset. The numerator corresponds to each year of the asset's useful life, applied in reverse order. The last year of an asset's useful life is the numerator for the first year's fraction. The yearly fractions for the tour bus with a five-year useful life are calculated as follows:

Year		Fraction
1	$\frac{5}{1+2+3+4+5} = \frac{5}{15} = \frac{1}{3}$	
2	$\frac{4}{1+2+3+4+5} = \frac{4}{15} = \frac{4}{15}$	
3	$\frac{3}{1+2+3+4+5} = \frac{3}{15} = \frac{1}{5}$	
4	$\frac{2}{1+2+3+4+5} = \frac{2}{15} = \frac{2}{15}$	
5	$\frac{1}{1+2+3+4+5} = \frac{1}{15} = \frac{1}{15}$	

The above method of calculating the denominator of the fraction is practical only when the asset's useful life is short. For longer useful lives the following formula should be used:

$$\text{sum of years} = \tfrac{1}{2}[N(N+1)]$$

where N is the estimated useful life of the asset in years.

Once the yearly fraction is determined, it is applied according to the follow-

TABLE 14.4. Sum-of-the-Years'-Digit Method for Depreciating Tour Bus

Year	Depreciable base		Fraction		Depreciation expense	Accumulated depreciation	Net book value
1	$10,000	×	5/15	=	$3,333	$ 3,333	$8,667
2	10,000	×	4/15	=	2,667	6,000	6,000
3	10,000	×	3/15	=	2,000	8,000	4,000
4	10,000	×	2/15	=	1,333	9,333	2,667
5	10,000	×	1/15	=	667	10,000	2,000

ing formula to calculate the annual sum-of-year's-digit depreciation:

$$\frac{\text{annual depreciation}}{\text{expense}} = \frac{\text{yearly}}{\text{fraction}} \times \frac{\text{cost less}}{\text{salvage value}}$$

Table 14.4 indicates the annual depreciation expense, accumulated depreciation, and net book value of the tour bus, which has a $12,000 cost, a $2,000 salvage value, and a five-year useful life.

COMPARISON OF DEPRECIATION METHODS

Table 14.5 indicates the annual depreciation expense for the hypothetical tour bus under the four depreciation methods.

As can be verified by the reader, the two accelerated-depreciation methods result in the depreciation of more than half of the tour bus' depreciable base during the first half of its useful life. These methods should, therefore, be used to depreciate assets whose cost expires more rapidly in their early years than in their later years of life. The straight-line method results in equal annual depreciation expense over an asset's useful life and should be used to depreciate assets that lose their value at a constant rate over time. The units-of-output method apparently produces an erratic depreciation expense pattern. However, this pattern is due to the fluctuations in tour bus usage and is based on a constant rate of depreciation per mile of operation. This method should be used when an asset's loss of value is directly proportional to the amount of use it is given, thereby relating depreciation to the asset's productive output. It should be used to depreciate assets whose cost expires in direct proportion to the wear and tear caused by usage.

Figures 14.2 and 14.3 show graphically the results of plotting the depreciation amounts shown in Table 14.5. Notice how depreciation expense is high in the early years of the tour bus' life and then decreases sharply under the

TABLE 14.5. Comparative Depreciation Expense Chart

Year	Straight-line	Units-of-output	Double-declining-balance	Sum-of-the-years'-digits
1	$ 2,000	$ 2,000	$ 4,800	$ 3,333
2	2,000	1,000	2,880	2,667
3	2,000	3,000	1,728	2,000
4	2,000	2,500	592[a]	1,333
5	2,000	1,500		667
Total	$10,000	$10,000	$10,000	$10,000

[a]Depreciation required to arrive at salvage value.

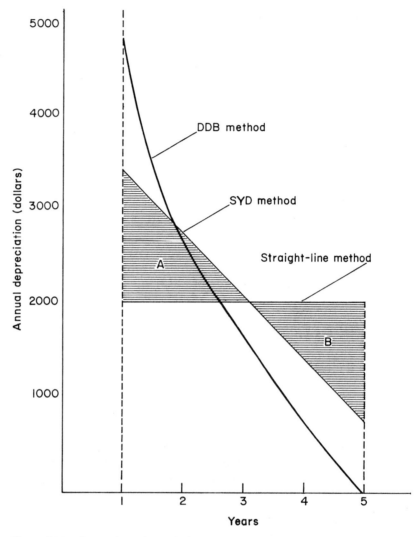

Figure 14.2. Comparison of straight-line and accelerated depreciation methods.

double-declining-balance and sum-of-years'-digits depreciation methods. In contrast, the straight-line rate (it is actually a straight line on the graph) remains constant throughout the life of the asset. Figure 14.3 indicates that depreciation expense under the units-of-output method fluctuates according to the tour bus' annual mileage. This is consistent with the way depreciation is calculated under this method.

GROUP DEPRECIATION

It is practical to calculate depreciation for each individual item in a property and equipment category only when there are not many. When there are many items of property or equipment in an asset category and straight-line or declining-balance depreciation is used, it is more convenient to depreciate them as a group. Because they will probably have different useful lives and salvage values, an average of their useful lives should be used and the assets should be depreciated as a group down to their total salvage value. An example, with corresponding assumptions, is given in Tables 14.6 and 14.7. In this case, the average useful life is $12/3 = 4$ years; the straight-line depreciation rate is ¼ or 25%; and the total salvage value is $5,000.

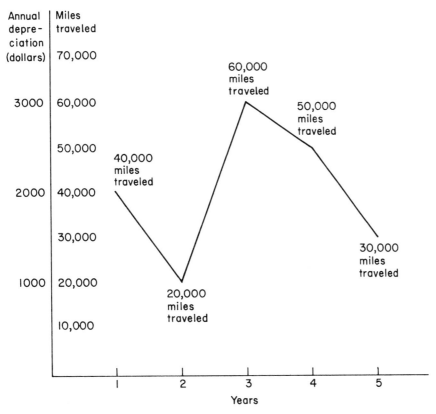

Figure 14.3. Units-of-output depreciation method.

TABLE 14.6. Assumptions For Group Depreciation— Tour Buses

Asset	Cost	Useful life (years)	Salvage value
Tour bus 1	$10,000	5	$ 0
Tour bus 2	5,000	2	1,000
Tour bus 3	14,000	5	4,000
Total	$29,000	12	$5,000

TABLE 14.7. Group Straight-Line Depreciation

Year	Group cost	Depreciable base		Straight-line rate		Depreciation expense	Accumulated depreciation	Net book value
1	$29,000	($29,000−5000)	×	0.25	=	6,000	$ 6,000	$23,000
2	29,000	(29,000−5000)	×	0.25	=	6,000	12,000	17,000
3	29,000	(29,000−5000)	×	0.25	=	6,000	18,000	11,000
4	29,000	(29,000−5000)	×	0.25	=	6,000	24,000	5,000

FRACTIONAL-YEARS DEPRECIATION

When property or equipment is acquired on a date other than the beginning of an entity's accounting year, fractional-years depreciation must be used in order to include the proper amount of depreciation in each accounting period. For example, if a restaurant on a calendar accounting year purchases an oven on September 1, 1987, then ⅓ of the oven's first-year depreciation must be recorded in the accounting year ended December 31, 1987, and ⅔ in the 1988 accounting year. The example in Tables 14.8 and 14.9 serves to clarify this procedure. It shows the annual depreciation expense for a restaurant that is on an accounting year beginning September 1 (the date on which the oven was purchased) as opposed to that of a company on a calendar accounting year. The sum-of-years'-digits depreciation method is used.

TABLE 14.8. Restaurant on Fiscal Year September 1– August 31

Year	Depreciation year dates	SYD annual depreciation expense[a]
1	Sept. 1, 1987–Aug. 31, 1988	$ 3,333
2	Sept. 1, 1988–Aug. 31, 1989	2,667
3	Sept. 1, 1989–Aug. 31, 1990	2,000
4	Sept. 1, 1990–Aug. 31, 1991	1,333
5	Sept. 1, 1991–Aug. 31, 1992	667
Total		$10,000

[a]Assume the oven cost $10,000 and had no salvage value.

TABLE 14.9. Restaurant on Calendar Year January 1–December 31

Year	Depreciation year dates	Fractional depreciation	Annual depreciation expense
1	Sept. 1, 1987–Aug. 31, 1988	1/3 ($3,333)	$ 1,111
2	Sept. 1, 1988–Aug. 31, 1989	2/3 ($3,333)+1/3 ($2,667)	3,111
3	Sept. 1, 1989–Aug. 31, 1990	2/3 ($2,667)+1/3 ($2,000)	2,444
4	Sept. 1, 1990–Aug. 31, 1991	2/3 ($2,000)+1/3 ($1,333)	1,778
5	Sept. 1, 1991–Aug. 31, 1992	2/3 ($1,333)+1/3 ($667)	1,111
6	Sept. 1, 1992–Aug. 31, 1993	2/3 ($667)	445
Total			$10,000

RECORDING THE COST EXPIRATION OF CHINA, GLASSWARE, SILVER, LINEN, AND UNIFORMS

China, glassware, silver, linen, and uniforms are assets with very short lives when compared to other property and equipment. Because of their special nature, cost expiration of assets in this category usually occurs because of (1) physical deterioration due to wear and tear and/or pattern obsolescence, and (2) physical disappearance due to theft or breakage.

Therefore, a two-step procedure is required to record their cost expiration.

When china, glassware, silver, linen, and uniforms are purchased, and before removal from their original containers, they are placed in a reserve stock account. Items in this account do not undergo cost expiration. As they are placed in service, these items are transferred to a separate account where they undergo periodic cost adjustment in order to reflect their used condition. This adjustment is usually made in annual increments as indicated in Table 14.10. The increments vary according to the age of the establishment, and not according to the age of the assets themselves. If cost expiration were not calculated in this manner, the constant turnover of assets in this account would not allow any cost expiration to accumulate.

During each of the first five years of an establishment's existence the cost of china, glassware, silver, and linen as reflected in the "stock in use" account is reduced by the adjustment amounts shown in the table and a charge for an equal amount is made to the china, glassware, silver, and linen expense accounts. Uniforms have such short lives that their full value is expensed when they are taken out of the reserve stock account and placed in service.

The second required adjustment involves recording cost expiration due to physical disappearance. A count of the assets is made and the original cost of all missing items is included in the cost expiration expense account, less any cost adjustment previously made to record physical deterioration.

The two procedures described constitute one manner of accounting for china, glassware, silver, linen, and uniforms. There are other methods of accounting for the cost expiration of these assets, but the above method serves to present the value of the items in this account most fairly, recognizing inventory losses when they occur, without going to the extreme of tracking each individual item.

The following example should serve to illustrate the operation of the preceding method of accounting for china, glassware, silver, linen, and uniforms. Assume a two-year-old establishment purchases $1,000 worth of china plates. Further assume that $500 worth of these are put into service and that only $400 worth (original cost) are still in existence at the end of the year according to a physical count. The journal entries to record these events would be as shown in Figure 14.4.

Notice that when they are put into service the new plates receive an adjustment of 10%, 5% for each year the establishment has been in existence. Also notice that in journal entry [3] the cost of the missing plates that was expensed represented the cost after making the adjustment for the age of the establishment. This $90 cost was calculated by deducting the 10% adjustment made in journal entry 2 from the $100 original cost of the missing plates.

The cost expiration expense of china, glassware, silver, linen, and uniforms

TABLE 14.10. Annual Cost Adjustment Table (%) for China, Glassware, Silver, and Linen

Age of establishment	China	Glassware	Silver	Linen
Year 1	5	0	10	16-2/3
Year 2	5	0	10	16-2/3
Year 3	5	0	10	16-2/3
Year 4	5	0	10	0
Year 5 and beyond	5	0	10	0

Note: Amounts shown above are annual adjustments as a percentage of cost. For example, a two-year-old establishment would use a 10% (5% + 5%) adjustment factor for china.

	Dr	Cr
[1]		
China, glassware, silver, linen and uniforms—reserve stock	1,000	
Cash		1,000
To record purchase of $1,000 worth of plates		
[2]		
China, glassware, silver, linen, and uniforms—stock in use	500	
China, glassware, silver, linen expense	50	
China, glassware, silver, linen, and uniforms—reserve stock		500
China, glassware, silver, linen and uniforms—stock in use		50
To record putting into service $500 worth of plates, and to adjust their cost by 10% per age of the establishment (two-years old)		
[3]		
China, glassware, silver, linen expense	90	
China, glassware, silver, linen, and uniforms—stock in use		90
To record, at the end of third year, shortage of plates with an original cost of $100 ($100 original cost minus 10% adjustment factor expensed when plates were put into service)		

Figure 14.4. Journal entries to record purchase, putting into service, and shortage of china plates.

appears in two accounts on the room and food and beverage department income statements: (1) china, glassware, silver, and linen, and (2) uniforms.

The cost expiration of these assets is deducted directly from the asset account. No contra-asset account is used. Therefore, the china, glassware, silver, linen, and uniforms account appears after the accumulated depreciation and amortization account on the balance sheet according to the USAH.

AMORTIZATION OF LEASEHOLD AND LEASEHOLD IMPROVEMENTS

Leasehold and leasehold improvements are a significant asset category in the hospitality industry. Their useful life is usually limited by the length of the lease contract, although in the case of longer leases physical deterioration may be the life-limiting factor.

Amortization of leasehold and leasehold improvements is always calculated on a straight-line basis. The journal entry to record amortization, assuming amortization of $1,000 is required and using an accumulated amortization contra-asset account, is made as follows:

	Dr	Cr
Amortization expense	1,000	
Accumulated amortization		1,000
To record $1,000 amortization of leasehold improvements		

DISPOSAL OF PROPERTY AND EQUIPMENT

Property and equipment may be disposed of by (1) sale, (2) retirement, (3) exchange, or (4) accidental destruction. Different accounting procedures are required to record each method of disposal, as shall be explained subsequently.

Sale of Property and Equipment

When property or equipment is sold, its cost must be deducted from the appropriate asset account and its related accumulated depreciation from the appropriate contra-asset account. Additionally, any gain or loss must be reported on the income statement. This gain or loss is the difference between the asset's net book value (NBV) and its sale price.

The entry to record the sale of a freezer with a cost of $12,000 and accumulated depreciation of $10,000 is shown below. The freezer is sold for $3,000 in cash.

	Dr	Cr
Cash	3,000	
Accumulated depreciation	10,000	
Equipment		12,000
Gain on sale of property		1,000

To record sale of freezer for $1,000 above its net book value

The above gain was calculated as follows:

Cost of freezer	$12,000
Less:	
Accumulated depreciation	10,000
Net book value	$ 2,000
Sale price	$ 3,000
Less:	
Net book value	2,000
Gain on sale	$ 1,000

A loss would be calculated similarly.

To comply with GAAP, a special account called "gain or loss on sale of property" is provided by the USAH to report such transactions. Since sales of property or equipment are considered to occur infrequently, APB Opinion No. 30 requires that gains or losses from such sales must be reported separately on the income statement, after all normal operating revenues and expenses and before extraordinary items. This opinion states: "A material event or transaction that is unusual in nature or occurs infrequently but not both, and therefore does not meet both criteria for classification as an extraordinary item, should be reported as a separate component of income from continuing operations. . . . Such items should not be reported . . . net of income taxes."[2]

In the case of certain hotel or restaurant chains that are constantly buying and selling properties, gains and losses from such sales do occur frequently and are considered usual because they involve the operating assets of the corporation. Therefore, they may be reported along with other ordinary operating revenues or expenses as part of the normal operations of the company.

Retirement of Property and Equipment

Property or equipment is retired when it cannot be sold or exchanged. Ideally, management should have foreseen this event, and the asset should be fully depreciated to a net book value of zero. Assuming this to be the case, the entry to retire a fully depreciated oven that cost $8,000 is shown below:

	Dr	Cr
Accumulated depreciation	8,000	
Equipment		8,000

To record retirement of a fully depreciated oven

[2]American Institute of Certified Public Accountants, *Accounting Principles Board Opinion No. 30,* "Reporting the Results of Operations" (June 1973), Par. 26.

When an asset is netted against an amount in its related contra-asset account, thereby removing both amounts from a company's books, the asset is said to be written off against its accumulated depreciation account.

If an asset is not fully depreciated upon retirement then its write-off produces a loss. The entry to record the write-off of an oven that cost $8,000 and has accumulated depreciation of $6,000 is presented below:

	Dr	Cr
Loss on retirement of equipment	2,000	
Accumulated depreciation	6,000	
Equipment		8,000

To record retirement of an oven with a net book value of $2,000

If it is not independently significant, the gain or loss on retirement of property may be reported on the income statement along with gains or losses from sales of property in a combined classification called "gain or loss on disposal of property."

Exchanges of Properties

Property and equipment may be exchanged for (1) similar property and equipment (a tour bus for a tour bus), or (2) dissimilar property and equipment (a tour bus for a freezer). When similar assets are exchanged APB Opinion No. 29 considers the exchange does not interrupt the original revenue-generating process of the initial asset, and so a gain from such an exchange is not recorded. In keeping with the concept of conservatism, however, losses are recorded. On the other hand, when a dissimilar exchange occurs, both gains and losses are recorded.

When a loss results, the entries to record exchanges of both similar and dissimilar property and equipment are the same. The entry to record the exchange of kitchen equipment (with a cost of $12,000 and accumulated depreciation of $10,000) plus $500 in cash, for other equipment, similar or not, with a price of $1,000 is shown below.

	Dr	Cr
Loss on exchange of property	1,500	
Equipment (to record new asset)	1,000	
Accumulated depreciation (original equipment)	10,000	
Cash		500
Equipment (original equipment)		12,000

To record exchange of similar or dissimilar property at a loss

The same procedure is used to record a gain from a dissimilar exchange, except that instead of debiting the "loss on exchange of assets" account, any gain would be recognized by crediting the account "gain on exchange of assets." A gain results when the NBV of the asset given is less than its recognized fair market value (FMV), usually determined by its trade-in allowance.

When similar exchanges of property occur and the trade-in allowance on the old property or equipment is greater than its net book value, then the gain is not recognized and the new property or equipment is recorded at the net book value of the old property or equipment.

Accidental Destruction of Property or Equipment

The accidental destruction of property may be total or partial, and it may or may not be covered by insurance. All four situations will be dealt with here.

Total Destruction. In the case of total destruction the amount of the loss is equivalent to the net book value of the asset less any scrap value that can be realized. If there is any insurance coverage, it too must be deducted from the loss. Assume that a kitchen whose equipment cost $200,000 and had accumulated depreciation of $150,000 is totally gutted by fire. Further assume that the scrap value of the burned equipment is $5,000 and the insurance coverage amounts to $35,000. The fire loss would be calculated as follows:

Kitchen equipment cost	$200,000
Less: accumulated depreciation	150,000
Less: realizable scrap value	5,000
Less: insurance coverage	35,000
Net loss due to fire	$ 10,000

It would be recorded with the following entry:

	Dr	Cr
Scrapped property	5,000	
Insurance indemnity receivable	35,000	
Accumulated depreciation	150,000	
Loss due to fire	10,000	
Equipment		200,000
To record total destruction of kitchen equipment by fire		

If the kitchen equipment had not been insured, then no indemnity payment would be forthcoming and the loss would be $45,000 ($200,000 − $5,000 − $150,000).

Partial Destruction. In the previous example the kitchen equipment was totally destroyed. In the case of partial destruction, assuming the asset will be restored to its original condition, the same procedure is followed except that the value of the damaged portion of the property or equipment is expensed without reducing the accumulated depreciation account. The cost of restoring the property and equipment is subsequently debited to the appropriate asset account. Assume that a $200,000 cafeteria building with accumulated depreciation of $100,000 suffers $30,000 worth of fire damage. Further assume that items with a realizable scrap value of $1,000 were recovered after the fire and that insurance coverage on the damaged portion of the building is $20,000. The entry to record this event is:

	Dr	Cr
Scrapped property	1,000	
Insurance indemnity receivables	20,000	
Loss due to fire	9,000	
Building		30,000
To record partial destruction of cafeteria by fire		

The subsequent cost of restoring the cafeteria is debited to the building account. If the cost to restore is greater than the loss, then the annual depreciation expense must be increased accordingly.

INCOME TAX CONSIDERATIONS IN ACCOUNTING FOR PROPERTY AND EQUIPMENT

This chapter has dealt with the procedures of accounting for property and equipment according to GAAP. However, the Internal Revenue Code (IRC), the compendium of laws governing the calculation of taxable income, in an effort to provide tax relief to businesses, permits certain accounting procedures related to property and equipment which provide a lower current tax liability than that recognized under GAAP. This allows a company to postpone the payment of a portion of its taxes due. Certain other tax provisions, while not allowing a postponement of taxes due, permanently reduce a company's tax rate.

Accelerated Depreciation

The most commonly used method of postponing tax payments involves accelerating the depreciation of property and equipment when calculating taxable income. Taxable income is the income reported on a company's tax return and is calculated according to the stipulated rules of the Internal Revenue Code. The Accelerated Cost Recovery System (ACRS), incorporated in the Economic Recovery Tax Act (ERTA) of 1981, allows the recovery of the cost of property and equipment over a period shorter than its useful life. This procedure cannot be used when calculating earnings before income taxes (also called book income) for financial reporting purposes because it violates the matching concept. A realistic depreciation method, based on an asset's actual useful life, must be used to calculate book income.

As a result of this, taxable income will be lower than book income during the early part of an asset's life. Also, income tax payable, the tax actually paid to the government in the current accounting period, will be lower than income tax expense (sometimes called "provision for income taxes"), which is obtained by applying the current tax rate to book income. The relationship is reversed during the latter part of an asset's life, when the asset is fully depreciated for tax purposes and taxable income is greater than book income.

This can be observed in the example in Tables 14.11 and 14.12. In this example, an asset with a cost of $10,000 and no salvage value is depreciated over three years (using percentages provided in ACRS depreciation tables) for purposes of calculating taxable income and income tax payable. It is depreciated using the straight-line depreciation method over its useful life of five years for purposes of calculating book income and income tax expense. An income tax rate of 40% is assumed.

TABLE 14.11. Calculation of Book Income and Income Tax Expense

Year	Earnings before depreciation and taxes	Straight-line depreciation	Book income	Income tax expense
1	$10,000	$ 2,000	$8,000	$ 3,200
2	10,000	2,000	8,000	3,200
3	10,000	2,000	8,000	3,200
4	10,000	2,000	8,000	3,200
5	10,000	2,000	8,000	3,200
		$10,000		$16,000

TABLE 14.12. Calculation of Taxable Income and Income Tax
Payable

Year	Earnings before depreciation and taxes	ACRS depreciation	Taxable income	Income tax payable
1	$10,000	$ 2,500	$ 7,500	$ 3,000
2	10,000	3,800	6,200	2,480
3	10,000	3,700	6,300	2,520
4	10,000	0	10,000	4,000
5	10,000	0	10,000	4,000
		$10,000		$16,000

Notice that income tax expense is greater than income tax payable during the first three years of the asset's useful life but is lower than income tax payable during the last two years. The process of accelerating depreciation has allowed this company to defer paying some income taxes until years 4 and 5, when income tax payable exceeds income tax expense because it is paying the $1,600 of taxes that were deferred in years 1–3. The annual tax deferral during these years is shown in Table 14.13. The deferred income tax amount of $1,600 is paid in years 4 and 5 at the rate of $800 ($4,000 − $3,200) per year.

The journal entry to record income tax expense in year 1 of the asset's life is:

	Dr	Cr
Income tax expense	3,200	
Income tax payable		3,000
Deferred income taxes		200

To record income tax expense during the first year
of the asset's life

After the third year of the asset's useful life, income tax payable is $4,000. This is more than income tax expense because the previously deferred income taxes are now becoming due, and so the deferred income tax account is debited $800 ($4,000 − $3,200) in years 4 and 5 of the asset's life.

Income tax expense is recorded on the income statement since it represents the tax corresponding to book income. Income tax payable is recorded as a current liability, since it is the amount of tax to be paid in the current accounting period. The deferred income tax payable is reported after long-term liabilities on the balance sheet, as explained in Chapter 11.

TABLE 14.13. Deferred Taxes

Year	Income tax expense	Income tax payable	Deferred income tax credits <Debits>	Balance in deferred income tax account
1	$3,200	$3,000	$200	$ 200
2	3,200	2,480	720	920
3	3,200	2,520	680	1,600
4	3,200	4,000	<800>	800
5	3,200	4,000	<800>	0

Investment Tax Credit

As of this writing, the Internal Revenue Code also provides tax relief to businesses through the investment tax credit (ITC). A tax credit is deductible from the amount of income tax payable rather than being treated as a deductible expense used in determining taxable income. The investment tax credit varies from 4 to 10% of the cost of non-real estate property and equipment purchased, depending on how long it is owned and on whether or not an optional reduction in the depreciable base of the asset is taken. The investment tax credit is also subject to certain limitations when used property is purchased.

If a building is considered a historic structure, a credit of up to 25% is allowed on all expenditures incurred in rehabilitating the building. This provides opportunities for hospitality firms to convert historic sites to hospitality use. An additional credit is also allowed for energy-saving investments.

Companies that take advantage of these latter two investment tax credits must reduce the depreciable base of the affected assets by 50% of the investment tax credit. The use of an ITC results in a permanent reduction in a firm's tax rate. No deferred income tax account is required unless a method called the "reserve method" is used to record the investment tax credit on a company's books, in which case an investment tax credit contra-asset account is created and amortized over the life of the asset.

Capital Gains Tax

When business property and equipment owned by a company for more than six months is sold at a gain, the normal income tax rate for the firm is not applicable to this gain. A tax rate lower than the standard rate may be used and is called the capital gains tax rate. The rate varies for sole proprietorships, partnerships, and corporations. This tax provision results in a permanent reduction in the amount of tax that must be paid in the current period, and not just a postponement. Therefore, no income tax payment is deferred to future accounting periods.

Income Tax Treatment of Property and Equipment Exchanges

The Internal Revenue Code does not allow the recognition of gain or loss on exchanges of similar (like-kind) property although it does allow such recognition in dissimilar exchanges. For tax-reporting purposes, the unrecognized loss is added to the fair market value of the equipment received in the exchange. In the kitchen equipment exchange example presented earlier in the chapter, the cost of the new equipment for tax purposes would be $2,500. Thus, instead of being recognized immediately, for tax purposes the loss will be recognized over the life of the asset as the additional asset cost produced by the loss is gradually depreciated. In this case a "deferred income tax charges" account would have to be created. Such an account would appear in the "other assets" classification on the balance sheet.

FINANCIAL STATEMENT PRESENTATION OF PROPERTY AND EQUIPMENT

Financial reports designed primarily for management, such as those prepared according to the USAH, present property and equipment and their related accounts in greater detail than is meaningful to interested parties. It is

Assets			1981	1980
			(in thousands)	
Property and Equipment:	Flight equipment	Ground property and equipment		
Cost				
1981	$2,639,351	$450,776	3,090,127	
1980	2,388,808	372,793		2,761,601
Accumulated depreciation				
1981	$1,157,745	$197,481	1,355,226	
1980	1,031,681	177,091		1,208,772
			1,734,901	1,552,829
Advance payments for new equipment			149,628	90,952
			1,884,529	1,643,781

Figure 14.5. Delta Air Lines, Inc. presentation of property and equipment.

management's responsibility, therefore, to condense financial information in a manner that will enable these interested parties properly to evaluate the financial position of the firm and the results of its operations. The presentation of property and equipment in the 1981 financial statements of Delta Air Lines, Inc. is shown in Figure 14.5 as an example of how this can be accomplished.

QUESTIONS

1. What is depreciation?
2. What three factors must be taken into account in determining the useful life of an asset?
3. What types of expenditures should be included in the cost of newly purchased property and equipment?
4. In what circumstances should expenditures related to property and equipment be capitalized?
5. Should a gain or loss be recognized when similar assets are exchanged? when dissimilar assets are exchanged?
6. What is the net book value of an asset that cost $2,000 and has accumulated depreciation of $500? Will a gain or a loss result if this asset is sold for $900?
7. Why are certain depreciation methods called accelerated-depreciation methods? Name them.
8. Under what circumstances should each of the four depreciation methods described in this text be used to record the cost expiration of assets?
9. What is a deferred income tax payable account? When is it necessary to create such an account on the balance sheet?
10. What is an acceptable method for recording the cost expiration of china, glassware, silver, and linen? Describe it.
11. What is the investment tax credit? When is capital gains tax applicable?

EXERCISES

1. Determine which of the following expenditures should be capitalized and prepare the journal entry to record each expenditure. Assume all cash payments.
   (a) Fumigated a hotel for $1,000. The fumigation is guaranteed to eliminate cockroaches for three months.
   (b) Paid $5,000 for annual painting of a motel.
   (c) Rewired a restaurant at a cost of $2,000.

(d) Constructed a wall to divide the banquet hall into two rooms at a cost of $10,000.

(e) Paid $3,000 to remove rubble from an empty lot on which a restaurant will be constructed.

(f) Spent $6,000 to insulate a hotel in order to reduce energy costs.

2. Prepare journal entries to record the following transactions.

   (a) Exchanged a computer that cost $8,000 and had accumulated depreciation of $4,000 for another computer with a fair market value of $3,000.

   (b) Exchanged a refrigerator with a cost of $2,000 and accumulated depreciation of $500 for an oven with a fair market value of $1,000.

   (c) Exchanged a pick-up truck that cost $7,000 and had accumulated depreciation of $2,000 for a freezer with a fair market value of $5,500.

   (d) Sold an airplane that cost $20,000,000 and had accumulated depreciation of $15,000,000 for $6,000,000 cash.

   (e) Sold a building (previously used as a fast-food restaurant) that cost $150,000 and had accumulated depreciation of $80,000 for $60,000.

3. A hamburger broiler with a conveyor cost $20,000 and had accumulated depreciation of $5,000. It was exchanged for a smaller, more efficient model with a fair market value of $14,000.

   (a) Record the exchange according to GAAP.

   (b) Record the exchange for income tax reporting purposes.

   (c) Assume the new broiler has a three-year useful life and no salvage value. Calculate annual depreciation using the straight-line method as you would to report book and taxable income and fill in the information on the following chart.

| | Depreciation | | | Loss plus |
Year	For tax reporting	For book income	Loss on exchange	book depreciation
1				
2				
3				
Totals				

   (d) Explain why total accumulated depreciation for tax-reporting purposes is the same as total book depreciation plus the loss on the exchange.

4. The Campos Restaurant purchased a lunch van for $30,000 on June 30, 1987. The salvage value of the van is $5,000 and its useful life is 3 years. It is to be depreciated using the sum-of-years'-digit method.

   (a) Calculate the restaurant's annual depreciation expense for the van over its useful life based on the fact that the restaurant's fiscal year ends September 30. Round to nearest dollar.

   (b) What would the depreciation expense over its remaining life be if, after using the van for 12 months, additional partitions for sandwiches were built into it on June 30, 1988, at a cost of $2,000. Assume the useful life of the partitions is equal to the remaining useful life of the van.

5. On November 30, 1989 the Trundmore Restaurant purchased an automobile in a city 300 miles away for $9,000. The sales tax was $450 and the owner had to pay a driver $100 to drive it 300 miles to the restaurant. The car has an estimated useful life of five years, a salvage value of $1,000, and is depreciated using the sum-of-years'-digits method. The restaurant's fiscal year ends on March 31.

   (a) Assume the car was sold on March 31, 1991, for $6,000. Prepare the journal entry to record the sale.

   (b) Assume the car was not sold, but was demolished in an accident on March 31, 1992. If the car insurance paid $3,000, prepare the required journal entry to write off the car.

PROBLEMS

1. The Garden Restaurant, whose fiscal year ends on June 30, purchased a new oven for $5,000 on March 31, 1989. The oven was purchased and transported at a cost of $500. A sales tax of $250 was paid and transportation insurance cost $50. It also cost $450 to prepare the site where the oven was to be installed and certain expenses involved in testing the oven prior to commercial use amounted to $100. The room where the oven was installed was due for its annual coat of paint, which was done at a cost of $250.

   (a) Prepare the journal entry or entries to record all of the above expenditures.

   (b) Calculate depreciation expense for the oven using the double-declining-balance method for the fiscal years ended June 30, 1989 and 1990. Assume a five-year useful life and a $500 salvage value.

   (c) Assume the oven was exchanged, on June 30, 1990, for a freezer with a price of $4,000. Prepare the entry to record this exchange.

2. The Villamar Tour Bus Company purchased a small tour bus for $15,000 on April 30, 1989, the company's fiscal year end. Management estimates that it will be in usable condition for only 100,000 miles after a major overhaul, which cost $3,000. Its salvage value is estimated to be $1,000. Management expects to operate the bus as follows:

Fiscal year ended	Miles covered
April 30, 1990	20,000
April 30, 1991	40,000
April 30, 1992	25,000
April 30, 1993	15,000

   (a) Calculate the annual depreciation for each year of the life of the bus using the four depreciation methods explained in this chapter. Assume a four-year life where needed.

   (b) What is the effect of the different depreciation methods on net income?

   (c) Which depreciation method is best to use in this situation? Explain.

   (d) Under what operating circumstances would the straight-line depreciation method achieve the same results as the units-of-output depreciation method?

3. The Moors Hotel purchased an adjacent tract of land and is building an extension to the hotel on the land. The building work was divided into two identical sections, one of which was completed on October 31, 1989.

   All the following expenditures were charged to the building account. You are reviewing the account on December 31, 1989—the hotel's fiscal year end.

Cost of original hotel building	$2,562,000
Land appraisal fee	1,000
Title search	200
Attorney's fee related to purchase of land	800
Cost of land	700,000
Cost of demolishing previous structure on land	20,000
Cost of leveling land	13,000
Cost of laying building foundations	80,000
Cost of reducting the air-conditioning system of the original Moors Hotel building	30,000
Cost of air-conditioning unit for new addition	60,000
Freight cost of air-conditioning unit	1,500
Cost to install air conditioner	1,000
Cost of testing air conditioner	200
Cost of purchasing new freezer for original hotel	2,500
Architectural drawings	25,000
Construction materials	807,632
Construction labor	547,321
Total in building account	$4,852,153

In addition to the above expenses a company employee whose salary was $30,000 per year spent six months exclusively supervising this construction. His salary has been charged to the salaries and wages account. Also, the company borrowed funds specifically to finance this construction and had paid interest on these funds of $122,000, which was charged to the interest expense account as of December 31, 1989.

(a) Should all of the expenditures charged to the building account be in that account? If not, what other accounts should have been charged with some of these expenditures? Were any expenditures charged to other accounts that should have been charged to the building account?

(b) Prepare a worksheet as follows:

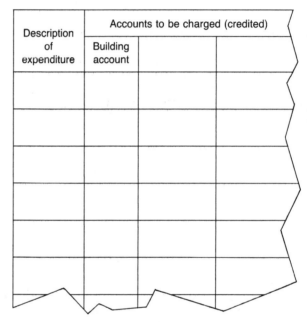

Enter the names of the correct accounts to be charged across the top of the worksheet. Then enter each expenditure amount in the column corresponding to the account where it belongs. Credit accounts from which amounts must be removed by using brackets.

(c) Based on the above worksheet prepare one entry to correct all the misrecorded amounts.

4. The Riverside Inn owns the following property and equipment:

Description	Cost	Useful life (years)	Salvage
Tractor-mower	$ 800	5	$ 100
Pick-up truck	7,000	7	2,000
Automobile	10,000	6	3,000
Oven	4,000	5	500
Broiler	6,000	4	700
Refrigerator	3,000	3	400
Building	250,000	25	50,000

(a) Can any of the above assets be depreciated as a group? Explain.

(b) What depreciation methods may be used to depreciate those assets that can be grouped together? Explain.

(c) Calculate the annual depreciation expense of those assets that may be depreciated as a group. Do this for each one of the depreciation methods that can be applied to property and equipment on a group basis. Prepare two worksheets similar to the ones presented in this chapter for each asset category.

5. The Grass Roots Restaurant opened its doors for business two years ago, on July 1, 1987. It uses the most fair method of recording cost expiration in its china, glassware, silver, linen, and uniforms account. Below are listed some events related to china, glassware, silver, and linen that have taken place since that date.

   A. Prepare the journal entry or entries required to record each event.

   (a) July 1, 1987 Purchased $20,000 worth of china, of which $10,000 worth was put into service immediately.

   (b) October 1, 1987 Took physical inventory of china, glassware, silver, and linen and found that china with an original cost of $2,000 was missing.

   (c) June 30, 1988 Took physical inventory of china, glassware, silver, and linen and found that china with an original cost of $3,000 was missing, then adjusted and closed the accounting books.

   (d) June 30, 1989 Took physical inventory of china, glassware, silver, and linen and found china with an original cost of $3,000 was missing. Adjusted and closed the books.

   (e) June 30, 1990 Took physical inventory of china, glassware, silver, and linen and found china with an original cost of $2,000 was missing; then adjusted and closed the accounting books.

   B. Show the above transactions and adjustments in the china, glassware, silver, linen and uniforms stock in use general ledger account. (Use "T" account format.)

15

Inventories

The principal source of revenue for the hospitality industry in general is the sale of services such as lodging and travel. Only in the restaurant industry subsector is the sale of food and beverages the primary source of revenue. Even then, because food is highly perishable, only small amounts are kept on hand. Supplies and spare parts inventories also tend to be of limited economic significance. Consequently, hospitality industry firms tend to have small inventories relative to their total assets.

Nevertheless, for those firms that do have food and beverage inventories, the use of proper accounting procedures to record their purchase and consumption is essential in order to determine cost of sales accurately. When profit margins are small, the method used to account for these inventories may make the difference between reporting a profit or a loss. This chapter explains the proper procedures for recording the acquisition of inventories as well as the acceptable methods of valuing inventories and determining cost of sales according to GAAP.

The procedures for recording the physical flow of inventories under the periodic- and perpetual-inventory systems are explained first, including an explanation of the proper method of recording employee meals. The proper accounting treatment of inventory transportation costs, returned inventory, and purchase discounts is then discussed. Next, the procedures involved in inventory valuation are presented as well as the impact of the different inventory valuation methods on the determination of cost of sales. The effect of inventory valuation errors on net income is then analyzed and the income tax impact of the different methods of accounting for inventories is reviewed. Finally, an example of the financial statement presentation of inventories is presented.

RECORDING INVENTORIES AND DETERMINING COST OF SALES

The most succinct and authoritative definition of the types of inventories used by hospitality industry firms is given in Accounting Research Bulletin (ARB) No. 43: "inventory is used herein to designate the aggregate of those items of tangible personal property which [1] are held for sale in the ordinary course of business, . . . or [3] are to be currently consumed in the production of goods or services to be available for sale."[1]

In a hospitality firm, inventories for sale may include (1) food, (2) bev-

---

[1]American Institute of Certified Public Accountants, Committee on Accounting Procedure, Accounting Research and Terminology Bulletins, *Accounting Research Bulletin No. 43,* Final Edition (Sept. 1961), p. 27.

erages, (3) sundry merchandise for sale (candy, souvenirs, etc.), and (4) equipment for sale (to franchisees). Inventories not for sale (to be consumed by the hospitality entity itself) may consist of (1) spare parts and (2) supplies.

Spare parts inventories are usually associated with airlines and other transportation-oriented firms with a large investment in equipment. Supplies inventories in the hospitality industry include guest gratuities, office, advertising, maintenance, and—the most important category—housekeeping (cleaning) supplies. Housekeeping supplies consist of brooms, detergents, dishwashing compounds, disinfectants, insecticides, mops, pails, polishes, soaps and any other materials used in cleaning.

The procedure of accounting for supplies inventory and supplies expense was explained in Chapter 7 and the accounting procedures related to spare parts are discussed in a later section of this chapter. Here we describe the procedures for valuing and recording inventories for sale.

Two steps are involved in measuring inventories: (1) determining the number of physical units in inventory, and (2) determining the value of these units.

In order to determine the number of units in inventory, their physical flow must be recorded and controlled. In order to value the units in inventory, some assumptions must be made regarding the flow of inventory costs, which (as explained in a later section) is not always the same as the physical flow of the individual inventory items.

The two systems for recording and controlling the physical flow of inventory units are the periodic-inventory system and the perpetual-inventory system. Under the periodic-inventory system, purchases are recorded as they occur but inventory issues are not recorded until the end of the accounting period, whereas under the perpetual-inventory system, both purchases and issues are recorded as they occur.

PERIODIC-INVENTORY SYSTEM

Because under the periodic-inventory system inventory issues are not recorded as they occur, it is impossible to know how much of each inventory item is on hand unless a physical-inventory count (called "taking a physical inventory") is made. Since this involves time and labor, it is practical to take a physical inventory only on a periodic basis, usually at the end of the accounting period, when it is required to determine cost of sales. Also, since inventory issues are not controlled, less paperwork and less physical control over inventories are involved in the application of the periodic-inventory system. Therefore, it is the preferred system for controlling inventories containing many different items of low individual value to which employees must have ready access, such as the food in a kitchen storeroom.

Although simpler to maintain than a perpetual inventory, the periodic-inventory system has the following disadvantages: (1) it does not provide continuous information concerning inventory quantities on hand, and (2) a simultaneous inventory count of all items is required every time financial statements are prepared in order to determine cost of sales.

Accounting for Periodic Inventories

In Chapter 7 we learned that cost of sales is calculated in the manner shown next.

```
            Beginning inventory
   Plus:    Purchases
            Product available for sale
   Less:    Ending inventory
            Cost of sales
```

Under the periodic-inventory system, purchases are debited to an account called "purchases," rather than to the inventory account directly. The amount in the inventory account throughout the entire accounting period reflects the inventory at the time the physical count was made at the end of the previous accounting period and is called the "beginning inventory." In order to determine the current period's cost of sales, a calculation such as the above is required based on a new physical inventory taken at the end of the current accounting period. This inventory is called the "ending inventory." The inventory account is adjusted to reflect this ending inventory amount and remains constant until the next physical inventory is taken at the end of the following accounting period. Because issues are not recorded until the end of the accounting period, it is impossible to determine cost of sales for each sale individually.

The example in Figure 15.1 shows the cost of sales calculations under the periodic-inventory system for the initial two months of a restaurant based on the food purchases and physical-inventory counts specified. Notice that the first month's ending inventory becomes the following month's beginning inventory.

The entries to record the above inventory purchases and cost of sales are given in Figure 15.2. The cost of sales entries close out the purchases account to the cost of sales account, thus preparing it for recording the following period's purchases. They also adjust the inventory account to the physical inventory taken at the end of the period. At the end of the first month, the ending inventory amount is $2,000 greater than the beginning inventory amount, and so the inventory account is debited. At the end of the second month the opposite is true, and so the inventory account is credited.

EMPLOYEE MEALS

In the hospitality industry, employee meals are often provided to employees while at work. The USAH includes these meals in the employee benefits account.

		Cost of sales
First month		
Beginning inventory	0	
Plus: Purchases	$10,000	
Product available for sale	10,000	
Less: Ending inventory	−2,000	$ 8,000
Second month		
Beginning inventory	$ 2,000	
Plus: Purchases	12,000	
Product available for sale	14,000	
Less: Ending inventory	1,000	$13,000

Figure 15.1.   Purchases and physical-inventory amount.

	Dr	Cr
First month		
Food purchases	10,000	
Cash		10,000

To record the first month's food purchases using the periodic-inventory method

	Dr	Cr
Cost of sales	8,000	
Food inventory	2,000	
Food purchases		10,000

To record the first month's cost of sales using the periodic-inventory method

	Dr	Cr
Second month		
Food purchases	12,000	
Cash		12,000

To record the second month's food purchases using the periodic-inventory method

	Dr	Cr
Cost of sales	13,000	
Food inventory		1,000
Food purchases		12,000

To record the second month's cost of sales using the periodic-inventory method

Figure 15.2. Entries to record inventory purchases and cost of sales.

Nevertheless, when the periodic-inventory system is utilized, the food and beverage consumed in employee meals are automatically included in cost of sales because they will be missing when the physical inventory is taken. A separate record of food and beverage consumed for employee meals must be maintained so that these amounts may be deducted from cost of sales and included in employee benefits through an entry such as the following:

	Dr	Cr
Employee benefits	350	
Cost of sales		350

To record $350 worth of food consumed for employee meals

If the above entry is not made, the familiar cost of sales calculation produces cost of food and beverages consumed, not cost of food and beverages sold. It is not until after deducting the cost of employee meals from cost of food consumed that it becomes a true cost of sales amount. This relationship is clarified in the condensed food and beverage department income statement in Figure 15.3.

FREIGHT-IN, PURCHASES RETURNS AND ALLOWANCES, AND PURCHASE DISCOUNTS

Inventories should be recorded at their purchase cost plus other acquisition costs, such as transportation, transportation insurance, taxes, storage, and purchasing and receiving costs. However, for the sake of expediency, only costs related to transporting inventory to the purchaser's business location are included in the inventory account. Other inventory acquisition costs such as storage, purchasing costs, and receiving costs, are reported directly on the

Revenue		$25,000	
Cost of sales			
Beginning inventory	$ 2,000		
Purchases	11,000		
Ending inventory	−3,000		
Cost of food and beverages consumed	10,000		
Less: Cost of employee meals	300		
Cost of food and beverages sold		9,700	
Gross profit			$15,300
Expenses			
Salaries and wages	$ 2,000		
Employee benefits			
(including employee meals)	1,100		
Total payroll & related expenses		$ 3,100	
Other expenses		6,000	9,100
Departmental income			$ 6,200

Figure 15.3.   Food and beverage department income statement.

income statement because they are difficult to identify with individual inventory items.

When inventory is purchased FOB (free on board) point of origin, as opposed to FOB destination, the supplier is responsible for placing it free on board the shipping vehicle at the shipper's location and the purchaser must pay the freight to his own place of business.[2] This expense is called freight-in and increases the cost of products available for sale. Any inventory that is returned to a supplier or for which an allowance is received from the supplier represents a reduction in the cost of products available for sale.

Under the perpetual-inventory system these increases or reductions in the cost of products for sale are debited or credited to the inventory account directly so that this account will reflect the cost of the inventory actually on hand. The cost of the affected inventory items will also be adjusted on their individual perpetual-inventory cards.

Freight-in of $500 and purchases returns and allowances of $300 on beverage inventory purchases would be recorded as follows under the perpetual-inventory system:

	Dr	Cr
Beverage inventory	500	
Cash		500

To record $500 of freight charges for beverage purchased using the perpetual-inventory system

	Dr	Cr
Accounts payable	300	
Beverage inventory		300

To record $300 of returned beverages using the perpetual-inventory system

Under the periodic-inventory system the inventory account does not reflect the current value of inventories. Consequently, there is no advantage in post-

---

[2]Inventory purchased FOB point of origin should be recorded in an account called "purchases-in-transit" until it is received.

ing freight-in and purchases returns and allowances directly to the inventory account. It is much more important for management to know the amount paid for freight-in, the better to control this expense. Management should also be watchful of purchases returns since the process of returning products generates additional handling and shipping expenses for the firm.

Under the periodic-inventory system, therefore, freight-in is debited to an account called "freight-in" and purchases returns and allowances are credited to an account called "purchases returns and allowances" as follows:

	Dr	Cr
Freight-in	500	
Cash		500

To record $500 of freight charges for beverage purchased using the periodic-inventory system

	Dr	Cr
Accounts payable	300	
Purchases returns & allowances		300

To record $300 of returned beverages using the periodic-inventory system

Purchase discounts are usually granted by suppliers for prompt payment of their accounts. As stated earlier, the payment due date and discount period may be abbreviated on a supplier's invoice as, e.g., $2/10$, net 30, which means a 2% discount will be granted if payment is made within 10 days, otherwise the full amount of the invoice must be paid in 30 days. Because of the savings involved in taking discounts on purchases, they are recorded in a separate account called "purchases discounts," where management can keep them under observation.

Thus, the payment of $10,000 worth of invoices on which a 2% discount had been earned would be recorded as follows:

	Dr	Cr
Accounts payable	10,000	
Purchases discounts		200
Cash		9,800

To record payment of $10,000 worth of invoices with a 2% discount

Although theoretically discounts, freight-in, and returns and allowances should be apportioned between inventory and cost of sales, these amounts usually are not material. Therefore, under the periodic-inventory system they are closed to cost of sales at the end of the accounting period.

An alternative procedure is to record the purchases discounts account separately on the income statement as "other revenue." Including this account on the income statement calls more attention to it, encouraging management to pay bills within the discount period. The closing of freight-in, returns and allowances, and purchases discounts to cost of beverage sales during the month of January is demonstrated in the cost of sales entry shown in Figure 15.4.

PERPETUAL-INVENTORY SYSTEM

Under the perpetual-inventory system, both purchases and issues are recorded as they occur. Management therefore knows at all times the quantity of each inventory item in stock without having to take a physical inventory. This constant control over inventories enables a manager to keep lower quantities

Assumptions		
December 31: Beverage inventory		$ 1,000
January 31: Beverage inventory		4,000
Beverage purchases during January		10,000
Freight-in on beverage purchases		500
Beverage returns during January		300
Discounts on purchases		200

	Dr	Cr
Cost of sales	7,000	
Beverage inventory	3,000	
Purchases returns & allowances	300	
Purchases discounts	200	
Beverage purchases		10,000
Freight-in		500
To record beverage cost of sales during the month of January		

Figure 15.4. Beverage cost of sales.

in stock without running out, thereby permitting a reduction of investment in inventories. In order to maintain this type of control, however, the following additional reports and subsidiary ledger are required, as well as additional personnel to maintain physical control over inventories and send these reports to the accounting department: (1) daily inventory receipts report, (2) daily report of inventory issues, (3) perpetual-inventory cards.

Samples of the above are shown in Figure 15.5. The two reports are prepared and remitted to the accounting department by a storeroom clerk, who also updates the perpetual-inventory card. Perpetual-inventory cards constitute a subsidiary ledger for the inventory control account that enables management to know the detailed composition of this account at any time. To reduce the risk of exhausting an item completely, the perpetual-inventory card has a minimum quantity at the top, indicating to the storeroom clerk when to reorder that particular item. Large firms have computerized their perpetual inventory, but the information reported by the computer concerning individual items is the same as that maintained on perpetual-inventory cards.

A perpetual-inventory card should show the (1) number of units received and their cost, (2) number of units issued and their cost, (3) balance on hand in units and their cost. Under the FIFO and LIFO inventory valuation methods (to be described later in this chapter), separate lines should be used in the balance column to record units having different costs, as shown in Figure 15.5.

Because of the additional control provided by the perpetual-inventory system, it is best used to control inventories of high-value items, such as wines, which justify the additional administrative cost of this inventory system.

Accounting for Perpetual Inventories

Under the perpetual-inventory system, inventory purchases are debited directly to the inventory account and issues are credited to the inventory account based on the daily receipts and issues reports. Because the amount of inventory purchased and consumed is known on a continuous basis, the inventory account does reflect the actual amount of inventory on hand at all times. The cost of sales account is also current because inventory issues are recorded as they occur.

Daily Inventory Receipts Report

Storeroom no: _____
Date: _____

Qty.	Description	Supplier	Unit price	Total amount

Storeroom clerk
(signature)

Daily Report of Inventory Issues

Storeroom no.: _____
Date: _____

Qty.	Description	Requisitioning department	Unit price	Total amount

Storeroom clerk
(signature)

Perpetual-Inventory Card—FIFO Valuation Method

Item name: Frozen turkeys   Inventory minimum: 2

Date	Receipts	Issues	Unit cost	Total cost	Balance Units	Balance Unit cost	Balance Total cost
3-1-85	2	—	10.00	20.00	2	10.00	20.00
3-2-85	5	—	10.50	52.50	2	10.00	
					5	10.50	72.50
3-2-85	—	2	10.00	20.00			
		1	10.50	10.50	4	10.50	42.00
3-8-85		1	10.50	10.50	3	10.50	31.50

Figure 15.5. Perpetual-inventory system records.

To record a $10,000 cash inventory purchase under the perpetual-inventory system, the following entry would be made:

	Dr	**Cr**
Inventory	10,000	
Cash		10,000

To record the purchase of $10,000
worth of inventories using the perpetual-inventory system

Under the perpetual-inventory system the entry to record the day's sales is accompanied by an entry to record the day's cost of sales, based on the inventory issues reports, as follows: Assume cash sales of $9,000 and cost of sales of $3,000:

	Dr	**Cr**
Cash	9,000	
Sales		9,000

To record day's sales

	Dr	**Cr**
Cost of sales	3,000	
Inventory		3,000

To record day's cost of sales

It is not necessary to take a physical inventory in order to determine cost of sales, because the information is available from the inventory issues report.

Since errors can occur in maintaining individual perpetual-inventory cards or because the physical control over inventories may become lax, it is recommended that physical-inventory counts of each inventory item be taken at least annually even under the perpetual-inventory system. One great advantage of the perpetual-inventory system is that a simultaneous count of all items at year end is not necessary in order to determine cost of sales. The amount of each item that should be on hand is known from the perpetual-inventory cards. Therefore, a few items may be counted at a time and the count compared to each item's perpetual-inventory card. The physical inventory may be taken gradually throughout the year when personnel have the spare time available, thereby avoiding the interference with the normal operation of the business produced by a general inventory at year end.

SPARE PARTS INVENTORIES

Spare parts inventories tend to be critical to the operations of a business. Consequently, the pereptual-inventory system is usually used to control them. This method provides management with a continuous record of spare parts availability and assures timely reordering.

As spare parts are consumed they are credited to the spare parts inventory account and charged to the repairs expense account.

INVENTORY VALUATION METHODS

We have discussed the two systems of controlling the physical flow of inventories. This physical flow, however, does not always match the flow of costs associated with individual inventory items. For instance, in a room full of wine bottles, all of the same vintage, vineyard, and bottler, it may be impossible or impractical to maintain a record of which bottles were purchased first and which last. If the purchases were made at different prices, some practical assumption must be made regarding the assignment of costs to each individual bottle as it is consumed.

Four different methods acceptable under GAAP for assigning such costs are discussed here:

1. Specific-units method
2. Weighted-average method
3. FIFO (first-in–first-out) method
4. LIFO (last-in–first-out) method

The specific-units method assigns actual costs to each specific unit. It is only practical for valuing inventories containing a few high-cost units, such as

TABLE 15.1. Chateau d'Yquem Wine Inventory Transactions

Transaction date	Units purchased	Unit cost	Total cost of units purchased	Sales	Units in inventory
May 1	2	$100	$ 200		2
5	5	105	525		7
10				3	4
15	2	115	230		6
17	4	120	480		10
20				5	5
31	6	125	750	–	11
Total	19		$2,185	8	

elaborate cakes or very expensive wines. The weighted-average method assigns an average cost to each inventory item, determined by dividing the total cost of the inventory by the total units in inventory. The FIFO method assigns the cost of the first items purchased to the first items sold, so that the oldest costs flow through to cost of sales first. The LIFO method assigns the cost of the last item purchased to the first item sold. In this case, the most recent costs are allowed to flow through to cost of sales first. These four inventory valuation methods will be explained based on the inventory data for a Chateau d'Yquem wine presented in Table 15.1. The periodic-inventory system for measuring product flow will be assumed.

Although the specific-units and FIFO inventory valuation methods generate the same cost of sales under both perpetual- and periodic-inventory systems, the weighted-average and LIFO inventory methods produce different results under the two systems, which will be explained where appropriate.

Specific-Units Valuation Method

Under the specific-units method the actual cost of each bottle sold is allowed to flow through to cost of sales. Thus, referring to Table 15.1, if two bottles came from those on hand at the beginning of May, two came from the purchase on May 5, and four came from the purchase on May 17, then the ending inventory and the cost of sales would be calculated as shown in Figure 15.6. This is verified by the familiar cost of sales calculation as follows:

Beginning inventory	0
Purchases	$ 2,185
Product available for sale	2,185
Ending inventory	−1,295
Cost of sales	$ 890

The specific-units method of inventory valuation is only practical for use with readily differentiable high-value items that can easily be associated with their actual cost. It would be ridiculous, for instance, to assign each individual potato in a bushel a specific unit cost.

Weighted-Average Valuation Method

Under the weighted-average method of determining the flow of inventory costs, the total cost of all units in inventory is divided by the total number of units on hand in order to arrive at the weighted-average cost per unit for

Ending Inventory—Specific-Units Method

Date purchased	Quantity		Unit cost		Total cost
May 5	3	×	$105	=	$ 315
15	2	×	115	=	230
31	6	×	125	=	750
Total	11				$1,295

Cost of Sales

Date sold	Units sold	Date purchased	Unit cost		Total cost
May 10	3	May 1	2 × $100		
		5	1 × 105	=	$305
20	5	5	1 × 105		
		17	4 × 120	=	585
Total	8				$890

Figure 15.6. Specific-units valuation method.

calculating cost of sales. Under the periodic-inventory system this calculation for the entire period is made at the end of the period. Figure 15.7 shows the weighted-average unit cost of the Chateau d'Yquem wine inventory calculated under the periodic-inventory method on the basis of the data presented in Table 15.1.

Notice that under the periodic-inventory system the cost of sales is not deducted until the end of the period, when the physical inventory is taken. Under the perpetual-inventory system the weighted-average unit cost at the time of each sale is deducted from the cumulative inventory value as sales occur, resulting in a slightly lower cost of sales in times of inflation.

The procedure for determining the inventory cost on May 5 is shown below as an example of how to make a weighted-average inventory calculation.

Date purchased	Units purchased		Unit cost		Total cost
May 1	2	×	$100	=	$200
5	5	×	105	=	525
Total	7				$725

The weighted average (rounded to the nearest dollar) is then given by

$$\frac{\text{cumulative inventory value on May 5}}{\text{total units in inventory}} = \frac{\$725}{7} = \$104$$

Using the cumulative ending inventory value at May 31 of $1,265 (see Figure 15.7), the cost of sales for the month can be calculated as follows:

Beginning inventory	0
Purchases	$ 2,185
Product available for sale	2,185
Ending inventory	−1,265
Cost of sales	$ 920

The weighted-average inventory valuation method dampens the effect of price fluctuations throughout an accounting period. This method generates a cost of sales amount and inventory values that are intermediate between those produced by the FIFO and LIFO inventory valuation methods.

Chateau d'Yquem Wine

Weighted-Average Unit Cost

Date	Units Purchased	Units Sold	Unit cost	Transaction value	Cumulative value in purchases account	Cumulative total units purchased	Weighted-average unit cost
May 1	2		$100	$200	$ 200	2	$100
5	5	Not	105	525	725	7	104
10		recorded					
15	2	under	115	230	955	9	106
17	4	periodic	120	480	1,435	13	110
20		inventory					
31	6		125	750	2,185	19	115
Total	19						

Ending Inventory Valuation

Weighted-average cost	×	Units in inventory per physical count	=	Weighted-average value of ending inventory
$115	×	11	=	$1,265

Figure 15.7. Weighted-average unit cost calculated by the periodic-inventory method.

First-in–First-out (FIFO) Valuation Method

The first-in–first-out (FIFO) method of inventory valuation allows the oldest costs to flow through to cost of sales, applying the most recent costs to products remaining in inventory. Figure 15.8 shows the Chateau d'Yquem ending inventory and cost of sales under the FIFO valuaton method.

This is verified by the familiar cost of sales calculation as follows:

Beginning inventory	0
Purchases	$ 2,185
Product available for sale	2,185
Ending inventory	−1,345
Cost of sales	$ 840

Because it allows the oldest costs (lower than current costs in times of inflation) to flow through to cost of sales, the FIFO method of inventory valuation generates the lowest cost of sales in an inflationary economic environment, and the highest inventory value.

Last-in–First-out (LIFO) Valuation Method

The last-in–first-out (LIFO) inventory valuation method allows the most recent costs to flow through to cost of sales and applies the oldest costs to products remaining in inventory. Figure 15.9 shows the Chateau d'Yquem ending inventory and cost of sales under the LIFO method. This can be verified by the familiar cost of sales calculation as follows:

Beginning inventory	0
Purchases	$ 2,185
Product available for sale	2,185
Ending inventory	−1,195
Cost of sales	$ 990

Ending Inventory—FIFO Method

Date purchased	Units in FIFO inventory		Unit cost		FIFO inventory value
May 15	1	×	$115	=	$ 115
17	4	×	120	=	480
31	6	×	125	=	750
Total	11				$1,345

Cost of Sales

Date sold	Units sold	Date purchased	Unit cost		Total cost
May 10	3	May 1	2 × $100		
		5	1 × 105	=	$305
20	5	5	4 × 105		
		15	1 × 115	=	535
Total	8				$840

Figure 15.8. FIFO valuation method.

Notice that since cost of sales is calculated at the end of the accounting period under the periodic-inventory system, the cost of May 31 purchases is applied to sales on May 10 and May 20 as if the sales had been made at the end of the month. If a perpetual inventory were being used, the cost of sales for each sale would be recorded when it occurred, on the basis of the latest purchase costs prior to the sale, thereby generating a slightly lower cost of sales in times of inflation.

In an inflationary economic environment, the LIFO inventory valuation method generates the highest cost of sales and the lowest inventory value because it allows the most recent costs (the most inflated) to flow through to cost of sales and assigns the oldest (the lowest during inflation) to inventories.

Ending Inventory—LIFO Method

Date purchased	Units in LIFO inventory		Unit cost		LIFO inventory value
May 1	2	×	$100	=	$ 200
5	5	×	105	=	525
15	2	×	115	=	230
17	2	×	120	=	240
Total	11				$1,195

Cost of Sales

Date sold	Units sold	Date purchased	Unit cost		Total cost
May 10	3	May 31	3 × $125	=	$375
20	5	31	3 × 125		
		17	2 × 120	=	615
Total	8				$990

Figure 15.9. LIFO valuation method.

COMPARISON OF INVENTORY
VALUATION METHODS

In order to visualize better the effects on net income of the four inventory valuation methods discussed in this text, they are presented in the context of a partial income statement in Table 15.2.

In Table 15.2 it is easy to verify that the weighted-average inventory valuation method produces cost of sales and ending inventory amounts that are intermediate between the corresponding FIFO and LIFO amounts. This is due to the moderating effect produced by averaging costs when they are either increasing due to inflation or declining in recessionary times.

It is also evident that because the data presented in Table 15.1 assumed a period of rising prices (inflation), the FIFO inventory valuation method produces the lowest cost of sales and highest ending inventory value. It allows the oldest and lowest costs to flow through to cost of sales. In contrast the LIFO inventory valuation method allows the most recent, highest costs to flow through to cost of sales. Hence it generates the highest cost of sales and lowest inventory valuation. If prices were declining the opposite would be true concerning FIFO and LIFO inventory valuation, although the weighted-average method would still produce intermediate cost of sales and inventory values. The specific-unit valuation method is not subject to any type of predictability. In our example it produced a cost of sales higher than FIFO and lower than the weighted-average method because mostly older, low-cost bottles were sold. Depending upon which specific units are sold (high cost or low cost) this method can generate a cost of sales anywhere between the FIFO and LIFO methods.

A review of Table 15.2 indicates that the value assigned to ending inventory is a critical factor in determining cost of sales. As the ending inventory value increases, cost of sales decreases. Accounting Research Bulletin No. 43 states: "the major objective in selecting a method shall be to choose the one which, under the circumstances, most clearly reflects periodic income."[3] Thus, priority should be given to realistic income determination as opposed to realistic inventory valuation when selecting an inventory cost flow method. Since the LIFO inventory valuation method allows the most recent costs to flow through to cost of sales, it would seem to meet this requirement best in periods of changing prices.

TABLE 15.2.   **Comparative Gross Profit Calculations Based on Four Inventory Valuation Methods**

	FIFO	Weighted average	LIFO	Specific units
Sales	$ 2,000	$ 2,000	$ 2,000	$ 2,000
Cost of sales				
Beginning inventory	0	0	0	0
Purchases	2,185	2,185	2,185	2,185
Product available for sale	2,185	2,185	2,185	2,185
Ending inventory	−1,345	−1,265	−1,195	−1,295
Cost of sales	840	920	990	890
Gross profit	$ 1,160	$ 1,080	$ 1,010	$ 1,110

[3]American Institute of Certified Public Accountants, Committee on Accounting Procedure, Accounting Research and Terminology Bulletins, *Accounting Research Bulletin No. 43,* Final Edition (Sept. 1961), p. 29.

However, although FIFO tends to overstate income in times of rising prices and understate income when prices are declining it is the simplest inventory valuation method to use. When the difference in net income produced by the FIFO and LIFO inventory methods is not material, most companies will tend to use the FIFO method. This is particularly true in the hospitality industry where inventories are usually perishable and small. Hospitality entities tend to consume all of their inventories even back to the oldest cost layers, thus diminishing the potential difference between the FIFO and LIFO valuation methods.

The income tax considerations involved in the selection of inventory valuation methods are discussed later in this chapter.

LOWER OF COST OR MARKET

Although inventories are recorded at cost, in periods of recessionary prices, and sometimes due to physical deterioration or obsolescence, the market value of inventories may decline below their original cost. When this occurs, ARB No. 43 states that inventories should be reported at their market value, recognizing the loss on the income statement in compliance with the principles of conservatism and matching.

The market value of inventories is their replacement cost. Since this is an estimate, ARB No. 43 places an upper and a lower limit on market value to prevent exaggeration, by stating that the market value of inventories:

- cannot be higher than their net realizable value (NRV)
- cannot be lower than net realizable value less a normal profit margin

Net realizable value is the value received upon the sale of inventories net of any expenses incurred in their sale. Thus if a $500 advertisement were required to sell 10 bottles of wine at $300 each, their net realizable value would be $3,000 (10 × $300) less the $500 cost of the advertisement, or $2,500.

The lower-of-cost-or-market value (LCM) of an inventory can be calculated for (1) each individual item, (2) each category of items (soups, meats, etc.), (3) the inventory taken as a whole. ARB No. 43 indicates that the item-by-item method is to be preferred when feasible.

Table 15.3 indicates how each of these procedures is applied. The first two columns after the description column indicate the cost and the market value of each item in inventory. The three columns to the right indicate the value of the total inventory when lower of cost or market is applied on an item-by-item basis, on an individual category basis, or to the entire inventory taken as a whole.

It should be noted that the concept of conservatism does not allow inventories to be marked up again should their market value increase at a later date.

After the lower of cost or market has been determined, the loss is recorded in an income statement account called "loss on markdown of inventory to LCM." The credit entry is recorded either as a direct reduction of the inventory account or in an inventory contra-asset account called "allowance for markdown of inventory to LCM."

The direct-inventory-reduction method is preferable under the periodic-inventory system because the cost of sales calculation is less cumbersome without the allowance for markdown contra-asset account. It is better to use the allowance contra-asset account under the perpetual-inventory system because

TABLE 15.3. Calculation of Lower of Cost or Market: Three Methods

Description	Cost	Market value	Lower-of-cost-or-market basis		Whole inventory
			Individual		
			Item	Category	
Soups					
Vegetable	$ 1,000	$ 1,100	$ 1,000		
Tomato	2,000	1,800	1,800		
	3,000	2,900		$ 2,900	
Meats					
Beef	5,000	4,750	4,750		
Chicken	3,100	3,375	3,100		
	8,100	8,125		8,100	
Total	$11,100	$11,025			$11,025
Comparison values			$10,650	$11,000	$11,025

it permits a lump sum adjustment of inventories at the end of each accounting period, without having to change item costs on each individual perpetual-inventory card.

THE PHYSICAL INVENTORY COUNT

As you have learned, the correct valuation of inventories depends on recording accurately the physical flow of inventory items. When using the periodic-inventory system, the only way of recording inventory consumption is to take a physical inventory at the end of the period. This procedure must therefore be executed with care. Taking a physical inventory involves the following steps:

1. Prepare appropriate inventory sheets.
2. Control access to the area being inventoried (during the entire inventory period) and keep a control sheet of the amount, date, and time of all inventory items entering or leaving the area.
3. Count all items in the area and keep a record of the date and time each item was counted.
4. Adjust the physical count for all inventory items that entered or left the area between the date and time of the count and the inventory cutoff date.
5. Assign costs to the items in the inventory using an acceptable inventory valuation method such as specific units, FIFO, weighted average, or LIFO, and calculate the total cost of the inventory.

A sample inventory count sheet is presented in Figure 15.10. The adjustment columns in the inventory count sheet are necessary due to the impossibility of taking an inventory of a large number of products exactly at the inventory cutoff time. In the physical inventory sheet shown in Figure 15.10, the cutoff time is midnight, December 31. Since the items to be counted were so numerous, the inventory was taken on December 31 and January 1, between 8:00 A.M. and 5:00 P.M. The time span between the time of the physical count and the inventory cutoff time may require that one of four types of

Stock no.	Description of item	Date and time of count	Quantity counted	Adjustments				Qty. at cutoff date	Unit cost	Total cost
				Out	In	Out	In			
446J	Canned vegetable soup	Dec. 31 4:55 P.M.	4	(1)	10			13	0.30	3.90
447J	Canned chili	Dec. 31 5:00 P.M.	5					5	0.55	2.75
448J	Canned carrots	Jan. 1 8:00 A.M.	16	1	(10)			7	0.40	2.80

Figure 15.10. Sample inventory count sheet.

potential adjustments be made to the actual physical count. When the physical count is made before the inventory cutoff date:

1. Add to the physical count any items received after the count is made.
2. Subtract from the physical count any items issued after the count is made.

When the physical count is made after the inventory cutoff date:

3. Add to the physical count any items issued after the inventory cutoff time.
4. Subtract from the physical count any items received after the inventory cutoff time.

For example, on the inventory count sheet shown above, 4 cans of vegetable soup were counted at 4:55 P.M. on December 31. Between 4:55 P.M. and midnight, 1 can was consumed and 10 cans were received, and so the physical count at 4:55 P.M., December 31, must be adjusted to show the correct inventory at midnight, December 31, as follows:

December 31	Number of cans
Physical inventory count at 4:55 P.M.	4
Less: Consumed between 4:55 P.M. and midnight	−1
Plus: Received between 4:55 P.M. and midnight	+10
Inventory in stock at midnight, December 31	13

Opposite adjustments would be made if the physical inventory count had been taken after the midnight cutoff time on December 31.

Any items purchased FOB point of origin that have been shipped by the supplier but not received by the purchaser constitute purchases-in-transit and should be included in the physical inventory count. As noted earlier, title to these items passed to the purchaser upon delivery by the supplier to the transportation company.

After the physical quantities in inventory have been determined, unit costs are assigned and the total inventory cost is determined by adding the total cost of all inventory items. This may be done on the same sheet used for making the inventory count or on separate value computation worksheets.

When the inventory value from a physical inventory differs from the inventory value on the books under the perpetual-inventory system, the books must be adjusted to the physical count by debiting or crediting an account called inventory shortages and overages, which appears on the income statement.

SOURCES OF ERRORS IN INVENTORY VALUATION

Errors in valuing inventories have as many sources as there are steps in the computation process. Some of these sources are listed below:

- No company policy requiring occasional physical inventory counts to verify perpetual-inventory cards.
- Errors in making the physical inventory count.
- Errors in recording the physical count on value computation sheets (the sheets on which quantities are multiplied by cost) when such sheets are used.
- Errors in applying purchase costs according to the inventory valuation method selected.
- Errors in recording freight-in and purchases returns when computing costs.
- Mathematical errors on value computation sheets or physical count sheets.
- Improper physical control of inventory while making the inventory count.
- When a perpetual inventory is used, unauthorized personnel may have access to a storeroom and fail to record issues.
- When using a computerized system, errors may be made in entering amounts.
- When a perpetual-inventory system is used, errors may be made in entering receipts and issues on the perpetual-inventory cards.
- When a periodic-inventory system is used, errors may be made in entering purchases.

It is no coincidence that some of the sources of errors mentioned above, if avoided, will not only result in the correct evaluation of inventories at year end, but will also promote good physical control over inventories throughout the year. Avoiding errors in these areas is known as exercising good "internal control." The objectives of internal control are to safeguard the assets of an entity and to avoid misinformation. The effects of inventory valuation errors on reported management results are highlighted in the following section.

Impact of Inventory Valuation Errors

The inverse relationship between inventories and cost of sales should have been clearly established in the reader's mind by now. Given a specific amount of product available for sale, the higher the ending inventory value, the lower will be the cost of sales and the higher the current period net income.

Thus, if the current period's inventory is understated the current period's cost of sales will be overstated. Also, since the current period's ending invento-

TABLE 15.4. Gourmet Restaurant

	Year 1	Year 2	Year 3
Sales	$1,500,000	$1,500,000	$1,500,000
Correct value of			
Beginning inventory	100,000	100,000	100,000
Food purchases	500,000	500,000	500,000
Ending inventory	100,000	100,000	100,000

TABLE 15.5. Food Inventory Understated in Year 2

	Year 1	Year 2	Year 3
Sales	$1,500,000	$1,500,000	$1,500,000
Correct value of			
Beginning inventory	100,000	100,000	50,000
Food purchases	500,000	500,000	500,000
Food available for sale	600,000	600,000	550,000
Ending inventory	−100,000	−50,000	−100,000
Cost of sales	500,000	550,000	450,000
Gross profit	$1,000,000	$ 950,000	$1,050,000

ry is the following period's beginning inventory, an understatement in the current period's inventory will produce an understatement in the subsequent period's cost of sales.

The effects of inventory valuation errors on the current and subsequent period's gross profit and corresponding net income, are demonstrated by the examples given in Tables 15.4–15.7. They indicate the effects on gross profit of (1) undervaluation, (2) correct valuation, and (3) overvaluation of inventories based on the data from the Gourmet Restaurant.

In Table 15.5, an understatement of ending inventory in year 2 results in an overstatement of cost of sales in year 2 and an understatement of cost of sales in year 3. The opposite occurs in Table 15.7, where an overstatement of the current period's inventory occurs. Only the example of Table 15.6, in which inventories are correctly valued, shows the correct gross profit for all three years.

Errors in current inventory valuation should therefore be diligently avoided. Their effect will be felt over a two-year period with possible negative consequences respecting the company's credit rating and income taxes payable, in addition to the unfavorable emotional impact of earnings fluctuations on the owners of the business.

TAX CONSIDERATIONS IN ACCOUNTING FOR INVENTORIES

Since the various methods of inventory valuation result in different cost of sales amounts, they also have a direct bearing on the amount of income taxes paid. From a tax-planning point of view, it is evident that in times of inflation the LIFO method of inventory valuation tends to minimize net income because it allows the most recent cost (the highest in times of inflation) to flow through

TABLE 15.6. Food Inventory Correctly Stated in Year 2

	Year 1	Year 2	Year 3
Sales	$1,500,000	$1,500,000	$1,500,000
Correct value of			
Beginning inventory	100,000	100,000	100,000
Food purchases	500,000	500,000	500,000
Food available for sale	600,000	600,000	600,000
Ending inventory	−100,000	−100,000	−100,000
Cost of sales	500,000	500,000	500,000
Gross profit	$1,000,000	$1,000,000	$1,000,000

TABLE 15.7. Food Inventory Overstated in Year 2

	Year 1	Year 2	Year 3
Sales	$1,500,000	$1,500,000	$1,500,000
Correct value of			
Beginning inventory	100,000	100,000	150,000
Food purchases	500,000	500,000	500,000
Food available for sale	600,000	600,000	650,000
Ending inventory	−100,000	−150,000	−100,000
Cost of sales	500,000	450,000	550,000
Gross profit	$1,000,000	$1,050,000	$ 950,000

to cost of sales. The FIFO method maximizes net income in times of inflation because it allows the oldest costs (lowest in times of inflation) to flow through to cost of sales, and the weighted-average inventory method produces an intermediate net income. The specific-units valuation method is unpredictable because the cost of sales under this method depends on which specific units are actually sold. If a firm wishes to postpone its tax payments as long as possible, it will use the LIFO method of inventory valuation in order to minimize taxable income. Use of the LIFO inventory valuation method in calculating taxable income for tax reporting purposes has one drawback. When this method is used to calculate taxable income, the IRS requires that it also be used to calculate book income for financial reporting purposes. A manager is thus required to minimize the net income reported to stockholders.

Also, the LIFO inventory valuation method is very complex to use because of present IRS regulations. Consequently, about as many firms use the FIFO inventory valuation method as use the LIFO method, despite the tax advantages of the latter. Because of the low amounts of inventory carried by the typical hospitality firm, the tax savings provided by using the LIFO method are usually not significant.

The IRS allows the markdown of inventories to LCM with the recognition of the related loss on the tax return as long as the inventories so marked down are actually scrapped. This is usually the case when dealing with perishables such as food. Otherwise, the markdown cannot be made and the loss cannot be recognized for tax reporting purposes, even though GAAP may require the markdown for financial reporting purposes. In this case a deferred income tax charges account, the opposite of a deferred income tax payable account, must be created and listed under "other assets" on the balance sheet. It is amortized as the marked-down inventory is gradually consumed.

FINANCIAL STATEMENT PRESENTATION
OF INVENTORIES

As stated earlier, financial information should be summarized for the sake of clarity when preparing financial statements for external reporting purposes. There are, however, certain minimum disclosures that cannot be omitted. The disclosure requirements for inventories will be covered in Chapter 19. The 1980 financial statement presentation of inventories by Wendy's International, Inc., a fast-food restaurant chain, is presented in Figure 15.11. Note that inventories are presented in the current asset section of the balance sheet

December 31	1980	1979
Assets		
Current assets		
Cash	$ 5,875,439	$ 2,285,180
Short-term investments, at cost, which approximates market	7,012,267	12,656,352
Accounts receivable	5,514,180	4,902,746
Inventories and other	6,305,129	2,581,528
	24,707,015	22,425,806

Figure 15.11. Wendy's International, Inc. 1980 financial statement presentation of inventories. In the notes to the statement appears the note that "inventories are stated at lower of cost (first-in, first-out) or market, and consist of restaurant food items and paper supplies."

according to their order of liquidity with respect to other current assets, and on a comparative basis (the previous year inventory amounts should be shown.) Also, when they are material, the different inventory categories should be disclosed separately (food and beverages, supplies, etc.).

QUESTIONS

1. ARB No. 43 describes two broad inventory classifications. What are they?
2. Why is there sometimes a difference between the physical flow of inventories and the flow of inventory costs?
3. What are the two methods of recording the physical flow of inventories? How do they differ?
4. What are the advantages and disadvantages of each of the two methods of recording the physical flow of inventories? Under what circumstances should each method be used?
5. What is the difference between beginning and ending inventory? Explain the relationship between the ending inventory of an accounting period and the beginning inventory of the following accounting period.
6. How do you determine cost of sales under the periodic-inventory method? Under the perpetual-inventory method?
7. What does it mean to take a physical inventory?
8. What costs are charged to the inventory account when recording inventories?
9. In what account should employee meals be recorded? How is this done under the periodic- and perpetual-inventory methods?
10. When is cost of sales recorded under a periodic-inventory system? Under a perpetual-inventory system?
11. Under the periodic-inventory system, to what account are freight-in, purchases returns and allowances, and purchase discounts closed? At what point of the accounting cycle is this done?
12. Which inventory valuation method tends to minimize net income in an inflationary economy? Which method generates the largest net income in an inflationary economy? Explain.
13. If inventories are understated at the end of year 1, what effect will that have on the income statements for years 1 and 2, and on the balance sheet at the end of year 2?
14. What are the allowable upper and lower limits for determining market value specified by ARB No. 43 when marking inventories down to LCM?
15. What four types of adjustments may have to be made on the inventory sheet when taking a physical inventory?

EXERCISES

1. Suppose you purchased 75 bottles of Burgundy from three different bottlers as follows:

		Total cost
Jan 1	25 bottles at $50	$1250
15	25 bottles at $75	1875
30	25 bottles at $100	2500

   (a) If you used the specific unit method of inventory valuation and you sold 50 bottles in January, which bottles would you sell first if you wish to:
   (1) Maximize your net income?
   (2) Minimize your net income?
   (b) Calculate the cost of sales for the 50 bottles sold using the FIFO and LIFO inventory valuation methods.
   (c) Does the FIFO method tend to maximize net income in this example? Why?

2. Which of the following inventory unit costs would you select under the item-by-item basis of determining lower of cost or market?

Item	Cost	Net realizable value	Market value	Net realizable value less normal profit
Caviar	$ 5.45	$ 9.00	$ 5.25	$ 5.40
French bread	1.20	1.10	1.05	0.70
Bordeaux wine	40.50	30.00	35.00	10.00
Tomato soup	0.90	2.70	0.85	0.95
Gouda cheese	20.00	40.00	30.00	13.00

3. Your inventory cutoff time was midnight on March 31 but you required between 8:00 A.M. and 5:00 P.M. on March 31 and between 8:00 A.M. and 5:00 P.M. on April 1 to take the entire physical inventory. The activity that occurred between the time of your physical count indicated on the inventory count sheet shown here and the inventory cutoff time is listed below for four inventory items. Based on this activity make the required adjustments to your physical count and determine the correct amount in inventory at the inventory cutoff time.

Inventory Count Sheet

Stock no.	Description item	Date and time of count	Quantity counted	Adjustments Out	Adjustments In	Quantity at cutoff time
688P	Onions	Mar. 31 4:55 P.M.	30 lb			
689P	Carrots	Mar. 31 5:00 P.M.	20 lb			
690P	Potatoes	Apr. 1 8:00 A.M.	100 lb			
691P	Cauliflower	Apr. 1 8:05 A.M.	20 lb			

   Activity between time of count and cutoff time:
   (1) At 6:00 P.M. on March 31, 10 lb of onions were received.
   (2) At 10:00 P.M. on March 31, 5 lb of carrots were consumed.
   (3) At 5:00 A.M. on April 1, 8 lb of potatoes were consumed.
   (4) At 7:30 A.M. on April 1, 10 lb of cauliflower were received.

4. The following three-years' income statements for the No-A-Count Restaurant reflect a $10,000 overstatement in the 1986 ending inventory:

	1986	1987	1988
Sales	$600,000	$650,000	$630,000
Cost of food and beverages sold	170,000	205,000	189,000
Gross profit	430,000	445,000	441,000
Expenses	330,000	350,000	335,000
Net income	$100,000	$ 95,000	$106,000

(a) Prepare corrected income statements for 1986, 1987, and 1988 after eliminating the $10,000 ending inventory overstatement error in 1986.

(b) Calculate and explain the effect of this inventory valuation error on No-A-Count Restaurant's owner's equity for 1986, 1987, and 1988.

5. The Fish-R-Fresh Restaurant chain's fish inventory was determined to be $1,205,439 by physical count on November 30, 1987. It was discovered later that the following information had not been considered in calculating this inventory:

(1) $127,462 worth of fish had been purchased FOB point of origin but had not yet been shipped as of November 30, 1987.

(2) $89,776 worth of fish had been purchased FOB destination and was en route to the restaurant chain's warehouse on November 30, 1987.

(3) $69,435 worth of fish had been purchased FOB point of origin and was en route to the restaurant chain on November 30, 1987.

(a) What is the correct fish inventory value for the Fish-R-Fresh Restaurant chain?

(b) What effect will this correction have on the current year's net income?

(c) What would have been the effect on the following year's net income if this correction had not been made?

PROBLEMS

1. Prepare journal entries to record the following transactions of the Swan Song Restaurant under the (a) periodic- and (b) perpetual-inventory systems. Record end-of-period cost of sales entry where appropriate and prepare closing entries. Assume the purchase discounts account is not closed to cost of sales and that freight and insurance on returns are charged back to the supplier. Round amounts to the nearest dollar.

(1) Purchased 20 frozen ducks on 2/10, net 30 credit terms for $10 each FOB suppliers warehouse.

(2) Paid $15 freight and $5 insurance for above 20 ducks.

(3) Returned 1 duck because it was a turkey.

(4) Sold 5 of the above ducks for $200.

(5) Paid for the above ducks within the discount period.

2. Assume the L.E. Tist Restaurant made the following transactions and uses the perpetual-inventory system:

Sept. 4 Purchased 5 chickens at $3.00 each.

6 Sold 3 chickens.

10 Purchased three chickens at $3.50 each.

15 Purchased 10 chickens at $4.50 each.

20 Sold 5 chickens.

25 Sold 4 chickens.

(a) Prepare a perpetual-inventory card such as the one shown in Figure 15.5 and enter the above transactions on the card, assuming the FIFO inventory valuation method is used. Be sure to record the sales and show the unit costs of different cost units on separate lines of the card.

(b) Prepare another perpetual-inventory card for the above transactions assuming the LIFO inventory valuation method is used.

(c) Prepare a third perpetual-inventory card for the above transactions assuming the weighted-average inventory valuation method is used.

(d) Prepare the cost of sales entry (or entries) to record the sale on September 20 using the FIFO inventory valuation basis.

3. Based on the following inventory values, answer the questions below:

	1986	1987	1988
FIFO	$100,000	$ 90,000	$115,000
Market value	90,000	85,000	125,000
LIFO	95,000	100,000	110,000

(a) Which inventory valuation method (FIFO or LIFO) would you prefer if you want to:
(1) Maximize net income in 1986?
(2) Minimize net income in 1986?
(3) Maximize net income in 1987?
(4) Minimize net income in 1987?
Explain your answers to the above.

(b) Which of the following statements best describe the movement of prices within each of the three years—1986, 1987, and 1988:
(1) Prices increased from the beginning to the end of the year.
(2) Prices decreased from the beginning to the end of the year.
(3) Prices went up in the first half of the year and down in the second half of the year.
Explain your answers to the above.

4. Following are listed the sales and purchases of Chianti Wine made by Mr. Xavier Camp's Restaurant in January, February, and March, 1986. Assume there was no beginning inventory and that the periodic-inventory system is in use.

Transaction date 1986	Units purchased	Unit cost	Total cost	Unit sales
Jan. 10	20	$2.00	$40.00	
Jan. 13				8
Jan. 15	5	2.10	10.50	
Jan. 18				9
Jan. 26	6	2.10	12.60	
Feb. 4				4
Feb. 10	7	2.15	15.05	
Feb. 20				7
Feb. 28	7	2.20	15.40	
Mar. 15				9
Mar. 20	5	2.30	11.50	
Mar. 23				7
Mar. 30				6

(a) Prepare abbreviated income statements showing sales, cost of sales (based on the periodic-inventory system), and gross profit for each of the three months individually and for the three-month period as a whole, using the FIFO, weighted-average, and LIFO valuation methods. Assume the sales price is $6 per unit for all sales. When calculating weighted average round amounts to nearest hundredth of a cent.

(b) How does gross profit change from month to month under the three valuation methods? Explain. How is the overall gross profit for the entire three-month period affected by the use of the three different inventory valuation methods? Explain.

5. The following mistakes were made by the Mary Penin Restaurant in accounting for its food and beverage inventory as of December 31, 1986, the restaurant's year end. (The accounting records have already been adjusted to the physical inventory count.)

(1) Food amounting to $1,200 was purchased and recorded on the books on December 28, 1986, FOB point of origin, but had not been received when the physical inventory was taken and was therefore excluded from the inventory count.

(2) When the physical inventory sheets were totaled, one sheet was added incorrectly. An incorrect amount of $1,000 was used as a column total instead of the correct amount of $500.

(3) The Mouton-Cadet wine inventory was taken on January 1, 1987 and amounted to $5,600. Because of poor inventory-taking procedures, $1,000 worth of this wine was taken to the ballroom from inventory between midnight December 31, 1986 (the inventory cutoff date) and the time of the physical count, without being detected by those in charge of taking the inventory.

(4) The wrong invoice was used to determine the value of the Spanish ham inventory. Consequently, the 100 hams in inventory were erroneously valued at $25 each instead of $35 each, the correct amount.

(5) In order to avoid bothering the chefs during their preparations for midnight dinner on December 31, 1986, the food in the kitchen pantry was counted on December 30, 1986. No control was kept of the amount of food consumed subsequently in preparing the midnight dinner. The value of the food consumed during the dinner was $15,000.

(a) On the worksheet presented below indicate the effect of each error on inventory, cost of sales, and gross profit for the years 1986 and 1987. Indicate amounts to be subtracted in each column by using parentheses.

1986			
Mistake	Inventory	Cost of sales	Gross profit
(1)			
(2)			
(3)			
(4)			
(5)			

1987			
Mistake	Inventory	Cost of sales	Gross profit
(1)			
(2)			
(3)			
(4)			
(5)			

(b) Based on the above analysis prepare appropriate entries to correct the errors in 1986 and 1987. Assume 1986 closing entries have already been made.

16

Receivables and Payables

Because of the transient nature of its clientele, the hospitality industry relies primarily on cash sales. Although credit sales are growing in the industry due to the expanding presence of credit card companies, hospitality firms tend to have trade accounts receivable approximately equivalent to only 3% of total assets, although accounts receivable may assume greater proportions in some hotels and restaurants. Similarly, as noted earlier, inventories, which are usually purchased on credit, tend to be small in the hospitality industry, resulting in accounts payable of lesser dollar magnitude.

Nevertheless, due to the fact that accounts receivable are converted into cash fairly quickly in the hospitality industry, a small investment in accounts receivable can increase sales and profits considerably, with only a slight increase in risk to hospitality firms when proper credit and collection policies are applied. Likewise, taking advantage of the full discount period to pay accounts payable not only enables a firm to earn appreciable discounts, but also provides interest-free funds to help finance accounts receivable.

Although trade accounts receivable and accounts payable are the most significant components of the receivables and payables accounts in terms of their impact on the operations of a hospitality firm, they are not the only nor the largest components of these account groups. This chapter therefore takes into consideration nontrade accounts receivable and notes receivable as well as other payables, such as accrued liabilities, taxes payable, short-term notes payable, dividends payable, unearned revenue, and long-term debt. Additionally, other related items, such as deferred taxes payable and contingent liabilities are discussed.

In this chapter the various accounts in the receivables group are first defined, including a discussion of certain credit and collection procedures. The allowance method of accounting for uncollectible accounts is then explained, including an explanation of the procedures for writing off an uncollectible account. This is followed by a discussion of the direct write-off method of accounting for uncollectible accounts.

The unique aspects of credit card sales and a brief overview of pledging, assigning, and factoring accounts receivable are discussed after this, followed by an explanation of notes receivable and the process of discounting them. The various accounts in the current liability classification will then be dealt with.

Long-term debt, deferred income taxes payable, and contingent liabilities are covered next, concluding the chapter with the balance sheet presentation of receivables, payables, and their required disclosures.

TYPES OF RECEIVABLES

The receivables account group can be subdivided into the following three major categories:

1. Trade accounts receivable
2. Other accounts receivable
3. Notes receivable

Trade accounts receivable represent amounts due the hospitality firm for goods sold or services rendered, and originate as the result of credit sales. Other accounts receivable include all nontrade accounts receivable such as loans to employees, refunds receivable, and interest receivable. Notes receivable are receivables that are evidenced by a note signed by a party who has received services or property from the hospitality firm.

Although credit sales imply an additional risk for a business entity, without credit sales growth in the hospitality industry would be greatly impaired. When sales are made on credit the hospitality firm receives a commitment of future payment instead of immediate cash payment. In order to engage safely in making such sales, therefore, a firm should apply certain credit and collection policies to reduce the risk of subsequent nonpayment:

- Establish internal procedures for authorizing credit, such as (1) investigating the client's credit history and (2) requiring an officer's authorization before granting credit
- Establish specific collection procedures to remind customers of amounts that are due

In larger firms, a credit department is established to assume responsibility for implementing the policies enumerated above. Proper control of credit enables a firm to minimize losses due to nonpayment and to maximize profits earned on credit sales.

Nevertheless, it is nearly impossible to avoid such losses altogether and it is difficult to ascertain the amount of current accounts receivable that will become uncollectible in the future. Management usually does not become aware of the uncollectibility of an account until a subsequent accounting period, since the creditworthiness of each client is well established at the time of the sale if proper credit policies are applied.

This is problematical because the matching concept requires that expenses be matched with the revenue they help to generate. In order to comply with this concept, management must offset against current revenues potential future losses due to the uncollectibility of some current accounts receivable.

ALLOWANCE METHOD OF RECORDING
BAD DEBTS EXPENSE

The allowance method of recording uncollectible accounts enables management to estimate future losses on accounts receivable. Under this method, an estimate of future uncollectible accounts is made and entered in a contra-asset account called "allowance for doubtful accounts." This account appears immediately below accounts receivable on the balance sheet as follows:

Accounts receivable	$100,000
Less: Allowance for doubtful accounts	2,000
Net accounts receivable	$ 98,000

The debit entry is made to an account called bad debts expense on the income statement. The allowance for doubtful accounts is recorded by the adjusting entry shown below:

	Dr	**Cr**
Bad debts expense	2,000	
Allowance for doubtful accounts		2,000

To provide an allowance for doubtful accounts and record bad debt expense of $2,000

Two alternative allowance methods are available to help management make a more accurate estimate of future uncollectible accounts: (1) the percentage-of-sales method, and (2) the accounts receivable aging method.

The percentage-of-sales method focuses on the income statement and is based on determining what percentage of the current year's sales will be uncollectible. Management estimates the percentage of previous annual sales that have been uncollectible and multiplies the current year's sales by this percentage rate. If management found that on average 2% of the previous three years' sales were uncollectible, the current year's sales would be multiplied by 2% in order to determine the amount by which the allowance for uncollectible accounts should be increased. This is demonstrated below:

Year	Sales	**Actual uncollectible accounts**	**Average uncollectible percentage**
1988	$ 650,000	$19,500	
1989	890,000	15,300	
1990	1,120,000	18,400	
	$2,660,000	$53,200	2%

The average uncollectible percentage is then found by dividing:

$$\frac{53,200}{2,660,000} \times 100 = 2\%$$

Assuming this year's sales are $1,400,000, the entry to record management's estimate of uncollectible accounts is indicated below:

	Dr	**Cr**
Bad debts expense	28,000	
Allowance for doubtful accounts		28,000

To record 2% bad debt expense on 1991 sales of $1,400,000

The accounts receivable aging method focuses on the balance sheet and attempts to estimate the percentage of current accounts receivable that is likely to be uncollectible. In order to arrive at this estimate, an aging schedule of accounts receivable is prepared. This is a worksheet such as the one illustrated in Figure 16.1, in which each outstanding account is listed according to its age. Management estimates the percentage of each age category believed to be uncollectible and prepares a worksheet as in Figure 16.2. The accounts receivable aging schedule indicates that the allowance for doubtful accounts should have a credit balance of $742. If we assume that the account has a $300

Client	Amount due	Current	*Current* 1–30	Days past due 31–60	61–90	Over 90
John Wirth	$ 1,200			$1,200		
Karmon, Inc.	20,000	$10,000	$6,000	4,000		
William Blye	650				$650	
Patricia Velez	520					$520
	$22,370	$10,000	$6,000	$5,200	$650	$520

Figure 16.1. Accounts receivable aging schedule.

credit balance from previous years, then only $442 need be added in the current year as shown below:

Estimated uncollectible Accounts receivable	$ 742
Balance in the allowance for doubtful accounts from previous years	−300
Required current year adjustment	$ 442

The $442 adjustment calculated above is recorded as follows:

	Dr	Cr
Bad debts expense	442	
Allowance for doubtful accounts		442
To adjust the allowance for doubtful accounts per the accounts receivable aging schedule		

As we shall see later, if management has underestimated the amount of uncollectible accounts in the past, the allowance for doubtful accounts will end up with a debit balance. This debit balance should be added to the amount considered uncollectible per the accounts receivable aging schedule to record the new, current allowance for doubtful accounts.

Generally, both the percentage-of-sales method and the accounts receivable aging schedule method are used by a firm at different stages of the accounting cycle. Throughout the year the percentage-of-sales method is applied because of its simplicity. At year end, an aging schedule is prepared to adjust the allowance for doubtful accounts with greater accuracy, and also to revise the percentage of sales considered uncollectible based on any changes in the company's most recent collection experience.

Account age	Amount	Percentage uncollectible[a]	Allowance for uncollectible accounts
Current	$10,000	1	$100
Days past due			
1–30	6,000	3	180
31–60	5,200	4	208
61–90	650	15	98
Over 90	520	30	156
	$22,370		$742

[a]Based on previous years' experience.

Figure 16.2. Calculation of allowance for uncollectible accounts.

Writing Off an Uncollectible Account

The allowance for doubtful accounts is recorded on the basis of estimates. When a customer goes into bankruptcy or gives evidence in some other way that it will be impossible to collect all or part of the amount owed the firm, then the loss on that account becomes a certainty. It is misleading to include such customers in accounts receivable, and so their account must be written off the books. Since, under the allowance method, bad debts expense has already been charged, such accounts must be written off against the allowance for doubtful accounts. Assuming Rolf Auslin owed the firm $1,000 and was declared bankrupt, and was thus unable to pay any of his debt, the entry to write off his account would be made as follows:

	Dr	Cr
Allowance for doubtful accounts	1,000	
Accounts receivable		1,000
To write off Rolf Auslin's account receivable due to his bankruptcy		

Thus, if management has underestimated the amount of uncollectible accounts, the allowance for doubtful accounts will end up the year with a debit balance, which must be adjusted according to the aging schedule.

When a customer whose account was previously written off as uncollectible later pays all or part of the account, the above entry is reversed and a second entry to record collection of the restored account is made as follows:

	Dr	Cr
Accounts receivable	500	
Allowance for doubtful accounts		500
To restore $500 of Rolf Auslin's account previously written off		
Cash	500	
Accounts receivable		500
To record collection of Rolf Auslin's account		

DIRECT WRITE-OFF METHOD OF RECORDING BAD DEBTS EXPENSE

The direct method of recording bad debts expense requires waiting for an account to be proven uncollectible before it is charged to bad debts expense. Since this may occur in a period subsequent to the one in which the account was created and its related revenue was recorded, this method does not comply with the matching principle.

Under this method an allowance for doubtful accounts is created. The write-off is recorded as follows:

	Dr	Cr
Bad debts expense	400	
Accounts receivable		400
To write off a $400 uncollectible account under the direct write-off method		

Although it is not acceptable for financial-reporting purposes, this method is allowed by the IRS for tax-reporting purposes.

ACCOUNTS RECEIVABLE CREDIT BALANCES AND CREDIT SALES TO SUPPLIERS

The account of a customer who overpays will have a credit balance. In such cases, the account should be included in accounts payable when preparing financial statements. It would be misleading to offset this credit amount against the accounts receivable debit balance, because the overpayment represents an amount actually owed by the firm.

Likewise, a firm cannot offset accounts payable generated by purchases from a supplier against accounts receivable generated by sales to the same supplier. Even though both the sales and purchase transactions occurred with the same firm, the receivable must be shown as a current asset and the payable must be shown as a current liability on the financial statements.

CREDIT CARD SALES

Credit card companies assume the risk of granting credit to their cardholders, thereby relieving the hospitality firm of this risk. In return for this service they charge member firms a percentage of sales effected through their cards. This percentage becomes an expense of the member firm.

For example, a $200 credit card sale is recorded by debiting the accounts receivable account of the credit card company as follows:

	Dr	Cr
Accounts receivable (credit card)	200	
Sales		200
To record a $200 sale through a credit card		

At the time the sale is made, the customer signs a sales slip, which is sent to the credit card company for payment. Payment is made for the amount of the sale less a commission. Assuming a 3% commission on the above sale, the entry to record payment by the credit card company is made as follows:

	Dr	Cr
Cash	194	
Credit card commission expense	6	
Accounts receivable		200
To record payment by a credit card company of a $200 sales slip less 3% commission		

Some credit card companies, such as Visa and Master Card, sometimes arrange with local banks to have the bank deposit funds in a company's account when the company delivers its credit card sales slips to the bank, thus avoiding mailing delays. In these circumstances the credit card sales slips are sent to the bank in the form of a normal deposit by the company, and the entry to record the deposit is made as follows:

	Dr	Cr
Cash	194	
Credit card commission expense	6	
Sales		200
To record credit card sales slip deposits when a direct payment agreement exists with a local bank		

PLEDGING, ASSIGNING, AND FACTORING ACCOUNTS RECEIVABLE

Sometimes firms have such great cash needs that they cannot wait to collect accounts receivable. Three methods of obtaining some cash for their accounts receivable are available to such firms, namely pledging, assigning, and factoring their accounts receivable.

When accounts receivable are pledged they are used as collateral for a loan, which is repaid, plus interest, from any source the borrower wishes to use. The full amount of the pledged accounts serves as collateral for the loan until it is paid completely. In case of default the lender can sell any accounts pledged to recover the amount owed.

When accounts receivable are assigned, the lender takes charge of the collection of the assigned accounts and collects the loan principal and interest plus a service commission. The borrower still assumes the loss from any uncollectible accounts.

When they are factored, accounts receivable are sold to the lender. The lender is responsible for collecting the accounts and assumes any bad debt losses. Consequently, the lender charges a higher commission than when the accounts are merely assigned. Also, until all accounts have been collected the lender only remits 80–90% of the collections to the borrower as protection against sales returns and allowances.

NOTES RECEIVABLE

Often, when a customer cannot pay the amount owed within the normal credit period, either because of the large volume of business involved or because of temporary cash shortages, the hospitality firm may extend the credit period by asking the client to sign a promissory note. Notes have two advantages over accounts receivable: (1) they are interest-bearing, and (2) they are negotiable instruments, legally transferable to a lender by endorsement. These two attributes facilitate a firm's converting its notes into cash and recompense it for the time value of the money being used by the customer.

To be negotiable a note must meet four conditions:

1. It must be signed by the maker (customer–borrower).
2. It must contain an unconditional promise to pay or order someone other than the maker to pay a specific amount.
3. It must be payable on demand or at a specific future time.
4. It must be payable to bearer or to the order of someone named specifically (payee).

Notes receivable are recorded at their face value, i.e., the amount of the principal owed, exclusive of interest. Thus, if $1,000 of accounts receivable are converted into a note receivable due in six months and bearing interest of 12%, the note is recorded as follows:

	Dr	Cr
Notes receivable	1,000	
Accounts receivable		1,000

To record conversion of $1,000 in accounts receivable into a note receivable with a face value of $1,000

The accrual of three-months' interest is recorded as follows:

	Dr	Cr
Interest receivable	30	
Interest revenue		30

To accrue three-months' interest at 12%
on a $1,000 note receivable (3/12 × 0.12
= 0.03; 0.03 × $1,000 = $30)

When the note is paid, at the end of its six-month term, the following entry is recorded:

	Dr	Cr
Cash	1,060	
Interest revenue		30
Interest receivable		30
Notes receivable		1,000

To record collection of a $1,000 note receivable
plus six-months' interest at 12%

Discounting Notes Receivable

The principal advantage of having a customer sign a note receivable is that it can be converted into cash more easily than an accounts receivable. The procedure for doing this is called discounting and is accomplished by the hospitality firm endorsing the note to a lender. When a note receivable is discounted, the bank or other lender to whom the note is endorsed pays the borrower–endorser the face amount of the loan plus interest due on the note less the lender's discount. This discount varies according to the number of days the note will be held and the interest rate charged.

For example, let us assume that the $1,000, six-month note bearing 12% interest mentioned earlier was discounted at 18%, two months after it was received. In order to record the discounting of this note three calculations are required.

(1) We must calculate the face amount plus interest (maturity value) on the date the note is due:

Face amount	$1,000
Six months' interest at 12%	60
Maturity value of note	$1,060

(2) We must calculate the discount or interest the lender will deduct from the $1,060 maturity value of the note:

$$\text{lender's discount} = \$1{,}060 \times 0.18 \times \frac{120 \text{ days}}{360 \text{ days}} = \$64 \text{ (rounded)}$$

[*Note*: The number of days the lender will have to wait before receiving the principal back, plus interest (6 months − 2 months = 4 months; 4 months × 30 days = 120 days]

(3) We calculate the amount to be received by the borrower on the discounted note:

Maturity value	$1,060
Lender's discount	64
Discount proceeds	$ 996

The discounted note receivable can then be recorded as follows:

	Dr	Cr
Cash	996	
Interest expense	4	
Notes receivable discounted		1,000

To record receipt of proceeds from discounting $1,000 note receivable

In this example the amount received by the borrower is less than the face value of the note. If the amount received is greater than the face value of the note, the account "interest income" is credited for the difference.

The account "notes receivable discounted" is a contra-asset account and appears immediately under the notes receivable account on the balance sheet. This indicates to the reader of the financial statements that a potential liability for paying these discounted notes receivable exists until they are paid by the maker of the notes.

When the notes are paid, then the following entry removes it and its corresponding contra-asset account from the accounting records.

	Dr	Cr
Notes receivable discounted	1,000	
Notes receivable		1,000

To record payment of discounted notes receivable

Dishonored Notes Receivable

When the maker does not pay the note on its due date, the note is said to be dishonored. The note receivable plus the amount of unpaid interest must be returned to accounts receivable as follows:

	Dr	Cr
Accounts receivable	2,240	
Notes receivable		2,000
Interest revenue		240

To record dishonor of a $2,000 one-year note receivable bearing 12% interest

The unpaid interest revenue is accrued because it was earned. If periodic accruals are made during the year, the final accrual is proportionately reduced.

If the dishonored note has been discounted, the lender informs the hospitality firm (the borrower–endorser) that it must pay the note's maturity value plus a protest fee. The entries to record dishonor of the $1,000, six-month, 12% note receivable used in our discounting example previously are shown below:

	Dr	Cr
Accounts receivable	1,070	
Cash		1,070
Notes receivable discounted	1,000	
Notes receivable		1,000

To record payment of principal ($1,000), interest ($60), and protest fee ($10) on a dishonored note that had been discounted

As is evident from the above, when a note receivable is discounted by a hospitality firm, this firm continues to be responsible for payment of the note as guarantor, even though the net value of the note no longer appears on the firm's books. This type of liability is called a contingent liability because its becoming an actual liability is contingent upon the maker's default on the note. If the maker of the note pays the lender on time the note will never become a liability of the hospitality firm (borrower–endorser). Other contingent liabilities are discussed later in the chapter.

TYPES OF PAYABLES

Payables, as discussed in this text, include actual liabilities, which are divided into two groups called (1) current liabilities and (2) long-term debt, as well as certain potential future liabilities called contingent liabilities. Together, these comprise all amounts owed to others by a hospitality firm, as well as amounts that may become liabilities in the future. Actual liabilities include all the definite and specific obligations of a firm. Contingent liabilities are liabilities whose existence is contingent upon the occurrence of an uncertain event.

CURRENT LIABILITIES

Current liabilities are debts that are payable within one year of the balance sheet date. They include the following:

- Accounts payable
- Accrued liabilities
- Unearned revenue
- Taxes payable
- Dividends payable
- Short-term notes payable
- Current portion of long-term debt

Accounts payable, also called trade accounts payable, are amounts owed to suppliers for purchases of goods or services.

Accrued liabilities are actual liabilities that are entered by adjusting entry because they have not been invoiced. Some liabilities, such as interest on notes payable or vacations payable, are never invoiced. Other liabilities, such as electricity expense payable, must be accrued because receipt of the invoice does not usually coincide with the end of an accounting period.

Unearned revenue, such as customers' deposits, represents the value of goods or services that must be rendered in return for advance payments made by customers. For example, if the firm is to cater a wedding next month and the customer pays for it in advance, the payment is recorded as a customer's deposit, or unearned revenue. The realization concept does not allow such receipts to be considered as earned revenue untill the corresponding service has been rendered.

Taxes payable include both taxes owed by the firm directly and taxes collected from others for subsequent remittal to the federal and local governments. Income and property taxes payable are an example of the former. Sales taxes and taxes deducted from employees' pay fall into the latter category.

Corporations are not obliged to pay dividends unless the board of directors declares them. After they have been declared, however, there is usually a lapse of time before they are paid. Dividends payable represent dividends that

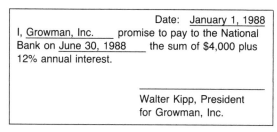

Date: <u>January 1, 1988</u>
I, <u>Growman, Inc.</u>   promise to pay to the National
Bank on <u>June 30, 1988</u>   the sum of $4,000 plus
12% annual interest.

_____
Walter Kipp, President
for Growman, Inc.

Figure 16.3.   Interest not included in face value of note.

a corporation is obligated to pay because they have been declared by the board of directors.

Short-term notes payable are promissory notes signed by the firm. They are usually given to suppliers for goods or services that will be paid for over a longer term than the supplier's normal credit period, or they are given to banks for short-term loans. The interest on notes payable may be stated separately on the face of the note as a percentage rate, or the actual amount of interest may be included in the face amount of the note.

An example of a $4,000 promissory note bearing 12% interest and due in 180 days is presented in Figure 16.3, with the interest stated separately, and in Figure 16.4, with the interest included in the face amount of the note.

When the interest is stated as a percentage rate, then the firm (borrower) receives the full face value of the note. A $4,000, 180-day note bearing 12% interest would be recorded as follows:

1988		**Dr**	**Cr**
Jan. 1	Cash	4,000	
	Notes payable		4,000

To record a $4,000, 180-day note when the interest is
not included in the face amount

When the interest is included in the note's face value, the note is recorded through the following journal entry:

1988		**Dr**	**Cr**
Jan. 1	Cash	4,000	
	Discount on notes payable	240	
	Notes payable		4,240

To record a $4,000, 180-day note with the interest amount in-
cluded in the face value of the note

In this case, the note would appear on the balance sheet as shown below:

Current Liabilities
Notes payable	$4,240	
Less: Discount on notes payable	240	$4,000

Date: <u>January 1, 1988</u>
I, <u>Growman, Inc.</u>   promise to pay to the National
Bank on <u>June 30, 1988</u>   the sum of $4,240.

_____
Walter Kipp, President
for Growman, Inc.

Figure 16.4.   Interest included in face value of note.

If the firm's accounting period ends on March 31, 1988, then interest payable would have to be accrued for each type of note as follows. For interest not included in the face value of the note:

1988		Dr	Cr
Mar. 31	Interest expense	120	
	Accrued interest payable		120

To accrue 90-days' interest on a $4,000, 12% note payable with interest not included in face value (12% × 90/360 × $4,000 = $120)

For interest included in the face value of the note:

1988		Dr	Cr
Mar. 31	Interest expense	120	
	Discount on notes payable		120

To accrue 90-days' interest on a $4,000, 12% note payable with interest included in face value (12% × 90/360 × $4,000 = $120)

Payment of the note and interest at the end of its 180-day term is recorded as follows for each type of note:

For interest not included in the face value of the note:

1988		Dr	Cr
June 30	Accrued interest payable	120	
	Interest expense	120	
	Notes payable	4,000	
	Cash		4,240

To record payment of note whose interest is not included in the face value

For interest included in the face value of the note:

1988		Dr	Cr
June 30	Interest expense	120	
	Notes payable	4,240	
	Discount on notes payable		120
	Cash		4,240

To record payment of note whose interest is included in the face value

The current portion of long-term debt is that portion of a firm's long-term debt that is due in the current year. If a firm owes $1,000,000 to be paid $100,000 annually, then the $100,000 installment due in the current year is reclassified as a current liability account called "current portion of long-term debt" as follows:

Long-term debt	100,000	
Current portion of long-term debt		100,000

To reclassify portion of long-term debt payable within the current year

LONG-TERM DEBT

Long-term debt is that portion of a firm's debt payable more then one year in the future. This is an important account classification in the hospitality industry because of the capital-intensive nature of the industry. Large amounts of long-term financing are needed to purchase the hotels, restaurants, airplanes, tour buses, etc. required by this expanding industry. Short-term notes, which might be renewable every six to twelve months, would be entirely inadequate for financing a hotel with a 40 year useful life. The major categories of long-term debt are

- Long-term notes payable
- Mortgages payable
- Bonds payable
- Long-term lease obligations (for capital leases)
- Deferred income tax payable

Long-Term Notes Payable

Long-term notes payable are similar to short-term notes payable except that they are due after one year from the balance sheet date.

Mortgages Payable

Mortgages payable are similar to long-term notes payable except that they offer the lender, as guarantee or collateral, a specific property, usually real estate. If the borrower defaults on the mortgage notes, the lender may take possession of the property or equipment pledged.

Mortgages payable are usually paid in equal monthly installments that include both principal and interest, necessitating the recording of the current portion of the mortgage obligation as a current liability. If a $100,000, 12% mortgage note were payable in $2,000 monthly installments, each installment would contain an interest portion and a principal portion as shown in Table 16.1.

Bonds

Bonds are debt instruments (usually long-term) that enable a hospitality firm to divide a large amount of debt into small discrete units (usually having a face value of $1,000), thus making them accessible to many small- and medium-sized lenders. Bonds may be collateral bonds (secured by some specific property or equipment) or they may be unsecured debentures (secured by the general credit-worthiness of the hospitality firm). They may be registered bonds (the owner's name is registered with the company, which mails the interest checks when due) or coupon bonds (the owner clips interest coupons

TABLE 16.1. Installments on $100,000, 12% Mortgage

Month	Monthly payment	Monthly interest[a] (12% annually)	Principal reduction	Principal balance
Loan date	—	—	—	$100,000
Jan. 31	$2,000	$1,000	$1,000	99,000
Feb. 28	2,000	990	1,010	97,990
Mar. 31	2,000	980	1,020	96,970
June 30	2,000	970	1,030	95,940

Note: All amounts rounded to nearest dollar.
[a]12%/12 months × principal balance.

off the bonds when due and deposits them in the bank). When a company issues sinking-fund bonds it must deposit certain amounts annually to be invested in income-producing investments for the purpose of paying the bonds when they mature. Serial bonds, though issued on the same date, do not all fall due on the same date. They are repaid gradually over a specified period of years, providing the lender with a constant cash flow over the repayment period.

Bonds may be further subdivided into subordinated and unsubordinated debentures. When a bond is subordinated it means that in the event of liquidation, it becomes payable only after all other liabilities have been discharged.

Convertible debentures may be convertible into a specific number of common shares at the bondholder's option, enabling the bondholder to participate in the growth of the company. Some bonds may also be callable at the option of the issuing firm, thereby enabling it to take advantage of lower current interest rates to refinance its debt.

The entries to issue bonds, pay interest on the bonds, and retire $1,000,000 worth of five-year bonds payable at maturity and bearing 12% interest are presented below:

	Dr	Cr
Cash	1,000,000	
Bonds payable		1,000,000
To issue $1,000,000, 12%, five-year bonds		
Interest expense	120,000	
Cash		120,000
To record annual interest payment on the 12% bonds		
Bonds payable	1,000,000	
Cash		1,000,000
To retire the bonds		

The above entries are valid only when bonds are issued or sold at their face or par value, the amount that will have to be repaid at maturity; this very seldom occurs, however. Usually bonds are issued at a discount from their par value or at a premium. The interest rate a firm will have to pay when it issues bonds to the public depends on two factors that cannot be accurately measured beforehand: (1) the prevailing interest rate on the day of the sale, and (2) the public's reaction to the firm's recent earnings history. Because of these uncertainties, issuing firms print bonds with a predetermined par value (usually $1,000) and with an interest rate percentage that is related to the bond's par value. For instance, annual interest of $120 is paid to the owner of a $1,000 (par value), 12% bond, regardless of what was paid for it.

At the time the bonds are sold, however, the public may demand more than 12% interest on the bonds. It is impractical to reprint new bonds, and so, instead of changing the stated interest rate on the bonds, they are sold for less than their par value (at a discount).

Similarly, if potential buyers are willing to earn less than 12% interest on their investment, then they will bid the issue price of the bonds up above their par value. If issued at a $77,000 discount or a $90,000 premium the $1,000,000, 12%, five-year bonds are said to be sold at 92.3 (percentage of par value) or 109 (percentage of par value) and would be recorded as follows, respectively:

	Dr	Cr
Cash	923,000	
Discount on bonds payable	77,000	
Bonds payable		1,000,000
To record sale of $1,000,000 in bonds, at a discount		

	Dr	**Cr**
Cash	1,090,000	
Bonds payable		1,000,000
Premium on bonds payable		90,000

To record sale of $1,000,000 in bonds, at a premium

Since the bonds were sold at a discount or premium, to adjust the face interest rate to the prevailing (effective) market rate at the date of sale, the interest expense on the books of the issuing company must reflect this effective interest rate, not the face rate. This is accomplished by amortizing the discount or premium over the life of the bond issue.

There are two ways of calculating the annual amortization amount: (1) straight-line amortization, and (2) effective-interest amortization.

The entries to record the annual interest payments for the $1,000,000, five-year bonds sold at a discount or at a premium using the straight-line amortization method are presented below:

	Dr	**Cr**
Interest expense	135,400	
Cash		120,000
Discount on bonds payable		15,400

To record annual interest payment on bonds payable sold at a discount

	Dr	**Cr**
Interest expense	102,000	
Premium on bonds payable	18,000	
Cash		120,000

To record annual interest payment on bonds payable sold at a premium

The annual amortization of the discount or premium is determined by dividing the discount ($77,000) or premium ($90,000) by the life of the bond issue (five years).

It is beyond the scope of this book to explain the effective-interest amortization method.

Long-Term Lease Obligations

In Chapter 14 we learned that the present value of the annual lease payments of certain long-term leases must be capitalized and included among the property and equipment category of the lessee (the party receiving and using the property). When the present value of these payments is recorded as property or equipment the corresponding credit entry is made to the long-term lease obligations account. The entry to record the capital lease of a building with lease payments having a present value of $270,000 is made as follows:

	Dr	**Cr**
Property under capital leases	270,000	
Long-term lease obligations		270,000

To record the capital lease for a building

At year end the current portion of the long-term lease obligations is reclassified to a current liability account on the balance sheet, as explained earlier.

Deferred Income Taxes Payable

In Chapter 14 we also learned that because the IRC allows a business to accelerate the deduction of certain expenses when calculating taxable income for income tax reporting purposes, part of a firm's income tax expense can be deferred for payment in later years. This deferred amount is recorded in an account called "deferred income taxes," often shown on a separate line after long-term liabilities, as explained in Chapter 11.

CONTINGENT LIABILITIES

A contingent liability is a potential future liability whose existence and amount cannot be definitely established. Before it can be considered a definite liability of the hospitality entity, some event of uncertain occurrence must take place to transform a contingent liability from a potential to an actual liability. For instance, a lawsuit directed against an entity does not mean the entity will necessarily lose and pay the lawsuit. Before the amount being sued for becomes an actual liability, the lawsuit must be won by the adversary and a judge must establish the specific amount to be paid. Thus, this liability is contingent upon losing the lawsuit.

A contingent liability also arises when an entity guarantees a debt of another entity, such as when receivables are discounted and the entity that made the sale is still responsible for any uncollectible accounts. Contingent liabilities usually do not appear on the balance sheet. Rather, their existence is disclosed in a note to the financial statements informing the reader that the company may have a significant additional liability in the future if a specific unfavorable event occurs.

Statement of Financial Accounting Standards No. 5, "Accounting for contingencies," states that a contingent liability should be presented on the balance sheet only if both of the following are applicable:

1. It is probable that the event upon which the liability is contingent will occur.
2. The absolute amount of the liability can be estimated with reasonable accuracy.

BALANCE SHEET PRESENTATION OF RECEIVABLES AND PAYABLES

Receivables

Receivables should be listed in the current assets section of the balance sheet in their proper order of liquidity in relation to the other current assets. The current assets section of Restaurant Associates, Inc. 1981 financial statements is shown in Figure 16.5 as an example of the typical balance sheet presentation of receivables. As seen in the figure, receivables are presented in their order of liquidity with respect to other current assets, after cash and short-term investments and before inventories. They are shown on a comparable basis with previous years' amounts and the allowance for doubtful accounts is specified.

If they were material, other accounts receivable or notes receivable would

RESTAURANT ASSOCIATES INDUSTRIES, INC. AND SUBSIDIARIES

ASSETS   IN THOUSANDS

	DECEMBER 26, 1981	DECEMBER 27, 1980
CURRENT ASSETS		
Cash	$ 701	$ 766
Short-term investments	3,633	3,817
Receivables, less allowance for doubtful accounts: 1981—$341; 1980—$372	4,372	3,694
Inventories	3,684	3,214
Prepaid expenses and supplies	1,267	1,239
Total current assets	13,657	12,730

Figure 16.5. Current assets section of financial statement.

have to be listed separately and any discounted notes would have to be indicated as in the following hypothetical example:

Accounts receivable	$5,000,000	
Less: Allowance for doubtful accounts	100,000	$4,900,000
Other receivables	$4,000,000	
Less: Notes receivables discounted	1,000,000	$3,000,000

Additionally, the notes to the financial statements should indicate

1. any material amounts due from a single customer,
2. any material amounts of accounts receivable discounted, pledged, or factored, along with the applicable terms and conditions,
3. the conditions, such as interest rate and other terms, of notes receivable and notes receivable discounted.

Payables

As an example of the balance sheet presentation of payables, the current and long-term liability sections of Denny's, Inc. 1980 financial statements are presented in Figure 16.6. Observe that the current liabilities classification includes accounts payable, income taxes payable, accrued payroll and related expenses, other accrued liabilities, and the current portion of long-term notes and lease obligations under capital leases. The long-term debt classification includes the noncurrent portion of long-term notes, long-term convertible debenture bonds, the noncurrent portion of obligations under capital leases, other liabilities (long-term), and deferred income taxes payable.

In relation to the above, the notes to the financial statements should disclose the following:

1. Terms, such as due dates, any assets pledged, sinking fund requirements, if any, and interest rate if not shown in the body of the financial statements.
2. The amount of the discount or premium on the sale of bonds.
3. Any unrecorded obligations such as commitments to make progress payments on property and equipment under construction, commitments to make future lease payments on operating leases, and contingent liabilities.

Figure 16.7, the note to Denny's, Inc. 1980 financial statements pertaining to long-term notes, demonstrates some of the aforementioned disclosures.

LIABILITIES AND SHAREHOLDERS' EQUITY	June 27 1980	June 29 1979
Current liabilities:		
Accounts payable	$ 21,339,000	$ 20,411,000
Income taxes	2,118,000	262,000
Accrued payroll and related expenses	17,207,000	14,566,000
Other accrued liabilities	30,694,000	22,041,000
Current maturities of notes and obligations under capital leases	9,545,000	12,314,000
Total current liabilities	80,903,000	69,594,000
Long-term notes	94,093,000	72,045,000
5½% subordinated convertible debentures	9,489,000	10,298,000
Obligations under capital leases	136,971,000	108,126,000
Other liabilities	16,312,000	9,438,000
Deferred income taxes	4,778,000	7,697,000
Shareholders' equity:		
Common stock, $1 par value; 8,714,787 shares issued and outstanding (8,701,887 shares in 1979)	8,715,000	8,702,000
Additional paid-in capital	22,065,000	21,903,000
Retained earnings	115,709,000	106,409,000
Total shareholders' equity	146,489,000	137,014,000
	$489,035,000	$414,212,000

Figure 16.6. Current and long-term liabilities section of financial statements of Denny's, Inc.

LONG-TERM NOTES

A summary of long-term notes, exclusive of current maturities, follows:

	1980	1979
Mortgage notes payable, 7% to 10½ %	$87,897,000	$68,553,000
9% unsecured note payable semi-annually through August 1983	2,180,000	3,180,000
Other, 11% to 11⅜%	4,016,000	312,000
	$94,093,000	$72,045,000

Principal amounts payable on the above notes are as follows: 1982–$7,151,000; 1983–$5,469,000; 1984–$4,044,000; 1985–$4,197,000; 1986–$4,533,000 and the balance thereafter.

Mortgage notes (which mature over various terms to 20 years) relate to land, buildings and equipment purchased or constructed by the Company. These obligations are payable in monthly and quarterly installments. At June 27, 1980, land, buildings, equipment and improvements with an aggregate net book value of approximately $125,302,000 were mortgaged under these obligations.

Under the Company's unsecured note agreement, it is required, among other things, to maintain a minimum amount of consolidated working capital and consolidated tangible net worth. Unrestricted consolidated retained earnings at June 27, 1980 amounted to $15,489,000.

Under the terms of the Company's unsecured revolving credit agreements, the Company may borrow up to $18,000,000. At June 29, 1979, outstanding borrowings under these credit lines totaled $5,500,000. There were no such borrowings outstanding at June 27, 1980. Borrowings under the revolving credit notes are at the prime rate of interest. The agreements provide the Company with up to $15,000,000 through September 30, 1987. The agreements require the maintenance of a specified current ratio and specified ratio of total debt to shareholders' equity.

The highest balance outstanding under lines of credit at any time during 1980 and 1979 was $6,000,000 and $5,500,000, respectively. The approximate average aggregate short-term borrowings outstanding during 1980 and 1979 were $2,388,000 and $1,540,000, respectively, and the approximately weighted average interest rate during 1980 and 1979 was 14.0% and 11.3%.

Included in "Other" above is a $3,670,000 loan denominated in a foreign currency. The loan is due quarterly through September 30, 1982.

Interest expense, net of capitalized interest, for the three years ended June 30, 1978, was as follows: 1978–$13,648,000; 1977–$11,304,000; 1976–$9,876,000. Deferred debt expense is being amortized on the interest method over the term of the related debt.

Figure 16.7. Long-term notes to the 1980 financial statements of Denny's, Inc.

QUESTIONS

1. Why do hospitality entities make credit sales? Is there any added expense when making credit sales?
2. How do uncollectible accounts affect the balance sheet under the allowance method? the income statement?
3. What are two ways of recording losses from bad debts? Which method is acceptable under GAAP? Why?
4. What are two ways of determining the allowance for uncollectible accounts? When is each method best applied?
5. What are three basic types of receivables? Define them.
6. What is the difference between an account receivable and a note receivable? When should a note receivable be used to extend credit?
7. What are two ways of collecting on credit card sales? What are the differences between the two?
8. Where do discounted notes receivable appear on the balance sheet?
9. When is a 180-day note dated January 1, 1989 due? Who is the maker of a note? Who is the payee?
10. What are current liabilities? Give four examples of current liabilities.
11. When might a hospitality entity report money received from clients as a current liability?
12. What is a contingent liability? Give two examples of contingent liabilities. When must a contingent liability be recorded on the balance sheet of an entity?
13. What is the difference between mortgage bonds, unsecured debentures, and subordinated debentures?
14. How do bond premiums and bond discounts arise?
15. What types of investments are bonds best used to finance?
16. What is the difference between the face interest rate on bonds and the effective interest rate?

EXERCISES

1. John Worthee owed the Spicey Palate Restaurant $560 on account. Since the account was 120 days past due and John Worthee could not be found, the restaurant decided to write off his account. After it had been written off, however, John Worthee mailed in a payment of $560.
   (a) Prepare the journal entry to write off John Worthee's account.
   (b) Prepare the journal entry to record the subsequent payment by John Worthee.
   (c) Explain the effect on net accounts receivable of writing off John Worthee's account.
2. Wiley Willy owed the Bastille Hotel $1,050. His account was 90 days past due and so the manager of the hotel asked him to sign a 90-day note dated June 30, 1988, bearing 12% interest.

   After holding the note for 30 days the manager of the hotel needed the cash and so he decided to discount the note at 15% interest.

   When the note was due, Wiley Willy could not be found.
   (a) On what date was the note due?
   (b) Prepare the journal entry to record the note receivable from Wiley Willy.
   (c) Prepare the journal entry to record discounting the note.
   (d) Prepare the journal entry to record the dishonor of the discounted note. Assume a $20 protest fee is charged.
3. A cruise line sold the following tour packages in January, 1988:

Quantity	Name of tour	Price
200	Caribbean Cruise	$1,200
1,000	West Coast Cruise	1,500
500	Gulf Cruise	800

Of these, 80% of the Caribbean and West Coast cruises and 50% of the Gulf cruises were to take place in 1988. The remaining cruises were for 1989.

(a) Prepare the journal entry to record the sale of the cruises in January 1988.

(b) Prepare the journal entry to record the cruises taken in 1988.

PROBLEMS

1. The Paydmor Hotel prepared a list of the following open accounts in 1987, indicating which ones it believes are collectible:

Invoice Date	Client	Amount
Jan. 1	Joe Weingard	$ 156
Jan. 15	Marylinn Ops	342
Feb. 5	Larry Warmon	98
Feb. 18	Stan Welton	998
Mar. 3	Karl Josephs	320
Mar. 8	Bill Gordner	144
Mar. 14	Frank Ross	788
Mar. 20	Mary Smith	842
Mar. 25	Orlin Thomas	1,120
Apr. 4	Grif Dugood	88
Apr. 16	Marvin Fenton	2,112
Apr. 28	Grace Filigree	1,642
May 10	Ron Stacroft	450
May 14	Philip Herrera	676
May 15	Cecilia Debayle	771
May 21	Steve Murhous	1,342
May 24	Griselda Ferguson	2,231

(a) Prepare an aging schedule for the above accounts.

(b) Based on the aging schedule as of May 31, 1987, prepare the journal entry to record the allowance for doubtful accounts. You are told that the amount of bad debts was underestimated in prior years and the allowance for doubtful accounts has a debit balance of $450. You are also told that based on prior experience 1% of current accounts, 1.5% of accounts 31–60 days past due, 2% of accounts 61–90 days past due and 20% of accounts more than 90 days past due are estimated to be uncollectible.

(c) Show how the above accounts receivable would appear on the balance sheet after recording the journal entry you made in part (b).

2. (a) Record the following transactions in the general journal of Flywait Airlines for 1989:

May 12   Sold $2,400 worth of tickets to the Trustworth Co. on credit.

May 20   Wrote off a $1,200 balance due from John Peilaiter.

May 31 $1,000 worth of tickets are used.

Jun. 5   Sold $5,200 worth of tickets to the L. Argess Co.

Jun. 10   Sold $2,400 worth of tickets to Mr. I. M. Slopei on credit.

Jun. 30 $3,100 worth of tickets are used.

Aug. 5   Received signed notes from Trustworth Co. and L. Argess Co. to cover their accounts receivable. The notes are 60-day notes and bear 10% interest.

Aug. 31   Discounted the note from L. Argess at 12%.

Aug. 31 $1,400 worth of tickets are used.

Sept. 2   Received $200 checks from John Peilaiter in the mail.

Sept. 5   Accrued interest on the notes receivable from Trustworth Co.

Sept. 30   Sold $3,100 worth of tickets on an international credit card to M. N. Ernest. The credit card company charges a 5% commission and has an arrangement with a local bank to reimburse Flywait Airlines when it deposits the credit slip. This commission is recorded when the credit slip is deposited.

Sept. 30 $3,500 worth of tickets are used.

Oct. 1   The credit slip for the sale to M. N. Ernest is deposited in the bank.

Oct. 5   The Trustworth Co. honors its note and pays all amounts due.

Oct. 5   The L. Argess Co. dishonors its note but promises to pay all amounts due, plus a $10 protest fee, in 10 days. Flywait Airlines accepts this oral promise and agrees not to charge any more interest.

Oct. 30   There is a $2,400 credit balance in the allowance for doubtful accounts.

Oct. 31 $1,100 worth of tickets are used.

(b) Prepare the journal entry to record bad debts expense assuming Flywait Airline's accounts receivable aging schedule indicates it should have a balance of $3,100 in its allowance for doubtful accounts.

(c) Assuming it had a $60,000 balance in trade accounts receivable before the above transactions, show the net amount of accounts receivable as it would appear on the balance sheet after the above transaction. Round amounts to nearest dollar.

3. The Swellmont Hotel Corporation sold two bond issues during 1989. Following are listed the transactions relating to these bond issues.

Jan. 1   Issued $3,000,000, 12%, 10-year bonds, dated January 1, 1989, interest payable on June 30 and December 31. The bonds were sold at 98.

Feb. 1   Issued $5,000,000, 10%, five-year bonds, dated February 1, 1989, interest payable on July 31 and January 31. The bonds were sold at 103.

Jun. 30   Paid interest due on the $3,000,000 bond issue and amortized the discount using the straight-line amortization method.

Jul. 31   Paid interest due on the $5,000,000 bond issue and amortized the premium using the straight-line amortization method.

Dec. 31   Paid interest due on the $3,000,000 bond issue and amortized the discount using the straight-line amortization method. Also accrued interest and amortization on the $5,000,000 bond issue.

(a) Record the above transactions in general journal entry format.

(b) Show how the bonds and interest payable would appear on the balance sheet at December 31, 1989.

Corporation Accounting

17

As stated earlier, the corporation is the major form of business enterprise in terms of economic power in the United States. It is also the most complex form of business entity. The reader should therefore be familiar with accounting procedures involved in the creation and general operation of a corporation that are unique with regard to this form of business entity.

In Chapter 4 we learned that the corporation is often the preferred form of business entity for the following reasons:

1. It offers the protection of limited liability to its stockholders.
2. It has a continuous life independent of its stockholders.
3. Only authorized corporate officers can make binding decisions on behalf of the corporation.
4. It provides the facility of raising funds by selling partial ownership rights in the form of stock certificates to a large number of investors.
5. It facilitates the subsequent transfer of partial ownership rights through the sale of stock certificates.
6. Its status as a separate legal entity allows it to enter into contracts and execute business transactions independently of its stockholders.

These advantages are offset by the following special problems presented by the corporate form of business organization:

1. Corporate income is taxed twice, once at the corporate level and again at the stockholder level, when dividends are received.
2. Corporations are more heavily regulated by the federal and state governments than are sole proprietorships.
3. They are more costly to organize.
4. The decision-making process is more involved because of the corporate structure.
5. The control of a corporation and its net income are diluted because usually corporate ownership is distributed among many stockholders.

In Chapter 4 we also learned that the unique accounting characteristics of a corporation are reflected in the owners' equity section of the balance sheet, which is called the stockholders' equity section. As was stated, this section can be broken down into two major subdivisions:

1. Capital invested by the stockholders as shown in the preferred stock, common stock, and additional paid-in capital accounts.
2. Capital earned by the corporation through its operations, as shown in the retained earnings account.

In this chapter we learn the accounting procedures involved in recording the formation of a corporation. We also learn the effect on the stockholders' equity section of the balance sheet of some other basic transactions, such as (1) recording the results of operations of a corporation, (2) paying dividends, and (3) recording transactions involving a corporation's stock.

First, the method of recording the costs involved in organizing a corporation is explained, followed by an explanation of common stock, preferred stock, par value, and accounting procedures for recording the issue and sale of stock. Following this, the accounting procedure for purchasing and reselling a corporation's own stock, called treasury stock, is discussed, including a discussion of the accounting procedures for retiring a corporation's stock.

Some transactions that affect the retained earnings account are then noted, including an explanation of appropriated retained earnings.

Next, the procedures involved in declaring and paying cash and stock dividends are discussed as well as their effect on the appropriate stockholders' equity accounts, followed by an explanation of stock splits. In conclusion, a more complete example of the statement of retained earnings than was shown in Chapter 4 is presented.

FORMING A CORPORATION

A corporation is a legal person, whose separate rights are recognized by law. Although each state has its own laws governing the creation of a corporation, usually two or more people (incorporators) must submit to the state an application accompanied by the articles of incorporation of the new entity. The articles of incorporation state the conditions under which the corporation will be formed, such as number of shares, par value and types of stock, voting and dividend rights of each type of stockholder, and the names and addresses of the original subscribers to its stock. Since a corporation is governed by a board of directors, a provisional board of directors is also named in the articles of incorporation.

Because of the complexities and subtleties involved in preparing the articles of incorporation, a lawyer is usually called upon to draw them up, to fulfill any other legal registration requirement, and to pay registration fees. An accountant may be called upon to design an accounting system for the corporation, and there may also be certain promotional fees involved in its conception.

All of these expenses of forming the corporation are called "organization costs." Since they will benefit the corporation over its entire life and are intangible in nature, the matching concept would require that they be capitalized as intangible assets and amortized gradually over the life of the corporation. Organization costs are included in the "other assets" classification of the balance sheet along with other intangible assets. Although a corporation's life is indefinite, in practice GAAP require that organization costs be amortized over no more than 40 years. A frequently used practical approach when organization costs are not material is to amortize them over five years, the shortest amortization period allowed by the IRS.

If the lawyers' fees for creating a corporation were $2,700, registration fees $500, accountant's fees $2,000, and promoter's fees $4,000, the entry to record organization costs would be as follows:

	Dr	**Cr**
Organization costs	9,200	
Cash		9,200

To record various organization costs totaling $9,200

To amortize these costs over a five-year life, the following entry would be made annually for five years:

	Dr	**Cr**
Amortization expense	1,840	
Organization costs		1,840

To amortize 1/5 of organization costs totaling $9,200

Organizational Structure

As stated previously, individual stockholders do not manage a corporation. Instead, a separate management team is created to run its affairs. The composition of this team varies from corporation to corporation but usually includes a board of directors and a team of operating executives such as a president, one or more vice-presidents, a treasurer, a secretary, a controller, and various other managers at different levels of the corporation's structure. The president, also known as the chief operating officer is responsible for all the day-to-day operations of the firm. The president may delegate responsibility for certain geographical areas (United States, Europe, etc.) or for certain types of activity (hotels, airlines, etc.) to the vice-presidents. The treasurer reports to the president and has overall responsibility for the corporations' funds. He or she is assisted in managing them by the controller, or chief accountant, who is in turn responsible for establishing accounting systems, establishing and implementing internal control procedures, preparing accounting records, tax returns, and other financial records. The secretary is responsible for fulfilling the corporation's legal requirements such as maintaining the minutes of stockholders' meetings and meetings of the board of directors, and recording stock transfers.

The stockholders exert control over the executives in charge of the day-to-day operations through the board of directors. The board of directors is elected by the stockholders, normally at an annual stockholders' meeting.

The board may have as many members as provided for in the articles of incorporation and is presided over by the chairman of the board, also known as the chief executive officer (CEO). It is responsible for selecting the corporation's president and for overseeing the activities of the corporation throughout the year.

In addition to voting for the board of directors, other matters having great impact on the corporation, such as merger decisions, may be voted upon by stockholders directly at stockholders' meetings. If stockholders cannot attend a stockholders' meeting, they may assign their right to vote to someone else. This is called a proxy vote.

TYPES OF STOCK

Although all the stockholders of a corporation are the owners of the corporation to some degree, each type of stock issued may have different stockholder rights assigned to it by the issuing corporation. Generally, there are two broad categories of stock: common stock and preferred stock, distinguishable by the differences in stockholder rights associated with them.

COMMON STOCK

The rights of common stockholders may include some or all of the following:

- The right to sell their shares to whom they wish
- The right to vote at stockholders' meetings
- The right to receive dividends when declared by the board of directors
- The right to share in the distribution of a corporation's assets upon liquidation in proportion to the number of shares owned
- The right of first refusal on a number of shares proportionate to their current ownership percentage if additional shares are issued and sold. This is known as a stockholder's preemptive right. Its purpose is to enable stockholders to maintain their original percentage ownership of a corporation's shares

Common stockholders do not necessarily enjoy all of these rights, nor do they necessarily enjoy them to the same degree. Before stock may be sold by a corporation the stock issue for each particular type of common stock must be authorized by the state. When the authorization is requested, the stockholder rights attached to those shares must be specified.

All corporations must issue some common stock with the right to vote because such voting shares are necessary to elect a board of directors, which will create a management structure for the corporation. When different groups of common stock give different rights to stockholders they are differentiated by calling them type A common, type B common, etc.

PREFERRED STOCK

The rights of preferred stockholders usually differ from the rights of common stockholders in three ways:

1. Preferred stockholders do not have voting rights.
2. Preferred stockholders do not share in the corportation's growth. They are only entitled to the fixed dividend amount specified on the face of their stock certificates. Also, in case of liquidation the preferred stockholders are only entitled to a distribution of the corporation's assets up to the liquidation value specified on the preferred stock certificate.
3. Preferred stock derives its name from the fact that preferred stockholders have the right to receive their fixed dividend before common stockholders receive any dividend at all. Upon liquidation, preferred stockholders also have the right to receive the liquidation value of their stock before common stockholders receive any assets from the corporation.

There are many types of preferred stock, such as noncumulative, cumulative, nonparticipating, participating, and convertible. No dividends may be paid by a corporation unless declared by its board of directors. Thus, if in any year the board of directors does not deem it to be in the best interest of the corporation to declare a dividend on preferred stock, the preferred stockholders will not receive a dividend in that year. If the preferred stock is noncumulative, the stockholders lose their right to receive this dividend in future years. In the case of cumulative preferred, this right is never lost and the dividend accumulates from year to year so that the following year preferred stockholders are entitled to two years' dividends before any dividends can be declared on common stock. Unpaid dividends on cumulative preferred stock are said to be "in arrears." Dividends in arrears must be disclosed. Also, preferred stock is nonparticipating, that is, the preferred stockholders are entitled only to the fixed dividend amount specified on their stock certificate and do not have the right to share in the future earnings growth of the corporation. Owners of participating preferred stock do have this right, however. After they have received their preferred stock dividend they are entitled to participate with common stockholders in any dividends declared on common stock.

Finally, certain preferred stock issues give their stockholders the right to convert their shares into a specified number of shares of common stock. Such stock is called convertible preferred stock.

PAR VALUE

When a corporation is formed or a new stock issue is authorized, the board of directors arbitrarily assigns the minimum legal capital in the corporation per share of stock. This amount is called the "par value" of each share of stock and is printed on the face of each stock certificate. The total par value of all the outstanding shares is called the legal capital of the corporation. It is the minimum amount of capital that creditors of the corporation have the right to expect to be invested in the corporation. Thus, if stock with a par value of $10 is issued for $8, the creditors of the corporation can demand legally that all the stockholders invest the additional $2 per share to pay the corporation's debts.

In order to avoid this dilemma and sometimes to avoid giving the impression that the par value is the true value of a stock, some corporations issue "no-par" stock. However, a few states require that a minimum issue price be given to no-par stock to protect the creditors. This minimum issue price is called "the stated value" of the stock.

It should be understood by the reader that the par or stated value of a stock is not the value at which it is sold. The selling price of a stock may be higher or lower than the par or stated value depending upon the demand for the stock on the day it is sold. The higher the earnings expectations for the corporation selling the stock, the greater will be the demand for the stock and consequently the higher its selling price will be. Stocks that are listed on the major stock exchanges, such as the New York Stock Exchange and the American Stock Exchange, have a ready and liquid market allowing for constant daily price fluctuations to occur in the stock in response to recent news concerning the company or the economy. Therefore, it is impossible to know beforehand what the selling price at the issue date will be. The par value is fixed far enough below the market value of a stock to assure that a sudden market drop will not result in its being sold below par.

Par value is especially significant with regard to preferred stock because in the absence of a specifically stated liquidation value, it represents the liquidation value of a share. Also, preferred dividends are sometimes expressed in terms of a percentage of par value.

ISSUING STOCK

Before stock can be issued or sold the shares must be authorized by the state. The original stock issue is included in the articles of incorporation and is authorized when the corporation is registered with the state. After a stock issue is authorized it may be sold to investors, thereby becoming stock that is issued and outstanding. When all of the shares authorized originally have been issued, subsequent issues must be authorized both by the board of directors and by the state.

If 1,000,000 shares of common stock with a par value of $1 are authorized and 500,000 shares are sold, the sale would be recorded as follows:

	Dr	Cr
Cash	500,000	
Common stock		500,000
To record the sale of 500,000 shares of $1 par common stock at $1 per share		

They would appear in the stockholders' equity section of the balance sheet as shown below:

Stockholders' equity

Common stock—$1 par, 1,000,000 shares authorized, 500,000 shares issued and outstanding	$500,000

In the above example the common stock was sold at its par value of $1. When it is sold for more than its par value, the amount paid in excess of par is recorded in a separate account called additional paid-in capital. If the above company had sold its shares at $1.50 per share they would be recorded through the following journal entry:

	Dr	Cr
Cash	750,000	
Common stock		500,000
Additional paid-in capital		250,000
To record the sale of 500,000 shares of $1 par common stock at $1.50 per share		

They would appear in the stockholders' equity section of the balance sheet as shown below:

Stockholders' equity

Common stock—$1 par value, 1,000,000 shares authorized, 500,000 shares issued and outstanding	$500,000
Additional paid-in capital	250,000

The additional paid-in capital of $250,000 corresponds to the $0.50 ($1.50 selling price less $1.00 par value) per share collected in excess of the par value of each share times the number of shares sold (500,000 shares × $0.50 = $250,000).

Because of the additional demands that can be made on stockholders when stock is sold below par, it is illegal in most states to do so. The account "discounts on the sale of common stock" indicating that the stock was sold below par, therefore, seldom appear on balance sheets.

If the above company sold 200,000 shares of $2.00 par value preferred for $3.00 per share, they would be recorded in the same way as the sale of common stock, except that preferred stock is always listed first in the stockholders' equity section of the balance sheet. After the above sales of preferred and common stock the stockholders' equity section would appear as follows:

Stockholders' equity

Preferred stock—$2 par value, 5% non-cumulative, 200,000 shares authorized, issued and outstanding	$ 400,000
Additional paid-in capital—preferred stock	200,000
Common stock—$1 par value, 1,000,000 shares authorized, 500,000 shares issued and outstanding	500,000
Additional paid-in capital—common stock	250,000

When no-par common stock is sold, the full selling price of the stock is recorded in the stock account. In this case there is no additional paid-in capital.

Sometimes corporations will sell stock to be paid for in the future, or in installments. When investors agree to purchase stock in this manner, an asset account called "subscriptions receivable on sale of stock" is created as well as an equity account called "stock subscribed." For example, if investors agree to buy 50,000 shares of $5 par value preferred stock for $6 per share, the following journal entry would be made to record this agreement:

	Dr	Cr
Subscription receivable on sale of preferred stock	300,000	
Preferred stock subscribed		250,000
Additional paid-in capital—preferred stock		50,000
To record agreement to purchase 50,000 shares of $5 par preferred at $6 per share		

When the subscribed stock is fully paid for, the stock certificates are issued and the amount recorded in the preferred stock subscribed account is transferred to a preferred stock account.

Sometimes stock is exchanged for assets other than cash, or for services. In this case the entry to record the sale of stock includes a debit to the accounts of the assets or services being received. For example, the exchange of 50,000 shares of $1 par value common stock for land with a market value of $75,000 is recorded as follows:

	Dr	Cr
Land	75,000	
Common stock		50,000
Additional paid-in capital—common stock		25,000
To record the exchange of 50,000 shares of $1 par common stock for land worth $75,000		

When stock is exchanged for noncash assets or services, a problem arises in determining the exchange values for the transaction. The proper procedure is to record the exchange at either the market value of the asset or service received, or at the market value of the stock sold, whichever is more easily determinable accurately.

TREASURY STOCK

Sometimes it is advisable for a corporation to repurchase its own stock. It may use this stock for employee stock purchase plans, to increase or decrease the control of certain stockholders, or simply as a good investment, if it feels the market price of its stock is unreasonably low. The stock a corporation repurchases is called "treasury stock."

Treasury stock reduces the number of shares outstanding but not the number of shares issued. Issued shares can only be reduced by retiring or cancelling them. Also, treasury stock is not entitled to vote or to receive dividends.

The acquisition of treasury stock is always recorded at cost and is presented on the balance sheet as a reduction of stockholders' equity. The cost of repurchased stock is recorded in an account called treasury stock, to be deducted at the bottom of the stockholders' equity section.

Suppose our hypothetical corporation repurchased at $2 per share 10,000 shares of the $1 par common stock it had originally sold for $1.50. This transaction would be recorded as follows:

	Dr	Cr
Treasury stock	20,000	
Cash		20,000
To record purchase of 10,000 shares of treasury stock at $2 per share		

This purchase of treasury stock would appear as follows in the stockholders' equity section of the balance sheet:

Stockholders' equity

Common stock—$1 par value, 1,000,000 shares authorized, 500,000 shares issued, 490,000 shares outstanding	$500,000
Additional paid-in capital	250,000
	750,000
Less: Treasury stock at cost	20,000
Total stockholders' equity	$730,000

If 5,000 shares of the above treasury stock were reissued at $3, $1 more than their purchase price, the treasury stock account is credited for the amount of the original purchase price of $2 and the additional paid-in capital–treasury stock account is credited for the difference from the original purchase price as follows:

	Dr	Cr
Cash	15,000	
Treasury stock		10,000
Additional paid-in capital—treasury stock		5,000
To record the reissue of 5,000 shares of treasury stock at $3 per share when the original purchase was $2 per share		

When treasury stock is reissued at a price lower than its original purchase price, the difference between the original purchase price and the reissue price is debited to the additional paid-in capital–treasury stock account. If this account does not have a balance sufficient to absorb this difference, the retained earnings account is debited for the remaining amount.

Retiring Treasury Stock

A corporation may wish to retire or cancel some of its treasury stock. This is done by reducing all balances in the capital stock account, additional paid-in capital account, and treasury stock account related to the stock being cancelled. Any net debit difference is debited to retained earnings, and any net credit difference is credited to an account called "capital from stock retirement," which appears in the stockholders' equity section following the additional paid-in capital–common stock account.

RETAINED EARNINGS

The retained earnings account normally consists of the cumulative total of all prior periods' net earnings and losses, less any dividends declared. As stated earlier, this account may also be affected by adjustments of prior periods' transactions, some treasury stock transactions, and, in some cases, the retirement of stock. Furthermore, as we shall see, a portion of retained earnings may be appropriated, or designated, by the board of directors for a special use.

Net income is recorded in the retained earnings account by debiting the income summary account and crediting the retained earnings account as explained in Chapter 8. A $40,000 net income would be recorded as follows:

	Dr	**Cr**
Income summary	40,000	
Retained earnings		40,000
To close $40,000 of net income to retained earnings		

A net loss would be recorded by crediting the income summary account and debiting the retained earnings account. If a corporation's losses exceed its retained earnings, this account is reported as a deficit.

Although the amount of retained earnings is not indicative of a corporation's total previous earnings (dividends and other nonoperating transactions may have reduced this amount), it is important because no dividends may be declared in excess of the current retained earnings of an ongoing corporation. Sometimes a corporation's board of directors may decide not to use a portion of retained earnings for the distribution of dividends. It will communicate this fact to the reader of the financial statements by appropriating or setting apart this portion of retained earnings. If $500,000 is appropriated and if it is being set aside for future property acquisitions, it would be recorded as follows:

	Dr	**Cr**
Retained earnings	500,000	
Retained earnings—appropriated		
for acquisition of properties		500,000
To record appropriation of retained earnings for future property acquisition per resolution of the board of directors		

Other reasons for appropriating retained earnings might be

- Restrictions on the payment of dividends imposed by creditors or as part of the stipulations of a bond issue.
- To provide for the possible future loss of a lawsuit against the company.
- To meet the requirements of certain state laws concerning the amount of capital a corporation must maintain.

The $500,000 appropriation of retained earnings would appear as follows in the stockholders' equity section of a balance sheet:

Stockholders' equity

Common stock—$5 par value 100,000 shares authorized, issued and outstanding	$ 500,000
Retained earnings	
Appropriated for property acquisition	500,000
Unappropriated	800,000
Total stockholders' equity	$1,800,000

An alternative method of presenting appropriated retained earnings is simply to footnote the retained earnings account in the financial statements. This would appear as follows for the preceding example:

Retained earnings (Note 8) $1,300,000

Note 8 would explain the purpose and the extent of the appropriation of retained earnings.

CASH DIVIDENDS

Dividends are the partial or total distribution of a corporation's earnings to its stockholders in proportion to the number of shares each stockholder owns. No dividends may be declared in excess of a corporation's retained earnings unless the corporation is being liquidated, in which case they are called liquidating dividends. Dividends may be paid annually, quarterly, or at any other time determined by the board of directors. Although normally dividends are paid in cash, they may also be distributed in the form of assets, such as stock in other corporations owned by the corporation distributing the dividend.

Corporations are not obliged to pay dividends. If the board of directors does not deem it in the best interest of the corporation to do so, the corporation need not pay any dividend, even on preferred stock. No dividends may be paid to common stockholders, however, until the full dividend due has been paid to the preferred stockholders. The amount of this dividend is designated on the preferred stock certificate either as an absolute dollar amount or as a percentage of the par value of the stock. Thus the term "preferred stock—$10 par value, 5% noncumulative" indicates a preferred stock with a $10 par value and paying a noncumulative dividend of $0.50 per share (5% of $10). Alternatively, the absolute amount ($0.50) of the dividend might be specified on the stock certificate.

When a dividend is to be paid, three dates are of significance: (1) the declaration date, (2) the date of record, and (3) the payment date. The declaration date is the date the dividend is declared by the board of directors. When a dividend is declared it becomes a liability of the corporation and must be recorded as such. The date of record is usually determined by the board of directors at the time the dividend is declared. This is the date used to determine ownership of a stock for the purpose of receiving the dividend. For instance, if the date of record is October 3, 1987 and a stockholder sells stock on October 2, 1987, then the new stockholder is entitled to the dividend. The payment date is the date the dividend is actually paid.

Suppose a corporation had the following capital structure and the board of directors decided to pay $200,000 in dividends:

<table>
<tr><td colspan="2">Stockholders' equity</td></tr>
<tr><td>Preferred stock—$20 par value, 3% cumula-
tive, 100,000 shares, authorized, issued
and outstanding</td><td>$ 2,000,000</td></tr>
<tr><td>Additional paid-in capital—preferred stock</td><td>1,000,000</td></tr>
<tr><td>Common stock—$10 par value, 1,000,000
shares authorized, issued and outstanding</td><td>10,000,000</td></tr>
<tr><td>Retained earnings</td><td>1,000,000</td></tr>
<tr><td>Total stockholders' equity</td><td>$14,000,000</td></tr>
</table>

The preferred stockholders would receive $60,000 in dividends (3% of the $2,000,000 total par value of preferred stock outstanding) and the common stockholders would receive the remaining $140,000 in dividends. If the declaration date is June 15, 1988, the date of record is July 15, 1988, and the payment date is August 15, 1988, the following entries would be required to record this dividend:

	Dr	Cr
Declaration date		
June 15, 1988		
Retained earnings	200,000	
Dividends payable on preferred stock		60,000
Dividends payable on common stock		140,000
To record declaration of cash dividends, 3% of $2,000,000 par to preferred stockholders and $0.14 per share to common stockholders		
Date of record		
July 15, 1988		
No entry required. The stockholders registered on the corporation's stock records as of the date will receive the dividend.		
Payment date		
August 15, 1988		
Dividends payable on preferred stock	60,000	
Dividends payable on common stock	140,000	
Cash		200,000
To record payment of $200,000 in cash dividends		

STOCK DIVIDENDS

If the board of directors wishes to (1) make a nontaxable distribution to stockholders, (2) make a distribution that will indicate the increase in stockholders' equity without using the corporation's cash, or (3) reduce the market price of the stock by increasing the number of shares outstanding, it can declare a stock dividend instead of a cash dividend. A stock dividend does not reduce stockholders' equity since no assets are distributed. The only effect of a stock dividend is that retained earnings equivalent to the amount of the fair market value of the stock on the declaration date is transferred to the capital stock accounts in the stockholders' equity section, the par value to the stock account, and any excess to the additional paid-in capital account.

We shall use a corporation with the following capital structure as an example:

Stockholders' equity	
Common stock—$10 par value, 250,000 shares authorized, 100,000 shares issued and outstanding	$1,000,000
Additional paid-in capital	500,000
Retained earnings	1,500,000
Total stockholders' equity	$3,000,000

The entries to record a 10% stock dividend declared by the board of directors of the above company on April 15, 1989 with the stipulation that April 30, 1989 was to be the date of record and May 15, 1989 the distribution date are shown next. Assume the stock has a market value of $25 on the declaration date.

	Dr	Cr
Declaration date		
April 15, 1989		
Retained earnings	250,000	
Stock dividends distributable		100,000
Additional paid-in capital		150,000

To record the declaration of a stock dividend on common stock:
    10% × 100,000 shares = 10,000 shares
    10,000 shares × $10 par value = $100,000
    10,000 shares × $15 excess of market
    value over par value = $150,000

Date of record
April 30, 1989
No entry required. The stockholders registered on the corporation's stock
records as of this date will receive the stock dividend.

Distribution date
May 15, 1989

	Dr	Cr
Stock dividends distributable	100,000	
Common stock		100,000

To record distribution of a stock dividend of 10,000 shares

After the stock dividend is distributed the corporation's stockholders' equity section would appear as follows:

Stockholders' equity

Common stock—$10 par value, 200,000 shares authorized, 110,000 shares issued and outstanding	$1,100,000
Additional paid-in capital	650,000
Retained earnings	1,250,000
Total shareholders' equity	$3,000,000

Notice that the total stockholders' equity has remained the same ($3,000,000). Also, each stockholder owns the same percentage of the corporation's total stock as before the stock dividend, even though more shares may be owned. The only substantial change that has occurred in the stockholders' equity section of the balance sheet is that $250,000 has been transferred from retained earnings to the common stock and additional paid-in capital—common stock accounts.

If a stock dividend is greater than 20–25% of a corporation's outstanding stock, it is assumed that the increased number of shares will have a materially depressing effect on the market price of the stock. Therefore, GAAP require that when such a large stock dividend is declared, the par value and not the market value of the shares be used to determine the amount of retained earnings to be transferred to the common stock account.

STOCK SPLITS

If the market price of a corporation's stock increases excessively, this makes it difficult for the numerous small investors to purchase the stock. Most investors are charged a lower commission when they purchase a round lot of 100 shares. One hundred shares of a $90 stock amounts to $9,000, which is an amount large enough to discourage the small investor from buying it.

Therefore, corporations often try to reduce the market price of their shares. They do this by effecting a stock split. In a stock split every stockholder receives two or more new shares in exchange for every share owned. If the split is two-for-one two new shares are exchanged for every old one; if the split is three-for-one, three new shares are received for every old share, etc. In a two-for-one or a three-for-one split, the new shares have a par value, or stated value, that is one-half or one-third the par value of the original shares, respectively. The reduction in the par value depends on the extent of the split. If the split is four-for-one and the market price of an old share was $100, then each new share (after the split) will be worth $25 on the market. The par value of the shares will also be one-fourth the par value of the original shares. Since a corporation's account balances do not change as a result of a stock split, no journal entry is required to record the stock split, except a memo entry to record the new par value of the shares. The difference between a stock dividend and a stock split is that in the case of a stock dividend, a portion of retained earnings equivalent to the market value of the shares (or the par value in case of stock dividends of 20–25% or more) is transferred to the capital stock accounts.

STATEMENT OF RETAINED EARNINGS

In Chapter 4, the statement of retained earnings was presented in its simplest form as shown in Figure 17.1. In this chapter the reader has become aware that other events besides recording the results of operations and the payment of dividends affect the retained earnings account. Since the purpose of the statement of retained earnings is to show all the activity in this account, the effect of these other events on the retained earnings account must also be presented.

Three additional events that might affect the retained earnings account are (1) adjustments of a prior period's earnings (usually to correct an error), (2) declaration of a stock dividend, and (3) the sale of treasury stock at less than cost.

A more complex example of a statement of retained for the FRB Restaurant, Inc. might include the additional events listed below:

Additional Events

1. Depreciation expense was understated by $12,000 in 1988. The company's income tax rate is 40%, so that the after-tax effect of this additional depreciation expense on net income is $7,200. The company's expenses are increased by $12,000, thereby reducing taxable income by $12,000 and reducing the corresponding income tax by $4,800 (40% of $12,000).

FRB RESTAURANTS, INC.
Statement of Retained Earnings
For the Year Ended December 31, 1989

Beginning balance, December 31, 1988	$65,000
Add: Net income for year 1989	28,000
	93,000
Less: Dividends	8,000
Ending balance, December 31, 1989	$85,000

Figure 17.1. Simple form of statement of retained earnings.

FRB RESTAURANTS, INC.
Statement of Retained Earnings
For the Year Ended December 31, 1989

Beginning balance, December 31, 1988		$65,000
Less: Prior period correction of depreciation		
(net of $4, 800 tax effect)		7,200
Restated balance, December 31, 1988		57,800
Add: Net income for year 1989		28,000
		85,800
Less: Cash dividends	$ 8,000	
Stock dividends	15,000	
Treasury stock sold below cost	10,000	
Ending balance, December 31, 1989		33,000
		$52,800

Figure 17.2. Statement of retained earnings showing additional transactions.

2. A $15,000 stock dividend is declared in 1989.
3. Two thousand shares of treasury stock purchased for $20 per share are sold for $15 per share ($20 − $15 = $5 per share difference; $5 × 2,000 shares = $10,000 total difference between purchase and sales price). FRB Restaurants, Inc. made its original sale of stock at par value, and so it has no additional paid-in capital account.

The statement of retained earnings showing the above additional transactions is given in Figure 17.2. As was explained in Chapter 12, sometimes the statement of retained earnings is presented as a continuation of the income statement. FRB Restaurants, Inc.'s simple statement of retained earnings (without the additional transactions listed above) would appear as in Figure 17.3 when incorporated into the income statement.

FRB RESTAURANTS, INC.
Statement of Retained Earnings
For the Year Ended December 31, 1989
(presented as a continuation of the income statement)

Net income for year 1989	$28,000
Add: Beginning retained earnings, December 31, 1988	65,000
	93,000
Less: Dividends	8,000
Ending retained earnings, December 31, 1989	$85,000

Figure 17.3. Simple statement of retained earnings incorporated into income statement.

QUESTIONS

1. What are organization costs? How should they be recorded on the accounting books of a corporation?
2. What are three rights of common stockholders? How would you describe them?
3. What are three fundamental differences between common stock and preferred stock?
4. What are dividends in arrears? How should they be treated on the financial statements?
5. What is the significance of par value and why is it unwise for a corporation to issue stock at a price lower than its par value?
6. Who designates the board of directors of a corporation? What is the relationship between the board of directors and the management of a corporation?

7. What are four types of information that must be included in the articles of incorporation of a corporation?

8. What is meant when we say that a corporation's stock is authorized, issued, and outstanding?

9. What is the preemptive right of stockholders?

10. What is the difference in accounting treatment between a stock dividend of less than 20–25% and more than 25% of the outstanding stock?

11. What is the difference between a stock dividend and a stock split? —

12. What is treasury stock? Where should it appear in the stockholders' equity section of the balance sheet?

13. What is the significance of the following dates: (a) declaration date, (b) date of record, and (c) payment date?

14. What are retained earnings? What are appropriated retained earnings?

15. What is the journal entry to record the sale of 10,000 shares of no-par common stock for $87,642?

EXERCISES

1. Harry's Bar was authorized to issue 100,000 shares of $5 par common stock. It sold 50,000 shares at $7 per share.
   (a) Prepare the journal entry to record the sale.
   (b) Show the stockholders' equity section of the balance sheet immediately after the sale of the stock.

2. The stockholders' equity section of the Rodant Motel is presented below:

Stockholders's equity

Common stock, $10 par, 1,000,000 shares authorized, issued and outstanding	$10,000,000
Additional paid-in capital	2,000,000
Retained earnings	3,000,000
Total stockholders' equity	$15,000,000

   (a) Prepare the journal entry to record the purchase of 100,000 shares of treasury stock at $20 per share.
   (b) Show the stockholders' equity section of the balance sheet immediately after the purchase of the treasury stock.

3. The stockholders' equity section of the Ubiquitous Travel Agency Corporation is presented below:

Stockholders' equity

Preferred stock—$10 par, 10% participating, 200,000 shares authorized, 100,000 shares issued and outstanding	$ 1,000,000
Additional paid-in capital—preferred stock	500,000
Common stock—$5 par, 1,000,000 shares authorized, issued, and outstanding (except for 100,000 shares of treasury stock)	5,000,000
Retained earnings	10,000,000
	16,500,000
Less: Treasury stock at cost	1,000,000
Total stockholders' equity	$15,500,000

If the board of directors wishes to pay $3,000,000 in combined preferred and common stock dividends, how much will the shareholders receive (a) for each preferred share and (b) for each common share they own?

4. The Ponteverde Hotel Corporation was authorized to issue 42,000,000 common shares of $20 par value. It recently sold 500,000 shares for $12,500,000 and

exchanged 200,000 shares for land with an estimated market value of $6,000,000.

The Ponteverde Hotel Corporation is a well-established corporation and had sold 40,000,000 of the authorized common shares many years ago at $22 per share. Its stock is traded on the New York Stock Exchange, where a ready and liquid market exists for its shares. At the time the 200,000 shares were exchanged for the land, the Ponteverde Hotel's stock was selling for $25 per share.

(a) Prepare the journal entries to record the issue of the 700,000 additional shares of common stock.

(b) Show the stockholders' equity section of the balance sheet immediately after the issue of these shares. Assume the hotel has retained earnings of $30,000,000.

5. The Roundrib Restaurant reserved 20,000 shares of $10 par common stock for investors who subscribed to the stock at $12 per share on July 1, 1988. On October 30, 1988, the investors paid their stock subscriptions. Prepare journal entries to record:

(a) The subscription of the shares on July 1.

(b) The payment of the subscriptions on October 30.

(c) Assume the Roundrib Restaurant had 100,000 shares of $10 par authorized, of which 60,000 shares had been previously issued at $13 per share.

(d) Assume the company has $100,000 of retained earnings.

Show the stockholders' equity section of its balance sheet immediately after making the journal entry to record the subscription of an additional 20,000 shares as in part (a).

PROBLEMS

1. The Cucharita Restaurant Corporation was recently formed and has not begun operations yet.

(a) Prepare journal entries to record the following transactions:

June 1 Received an invoice from the lawyer who handled the incorporation for $2,000.

June 2 Received an invoice from the accountant who developed the accounting system for $3,000.

June 4 Received an invoice for a finder's fee of $5,000 from the person who brought together the original investors in the corporation.

June 10 Received a subscription commitment of $300,000 for 10,000 shares of $30 par, 5% preferred stock.

June 15 Sold 50,000 shares of $20 par common stock for $1,500,000.

June 20 Received payment for the preferred stock subscriptions.

June 30 Repurchased 5,000 shares of common stock at $25 per share.

July 1 Sold 2,000 shares of treasury stock at $15 per share.

(b) Show the stockholders' equity section of the Cucharita Restaurant Corporation's balance sheet immediately after recording all of the above transactions. Assume 50,000 preferred shares and 600,000 common shares authorized. Also, assume the company has a $30,000 accumulated deficit as of July 1, 1988.

2. The stockholders' equity section of the Sleepmore Hotel, Inc. as of August 31, 1987 is presented below. It is on a calendar year basis. The market value of a common share during the months of October and November was $20.

Stockholders' equity

Preferred stock—$5 par, 10% noncumulative 200,000 shares authorized, issued, and outstanding	$ 1,000,000
Common stock—$10 par 2,000,000 shares authorized, 1,000,000 shares issued and outstanding	10,000,000
Additional paid-in capital—common stock	2,000,000
Retained earnings	15,000,000
Total stockholders' equity	$28,000,000

(a) Prepare journal entries to record the following transactions on the corporation's accounting books:

Sept. 1   Purchased 100,000 shares of its own common stock for $1,500,000.

Sept. 3   Declared a cash dividend of $100,000 to preferred stockholders.

Sept. 30   Paid the cash dividend to preferred stockholders.

Oct. 15   Declared a common stock dividend of 90,000 shares to the common stockholders.

Oct. 30   Distributed the stock dividend to common stockholders.

Nov. 15   Declared a common stock dividend of 330,000 shares to the common stockholders.

Nov. 28   Distributed the 330,000 share stock dividend.

Dec. 26   10,000 shares of common stock are retired.

(b) Show the stockholders' equity section of the Sleepmore Hotel Corporation's balance sheet immediately after recording all of the above transactions.

3. The stockholders' equity section of the Condoga Hotel Corporations' balance sheet as of the corporation's fiscal year end, January 31, 1987, is presented below. For the first time since the company was formed no dividends were declared in the fiscal year ended January 31, 1987. The market value of a common share was $15 during the month of February, 1987.

Stockholders' equity

Preferred stock—$50 par, 5% cumulative, 100,000 shares authorized, issued, and outstanding	$ 5,000,000
Preferred stock—$20 par, 10% noncumulative, 50,000 shares authorized, issued, and outstanding	1,000,000
Additional paid-in capital—preferred stock	500,000
Common stock—$10 par, 900,000 shares authorized, issued, and outstanding (except for 100,000 shares of treasury stock)	9,000,000
Retained earnings	1,500,000
	17,000,000
Less: Treasury stock at cost	300,000
Total stockholders' equity	$16,700,000

(a) If the board of directors wishes to declare a dividend of $1,000,000 on February 5, 1987, how much must be distributed to each type of stockholder on a per share basis? Assume the date of record is February 15, 1987.

(b) Prepare the journal entry to record the declaration of this dividend and then prepare the journal entry to record the payment of this dividend.

(c) Prepare the journal entry to record the declaration of a stock dividend of 100,000 common shares on February 25, 1987.

(d) Prepare the journal entry to record the declaration of a stock dividend of 300,000 common shares on December 12, 1987.

(e) If the common stock were split five-for-one, what entry would have to be made on the accounting books of the corporation?

4. The retained earnings account of the XYZ Restaurant Corporation had a balance of $450,000 at the November 30, 1989 fiscal year end of the corporation. Based on the information given below, prepare a statement of retained earnings for the XYZ Restaurant Corporation at its November 30, 1990 fiscal year end. Ignore any information given below that does not affect retained earnings. The market value of a common share should be assumed to be $30 for all transactions listed.

Dec. 15, 1989   It was discovered after the books were closed that due to a calculation error the ending inventory of the corporation was overstated by $40,000 at November 30, 1989.

Jan. 15, 1990   The restaurant sold for $7,000 an oven that cost $12,000 and that had accumulated depreciation of $5,000.

March 12, 1990	A common stock dividend of 10,000 shares was declared. The par value of the common stock is $25 per share. There are 80,000 shares of common stock authorized, issued, and outstanding.
Aug. 1, 1990	10,000 shares of treasury stock that had been purchased for $15 per share were sold for $30 per share. The corporation has no additional paid-in capital accounts.
Sept. 2, 1990	The corporation repaid a $50,000 loan.
Oct. 12, 1990	The remaining treasury stock was retired. It consisted of 10,000 shares purchased at a cost of $30 per share. Its par value is $25 per share.
Nov. 30, 1990	The corporation earned a net income of $65,000 during the fiscal year ended November 30, 1990.

18

Responsibility Accounting

Responsibility accounting is a system of accounting used to evaluate the performance of individual managers and supervisors within an organization. Such a system is created by gathering all the accounts over which each manager or supervisor exercises direct control into separate groups called responsibility centers. By forming account groups in this way, in a manner consistent with the delegation of responsibility, the results of each manager's or supervisor's performance can be evaluated independently of the performance of the organization as a whole. This individualized feedback is essential in an organization because it provides the information that upper-level managers need to judge the efficiency with which lower-level personnel fulfill the responsibilities delegated to them.

This chapter first discusses the nature and goals of a business organization, as well as some criteria to be used in the departmentalization of an organization. Next, an explanation of the relationship to responsibility accounting of controllable and noncontrollable costs, and allocated and unallocated expenses is given. This is followed by an explanation of responsibility centers. The function of the chart of accounts and the various hotel income statement departmental account schedules as part of the responsibility accounting system is also discussed.

Subsequently, three ways of utilizing the information provided by a responsibility accounting system in evaluating a manager's performance are presented. The role of full-cost accounting in a responsibility accounting system is discussed next. In conclusion, the impact of responsibility accounting on financial statement disclosures required by GAAP is discussed.

NATURE AND GOALS
OF A BUSINESS ORGANIZATION

An organization can be defined as a group of people working together to achieve a common goal. The overall goal of management in a hospitality industry organization is to manage the assets of the entity as efficiently as possible while optimizing services rendered to its customers. In a market economy the degree of success achieved by management is ultimately evidenced by a firm's profitability.

Profit is determined by deducting expenses from revenues. Thus the higher a company's revenue and the lower its expenses, the greater its profit (net income). Profitability, as we shall use the term here, is not solely a measure of net income, but also depends on the amount of investment required to generate this net income. A company that earns a $2,000,000 net income with total assets of $40,000,000 is obviously managing its resources more efficiently

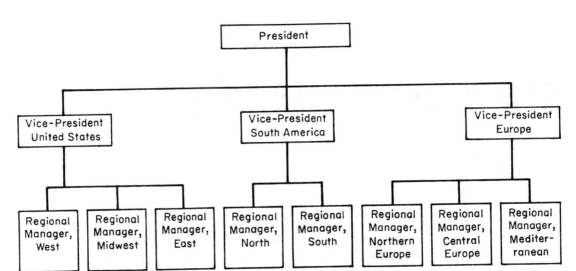

Figure 18.1.   Worldwide Hotel Corporation organization chart.

than one earning a $2,000,000 net income with total assets of $50,000,000. In measuring the profitability of a company, its earnings must be related to investment—this relationship is called return on investment (ROI).

To summarize the above, the organization's overall goal can be broken down into the following subsidiary goals:

- To maximize revenues
- To minimize expenses
- To minimize investment

The greater management's success in achieving its goals, the greater will be the firm's ROI. The person ultimately responsible for this is the organization's president. Since the president cannot perform all the functions required to attain the organization's goals, he or she must delegate part of the responsibility to other managers. These managers in turn delegate responsibility to others who assist them, so that gradually an organizational structure is created that looks somewhat like a pyramid, at the bottom of which are the individual hotel and restaurant employees. An organization chart of a typical hospitality entity is presented in Figure 18.1.

From Figure 18.1, it is evident that the president has delegated to subordinate managers responsibility for achieving a part of the overall goal for which the president is responsible. The president of the organization above is responsible for maximizing revenues, minimizing expenses, and minimizing investment for the organization as a whole. Responsibility for achieving these goals in the United States has been delagated to the vice-president of U.S. operations, who in turn has delegated responsibility to the Western, Midwest, and Eastern regional managers. Each regional manager has delegated responsibilities to the hotel managers, who in turn have delegated responsibilities to their department managers. Thus, the organization chart for the eastern region might end up looking like that in Figure 18.2 at the level of the individual hotel.

Notice that in Figure 18.2 some departments are connected to the organization by horizontal lines and others by vertical lines. This is due to the nature of each department's function. Those departments to which responsibility has

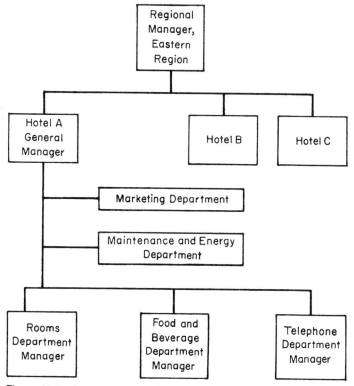

Figure 18.2. Individual hotel portion of organization chart.

been delegated for producing and selling food and beverages and rendering services to the public are called line departments. They are directly involved in producing revenue for the organization and are connected to the organization by vertical lines. Examples of these are the rooms department, food and beverage department and telephone department in the above chart. Other departments, such as the marketing and plant maintenance and energy departments, are responsible for assisting the line departments. They are connected to the organization by horizontal lines and are called staff departments.

In order to promote efficiency within an organization, regions, divisions, and departments must be created along functional lines so that all members of a particular region, division, or department have a common and logical goal. For example, not all members of the Eastern Region on the organization chart above would have a common goal if some of them were responsible for hotels in the Western region, nor would it be logical to have responsibilities crossing organizational lines in this manner. To achieve maximum efficiency, therefore, the delegation of responsibility in a responsibility accounting system must coincide with the organizational structure of the business entity.

CONTROLLABLE AND NONCONTROLLABLE COSTS

It is logical also that if managers or supervisors are made responsible for a certain activity they must be given control over the expenditures related to that activity. If a hotel restaurant manager is responsible for the restaurant's earnings, then he or she must be given the authority to control the restaurant's expenses. A restaurant manager cannot be held responsible for the restaurant's profit if expenses over which he or she has no control are included in the restaurant's income statement. For instance, if the hotel's personnel manager had the authority to hire and dismiss waiters and waitresses in the hotel's restaurant, the food and beverage department manager's performance could not be evaluated on the basis of the restaurant's earnings, because a large part of the payroll expenses used to calculate these earnings would not be under the food and beverage department manager's control.

A manager's performance may be fairly evaluated only on the basis of expenses or costs over which he or she has direct control. Such expenses are called controllable expenses insofar as that manager is concerned. Any account not controllable by a particular manager is called a noncontrollable expense insofar as that manager is concerned. The undistributed operating expenses and fixed charges, as listed in the USAH, are noncontrollable expenses insofar as the rooms department manager, food and beverage department manager, and the managers of other revenue-generating departments are concerned.

Nevertheless, all expenses and costs are controllable by managers at one level or other of the organization. Undistributed operating expenses are controllable by the managers of the administrative and general, marketing, guest entertainment, and property maintenance and energy departments. Both departmental expenses and undistributed operating expenses are controlled by the hotel's general manager through responsibility for and authority over each of the department managers. The hotel's fixed charges such as rent, depreciation, property insurance, and real estate taxes are controllable by the hotel owner or regional manager responsible for deciding the size and class of the hotel as well as its continued existence, although these are noncontrollable expenses insofar as the hotel manager or department managers are concerned.

ALLOCATED VERSUS UNALLOCATED EXPENSES

Equally as detrimental as the failure to establish clear-cut lines of control among responsibility center managers is the arbitrary allocation of one responsibility center's expenses to another responsibility center. In the case of the long-form hotel income statement, the undistributed operating expenses and fixed charges are incurred in part to service the hotel's line departments— the rooms department, food and beverage department, etc. Nevertheless, the line department managers cannot control these expenses. Thus it would distort the system of responsibility accounting to allocate or include undistributed operating expenses in the departmental income statement of the line departments, even though the line departments benefit from the services provided by these staff departments.

Suppose that rent expense was allocated to each hotel department and was one of the expenses used to evaluate the performance of the various department managers. Under these circumstances if the owner or regional manager of the hotel accepted a rent increase, this increase in rent expense and its negative effect on departmental profit would make it seem that the performance of the department managers had declined, even though they had no control over this expense and logically could not be held responsible for it. From the point of view of responsibility accounting, such an allocation is unfair. Rent expense is part of the fixed charges appearing on the hotel income statement prepared according to the USAH, is controllable by the owner or regional manager, and should only be used to evaluate the performance of the owner or regional manager.

RESPONSIBILITY CENTERS

Departments such as those described previously, with specific goals that the manager is responsible for achieving and whose costs and expenses are controllable by a manager or supervisor, are called responsibility centers. The reason for creating responsibility centers is twofold:

1. They enable upper-level management to delegate responsibility for a specific organizational goal to each department manager.
2. They enable upper-level management to obtain the necessary feedback concerning the performance of the responsibility center managers as reflected in the accounts associated with their departments.

In the hospitality industry, the three main objectives (maximizing revenues, minimizing expenses, minimizing investment) are achieved through four types of responsibility centers:

1. Profit centers, whose managers are responsible for maximizing revenues and minimizing expenses.
2. Revenue centers, whose managers are responsible for maximizing revenues.
3. Cost centers, whose managers are responsible for minimizing expenses.
4. Investment centers, whose managers are responsible for maximizing revenue, minimizing expenses, and minimizing investment.

These four types of responsibility centers are related to the long-form hotel income statement presented in Figure 18.3.

The rooms, food and beverage, and telephone departments are responsible for both maximizing sales and minimizing costs—they are profit centers. The store rentals department has no major direct identifiable expenses associated with it—it is a revenue center. The remaining departments are staff departments and do not generate revenues. Their managers' goal is to minimize expenses without curtailing services to the other hotel departments—they are cost centers. The hotel as a whole is an investment center because the objective of the owner or the regional manager responsible for its design is to minimize investment in property and equipment while maximizing the hotel's revenue-generating capacity and minimizing the hotel's expenses.

The performance of the line department managers can be evaluated on the basis of how well they maximize departmental income (departmental revenues minus departmental expenses). The performance of the staff departmental managers can be evaluated on the basis of how wisely they control their departments' expenses while maintaining or improving the quality of the services they render. The performance of the hotel manager, who is responsible for all the hotel's operated departments and controls expenses through the various department managers, but is not responsible for fixed charges, is evaluated on the basis of maximizing total income before fixed charges. Finally, the performance of the owner or regional manager, who determined the amount of the hotel's fixed charges when its class and size were decided, and

	Net revenues	Cost of sales	Payroll and related expenses	Other expenses	Income (loss)
Operated departments					
Rooms	$1,280,000		$200,000	$ 94,000	$ 986,000
Food and beverage	570,000	$188,000	227,000	65,000	90,000
Telephone	29,000		25,000	9,000	(5,000)
Store rentals	51,000				51,000
Total operated departments	1,930,000	188,000	452,000	168,000	1,122,000
Undistributed operating expenses					
Administrative and general			130,000	80,000	
Marketing			30,000	60,000	
Guest entertainment			25,000	70,000	
Property operation, maintenance and energy costs			27,000	108,000	
Total undistributed operating expenses			212,000	318,000	530,000
Income before fixed charges	$1,930,000	$188,000	$664,000	$486,000	592,000
Property taxes and insurance				72,000	
Interest				25,000	
Depreciation and amortization				$140,000	237,000
Income before income taxes					355,000
Income taxes					145,000
Net income					$ 210,000

Figure 18.3. Sample hotel long-form income statement.

who controls the hotel's revenue and expenses through its general manager, is evaluated on the basis of both net income and investment.

THE CHART OF ACCOUNTS AND DEPARTMENTAL ACCOUNT SCHEDULES

Since the proper functioning of a responsibility accounting system depends on grouping related accounts around responsibility centers, a system for identifying accounts by responsibility center is required. In practice, the accounts associated with each responsibility center are identified through their chart of accounts number. For instance, prefixes can be utilized to group accounts by responsibility center. In the sample chart of accounts presented in the appendix, all accounts associated with the rooms department and controlled by the rooms department manager have the prefix 10, accounts controlled by the marketing department manager have the prefix 75, and those associated with no specific department but applicable to the hotel as a whole have the prefix 00. Larger organizations may use an additional set of prefixes to identify expenses by regional responsibility centers.

Since the long-form income statement only includes departmental account totals, the USAH provides departmental account schedules for the various responsibility centers, each of which contains a detailed listing of the accounts controllable by each center's manager. The departmental account schedule for the food and beverage department is presented in Figure 18.4.

Since the food and beverage department is a profit center, its account schedule is a departmental income statement. The account schedule of a revenue

Revenue	
Food	$400,000
Beverage	171,000
Total	571,000
Allowances	2,000
Net revenue	569,000
Other income	1,000
Total	570,000
Cost of sales	
Cost of food consumed	160,000
Less cost of employees' meals	16,000
Net cost of food sales	144,000
Cost of beverage sales	44,000
Net cost of sales	188,000
Gross profit	382,000
Expenses	
Salaries and wages	184,000
Employee benefits	43,000
Total payroll and related expenses	227,000
Other expenses	
China, glassware, silver, linen	9,100
Contract cleaning	2,280
Kitchen fuel	5,130
Laundry and dry cleaning	1,710
Licenses	8,800
Music and entertainment	17,700
Operating supplies	18,860
Other operating expenses	1,200
Uniforms	220
Total other expenses	65,000
Total expenses	292,000
Departmental income (loss)	$ 90,000

Figure 18.4. Food and beverage departmental income statement.

center such as store rentals lists revenue accounts only, and the account schedule of a cost center such as the marketing department lists expense accounts only. The purpose of these departmental account schedules is twofold:

1. They group together those accounts for which department managers are responsible and that they can control.
2. They break down the departmental revenue and expense totals on the long-form income statement into their subaccounts. This account detail provides department managers a measure of control that would be lacking if they were only informed concerning total departmental revenue and total departmental expenses as they appear on the long-form hotel income statement.

In order to determine why their department's expenses are out of line, managers need to have detailed knowledge of where they are spending the department's funds. Otherwise, they may be prevented from using the authority to control their department's expenses by lack of knowledge regarding which expenses need to be controlled. A good responsibility accounting system must not only structure accounts in a manner consistent with the way authority is delegated, but must also provide the manager with sufficiently detailed information concerning departmental expenses to facilitate their effective control. The USAH attains both of these objectives effectively.

EVALUATING A MANAGER'S PERFORMANCE

After the accounts for which an individual manager is responsible have been segregated into responsibility centers, certain analytical techniques may be used to evaluate the manager's performance on the basis of the information reflected in these accounts. The three techniques discussed here are vertical analysis, budget variances, and rate of return analysis.

Vertical analysis involves expressing each revenue and/or expense account as a percentage of total departmental revenue in the case of revenue and profit centers, and as a percentage of total departmental expenses in the case of cost centers. Similarly, this procedure can be applied when analyzing an investment center's income statement by relating revenues and expenses appearing on the income statement to total sales. Vertical analysis may also be applied to an investment center's balance sheet by expressing the individual asset accounts as a percentage of total assets. In this way, any unusual variations in

Revenue		
Food	$400,000	70.2%
Beverage	171,000	30.0
Total	571,000	100.2
Allowances	2,000	0.4
Net revenue	569,000	99.8
Other income	1,000	0.2
Total	570,000	100.0
Cost of sales		
Cost of food consumed	160,000	28.1
Less cost of employees' meals	16,000	2.8
Net cost of food sales	144,000	25.3
Cost of beverage sales	44,000	7.7
Net cost of sales	188,000	33.0
Gross profit	382,000	67.0
Expenses		
Salaries and wages	184,000	32.3
Employee benefits	43,000	7.5
Total payroll and related expenses	227,000	39.8
Other expenses		
China, glassware, silver, linen	9,100	1.7
Contract cleaning	2,280	0.4
Kitchen fuel	5,130	0.9
Laundry and dry cleaning	1,710	0.3
Licenses	8,800	1.5
Music and entertainment	17,700	3.1
Operating supplies	18,860	3.3
Other operating expenses	1,200	0.2
Uniforms	220	0.0
Total other expenses	65,000	11.4
Total expenses	292,000	51.2
Departmental income (loss)	$ 90,000	15.8

Figure 18.5. Food and beverage departmental income statement showing vertical analysis.

revenue, expenses or asset account balances can be more readily identified. The vertical percentages calculated for the food and beverage department income statement presented earlier are shown in Figure 18.5.

Without the use of vertical analysis a 5 or 10% change in any account with relation to total sales might go unnoticed upon management review. Use of this technique makes it easier for upper-level managers to alert lower-level managers when certain expenses become excessive.

Another way to determine when revenues and/or expenses are unreasonably low or high is the use of a budget. A budget is a management estimate of what a responsibility center's revenues and/or expenses should be during the accounting year. Actual revenues and expenses are then compared to these budget estimates by subtracting the actual amounts from budgeted amounts. The differences between actual and budgeted amounts are called variances. If revenues are greater than estimated, or expenses are lower than estimated, the variance is favorable. In the opposite case the variance is unfavorable. With this technique, upper-level managers can alert lower-level managers concerning those accounts where unfavorable variances exist.

The variances from assumed budget amounts for the food and beverage department income statement presented earlier are shown in Figure 18.6. Unfavorable variances are shown in parentheses. Usually, budget estimates are made on a monthly basis, although they may also be prepared for the accounting year as a whole.

The above techniques are also useful in evaluating departmental totals within the framework of an investment center's overall income statement, such as the long-form income statement in the case of the USAH. If total departmental revenues are too low or if total departmental expenses are too high, this will show up when vertical or budgeting analysis is applied to the hotel income statement as a whole.

An investment center manager is not evaluated solely on the basis of maximizing earnings (net income). He or she must also control the amount of investment required to generate earnings. Therefore, as stated earlier, a hotel is evaluated as an investment center by relating net income to investment, which for purposes of this chapter will be considered to be total assets. This relationship can be expressed as follows:

$$\frac{\text{net income}}{\text{total assets}} = \text{return on investment (ROI)}$$

To evaluate the performance of the owner or regional manager as an investment center manager the percentage ROI of any particular hotel under his or her control can be compared to that of other hotels in the industry (industry averages) or, if the hotel is part of a large corporate group, to other hotels in its particular hotel chain. The performance of regional investment center managers can also be evaluated by comparing the ROI of the entire region under his or her control to the ROI of other regions within the corporate structure.

Furthermore, ROI can be compared to management estimates of future ROI (budgeted ROI) to determine if goals are being met, just as actual revenues and expenses are compared to budgeted revenues and expenses. If the percentage ROI is found deficient then the vertical and budgetary analysis of income statement accounts should reveal any expenses that are excessive. Also, vertical analysis of the assets on the balance sheet can help identify any types of assets in which excessive investment has been made.

	Actual amounts	Budgeted amounts	Variance (unfavorable)
Revenue			
Food	$400,000	$401,000	$(1,000)
Beverage	171,000	172,000	(1,000)
Total	571,000	573,000	(2,000)
Allowances	2,000	1,500	(500)
Net revenue	569,000	571,500	(2,500)
Other income	1,000	1,000	—
Total	570,000	572,500	(2,500)
Cost of sales			
Cost of food consumed	160,000	160,500	500
Less cost of employees' meals	16,000	16,300	(300)
Net cost of food sales	144,000	144,200	200
Cost of beverage sales	44,000	43,700	(300)
Net cost of sales	188,000	187,900	(100)
Gross profit	382,000	384,600	(2,600)
Expenses			
Salaries and wages	184,000	180,500	(3,500)
Employee benefits	43,000	40,200	(2,800)
Total payroll and related expenses	227,000	220,700	(6,300)
Other expenses			
China, glassware, silver, linen	9,100	9,000	(100)
Contract cleaning	2,280	2,200	(80)
Kitchen fuel	5,130	4,900	(230)
Laundry and dry cleaning	1,710	1,800	90
Licenses	8,800	8,800	—
Music and entertainment	17,700	17,400	(300)
Operating supplies	18,860	18,100	(760)
Other operating expenses	1,200	1,000	(200)
Uniforms	220	500	280
Total other expenses	65,000	63,700	(1,300)
Total expenses	292,000	284,400	(7,500)
Departmental income (loss)	$ 90,000	$100,200	$(10,200)

Figure 18.6. Food and beverage departmental income statement showing actual and budgeted amounts and variances.

RESPONSIBILITY ACCOUNTING VERSUS FULL-COST ACCOUNTING

The costs that we have been taking into account to evaluate managers' performance have been the costs they can control directly. When a responsibility system is designed correctly, those expenses for which managers are made responsible and over which they are given control are the expenses that can readily and directly traceable to their departments. Such expenses are called direct expenses of that department.

These direct expenses should be contrasted to other expenses, such as the undistributed operating expenses and fixed charges in a hotel, which are not directly traceable to the operated or line departments. It is not always possible to determine exactly how much electricity or depreciation expense is consumed by the rooms department or by the food and beverage department, for example. Expenses that cannot be directly traced to a department are called indirect expenses with regard to that department.

Although responsibility accounting is essential for the accurate evaluation of management performance, some people argue that departmental managers should be made aware of the full costs of operating their departments as noted in Chapter 12. This argument states that the indirect expenses (i.e., the undistributed operating expenses and fixed charges appearing on the hotel income statement) should be allocated or assigned to the appropriate hotel departments on an equitable basis. There is considerable merit in this point of view. However, such allocation of indirect expenses can make a responsibility accounting system deceiving.

It would be erroneous for an upper-level manager to conclude that certain lower-level managers were deficient in their performance on the basis of an increase in an indirect expense that has been allocated to their departments and that they cannot control. Perhaps an additional income or expense schedule should be prepared for department managers in which all hotel expenses are allocated to them. Such statements should be used only to provide guidelines regarding minimum levels of acceptable performance and only when cost allocation has been truly equitable. One of the problems with this approach is that it is very difficult to ascertain what constitutes equitable allocation. For instance, if the hotel owner constructs a banquet hall that is too large for the available market and if fixed charges are allocated to the various departments on the basis of square footage (an apparently equitable distribution), it would be illogical to conclude that the food and beverage department manager's performance is inadequate if this department did not generate sufficient departmental income to cover such excessive allocated fixed charges,which are beyond the manager's control.

A more logical approach would be to use allocated or full-cost statements as guides in determining pricing strategy. To this end, they should be prepared in two steps. First, fixed charges are allocated to all hotel departments, both line (revenue-generating) and staff (service) departments. Second, staff department expenses, including the previously allocated fixed charges, are allocated to the line departments. Line departments' income statements prepared in this fashion help to avoid underpricing by making the managers of these departments aware of the full costs involved in operating their departments, even though some of these costs are beyond their control. When utilized in this way, full-cost accounting is a useful complement to a responsibility accounting system, in that it helps a manager to know what minimum revenues must be generated in a department, which is after all, part of the manager's revenue-maximizing responsibility.

RESPONSIBILITY ACCOUNTING AND FINANCIAL STATEMENT DISCLOSURES

Financial accounting provides summary information to users of financial statements. Traditionally it has not always fallen within the scope of these statements to present information concerning individual business segments of a business entity. In 1976, however, the FASB issued statement No. 14, "Financial Reporting for Segments of a Business Enterprise." According to this statement, a hospitality entity must report separately in its financial statements any segment that according to special definitions given in FASB Statement No. 14 contributes 10% or more to the combined revenue or profit or loss of the entity as a whole, or represents 10% or more of the entire entity's assets. The statement reads, in part: "The term 'profit center' is used in this Statement to refer only to those components of an enterprise . . . for which information about revenue and profitability is accumulated. An enterprise's existing profit centers—the smallest units of activity for which revenue and expense information is accumulated for internal planning and control purposes—represent a logical starting point for determining the enterprise's industry segments."[1]

It is evident that in addition to providing necessary management information, a responsibility accounting system also serves as a basis and source of information concerning the distinct segments of an organization for financial reporting purposes.

QUESTIONS

1. What is a responsibility accounting system? What is a full-cost accounting system?
2. What are the three goals of a business organization?
3. What type of costs should be used to evaluate the performance of a manager in a responsibility accounting system? Explain.
4. What are allocated expenses? In what type of accounting system should expenses be allocated?
5. When and to what extent is it useful to allocate expenses?
6. What three analytical methods may be used to evaluate a manager's performance in a responsibility accounting system?
7. How many types of responsibility centers are there? Describe them and give an example of each in a hotel.
8. What is the difference between line and staff departments? Give an example of each in a hotel.
9. What are two reasons for creating responsibility centers?
10. How do the departmental account schedules in the USAH help improve a hotel's accounting system from the point of view of responsibility accounting?
11. What function of the chart of accounts is essential in constructing a responsibility accounting system?

EXERCISES

1. Assume a hotel has three restaurants, each of which has the accounts listed below. Prepare a chart of accounts for each restaurant as a separate responsibility center. Use the chart of accounts in the appendix as a guide and modify it as necessary to achieve your objectives.

   (a) Food and beverage sales
   (b) Cost of food and beverages sold
   (c) Salaries and wages
   (d) China, glassware, silver, and linen
   (e) Contract cleaning
   (f) Laundry and dry cleaning
   (g) Music and entertainment
   (h) Operating supplies
   (i) Other operating expenses
   (j) Uniforms

2. Of the following hotel revenue and expense accounts, which ones might be included and which ones would not be included in the rooms department profit center?

   (a) Contract cleaning
   (b) Property insurance
   (c) Operating supplies
   (d) Room revenue

[1]Financial Accounting Standards Board, *Statement of Financial Accounting Standards No. 14*, "Financial Reporting for Segments of a Business Enterprise" (Dec. 1976), Par. 13.

(e) Depreciation
(f) Uniforms
(g) China, glassware, silver, linen
(h) Interest

(i) Salaries and wages
(j) Property insurance
(k) Laundry and dry cle
(l) Commissions

PROBLEMS

1. On the long-form income statement of Miami Hotel identify by type responsibility centers as you can.

MIAMI HOTEL
Long-Form Income Statement

	Net revenue	Cost of sales	Payroll related expenses	Other expenses	Departmental income
Operated departments					
Rooms	$3,430,250		$ 573,500	$259,750	$2,597,000
Food and beverage	1,885,500	$566,750	819,500	214,000	285,250
Store rentals	110,750				110,750
Total operated departments	5,426,500	566,750	1,393,000	473,750	2,993,000
Undistributed operating expenses					
Administrative and general			378,431	102,819	
Marketing			150,237	202,763	
Guest entertainment			36,000	10,750	
Property operation, maintenance, and					
energy costs			384,832	193,168	
Total undistributed operating expenses			949,500	509,500	1,459,000
Income before fixed charges	$5,426,500	$566,750	$2,342,500	$983,250	$1,534,000
Property taxes and insurance				$198,000	
Interest				93,000	
Depreciation and amortization				254,000	545,000
Income before income taxes					989,000
Income taxes					400,545
Net income					$ 588,455

2. Prepare a vertical analysis of the income statement presented in Problem 1. Indicate line and staff positions. Indicate the responsibility centers for which each manager is responsible.

3. Prepare an organizational chart for Miami Hotel based on the income statement presented in Problem 1.

19

Understanding
Financial Statements

Throughout this book we have seen how the primary aim of accounting is to provide information for management and other interested parties, which will serve as a basis to make business decisions and to direct business activities.

As previously noted, financial statement users must be armed with a very good understanding of the nature and limitations of the accounting system in order to use the accounting information effectively to make economic business decisions. Once this knowledge is acquired, management and other users will be in a position of evaluating whether the data shown on the statements indicate good, bad, or indifferent performance as a basis to make sound business decisions.

It is of the utmost importance to recognize that financial statements are of no value unless they are properly understood. The analysis and interpretation of financial statements entails the compilation, comparison, study, and evaluation of financial and operating data. Financial analysis will help determine the overall position of the hospitality firm and establish future trends, thus clarifying and enhancing the usefulness of the financial statements.

Financial statements are read and interpreted in many different ways, depending on who is doing the reading—management, creditors, investors, or employees. All these users might emphasize a specific aspect of the firm's position. For example, a prospective investor will be primarily concerned with the company's earning prospects, whereas a creditor will be mainly interested in the determination of the hospitality firm's debt-paying ability.

Financial statement analysis employs various tools and techniques developed by business analysts as a means to assist financial statement users in the interpretation and understanding of key trends that serve as a guide for evaluating future business success. By using these tools, the users should gain insight into the company's operations and form an opinion about future performance. This is done by subjecting the financial data to scrutiny, looking for trends, and ascertaining strengths and weaknesses.

The purpose of this chapter is to introduce several analytical tools by which financial statements will be better understood, interpreted, and evaluated for decision-making purposes. We describe, to a limited extent, how these techniques are evaluated both by parties outside the hospitality firm and by the firm's own management.

First, current issues related to the major objectives of financial statement presentation for external reporting purposes are reviewed. Four major tools of financial statement analysis are discussed next: trend analysis, common-size analysis, ratio analysis, and funds analysis.

The next section of the chapter examines information contained in annual reports that is in addition to the financial statements. Accordingly, the auditor's opinion letter and the notes to the financial statements (footnotes) are reviewed in depth. These footnotes are dictated by the full disclosure principle of accounting with the basic objective of disclosing all items that might influence the decision-making process. Finally, this chapter discusses the nature and limitations of financial statements, which are to be fully recognized in order to perform an effective analysis and evaluation of financial and operating data.

OBJECTIVES OF FINANCIAL STATEMENT PRESENTATION

As noted in Chapter 2, since 1973 the FASB has taken over the primary responsibility for financial statement reporting requirements and the development of GAAP. Under a conceptual framework project intended to establish a basis for evaluating standards of financial accounting and reporting, the FASB has issued a series of pronouncements known as Statements of Financial Accounting Concepts (FAC).

FAC 1 ("Objectives of Financial Reporting by Business Enterprises"), which was issued in 1978, said that the objectives of financial statement presentation are to provide useful information (1) for credit and investment decisions, (2) in assessing cash flow prospects, and (3) about business economic resources, including claims to those resources and changes in them.

In FAC 2, issued in May 1980, the FASB emphasized the two primary qualities that make accounting information useful for decision-making purposes: relevance, which is the capability of the accounting information to make a difference in user decisions, and reliability, which means that the information must be verifiable and give a clear and accurate picture of a business's condition and performance.

As of this writing, the FASB has a proposal on the final phase of a conceptual framework concerning recognition and measurement concepts. In this proposal the FASB has endorsed, among other things, additional criteria for the recognition of revenues and gains, and a new distinction between earnings and comprehensive income. Earnings would be equivalent to net income as currently reported, except that it would exclude the cumulative effect of accounting changes. Comprehensive income, on the other hand, would include earnings, the cumulative effect of accounting changes, and certain other "nonowner changes in equity" (e.g., decline in market value of marketable securities).

Though no revolutionary changes in recognition and measurement are in sight, based on the aforementioned FASB proposal, the draft does foresee evolutionary changes. Furthermore, while describing the purposes and contents of the basic financial statements (the balance sheet, the income statement, and the statement of changes in financial position), the FASB recommended the presentation of one additional basic financial statement—the cash flow statement.

FINANCIAL ANALYSIS

No matter how relevant and reliable financial statements are, they only tell what happened to the hospitality firm during a particular period of time. Yet most financial statement users are concerned with what will happen to the firm in the future.

The future item that financial statement users are most interested in determining is earnings. Earnings provide a basis for creditors to lend funds to a restaurant or travel agency, and earnings, in most instances, make hotel and restaurant expansion possible. However, the prediction of earnings is rather uncertain, necessitating the use of certain analytical tools and techniques to facilitate the interpretation of key trends. These tools will aid in the evaluation of the financial condition and operating results of the hospitality firm as well as in the determination of earnings prospects.

Although the analysis and interpretation of financial statements is the subject of more specialized and advanced textbooks, it is helpful at this point to give an overview of the principal tools of financial analysis: trend analysis, common-size analysis (vertical and horizontal), ratio analysis, and funds analysis.

TREND ANALYSIS

Trend analysis involves the review of past performance in order to determine the direction in which the business appears to be headed. It is primarily used to predict earnings by forecasting future revenues and expenses. That is, past experience is projected into the future, taking into consideration known or planned changes.

It is important to note that analysis of trend results requires the use of comparative financial and operating data for several years. Looking at results over a period of time is usually far more meaningful than reviewing data for two consecutive periods, particularly if an unusual event distorted the figures for either of the two periods (e.g., an airline strike). Trend analysis will provide the reader with an added perspective in evaluating the firm's progress and in determining signs of future improvement or deterioration. In fact, trend analysis permits corrective action to be made prior to the actual occurrence of forecasted unacceptable operating results, thereby avoiding these anticipated unfavorable conditions.

In evaluating and analyzing trends we must keep in mind, however, that trends do not necessarily continue into the future, and thus other crucial factors are to be considered. For example, future poor economic conditions affecting travel might result in a decrease in room sales growth for a hotel in spite of a positive trend of sales growth denoted by trend analysis.

COMMON-SIZE ANALYSIS

Common-size analysis refers to expressing all financial statement items in percentage terms. These financial statements are often referred to as common-size statements. There are two types of common-size analysis: vertical analysis and horizontal analysis.

Vertical Analysis

Vertical common-size analysis compares all figures on the statement with a base figure selected from the same statement. On the balance sheet, all items (in both the asset and equity sections) are stated as a percentage of total assets. This will show the significant changes that have taken place in the composition of the various asset categories, showing the relative importance of individual assets as compared to total assets.

At the same time, by placing all items on the common-size income statement as a percentage of net sales, it is possible to see the relative significance of the various costs, expenses, and income items. Vertical analysis is also very helpful in bringing to the analyst's attention certain facts that otherwise might go unnoticed, as was explained in Chapter 18. If a restaurant's marketing costs go up by $25,000 over the previous period, for instance, this might appear as a major increase. However, when the common-size income statement of the restaurant is analyzed, it might indicate that marketing costs as a percentage of net sales were no higher than the previous year, evidence that there is no cause for concern.

Vertical analysis is, indeed, a very valuable tool when comparing several companies within the same segment of the hospitality industry. It is also helpful for comparing individual restaurants or hotel properties owned by a large chain, since vertical analysis would place various units of different size and volume on comparable terms.

Vertical common-size analysis is illustrated in Figure 19.1 using the condensed income statements of Regal Restaurant for the years ended December 31, 1987 and 1986.

We can see how the net income as a percentage of sales increased from 8.8% in 1986 to 9.2% in 1987. This was mainly attributable to the decreasing trend in cost of sales as a percentage of sales (from 40.1 to 37.9%), a possible result of improved control procedures, or an increase in menu prices in relation to food costs.

	Year ended Dec. 31		Year ended Dec. 31	
	1987	1986	1987	1986
Net sales	$980,000	$760,000	100.0%	100.0%
Cost of sales	371,000	305,000	37.9	40.1
	609,000	455,000	62.1	59.9
Other expenses	519,000	388,000	52.9	51.1
Net income	$ 90,000	$ 67,000	9.2	8.8

Figure 19.1. Vertical common-size analysis.

Horizontal Analysis

Horizontal common-size analysis compares all figures on one financial statement with the same account selected from a base year. It is useful in detecting trends in revenue, costs, and income items over time.

By showing changes between years in percentages, the evaluation of the relative significance of the changes that have taken place is greatly enhanced. To illustrate, an increase of $1,000,000 in the current year's sales will most likely be considered a reflection of normal growth if the preceding year's sales were $10,000,000 for a typical hotel company (a 10% increase). Conversely, the same $1,000,000 increase in sales would be viewed as extremely significant for the hotel if the previous year's sales were $2,000,000 inasmuch as it would represent a 50% increase.

In short, horizontal common-size analysis should enable financial statement users to gain insight into the trends, deficiencies, and strong points of a business.

RATIO ANALYSIS

Ratio analysis indicates the strengths and weaknesses of a hospitality firm by calculating basic relationships. A ratio is the mathematical expression of the relationship between two financial and/or operating figures. Nonetheless, a single ratio in itself is meaningless since it does not furnish a complete picture. The ratio becomes meaningful when compared with company or industry standards, or both.

Ratio analysis has become an integral part of most computerized financial analysis programs, demonstrating its widespread use. Ratios can serve as a guide for comparisons with historical data or industry performance, and to analyze trends. Management will select for further review any items showing material variance with hospitality industry standards (better known as hospitality industry averages) and/or company standards to determine the reason(s) for each major change. In this manner, problem areas in need of managerial attention are highlighted.

Ratio analysis can measure most aspects of a hospitality company's performance. In discussing ratios we identify four major types of evaluation based on ratio analysis: liquidity, solvency and leverage, profitability, and operating performance.

EVALUATION OF LIQUIDITY

Liquidity ratios measure the hospitality firm's ability to meet its short-term obligations as they become due, normally referred to as the firm's short-term debt-paying ability. In the evaluation of liquidity we assume that current assets are used for meeting payment of current liabilities.

Although the primary parties interested in the evaluation of the firm's current debt-paying ability are the short-term creditors, it is important to recognize that lack of liquidity in its more extreme form could lead to the dissolution of the hospitality company (i.e., bankruptcy) and thus will affect all financial statement users.

Three major measures of liquidity in the hospitality industry are the current ratio, the quick ratio, and the accounts receivable turnover.

Current Ratio

The current ratio is computed by dividing total current assets by total current liabilities. The computation of the current ratio for La Quinta Motor Inns, Inc. (La Quinta) for the years 1983 and 1982 is shown below:

	1983	**1982**
Current assets	$56,109,000	$47,027,000
Current liabilities	23,533,000	23,707,000
Current ratio	2.38 to 1	1.98 to 1

At 1983 La Quinta had approximately $2.38 of current assets for each dollar of current liabilities. As shown on its balance sheet (see Chapter 13), a major portion of La Quinta's current assets are short-term investments intended as a source of cash for the construction of specific properties ($44,182,000 in 1983; $37,210,000 in 1982).

While a low current ratio may spell potential financial trouble by suggesting that a hospitality firm is unable to pay its bills, a high current ratio may point to poor management if it reflects an excessive amount of cash on hand or too large an investment in receivables and inventories. In the latter case, it will suggest an unproductive use of assets.

As a result of the typical large investment in inventories and receivables, the industry average for the current ratio of commercial and industrial companies is normally 2 to 1. In the hospitality industry, on the other hand, due to the relatively small amounts of inventories, the industry average for the current ratio is 1 to 1. That is, an average firm in the hospitality industry would have $1 of current assets for each dollar of current liabilities. Therefore, the current ratios of La Quinta as of May 31, 1983 and 1982 serve as evidence of extremely high liquidity, resulting primarily from the large amounts of short-term investments.

Quick Ratio

The quick ratio (or acid-test ratio) supplements the current ratio by taking into consideration the composition of the current assets in the evaluation of liquidity. It measures the extent to which cash and near cash items (short-term investments and receivables) cover current liabilities, as follows:

$$\text{quick ratio} = \frac{\text{cash + short-term investments + receivables}}{\text{current liabilities}}$$

Thus the quick ratio will serve as a reflection of the hospitality firm's ability to pay its current liabilities by converting its most liquid assets into cash. Inventories and prepaid expenses are excluded from the calculation because they are not readily converted into cash.

In most segments of the hospitality industry, based on the small amounts and fast turnover of inventories (they are sold and converted into accounts receivable very quickly), the industry average has been somewhat less than 1 to 1 for the quick ratio.

Accounts Receivable Turnover

The accounts receivable turnover shows the number of times that accounts receivable is converted into cash during the period. It is obtained by dividing net sales by the average accounts receivable (the sum of the beginning and ending balances divided by 2), as follows:

$$\text{accounts receivable turnover} = \frac{\text{net sales}}{\text{average accounts receivable}}$$

The accounts receivable turnover ratio serves to assess the quality of the current and quick ratios in the evaluation of the hospitality firm's short-term debt-paying ability. This is done by determining the liquidity of receivables, that is, the likelihood of collection of the accounts without incurring a loss, since experience has indicated that the longer receivables remain uncollected, the higher the chances that they will not be collected in full.

In the hospitality industry, an average accounts receivable turnover is between 15 and 30 times. In other words, a typical hospitality firm will collect its average receivables between 15 and 30 times during the year (or between 12 and 24 days).

Other measures of the quality and liquidity of the receivables include average collection period and the accounts receivable percentage.

EVALUATION OF SOLVENCY AND LEVERAGE

A major aspect of financial analysis deals with the determination of the proportion of equity (common stock) and debt financing in a hospitality firm's capital structure, viewed as an indicator of the company's ability to meet its long-term obligations as they mature (both principal and interest).

Financial leverage refers to the use of borrowed funds with the major objective of increasing the owners well-being through increased returns. When leverage works to the advantage of the borrowing firm, it is said to be favorable or positive (when the return to the owners—common shareholders—is higher than the cost of borrowing—interest).

Solvency and leverage ratios measure the contribution of owners used to finance the hospitality firm's assets in relation to the financing provided by creditors. Obviously, if owners provide a small proportion of the firm's financing, the major risk of insolvency of the company will be borne by creditors.

Two principal ratios used to appraise the hospitality firm's long-term debt-paying ability are the debt-to-equity ratio and the interest coverage ratio.

Debt-to-Equity Ratio

The debt-to-equity ratio is an expression of the creditors' financing in relation to the owners' financing:

$$\text{debt to equity} = \frac{\text{total liabilities}}{\text{total equity}}$$

In making credit decisions, creditors prefer moderate debt-to-equity ratios inasmuch as the lower use of leverage would constitute a greater cushion against creditors' losses in the event of liquidation. Conversely, owners may seek high leverage in order to magnify earnings or because of the dilutive effect of raising new equity capital (loss of legal control).

Most businesses have a 1 to 1 debt-to-equity ratio (approximately), showing that 50% of their financing has been provided by creditors and the remaining 50% by owners. Hospitality firms, however, are highly leveraged companies, evidenced by an average debt-to-equity ratio of 2 to 1. That is, an average firm in the hospitality industry has $2 of debt financing for each dollar of equity financing. Some segments of the hospitality industry (e.g., airlines) have had average debt-to-equity ratios even higher than 2 to 1.

Interest Coverage Ratio

The interest coverage ratio measures the ability of the company to meet its annual interest costs. Failure to meet this obligation can bring legal action by creditors, which may lead to the dissolution of the hospitality firm.

The interest coverage ratio is determined by dividing earnings before interest and taxes (since interest was deducted in the computation of income before income taxes, it must be added back) by the annual interest charges, or:

$$\text{interest coverage} = \frac{\text{earnings before interest and taxes}}{\text{interest}}$$

Industry averages for interest coverage for typical hospitality firms have fluctuated between 2 and 5 times. The higher the interest coverage, the better the chances to obtain additional debt financing since it will represent a margin of safety for creditors.

EVALUATION OF PROFITABILITY

The evaluation of profitability centers around the measurement of a hospitality firm's ability to generate earnings from the available resources. This is done by relating earnings to sales, assets, and equity investment. It is based on the fact that both owners and long-term creditors measure the success of the firm by its ability to generate earnings.

Important measures of profitability in the hospitality industry include return on equity, return on assets, profit margin, and operating efficiency ratio. Additionally, the earnings per share, the price-earnings ratio and the dividend yield are very significant profitability measures for publicly owned companies in the hospitality industry.

Return on Equity

The return on equity or ROE is a fundamental measure of profitability from the standpoint of current and prospective investors. From their viewpoint, capital is invested with the primary objective of earning an acceptable return. ROE is calculated by dividing net income by the average shareholders' equity. The calculation of the return on equity for La Quinta for the year 1983 (based on the 1983 financial statements included in Chapter 13) is:

$$\text{return on equity} = \frac{\text{net income}}{\text{average shareholders' equity}} = \frac{\$13,456,000}{\$86,535,000} = 15.5\%$$

where the average shareholders' equity is calculated by

$$(93,746,000 + 79,324,000)/2 = 86,535,000$$

The above return on equity of 15.5% for 1983 would be somewhat lower than the five-year hotel industry average of 18.3%.[1] In fact, it represented a significant decline in ROE for La Quinta during that year, resulting primarily from the major impact of the economic downturn in certain geographical areas where a significant number of La Quinta properties are located. This showing reversed previous years' record-high levels of return on equity that served as evidence of La Quinta's overall success in achieving outstanding returns for its owners.

Return on Assets

Return on assets or ROA has been regarded as a measure of the return obtained on all the company's assets without consideration of the method used to finance them. It is computed as follows:

$$\text{return on assets} = \frac{\text{earnings before interest and taxes}}{\text{average assets}}$$

[1]"36th Annual Report on American Industry." *Forbes* (Jan. 2, 1984), p. 236.

In order to determine the total benefit (if any) of financial leverage, return on assets is compared with the annual interest rate on borrowed funds: If the return on assets is higher, leverage is said to be favorable.

Profit Margin

Profit margin expresses the net income per dollar of sale. It serves as an indication of the magnitude of protection against future losses resulting from decreases in sales revenue or increases in costs. The calculation of profit margin is made as follows:

$$\text{profit margin} = \frac{\text{net income}}{\text{net sales}}$$

Companies that tend to need a substantial investment in assets normally require a higher profit margin to offset the less effective utilization of resources in the generation of sales. For instance, a hotel company will generally require a higher profit margin than a restaurant due to the very significant investment in assets needed by the hotel firm.

The five-year industry average of the profit margin of hotel companies was reported in *Forbes* to be 4.7%,[2] whereas the five-year industry average for fast-food chains was reported as 4.2%,[3] and the average for sit-down restaurants is considerably lower.

Operating Efficiency Ratio

The operating efficiency ratio expresses the ability of a hotel firm to operate profitably by relating income before fixed charges to revenues:

$$\text{operating efficiency ratio} = \frac{\text{income before fixed charges}}{\text{total revenues}}$$

The operating efficiency ratio is, indeed, one of the most important profitability measures from the standpoint of operating management since it serves to appraise overall managerial performance.

For restaurants and other companies within the hospitality industry the operating income margin is regarded as the equivalent measure of operating profitability. This is done by relating operating income to revenues.

Earnings Per Share

Earnings per share (EPS) reflects management's success in achieving earnings for the owners. A rise in earnings per share will normally trigger an increase in market prices for publicly held companies. As a result, earnings per share has become the most widely published financial ratio of interest to all investors, both current and prospective.

The calculation of earnings per share for companies with a simple capital structure is fairly simple.

$$\text{earnings per share} = \frac{\text{net income less preferred dividends}}{\text{weighted average of common shares outstanding}}$$

[2]*Ibid.,* p. 236.
[3]*Ibid.,* p. 231.

However, publicly held companies with a complex capital structure will be required to make a number of adjustments (based on certain assumptions outlined in APB Opinion No. 15) in making the calculation of earnings per share, resulting in a rather difficult computation. A complex capital structure refers to special securities (such as debt or preferred stock that is convertible into common stock) in addition to common stock. As noted in Chapter 12, the complexities of calculating earnings per share for companies with a complex capital structure are not dealt with in this book.

Price-Earnings Ratio

The price-earnings ratio (P/E) serves as a reflection of how much the investing public is willing to pay for the company's prospective earnings. A high price-earnings ratio means that investors are confident in the company's future earnings prospects and are willing to pay a greater price in relation to the firm's current earnings.

The calculation of the price-earnings ratio is made by dividing market price per share by earnings per share. For example, if a hotel firm's common stock is traded at the price of $20 and its earnings per share for the most recent year is $2, the price-earnings ratio is computed as follows:

$$\text{price earnings ratio} = \frac{\text{market price per share}}{\text{EPS}} = \frac{\$20}{\$2} = 10$$

In this case, the investors are willing to pay $10 for each dollar of current earnings. Similarly, prospective investors will determine if the stock is priced too high or reasonably by comparing the price-earnings ratio against industry averages.

Generally, companies with ample opportunities for growth have very high price-earnings ratios. Conversely, companies with limited growth prospects have a low price-earnings ratio.

Dividend Yield

Dividend yield relates the current price of the company's common stock to the annual dividend:

$$\text{dividend yield} = \frac{\text{dividend per share}}{\text{market price per share}}$$

The dividend yield is of specific interest to investors whose primary objective is to receive a current return on their investment (in the form of dividends). Nevertheless, many successful hospitality firms invest their earnings for expansion purposes rather than distributing them as dividends. In those cases, the dividend yield will be relatively low.

Price-earnings ratios and dividend yields of selected companies in the hospitality industry are given in Table 19.1.

EVALUATION OF OPERATING PERFORMANCE

Activity and operating ratios measure the effective utilization of the hospitality firm's assets while relating business success to the company's ability to generate revenues and control expenses. Among the activity and operating

TABLE 19.1. Dividend Yields and Price/Earnings Ratios for Selected Companies in the Hospitality Industry[a]

Company	Dividend yield (%)	Price/earnings ratio
Holiday Inns	1.6	17
Jerrico	0.7	13
Resorts International	0.0	16
Denny's	2.0	13
United Airlines	0.0	44
McDonald's	1.4	13
U.S. Air Group	0.4	12
Wometco Enterprises	1.1	26
Hilton Hotels	3.1	15
Ralston Purina	3.3	10
Delta Air Lines	1.5	Def
MGM Grand Hotels	3.5	23
ARA Services	4.1	11
Ramada Inns	0.0	Def
Walt Disney	2.4	19
Caesars World	0.0	Def

Source: Forbes (Jan. 2, 1984).
[a] Def: deficiency.

measures used by hospitality firms in the evaluation of operating performance are inventory turnovers, cost percentages, annual occupancy percentages, average room rate, and average food check. A brief description of each of these measures is presented below.

Inventory Turnovers

Inventory turnovers show how rapidly goods (e.g., food and beverages) are being sold and replaced during the period. They are computed by relating the cost of sales to the average inventory (to eliminate seasonal fluctuations):

$$\text{inventory turnover} = \frac{\text{cost of sales}}{\text{average inventory}}$$

The main factors that affect the food and beverage inventory turnovers are

- Sales forecasting
- Purchasing policies
- Control procedures
- Property location
- Type of operation
- Perishable nature of food inventory

Whereas a low food inventory turnover can serve as an indication of overbuying, poor sales forecasting, waste, spoilage, or pilferage, or a combination of them, a higher turnover might not be desirable at all times. A high turnover can lead to dissatisfied customers if the firm runs out of inventory items constantly.

In addition to the foregoing, the beverage inventory turnover will depend on the "class" of operation. Luxury hotels and restaurants that carry a large assortment of wines and spirits will turn over their inventory at a very slow pace (possibly only three or four times a year). Conversely, an average commercial hotel or restaurant with a limited selection of wines and spirits will be turning over its inventory seven to nine times a year. (The average beverage inventory turnover reported was 7 times for 1982.[4])

Furthermore, the traditional large discounts taken by the hospitality industry for volume purchases of beverage inventories result in a slower beverage inventory turnover (lower) due to the overinvestment in inventories.

Cost Percentages

Both the food and the beverage percentages measure the relative efficiency of the food and the beverage operations by relating the cost of food or beverages sold to the revenues generated from the sale of food or alcoholic beverages:

$$\text{cost percentage} = \frac{\text{cost of sales}}{\text{sales}}$$

Food and beverage cost percentages are mainly affected by the adjustment of menu prices (or list prices), the product mix, control procedures (particularly in the kitchen and the bar), and purchasing policies.

Continuous review and evaluation of the beverage cost percentage is essential due to the high cost of the alcoholic beverages. In doing so, a major factor to be considered is the class of operation since this will affect the type of beverages sold. For instance, operations selling a high proportion of beer will normally have a higher beverage cost percentage in view of the fact that beer has a lower markup than most other liquors.

Lodging industry averages for food and beverage cost percentages are:

| Food cost percentages | 32–37% |
| Beverage cost percentages | 21–26% |

Annual Occupancy Percentage

The annual occupancy percentage measures the use of facilities through the generation of revenues from the sale of space. This is done by relating the total rooms sold to the rooms available for sale:

$$\text{annual occupancy percentage} = \frac{\text{rooms sold}}{\text{number of available rooms}}$$

Factors affecting occupancy include location, rate structure, management, seasonal nature of the operation, and the general state of the world, national, and local economies. As a result of recessionary economic conditions, for example, the overall occupancy percentage of U.S. lodging firms fell from 70.1% in 1981 to 66.0% in 1982.[5]

The calculation of the double occupancy percentage serves as an added measure of the profitable utilization of resources by the hotel operation. This results from the surcharge for the additional person in the room.

[4]Laventhol and Horwath, U.S. Lodging Industry Study. Exhibit 32 (1983), p. 68.
[5]*Ibid.*, p. 44.

Average Room Rate

The average room rate serves as an indication of the rate structure and/or salesmanship ability. It reflects the receipts per unit sold:

$$\text{average room rate} = \frac{\text{total room sales}}{\text{number of rooms sold}}$$

The rise of 11.3% in the average room rate in 1982 (to \$43.55) was higher than the increase in the consumer price index during that same year.

Average Food Check

The average food check is a widely used statistic in the food service industry. It measures the ability of the food operation to generate revenues by relating the food sales to the number of food covers (customers) served:

$$\text{average food check} = \frac{\text{food sales}}{\text{number of food covers}}$$

In addition to the activity and operating ratios enumerated and briefly discussed above, there are a multitude of operating measures designed to evaluate a hospitality company's operating performance. Some of those ratios include the average daily room rate per guest, food and beverage sales to room sales, payroll and related expenses to total revenue, and food and beverage departmental income to room sales.

FUNDS ANALYSIS

As stated in Chapter 13, the statement of changes in financial position reflects the sources and uses of funds (working capital) during an accounting period. Such a statement shows specifically where the resources of the hospitality firm have been obtained and how they have been used by management.

The statement of changes in financial position adds significantly to the understanding of what happened to the business during the year, providing insights into its financial and investing activities. In examining the details of the statement of changes in financial position, owners, creditors, and others can obtain data concerning changes in working capital, the dividend payment policies of the company, its investment in property and equipment, and the firm's financing policies.

The statement of changes in financial position provides clues to important future concerns such as future dividend policies, ability to meet future debt requirements, and sources of financing.

In general, the statement of changes in financial position serves as a summary of the overall investment and financing aspects of the hospitality firm, providing more reliable and credible evidence of the company's actions and intentions than any statements or speeches by its management.

Fund analysis encompasses a review of the major sources and uses of working capital appearing on the statement of changes in financial position. The sources of working capital can be divided into two main groups: internal—operations, and external—common stock, preferred stock, long-term debt, sales of property and equipment, or long-term investments. Funds generated by operations are, by far, the most significant since they reflect the firm's ability to finance expansion (additions to property and equipment) and meet future debt requirements internally.

Working capital is used for many different purposes: additions to property and equipment, dividends, repayment of long-term debt, purchase of long-term investments, etc.

It is evident that hospitality firms undergoing rapid growth (opening new areas, new hotels, or new restaurants) will show an extremely large proportion of working capital used for additions to property and equipment. It becomes very important to evaluate how the company's expansion is being financed, that is, through operations, long-term debt or common equity financing. In reviewing La Quinta's statement of changes in financial position included in Chapter 13 we determined, for instance, that La Quinta was expanding very rapidly, using most of its funds for additions to property and equipment and motor inns under development. This aggressive expansion had been primarily financed by long-term borrowings and by working capital provided by operations.

EXAMINATION OF SUPPLEMENTAL INFORMATION

As a means to acquire an adequate understanding of a hospitality firm's financial and operational data, it becomes important to examine certain supplemental information to the financial statements. The two main sources of supplemental information are the auditor's opinion and the notes to the financial statements (footnotes).

AUDITOR'S OPINION

Publicly owned corporations, companies whose securities are usually traded on a stock exchange (e.g., New York Stock Exchange) or over the counter, are required by federal securities laws to have their annual report audited by an independent CPA firm. Furthermore, there may be a legal need for an independent audit when raising new debt or equity capital or when borrowing money from a bank.

Indeed, the review of the CPA's report is a most essential step to be followed in understanding financial statements since it places the statements in proper perspective by providing the readers with crucial information concerning the "fairness" of the financial statement presentation.

The main purpose of the CPA audit is to provide external parties with a reasonable degree of assurance as to the validity of the information contained in the financial statements. CPAs examine sufficient evidential matter as a basis to express their professional opinion regarding the fairness of the financial statements. The audit steps entail the inspection and observation of invoices, bank statements, and other internal evidence, as well as external inquiries.

Again, it is important to recognize that the responsibility for financial statements (including footnotes) rests with management. Yet, the auditor's opinion adds credibility to the financial statements, serving as an indication of whether the financial statements have been prepared in accordance with GAAP and are fairly and consistently presented. Any departures are properly noted in order to enable readers better to interpret the statements.

The CPA's opinion letter includes a scope paragraph and an opinion para-

Auditors' Report

The Board of Directors
La Quinta Motor Inns, Inc.:

We have examined the combined balance sheets of La Quinta Motor Inns, Inc. as of May 31, 1983 and 1982, and the related combined statements of earnings, shareholders' equity and changes in financial position for each of the years in the three-year period ended May 31, 1983. Our examinations were made in accordance with generally accepted auditing standards and, accordingly, included such tests of the accounting records and such other auditing procedures as we considered necessary in the circumstances.

In our opinion, the aforementioned combined financial statements present fairly the financial position of La Quinta Motor Inns, Inc. at May 31, 1983 and 1982 and the results of its operations and the changes in its financial position for each of the years in the three-year period ended May 31, 1983, in conformity with generally accepted accounting principles applied on a consistant basis.

Peat, Marwick, Mitchell + Co.

San Antonio, Texas
July 20, 1983

Figure 19.2. Auditors' opinion.

graph. If, upon completion of the audit, the CPA is satisfied that the financial statements are fairly presented in accordance with GAAP, an unqualified (clean) opinion is issued. Figure 19.2 gives an example of an unqualified opinion covering the financial statements of La Quinta Motor Inns, Inc. for the years 1983 and 1982 (issued by Peat Marwick, Mitchell & Co., CPAs).

As can be seen in Figure 19.2, Peat Marwick, Mitchell & Co. attested that La Quinta's financial statements have been prepared in accordance with GAAP, presenting "fairly" the financial position, the results of operations and changes in financial position of La Quinta for the years 1983 and 1982.

If the opinion is other than unqualified (e.g., qualified, disclaimer of opinion, or adverse opinion) the financial statement users should proceed with caution. Readers should fully understand the reason(s) given by the auditors for their reluctance to issue a clean opinion on the fairness of the financial statement presentation.

NOTES TO THE FINANCIAL STATEMENTS

Notes to the financial statements (often referred to as footnotes) are considered an integral part of the statements. They are governed by the accounting principle requiring the full disclosure of all facts needed by statement users to reach informed conclusions, and thus make the financial statements not misleading.

These footnotes amplify and clarify the information contained in the three basic financial statements. As a result, it becomes evident that a review of the notes to the financial statements is essential for a complete and accurate interpretation of the hospitality firm's financial and operating data.

We shall examine some of the more significant footnotes, referring to the notes to the 1983 financial statements of La Quinta in Figure 19.3.

La Quinta Motor Inns, Inc.
Notes to Combined Financial Statements

(1) *SUMMARY OF SIGNIFICANT ACCOUNTING POLICIES*

Business and Basis of Presentation

The Company develops, owns and operates motor inns. The combined financial statements include the accounts of subsidiaries (all wholly owned) and unincorporated ventures in which the Company has an ownership interest and exercises legal, financial and operational control. All significant intercompany accounts and transactions have been eliminated in combination. Certain reclassifications of prior period amounts have been made to conform with the current year presentation.

Property and Equipment

Depreciation and amortization of property and equipment are computed using the straight-line method over the following estimated useful lives:

Buildings	30 years
Furniture, fixtures and equipment	4-10 years
Leasehold and land improvements	10-20 years

Maintenance and repairs are charged to operations as incurred. Expenditures for improvements are capitalized.

Deferred Charges

Deferred charges consist primarily of issuance costs related to industrial development revenue bonds, loan fees and motor inn preopening costs. Issuance costs are amortized over the life of the bonds using the interest method. The straight-line method is used to amortize preopening costs over five years and loan fees over the respective terms of the loans.

Income Taxes

Deferred income taxes arise principally from timing differences between financial reporting and income tax reporting of depreciation, preopening costs, construction loan interest, loan fees and gains realized on the sale of motor inns.

Investment tax credits are recorded as a reduction of the provision for income taxes in the year realized.

Earnings Per Share

Earnings per share are computed on the basis of the weighted average number of common and common equivalent (dilutive stock options) shares outstanding in each year after giving retroactive effect to the stock splits discussed in note 5. Weighted average shares used in the computation of earnings per share were 14,545,000 in 1983, 13,724,000 in 1982 and 12,540,000 in 1981. Primary and fully diluted earnings per share are not significantly different.

(2) *LONG-TERM DEBT AND CAPITAL LEASES*

Long-term debt, which is secured by substantially all property, equipment and motor inns under development, consisted of the following at May 31, 1983 and 1982:

	1983	1982
Mortgage loans maturing to year 2005 (10.3% weighted average)	$137,008,000	139,966,000
Construction line of credit (11.25%)	8,203,000	—
Industrial development revenue bonds, maturing 1984-2012 (11.5% weighted average)	71,276,000	46,653,000
Convertible subordinated debentures maturing in 2002 (10%)	25,000,000	—
Bank line of credit (10.5% at May 31, 1983)	1,344,000	4,323,000
Construction payables, including retainages	2,975,000	—
Capitalized leases maturing to year 1990 (12.1% weighted average)	3,564,000	4,608,000
Total	249,370,000	195,550,000
Less current installments	5,919,000	5,833,000
Net long-term debt	$243,451,000	189,717,000

Annual maturities for the four years subsequent to May 31, 1984 are as follows:

1985	$6,046,000
1986	8,180,000
1987	8,717,000
1988	8,975,000

Figure 19.3 (pp. 406–411).   Notes to combined financial statements, La Quinta Motor Inns, Inc.

The construction line of credit and certain construction payables are classified as long-term liabilities because they will ultimately be paid from the proceeds of long-term debt or from equity contributions by the Company's venture partners. The corresponding current installments and annual principal payments are based on the maturities of permanent financing commitments.

Borrowings under the bank line of credit are included in the above payments assuming such amounts are converted to a five-year term note to the extent allowable under the agreement and the balance into a one-year term note.

The agreements associated with the industrial development revenue bonds (IRB's) restrict the use of proceeds to specific qualified land or depreciable property as defined by the Internal Revenue Code and have certain other requirements so interest on the bonds will not be included in the taxable income of the holders thereof.

In June 1982 the Company sold $25,000,000 of 10% convertible subordinated debentures due 2002. The debentures are convertible into common stock at a conversion price of $20.94 per share and are redeemable by the Company beginning June 15, 1984 initially at 108% and thereafter at prices declining annually to 100% on and after June 15, 1992. The debentures are subordinated in right of payment to all existing and future senior indebtedness of the Company.

The Company has two long-term lines of credit aggregating $64,000,000. The construction line of credit, established for La Quinta Financial Corporation, a wholly owned subsidiary of the Company, may only be utilized to fund certain eligible construction costs. This agreement permits borrowings of up to $50,000,000 at ¾% above the current prime lending rate until October 31, 1983, at which date the Company may extend the maturity date to April 30, 1985 at 1¼% above the prime rate.

The bank line permits borrowings of up to $14,000,000 at the current prime lending rate until October 31, 1983, at which date the Company may (i) request an extension of the agreement subject to approval of the banks, (ii) convert the outstanding balance not to exceed $3,500,000 into a five-year term note payable in quarterly installments, and any additional outstanding balance into a one-year term note due October 31, 1984.

The lines of credit agreements require the maintenance of effective tangible net worth (shareholders' equity plus partners' capital) and subordinated

indebtedness, as defined, aggregating at least $90,000,000 plus an amount ($10,092,000 at May 31, 1983) equal to 75% of net earnings subsequent to May 31, 1982.

Both credit lines and agreements associated with IRB's contain certain covenants, the most restrictive of which preclude the following: payments of cash dividends, mergers, sales of substantial assets, incurrence of significant lease obligations or any material change in character of its business. The agreements require the maintenance of certain financial ratios in addition to those restrictions discussed above.

There are no formal requirements for compensating balances under the agreements; however, the Company attempts to maintain cash compensating balances, as desired by the banks, for the $14,000,000 line of credit aggregating 7% of the outstanding balance plus a fee of ½ of 1% of the unused portion. Such compensating balances aggregated $157,000 at May 31, 1983.

Property and equipment at May 31, 1983 and 1982 includes capitalized telephone, television and other capital leases aggregating $6,765,000 and $7,529,000, respectively, less accumulated amortization of $2,946,000 and $2,764,000, respectively. Future minimum obligations under these leases aggregate $4,419,000 and $6,076,000 at May 31, 1983 and 1982, respectively.

(3) UNINCORPORATED VENTURES

Summary financial information with respect to unincorporated ventures included in the combined financial statements follows:

	May 31	
	1983	1982
Current assets	$ 15,169,000	15,976,000
Current liabilities	12,567,000	10,994,000
Working capital	2,602,000	4,982,000
Net property, equipment and motor inns under development	148,405,000	126,738,000
Long-term debt	(107,143,000)	(99,500,000)
Other assets, net	3,145,000	4,104,000
Net assets	$ 47,009,000	36,324,000
Equity in net assets:		
Company	20,661,000	16,294,000
Partners	26,348,000	20,030,000
	$ 47,009,000	36,324,000

Figure 19.3 (*Continued.*)

	Years ended May 31		
	1983	1982	1981
Revenues	$62,667,000	58,418,000	44,385,000
Costs and expenses	49,355,000	45,388,000	34,962,000
Pretax earnings	$13,312,000	13,030,000	9,423,000
Equity in pretax earnings and losses:			
Company	7,088,000	6,913,000	5,094,000
Partners	6,224,000	6,117,000	4,329,000
	$13,312,000	13,030,000	9,423,000

(4) *INCOME TAXES*

The provision for income taxes consists of the following:

	Years ended May 31		
	1983	1982	1981
Current:			
Federal	$3,147,000	6,291,000	3,913,000
State	220,000	200,000	105,000
Deferred, resulting from:			
Accelerated depreciation	2,529,000	1,293,000	561,000
Construction loan interest	1,839,000	1,149,000	880,000
Installment sales	599,000	231,000	149,000
Other, net	637,000	109,000	132,000
Provision for income taxes	$8,971,000	9,273,000	5,740,000

The effective tax rate is lower than the statutory rate for the following reasons:

	Years ended May 31		
	1983	1982	1981
Tax expense at statutory rate	$10,316,000	9,919,000	6,602,000
Investment tax credit	(964,000)	(591,000)	(657,000)
Capital gains	(529,000)	(203,000)	(168,000)
Other, net	148,000	148,000	(37,000)
Provision for income taxes	$ 8,971,000	9,273,000	5,740,000

(5) *SHAREHOLDERS' EQUITY*

The Company authorized a four-for-three stock split in January 1982 and a five-for-four stock split in March 1981. Earnings per share, the weighted aver-

Figure 19.3 (*Continued.*)

age number of shares outstanding and the following information has been adjusted to give effect to each of these distributions.

The Company has stock option plans which provide for the granting of options to purchase an aggregate of 1,785,960 common shares. Options under the plans are issuable to certain officers and key employees at prices not less than fair market value at date of grant. Options are exercisable in four equal installments on successive anniversary dates of the date of grant and are exercisable thereafter in whole or in part. Options not exercised expire five to six years from the date of grant. Activity in the plans during the three years ended May 31, 1983 is summarized as follows:

	Number of shares	Option price ranges per share	Total option price
Outstanding May 31, 1980	693,945	$ .38- 6.75	3,063,000
Granted	352,167	6.65-11.40	3,476,000
Cancelled or expired	(75,368)	1.21-10.65	(418,000)
Exercised	(212,571)	.38- 6.68	(432,000)
Outstanding May 31, 1981	758,173	.79-11.40	5,689,000
Granted	140,067	11.82-19.00	2,148,000
Cancelled or expired	(53,519)	3.50-15.80	(539,000)
Exercised	(59,862)	.79-10.65	(320,000)
Outstanding May 31, 1982	784,859	1.43-19.00	6,978,000
Granted	81,455	15.63-20.69	1,468,000
Cancelled or expired	(21,140)	5.05-17.88	(261,000)
Exercised	(121,425)	1.43-15.84	(851,000)
Outstanding May 31, 1983	723,749	$3.87-20.69	7,334,000
Exercisable at May 31:			
1982	285,826	$1.43-11.18	1,916,000
1983	373,032	$3.87-19.00	2,872,000
Available for future grants at May 31:			
1982	182,850		
1983	122,535		

No charges have been made to earnings for these options. Upon exercise, the excess of the option price received over the par value of the shares issued, net of expenses and including the related income tax benefits, is credited to additional paid-in capital.

(6) PENSION PLAN

The Company has a pension plan covering substantially all employees. The Company makes annual contributions to the plan at least equal to the minimum deposit required under ERISA regulations. Effective January 1, 1983, pension costs were determined using an investment return assumption of 7.5% and a salary increase assumption of 6.5%. Prior to 1983, pension costs were determined using an investment return assumption of 6.5% and a salary increase assumption of 5%. These changes in assumptions did not have a significant effect on pension costs in 1983.

Total pension expense was $644,000 in 1983, $582,000 in 1982 and $449,000 in 1981, including amortization of past service cost over 40 years. A comparison of the accumulated benefits and net assets for the Company's plan is presented below as of the date of the latest actuarial valuation:

	January 1	
	1983	1982
Actuarial present value of accumulated benefits:		
Vested	$ 696,000	620,000
Nonvested	534,000	511,000
	$1,230,000	1,131,000
Net assets available for benefits	$3,532,000	2,236,000

The investment return assumption used in determining the actuarial present value of accumulated plan benefits was 8.5% in 1983 and 6.5% in 1982.

(7) OPERATING LEASES

A portion of the real estate and equipment utilized in operations is leased. Certain ground lease arrangements contain contingent rental provisions based upon revenues and renewal options at fair market values at the conclusion of the initial lease terms. The Company is a joint venture partner with a developer in an office building in which the Company has leased space. The Company's interest in the joint venture is accounted for by the equity method and is included in investments in the financial statements.

Future minimum rental payments, by year, required under operating leases that have initial or remaining noncancellable lease terms in excess of one year at May 31, 1983 follow:

1984	$ 1,516,000
1985	1,378,000
1986	1,245,000
1987	1,212,000
1988	753,000
Later years	4,723,000
Total minimum payments required	$10,827,000

Total rental expense for operating leases was $1,458,000 in 1983, $1,213,000 in 1982 and $1,028,000 in 1981.

(8) CONSTRUCTION COMMITMENTS

At May 31, 1983 the estimated additional cost to complete the construction of motor inns for which construction commitments have been made is $70,661,000. Funds in hand or committed are sufficient to complete these projects.

Motor inns under development at May 31, 1983 includes $17,772,000 representing the proceeds of industrial development revenue bonds. The use of such funds and $12,115,000 of current short-term cash investments is restricted to the costs of specific properties.

(9) CONTINGENCIES

The Company is a party to various lawsuits and claims generally incidental to its business. The ultimate disposition of these matters is not expected to have a significant adverse effect on the Company's financial position or results of operations.

Figure 19.3 (Continued.)

(10) *QUARTERLY FINANCIAL DATA (UNAUDITED)*

The unaudited combined results of operations by quarter are summarized below:

	First quarter	Second quarter	Third quarter	Fourth quarter
(Thousands of dollars, except per share data)				
Year ended				
May 31, 1983:				
Revenues	$30,985	27,347	24,507	30,539
Operating income	10,907	8,387	6,707	10,589
Net earnings	5,002	3,279	1,675	3,500
Earnings per share	.34	.23	.12	.24
Year ended				
May 31, 1982:				
Revenues	$26,556	24,985	23,260	27,855
Operating income	9,463	7,871	6,846	10,466
Net earnings	3,599	2,591	2,281	3,820
Earnings per share	.27	.20	.16	.27
Year ended				
May 31, 1981:				
Revenues	$20,356	19,488	19,096	23,825
Operating income	7,076	6,256	5,380	8,786
Net earnings	2,543	1,705	1,462	2,901
Earnings per share	.21	.14	.11	.23

Per share amounts have been adjusted for stock splits.

(11) *SUPPLEMENTARY INFORMATION TO DISCLOSE THE EFFECTS OF CHANGING PRICES (UNAUDITED)*

The following information is presented in accordance with the Statement of Financial Accounting Standards No. 33 (SFAS 33) FINANCIAL REPORTING AND CHANGING PRICES. SFAS 33 requires the use of two methods for estimating the effects of inflation on operations: "constant dollar" and "current cost". The constant dollar method uses the Consumer Price Index for All Urban Consumers to adjust the primary statements for the effects of general inflation. The current cost method measures the primary statements for effects of changes in the specific prices by applying internal estimates to the value of land and external indices to the cost of buildings and equipment. Both of these methods inherently involve the use of assumptions and estimates. Although these assumptions and estimates are believed to be reasonable, they are subjective judgements of management and should be viewed in that context and not as precise indicators of the effects of inflation.

Combined Statement of Earnings Adjusted for Changing Prices (Unaudited)
(Thousands of dollars)

	Year ended May 31, 1983		
	Primary Statements	Constant Dollar	Current Cost
Total revenues	$113,378	113,378	113,378
Cost and expenses:			
Depreciation and amortization	13,544	17,434	17,106
Partners' equity in earnings and losses	6,224	5,251	5,333
Provision for income taxes	8,971	8,971	8,971
Other expenses	71,183	71,183	71,183
	99,922	102,839	102,593
Net earnings	$ 13,456	10,539	10,785

Figure 19.3   *(Continued.)*

Five Year Comparison of Selected Supplementary Financial Data
Adjusted for Effects of Changing Prices (Unaudited)
(Thousands of dollars, except per share data)

	Years ended May 31				
	1983	1982	1981	1980	1979
Total revenues (historical)	$113,378	102,656	82,765	61,825	48,224
Constant dollar information:					
Total revenues	113,378	107,454	94,304	78,902	69,528
Net earnings	10,539	10,122	7,962	6,516	
Net earnings per share	.72	.73	.63	.55	
Net assets at year end	177,070	163,073	126,259	95,644	
Current cost information:					
Net earnings	10,785	10,647	8,548	7,338	
Net earnings per share	.74	.77	.68	.62	
Net assets at year end	216,962	180,458	136,672	93,589	
Net property and equipment, in average 1983 dollars	397,423				
Other Information:					
Purchasing power gain on net monetary items	6,389	10,267	13,807	17,690	
Excess (deficiency) of increases in specific prices over					
increases in the general price level	17,451	4,833	9,831	(4,326)	
Market price per common share at year end	24.88	19.00	15.94	6.15	4.84
Market price per common share at year end, expressed					
in constant dollars	$24.57	19.42	17.38	7.37	6.63
Average consumer price index	293.4	280.3	257.5	230.0	203.5

Figure 19.3 *(Continued.)*

Summary of Significant Accounting Policies

A particularly important footnote is the summary of the hospitality firm's accounting policies, usually the first note to the financial statements. According to APB Opinion No. 22, issued in 1972, "the information about the accounting policies adopted by a reporting entity is essential for financial statement users."[6]

Thus, the information in the statement of accounting policies is fundamental for understanding and evaluating the data contained in the statements. Further, it will be helpful in assessing the credibility and quality of earnings, and in comparative analysis.

The following are some of the most frequent disclosures found in the summary of significant accounting policies:

• Basis of preparing consolidated financial statements.
• Method of determining inventory cost and basis of stating inventories.
• A general description of the method(s) used in the computation of depreciation with respect to major classes of depreciable assets.
• Basis for accounting for revenue recognition and related costs (e.g., franchise fee revenue).

[6]American Institute of Certified Public Accountants, *Accounting Principles Board Opinion No. 22,* "Disclosure of Accounting Policies" (April 1972), Par. 8.

- Accounting methods and principles peculiar to the industry in which the reporting entity operates.
- Basis of presentation of earnings per share.
- Basis of allocating asset costs to current and future periods (e.g., deferred charges, goodwill).

(Note 1 to La Quinta's 1983 financial statements illustrates significant accounting policies, thereby providing a more detailed understanding of the preceding discussion.)

Commitments and Contingencies

An examination of commitments and contingencies is vital in assessing earnings prospects and probable future success of a hospitality firm. Contingencies refer to existing conditions whose ultimate effect is uncertain, and their resolution depends on specific future events. They include the cosigning of a note by another party, pending lawsuits, and tax assessments. Disclosures normally include the nature of the contingency and give an estimate of the possible loss (if any) or states that a reasonable estimate cannot be made.

The major commitments disclosed by a hospitality firm are construction, leasing, and restrictions pursuant to the terms of long-term debt agreements.

Disclosures of leasing commitments contain the general description of the leasing arrangement(s), including restrictions imposed by the lease agreement. For capital leases[7] (as defined by FASB Statement No. 13), the future minimum lease payments and the imputed interest rate are also disclosed.

(Notes 7, 8, and 9 to La Quinta's 1983 financial statements illustrate treatment of commitments and contingencies.)

Segment Reporting

The operations and assets of publicly held companies in the hospitality industry are to be apportioned into "reportable business segments" (if applicable), based upon FASB Statement No. 14 (Financial Reporting for Segments of a Business Enterprise), issued in December 1976 and discussed in Chapter 18. Disclosure includes revenue, operating earnings or losses, identifiable assets, depreciation expense, and capital asset expenditures relating to each segment or industry in which the company operates.

Pension Plans

When applicable, disclosure of the nature of the hospitality company's pension plan, describing the employee groups covered, funding policies, and provision for the current period pension cost, is needed. Other disclosure requirements for pension plans are governed by APB Opinion No. 8 and FASB Statement No. 36. (Note 6 to La Quinta's 1983 financial statements gives illustrative disclosures.)

Long-Term Debt Obligations

Important features and provisions of long-term obligations for each major type of debt are the general character of each issue, interest rates, assets

---

[7]Those leases transferring to the lessee the risks and benefits incident to ownership.

mortgaged, maturity dates and amounts; and restrictive debt agreements relating to working capital, dividends, or other restrictions.

(Note 2 to La Quinta's 1983 financial statements serves as an illustration of the type of disclosures pertaining to long-term debt.)

Subsequent Events

Disclosures of events that have occurred subsequent to the balance sheet date are required by GAAP to prevent the financial statements from being misleading. Examples of subsequent events are the purchase of new companies, mergers or business combinations, losses resulting from fire or other casualties, settlement of litigations, and the sale of bonds or capital stock.

Other Disclosures

Additional disclosures often found in notes to the financial statements of hospitality firms are as follows:

1. *Accounting changes.* This includes a clear explanation of the nature of and justification for changes in accounting principles, and their effect on earnings and on the related earnings per share amounts.
2. *Marketable securities.* Disclosure of the aggregate cost and aggregate market value with an indication as to which is the carrying amount.
3. *Stock options.* Disclosure of the status of the plan at the balance sheet date, including the number of shares under option, option price, and how many shares are exercisable is required. (See note 5 to La Quinta's 1983 financial statements.)
4. *Income taxes.* Disclosure of significant amounts of unused credits, the nature of significant differences between pretax accounting income (income before income taxes) and taxable income, and tax effects of timing differences.
5. *Supplementary information disclosing the effects of inflation on operational and financial data.* These supplementary data are required by large publicly owned companies having more than one billion dollars in assets or $125 million of investments in inventories and/or property and equipment. (See note 11 to La Quinta's 1983 financial statements.)

LIMITATIONS OF FINANCIAL STATEMENTS

As demonstrated, financial statements provide useful information for making rational decisions concerning the hospitality enterprise. However, financial statements have a number of shortcomings and weaknesses that all financial statement users must recognize during their evaluation and appraisal of the hospitality firm's financial and operating data. Some of these are enumerated and discussed below.

1. Conventional financial statements are prepared under a constant dollar assumption, which is, in fact, not valid since declines in purchasing power resulting from the changing value of the dollar (or inflation) are not taken into account.
2. Facts and conditions not specifically reflected on the financial state-

ments could have a major impact on the future of a hospitality firm. Some examples are changes in consumer tastes, seasonal nature of operations, management changes, and economic conditions. To illustrate, a change in an upper management position might serve as a basis for favorable earning projections, in spite of poor performance denoted by the historical financial statements.

3. Judgmental factors pertaining to diverse accounting treatments of inventory, depreciation, capitalizing vs. expensing expenditures, and the like make meaningful comparisons of hospitality firms doubtful.

4. Only those facts that can be expressed in monetary terms ($ U.S.) are included in the financial statements. As a result, a number of very significant items might not appear on the statements. For instance, the ability and expertise of hospitality firms' personnel, a prime hotel location, and the impact of political or economic factors are not included in the financial statements due to the nonmonetary nature of these data. Nonetheless, this information needs to be considered for a complete understanding of the hospitality firm.

QUESTIONS

1. What is the primary objective of financial statements? How do financial statement users accomplish this objective?
2. What is meant by financial analysis? Cite four major analytical tools.
3. What is the primary purpose of comparative analysis?
4. What is trend analysis?
5. What is common-size analysis? What are the two forms of common-size analysis?
6. What is ratio analysis? What are the most common evaluations done using ratio analysis?
7. In which ways is the liquidity of a hospitality company measured?
8. Is a high debt-to-equity ratio a sign of financial trouble for a hotel? Explain.
9. What are the most common measures of profitability and how do they differ?
10. Describe three common measures of operating performance in the hospitality industry.
11. What is funds analysis? What are the major sources and uses of working capital?
12. What is meant by an auditor's clean opinion? In which manner can a financial statement user evaluate the auditor's opinion letter concerning the fairness of the financial statements?
13. What is meant by full disclosure? How does full disclosure relate to the information contained in the notes to the financial statements?
14. What type of information is normally included in the "summary of significant accounting policies" footnote? List four examples.
15. What are commitments and contingencies? List two examples of each.
16. Describe three typical notes to hospitality firms' financial statements.
17. What are some limitations of financial statements? What are some of the influences that are not specifically reflected in the financial statements?
18. What is meant by the great diversity of accounting alternatives?

EXERCISES

1. What ratios or other analytical tools will assist in answering the following questions? Discuss each answer.
    (a) Is there adequate protection for short-term creditors?

(b) How liquid are the accounts receivable?
(c) Is there an overinvestment in inventories?
(d) Is the level of earnings adequate?
(e) How are the company's assets being financed?
(f) Are the shareholders receiving an adequate return on the money invested in the business?
(g) What is the overall efficiency of the food operation?

2. Go to your school library and locate the most recent annual report of a publicly held restaurant chain and a publicly owned hotel chain. Answer each of the following questions by using the information included in the annual reports:
(a) What was the net income earned per dollar of sale?
(b) Are foreign operations significant for the company?
(c) Who are the independent auditors of the company?
(d) Does the company use leverage to finance expansion?
(e) How does the company account for inventories?
(f) What is the firm's return on equity at the beginning and end of the year?
(g) What depreciation method(s) are used for property and equipment?
(h) Examine the company's commitments and contingencies.
(i) What is the significance of the company's commitments on lease obligations?

3. Z Company owns two restaurants, AZ and BZ, in the same city. Operating results for the current year for each restaurant follow:

	Restaurant AZ		Restaurant BZ	
Sales		$300,000		$400,000
Cost of sales	$110,000		$170,000	
Salaries and wages	120,000		155,000	
Other expenses	40,000	270,000	50,000	375,000
Net income		$ 30,000		$ 25,000
Customers served		110,000		120,000

The owners of the company are concerned that Restaurant BZ has higher sales and lower earnings than Restaurant AZ. Use common-size analysis to analyze both operations and comment about the results.

4. Consider the data for TRX Inn and answer the following questions:

	1987	1986	Industry average
Current ratio	2.9 to 1	1.9 to 1	1 to 1
Quick ratio	2.5 to 1	1.7 to 1	Somewhat less than 1 to 1
Accounts receivable turnover	5 times	5 times	15–30 times
Debt-to-equity ratio	3.12 to 1	3.59 to 1	2 to 1
Return on equity	9.6%	10.1%	15%
Number of times interest earned	2 times	3 times	5 times
Sales	$100,000	$80,000	Not applicable
Operating efficiency ratio	20%	21%	26%
Price/earnings ratio	11	9	10 times
Earnings per share	0.10	0.12	Not applicable

(a) Is it becoming easier for the company to pay its bills as they become due? Discuss.
(b) Is the total amount of accounts receivable increasing?
(c) Is the company employing leverage to the advantage of the common shareholders? Discuss.
(d) Are the investors confident about the future of the company? Discuss.
(e) Evaluate managerial performance. Speculate on the reasons accounting for improvements (or deterioration) in specific ratios.

PROBLEMS

1. The condensed balance sheet and income statements of Simple Restaurant are presented below:

SIMPLE RESTAURANT
Balance Sheet
December 31, 1987

Assets		Liabilities & shareholders' equity	
Current assets	$ 80,000	Current liabilities	$ 75,000
Investments	10,000	Long-term debt	270,000
Property and equipment	300,000	Common stock	50,000
Intangible assets	18,000	Retained earnings	13,000
Total	$408,000		$408,000

SIMPLE RESTAURANT
Income Statement
For the Year Ended December 31, 1987

Sales		$500,000
Cost of sales		150,000
Gross margin		350,000
Other operating expenses	$250,000	
Depreciation	30,000	
Interest	35,000	315,000
Income before income taxes		35,000
Income taxes		16,000
Net income		$ 19,000

Using ratio analysis, complete the following:
- (a) Evaluate the short-term debt-paying ability of Simple Restaurant.
- (b) Calculate the (1) debt-to-equity ratio and (2) interest coverage as a basis to evaluate Simple Restaurant's use of leverage.
- (c) Evaluate the ability of the company to generate earnings.
- (d) Discuss the firm's operating performance assuming that food is the only revenue-producing department and 100,000 customers were served in 1987.

2. Using the financial statements and auditors' report of Restaurant Associates Industries, Inc. (RA) (pp. 418–426), answer the following questions:
- (a) Did the amount of working capital increase or decrease from 1980 to 1981? By how much?
- (b) What was the largest source of resources in 1981 and 1980? Is this trend favorable?
- (c) Did the company's independent auditor think that the financial statements presented fairly the financial status of RA for the pertinent periods.
- (d) Did the current ratio improve from 1980 to 1981? Is this an indication of the firm's better debt-paying ability? Explain.
- (e) Discuss RA dividend policies.
- (f) Was RA undergoing material expansion during 1980 and 1981? How was expansion financed during this period?
- (g) Is the company employing leverage to the advantage of the owners of RA? Explain.
- (h) Did the capital structure of RA change from 1980 to 1981? Explain.
- (i) Is the earnings trend favorable? Explain.

3. Using the summary data taken from the financial statements of Glorious Inn for the past three years that appears next, do the following:

Current assets	$ 150,000	$140,000	$130,000
Total assets	1,000,000	800,000	700,000
Current liabilities	145,000	150,000	135,000
Long-term debt	800,000	500,000	450,000
Shareholders' equity	155,000	150,000	115,000
Sales	500,000	450,000	430,000
Net income	30,000	25,000	22,000
Interest expense	8,000	7,000	6,500

Required:

(a) Using the common measures to evaluate liquidity, determine the firm's short-term debt-paying ability.

(b) Is the company in a good position to borrow additional funds? (Assume an income tax rate of 50%).

(c) What is the ability of the company to generate earnings from the available resources?

(d) Using common-size analysis (vertical and horizontal analysis), comment on the significant trends indicated by the financial and operating data of Glorious Inn.

4. Using RA's financial statements presented in Problem 2, complete the following:

(a) An in-depth analysis of the major accounting policies of RA. Relate your discussion to the quality of earnings of RA.

(b) A review of other significant information revealed by the footnotes, indicating their possible impact on prospective earnings and financial position.

RESTAURANT ASSOCIATES INDUSTRIES, INC. AND SUBSIDIARIES

CONSOLIDATED BALANCE SHEET

ASSETS

	IN THOUSANDS	
	DECEMBER 26, 1981	DECEMBER 27, 1980
CURRENT ASSETS		
Cash	$ 701	$ 766
Short-term investments	3,633	3,817
Receivables, less allowance for doubtful accounts: 1981—$341; 1980—$372	4,372	3,694
Inventories	3,684	3,214
Prepaid expenses and supplies	1,267	1,239
Total current assets	13,657	12,730
PROPERTY AND EQUIPMENT		
Land	724	696
Buildings and improvements	3,094	2,744
Equipment, leasehold rights and improvements	25,100	25,458
Capitalized leases	203	203
	29,121	29,101
Less accumulated depreciation and amortization	14,278	14,498
	14,843	14,603
OTHER ASSETS		
Long-term notes receivable, less current portion	2,795	1,448
Excess of investment cost over net assets of acquired businesses	1,559	1,660
Liquor licenses	920	830
Other assets	539	432
Deferred charges	419	358
	6,232	4,728
	$ 34,732	$ 32,061

See notes to consolidated financial statements.

LIABILITIES AND SHAREHOLDERS' EQUITY

IN THOUSANDS

	DECEMBER 26, 1981	DECEMBER 27, 1980
CURRENT LIABILITIES		
Current installments of long-term debt	$ 833	$ 353
Accounts payable and accrued expenses	9,362	9,558
Income taxes payable	523	266
Total current liabilities	10,718	10,177
LONG-TERM DEBT (less portion due within one year included in current liabilities)	7,149	8,580
OTHER LIABILITIES (principally future costs of closed units)	1,800	1,625
SHAREHOLDERS' EQUITY		
Convertible preferred stock, par value $1 per share,		
Authorized 1,500,000 shares; issued and outstanding:		
5% Series A: 40,000 shares	40	40
5% Series B: 160,000 shares	160	160
$.40 Series C: 65,000 shares, assigned value $5 per share	325	325
	525	525
Common stock, par value $1 per share,		
Authorized 5,000,000 shares; issued and outstanding		
(net of treasury shares: 1981—175,776; 1980—190,289)		
1981—2,273,634 shares; 1980—2,194,721 shares	2,274	2,195
Additional paid-in capital	7,905	7,812
Retained earnings	4,361	1,147
	15,065	11,679
	$ 34,732	$ 32,061

RESTAURANT ASSOCIATES INDUSTRIES, INC. AND SUBSIDIARIES

CONSOLIDATED STATEMENT OF EARNINGS

IN THOUSANDS EXCEPT PER SHARE AMOUNTS

	YEAR (52 WEEKS) ENDED		
	DECEMBER 26, 1981	DECEMBER 27, 1980	DECEMBER 29, 1979
REVENUES			
Company owned and managed facilities	$ 119,577	$ 113,433	$ 101,754
Less: managed facilities	20,402	17,662	14,399
Company owned facilities	99,175	95,771	87,355
COSTS AND EXPENSES			
Cost of sales	62,595	61,345	56,470
Operating and administrative expenses	30,990	29,346	26,470
Depreciation and amortization	1,911	1,910	1,599
Interest expense	805	934	924
	96,301	93,535	85,463
INCOME BEFORE ITEMS BELOW	2,874	2,236	1,892
Gain on purchase of debentures	151	206	42
Gain (loss) on disposal of facilities	783	(278)	(280)
Income before extraordinary item and provision for income taxes	3,808	2,164	1,654
Provision for income taxes	1,458	659	619
Income before extraordinary item	2,350	1,505	1,035
Extraordinary item:			
Income tax benefit from loss carry-forwards	929	483	343
NET INCOME	$ 3,279	$ 1,988	$ 1,378
EARNINGS PER SHARE:			
Primary:			
Income before extraordinary item	$ .97	$ .64	$ .50
Extraordinary item	.38	.21	.16
Net income	$ 1.35	$ .85	$ .66
Fully Diluted:			
Income before extraordinary item	$ .93	$ .62	$ .47
Extraordinary item	.32	.20	.15
Net income	$ 1.25	$ .82	$ .62
Average shares used in earnings per share computations:			
Primary	2,432	2,340	2,092
Fully diluted	2,887	2,453	2,264

See notes to consolidated financial statements.

RESTAURANT ASSOCIATES INDUSTRIES, INC. AND SUBSIDIARIES

CONSOLIDATED STATEMENT OF CHANGES IN FINANCIAL POSITION

IN THOUSANDS

	YEAR (52 WEEKS) ENDED		
	DECEMBER 26, 1981	DECEMBER 27, 1980	DECEMBER 29, 1979
SOURCE OF FUNDS			
Income before extraordinary item	$ 2,350	$ 1,505	$ 1,035
Items not requiring working capital			
Depreciation and amortization	1,911	1,910	1,599
(Gain) loss on disposal of facilities	(783)	278	280
Gain on purchase of debentures	(151)	(206)	(42)
Working capital provided from operations exclusive of extraordinary items	3,327	3,487	2,872
Tax benefits from loss carry-forwards	929	483	343
Proceeds from disposal of facilities	2,740	784	1,569
Proceeds from stock options exercised	65	208	128
Proceeds from long-term debt	—	407	—
Proceeds from preferred stock issued	—	—	400
Other	2	3	2
	$ 7,063	$ 5,372	$ 5,314
APPLICATION OF FUNDS			
Additions to property and equipment	$ 3,585	$ 3,447	$ 2,646
Increase (decrease) in long-term notes receivable	1,347	(22)	370
Decrease in long-term debt	1,157	784	1,154
Increase in deferred charges	196	241	237
Decrease (increase) in liability for future costs of closed units	113	(26)	46
Increase in other assets	107	25	60
Additions to liquor licenses	90	—	—
Purchase of stock for options	82	—	—
Increase in working capital	386	923	801
	$ 7,063	$ 5,372	$ 5,314
INCREASE (DECREASE) IN WORKING CAPITAL			
Cash and short-term investments	$(249)	$ 992	$ 741
Receivables	678	440	269
Inventories	470	283	24
Prepaid expenses and supplies	28	(215)	345
Current installments of long-term debt	(480)	(128)	257
Accounts payable and accrued expenses	196	(297)	(721)
Income taxes payable	(257)	(152)	(114)
	$ 386	$ 923	$ 801

See notes to consolidated financial statements.

15

RESTAURANT ASSOCIATES INDUSTRIES, INC. AND SUBSIDIARIES

CONSOLIDATED STATEMENT OF SHAREHOLDERS' EQUITY

			IN THOUSANDS	
	PREFERRED STOCK	COMMON STOCK	ADDITIONAL PAID-IN-CAPITAL	RETAINED EARNINGS (DEFICIT)
BALANCE, December 30, 1978	$ 200	$2,019	$7,577	$(2,034)
Cumulative effect of retroactive change in accounting principle				(185)
Exercise of stock options		46	82	
Exchange of Series A for Series B preferred stock				
Series A preferred stock	(160)	—	—	—
Series B preferred stock	160	—	—	—
Issuance of Series C preferred stock	400	—	—	—
Stock dividend on Series B preferred stock	—	19	(19)	—
Net income	—	—	—	1,378
BALANCE, December 29, 1979	600	2,084	7,640	(841)
Exercise of stock options	—	89	119	—
Conversion of Series C preferred stock	(75)	22	53	—
Net income	—	—	—	1,988
BALANCE, December 27, 1980	525	2,195	7,812	1,147
Exercise of stock options	—	20	45	—
Purchase of Company stock for options exercised	—	(18)	(64)	—
Stock dividend on Series B and C preferred stock	—	15	50	(65)
Conversion of 10½% debentures	—	62	62	—
Net income	—	—	—	3,279
BALANCE, December 26, 1981	$ 525	$ 2,274	$ 7,905	$ 4,361

See notes to consolidated financial statements.

NOTES TO CONSOLIDATED FINANCIAL STATEMENTS

1. SIGNIFICANT ACCOUNTING POLICIES

BASIS OF CONSOLIDATION
The consolidated financial statements include the accounts of the Company and its subsidiaries, all of which are wholly owned. All significant intercompany balances and transactions are eliminated in the consolidation. Certain reclassifications have been made to the 1979 and 1980 financial statements to conform to the 1981 presentation.

INVENTORIES AND PREPAID EXPENSES
Inventories are carried at the lower of cost (first-in, first-out method) or market. Newsstand inventories are determined by the retail method.

When a restaurant is opened, the initial purchase of expendable equipment, such as china, glass and silverware, is set up as prepaid supplies and is not amortized; however, all replacements are expensed.

PROPERTY AND EQUIPMENT
Property and equipment are stated at cost. Additions, renewals and betterments of property and equipment are capitalized. The Company's internal design, construction and real estate expenditures which relate to property and equipment are capitalized and amortized over the useful lives of the respective assets. Depreciation is provided on a straight-line basis for financial reporting purposes.

Costs of leasehold rights and improvements are amortized on a staight-line basis over the periods covered by the leases.

DEFERRED CHARGES
All expenses related to the opening of new restaurants up to the time of opening are deferred and amortized on a straight-line basis for the three year period commencing with the date of opening. If a restaurant is sold, abandoned or subleased, the unamortized pre-opening expense is charged to operations.

16

EXCESS OF INVESTMENT COST OVER NET ASSETS OF ACQUIRED BUSINESSES

The Company amortizes the excess of investment cost over net assets of acquired businesses attributable to acquisitions subsequent to October 31, 1970 over periods of 10 to 40 years. Cost in excess of net assets acquired in connection with acquisitions prior to November 1, 1970 is not being amortized since in the opinion of management there has been no diminution in value.

LIQUOR LICENSES

Transferable liquor licenses which have a market value are carried at acquisition cost and are not amortized.

CLOSED UNITS

When a restaurant on leased premises is permanently closed or sold before lease expiration, the unrecovered cost of leasehold improvements, equipment and the estimated rental cost net of sublease income for the balance of the lease term is charged to operations in the year of closing. Provision for the loss is recorded as "Other Liabilities."

DEFERRED COMPENSATION PLAN

Future payments required under a plan of deferred compensation are being charged to operations over the period of expected service.

INCOME TAXES

The Company and its subsidiaries file a consolidated federal income tax return. Investment tax credits are used to reduce the provision for income taxes following the flow-through method of accounting.

2. ACCOUNTING CHANGE— ACCRUED COMPENSATED ABSENCES

Prior to 1981, the Company followed the common practice of accounting for the cost of employees vacation pay benefits in the period they were paid. Effective as of December 28, 1980, as a result of the Financial Accounting Standards Board Statement No. 43, the Company began accruing such benefits as they are earned. Financial statements for years prior to 1981 have been restated as required by the Statement, resulting in a decrease in retained earnings at December 30, 1978 of $185,000. The accounting change decreased previously reported net income by $20,000 ($.01 per share) in 1979 and $32,000 ($.01 per share) in 1980.

3. LONG-TERM NOTES RECEIVABLE

Long-term notes receivable at December 26, 1981 includes $2,282,000 of notes received principally in connection with the sale of restaurants and other properties. The notes come due from 1982 to 1990 and bear interest at rates of 5½% to 15%. Also included in this caption are notes due from officers of the Company which totaled $513,000 ($293,000 at December 27, 1980). These notes come due from 1985 to 1990 and bear interest at rates from 5% to 10%.

4. LONG-TERM DEBT

Long-term debt at December 26, 1981 and December 27, 1980 consisted of the following:

	IN THOUSANDS	
	1981	1980
9% convertible subordinated debentures due 1993 (a)	$4,819	$5,183
4⅞% convertible subordinated debentures due 1993 (b)	814	864
10½% convertible debentures due 1983 (c)	216	347
13% subordinated debentures due 1983 (d)	159	159
5½% to 11% mortgages collateralized by real estate, payable through 1995	1,569	1,602
Other notes with interest to 10%, payable in regular installments through 1991	384	626
Capitalized lease obligations due through 1983 with interest at 3% over prime rate	89	135
Revolving credit (e)	—	100
	8,050	9,016
Less unamoritzed discount on debentures	68	83
	7,982	8,933
Less portion due within one year	833	353
	$7,149	$8,580

The maturity of long-term debt is as follows:

1983	$574
1984	497
1985	452
1986	473

(a) The 9% debentures are convertible into common stock of the Company at a price of $16 per share. During 1981 and 1980, the Company purchased and retired $364,000 and $589,000 principal amount of 9% debentures, respectively. Annual sinking fund payments for the 9% debentures are required in the amount of $219,000 for the year 1984 and $354,000 per year thereafter.

(b) The 4⅞% debentures were issued in 1968 and are convertible into common stock of the Company at $41.25 per share. During 1981 and 1980, the Company purchased and retired $50,500 and $39,000 principal amount of 4⅞% debentures, respectively.

(c) The 10½% debentures are currently redeemable at face value and no further sinking fund payments are required. $64,000 of the principal balance is convertible into 32,000 shares of common stock.

(d) The 13% debentures are redeemable by the Company at face value.

(e) The Company may borrow up to $7 million at the prime interest rate under revolving credit agreements executed in 1981. The revolving credit agreements convert into five year term loan agreements at ¼% over prime rate upon maturity in July 1983. The prevailing prime rate at December 26, 1981 was 15.75%.

5. INCOME TAXES

The following table summarizes the provision for income taxes:

	IN THOUSANDS		
	1981	1980	1979
Current	$1,227	$ 659	$ 619
Deferred	231	—	—
	$1,458	$ 659	$ 619

A reconciliation of income taxes at the statutory rate to the effective rate for income taxes on the consolidated statement of earnings follows:

	IN THOUSANDS					
	1981		1980		1979	
Federal income taxes at statutory rate	$1,752	46%	$1,010	46%	$ 770	46%
Capital gains alternative tax benefit	(100)	(3)	—	—	—	—
Allowable tax credits	(500)	(13)	(374)	(17)	(308)	(18)
State income taxes net of federal tax benefits	311	8	95	4	137	8
Gain on purchase of debentures	—		(94)	(4)	—	
Other—net	(5)	—	22	1	20	1
	$1,458	38%	$ 659	30%	$ 619	37%

Deferred income taxes arising from differences between tax and financial reporting are as follows:

	IN THOUSANDS		
	1981	1980	1979
Installment sales	$ 231	$ —	$ —
Extinguishment of Company debt	118	—	—
Expenses deducted on financial statements not currently deductible on tax return	(119)	—	—
Other	1	—	—
	$ 231	$ —	$ —

Included in the extraordinary item, income tax benefit from loss carry-forwards, of $929,000 is $352,000 representing the reinstatement of deferred tax benefits.

6. ACCOUNTS PAYABLE AND ACCRUED EXPENSES

The following table itemizes the major items included in the accounts payable and accrued expenses caption in the consolidated balance sheet.

	IN THOUSANDS	
	1981	1980
Trade accounts payable	$5,521	$5,809
Sales taxes	621	541
Payroll taxes	271	389
Accrued expenses:		
Rent and utilities	994	1,048
Interest	233	258
Taxes	350	402
Other	1,372	1,111
	$9,362	$9,558

7. STOCK OPTIONS

On May 7, 1981, the shareholders approved the 1981 Employees' Stock Option Plan under which options may be granted for an aggregate of 200,000 shares of the Company's common stock prior to February 25, 1995. At the same time, the Company terminated the 1979 Employees' Stock Option Plan except for options then outstanding. All other Company employees' stock option plans had been previously terminated except for options outstanding at the time of termination. Generally, under the 1981 Plan, options may be exercised immediately but no later than ten years from the date of grant. Upon exercise of an option, 1/10 of the price must be paid in cash and the remainder in nine equal installments with interest at 5% per annum. The plans provide for the forgiveness, on each anniversary of the exercise date, of not less than 5% and not more than 10% of purchase price.

A summary of activity in the stock option plans follows:

	1981	1980	1979
Shares under option:			
Beginning of the year	148,100	177,550	151,100
Granted	86,250	84,600	80,000
Cancelled or surrendered	(4,500)	(24,850)	(7,850)
Exercised	(19,600)	(89,200)	(45,700)
Balance at end of year at prices of $1.75 to $6.75 per share	210,250	148,100	177,550
Shares available for grant at year end	152,750	41,400	120,000
Average price per share on options exercised	$3.30	$2.33	$2.80

8. SHAREHOLDERS' EQUITY

At December 26, 1981 a total of 910,159 shares of common

stock were reserved for:

Conversion of debentures	
4⅞%	19,721
9%	301,188
10½%	32,000
Conversion of preferred stock	194,250
Stock option plans	363,000
	910,159

As at December 26, 1981, under the indenture for the 9% debentures, the Company may not pay cash dividends or purchase stock in excess of $487,000. The funds available for the payment of cash dividends and purchase of Company stock are increased by future net earnings before extraordinary items and additions to capital stock accounts.

All series of convertible preferred stock are entitled to one vote per share. Attributes of all series of preferred stock issued and outstanding are as follows:

	CUMULATIVE PREFERRED STOCK		
	SERIES A	SERIES B	SERIES C
Conversion date	Nov. 1984	Nov. 1983	Nov. 1980
Preferred to common conversion rate	2 to 1	2 to 1	1 to 1.45
Call date	Nov. 1983	May 1984	May 1984
Call value	$1	$1	$5

Dividends of series B and C preferred stock can be paid in shares of common stock. Dividends in arrears for Series A preferred stock total $16,000.

9. COMMITMENTS AND CONTINGENCIES

OPERATING LEASE COMMITMENTS—PREMISES:

Aggregate minimum commitments for rental expenses and sublease income at December 26, 1981 were $23,531,000 and $7,352,000, respectively.

Minimum annual rentals under these operating leases are as follows:

	IN THOUSANDS	
	RENTS PAYABLE	SUBLEASE INCOME
1982	$ 3,598	$ 1,078
1983	3,063	966
1984	2,634	917
1985	2,379	894
1986	2,415	787
1987-1991	5,364	2,500
1992-1996	2,009	210
1997-2000	2,069	—
	$23,531	$ 7,352

Some of these leases provide for additional rentals based on a percentage of sales. The following table summarizes the rent expense, percentage rent expense above base minimum and sublease income for 1981, 1980 and 1979.

	IN THOUSANDS		
	1981	1980	1979
Rental expense	$6,251	$6,006	$5,805
Percentage rent expense above base minimum	3,031	2,766	2,662
Sublease income	612	736	765

10. GAIN (LOSS) ON DISPOSALS AND TERMINATIONS

The table below summarizes the sales, operating losses and gain (loss) on disposals attributable to sold or closed operations.

	IN THOUSANDS		
	SALES	OPERATING LOSSES	GAIN (LOSS) ON DISPOSALS
1981	$1,627	$255	$783
1980	2,253	165	(278)
1979	1,385	348	(280)

11. PENSION PLAN

Most of the Company's salaried employees, except for those of the Eastern Newsstands Division, are covered under a pension plan adopted during 1968 or under previously existing plans covering employees of certain subsidiaries. Employees of Eastern Newsstands are covered by a profit sharing plan. Total provision for pension costs was approximately $143,000 in 1981, $119,000 in 1980 and $124,000 in 1979 which includes amortization of past service cost over a period of 40 years. The contribution to Eastern Newsstands' profit sharing for 1981, 1980 and 1979 was $62,000, $57,000 and $52,000, respectively. The Company's policy is to fund pension costs accrued. The table below summarizes pension plan information as estimated by consulting actuaries.

	IN THOUSANDS		
	1981	1980	1979
Actuarial present value of accumulated plan benefits:			
Vested	$1,776	$1,658	$1,597
Non-vested	122	140	146
	$1,898	$1,798	$1,743
Net assets available for benefits	$1,058	$ 929	$ 796

Actuarial reports are dated January 1 of each year. The assumed rate of return used in determining the actuarial present value of accumulated benefits was 7% for 1981, 1980 and 1979. As per said reports, the unfunded past service cost for 1981, 1980 and 1979 approximated $1,030,000, $1,032,000 and $1,096,000, respectively. The actuarially computed excess of vested benefits over pension fund assets approximated $718,000 in 1981, $729,000 in 1980 and $801,000 in 1979.

12. EARNINGS PER SHARE

Primary earnings per share computations are based on the weighted average number of common and common equivalent shares outstanding. The Company's Series B and C convertible preferred stock have been deemed to be common stock equivalents and as such are included in the calculations of primary earnings per share. No material dilution would result from the exercise of the outstanding stock options in any of the years reported.

1981 fully diluted earnings per share were determined on the assumptions that all convertible debentures, the convertible preferred stock Series A and outstanding stock options were converted into common stock of the Company at the beginning of the year. 1979 and 1980 fully diluted earnings per share were determined on the assumptions that the 10½% convertible debentures and the con-

vertible preferred stock Series A were converted into common stock of the Company at the beginning of the year. Dilutive effects of other potentially dilutive securities and stock options were excluded from the 1979 and 1980 calculations since their effects are either anti-dilutive or not material.

13. OPERATIONS BY BUSINESS SEGMENT

	IN THOUSANDS		
	1981	1980	1979
Revenues:			
Foodservice	**$70,146**	$69,603	$63,076
Newsstands	**27,992**	25,645	23,999
Interest income	**1,037**	523	280
Total Revenues—Company owned facilities	**$99,175**	$95,771	$87,355
Operating profit:			
Foodservice	**$ 2,919**	$ 2,698	$ 2,571
Newsstands	**1,245**	1,356	1,239
Total operating profit	**4,164**	4,054	3,810
Gain on purchase of debentures	**151**	206	42
Gain (loss) on disposal of facilities	**783**	(278)	(280)
General corporate expenses	**(1,522)**	(1,407)	(1,274)
Interest expense	**(805)**	(934)	(924)
Interest income	**1,037**	523	280
Income before extraordinary item and provision for income taxes	**$ 3,808**	$ 2,164	$ 1,654
Identifiable assets:			
Foodservice	**$28,743**	$25,998	$24,945
Newsstands	**5,566**	5,708	5,177
Corporate	**423**	355	308
	$34,732	$32,061	$30,430
Capital expenditures:			
Foodservice	**$ 3,144**	$ 2,921	$ 2,320
Newsstands	**441**	526	326
	$ 3,585	$ 3,447	$ 2,646
Depreciation and amortization			
Foodservice	**$ 1,546**	$ 1,579	$ 1,290
Newsstands	**365**	331	309
	$ 1,911	$ 1,910	$ 1,599

REPORT OF INDEPENDENT ACCOUNTANTS
TOUCHE ROSS & CO.

To the Shareholders and Board of Directors of
Restaurant Associates Industries, Inc.
New York, New York

We have examined the consolidated balance sheet of Restaurant Associates Industries, Inc. and Subsidiaries as of December 26, 1981 and December 27, 1980 and the related consolidated statements of earnings, shareholders' equity and changes in financial position for each of the fiscal years in the three year period ended December 26, 1981. Our examinations were made in accordance with generally accepted auditing standards, and accordingly included such tests of the accounting records and such other auditing procedures as we considered necessary in the circumstances.

In our opinion, the financial statements referred to above present fairly the consolidated financial position of Restaurant

Associates Industries, Inc. and Subsidiaries at December 26, 1981 and December 27, 1980 and the consolidated results of their operations and the changes in their financial position for each of the fiscal years in the three year period ended December 26, 1981, in conformity with generally accepted accounting principles applied on a consistent basis after restatement for the change, with which we concur, in the method of accounting for compensated absences as discussed in Note 2 to the financial statements.

Touche Ross & Co.

February 26, 1982   Certified Public Accountants
                                     Newark, New Jersey

Appendix: Sample Chart of Accounts Based on USAH

ASSETS (100–199)

Current Assets (100–149)

102 Petty cash/cash on hand
104 Cash in bank
108 Marketable securities
110 Accounts receivable
112 Allowance for doubtful accounts
114 Notes receivable
118 Notes receivable discounted
120 Food inventory
122 Beverage inventory
124 Housekeeping supplies inventory
126 Rooms supplies inventory
128 Office supplies inventory
130 Prepaid rent
132 Prepaid insurance
134 Other prepaids
149 Other current assets

Investments (150–159)

151 Investments in subsidiaries
155 Other investments

Property and Equipment (160–189)

161 Land
163 Buildings
164 Accumulated depreciation—buildings
166 Leasehold and leasehold improvements
167 Accumulated amortization—leasehold and leasehold improvements
169 Equipment
170 Accumulated depreciation—equipment
175 Furniture and fixtures
176 Accumulated depreciation—furniture and fixtures
178 China, glassware, silver, linen, and uniforms

Other Assets (190–199)

191 Preopening expenses
193 Deferred expenses (charges)

195 Utility deposits
197 Goodwill
198 Other

LIABILITIES (200–299)

Current Liabilities (200–249)

201 Accounts payable
203 Notes payable—current portion
210 Mortgages payable—current portion
215 Unearned income
220 Federal and state income taxes
225 Accrued salaries and wages
230 Accrued interest
235 Accrued taxes
240 Dividends payable
245 Other current liabilities

Long-Term Debt (250–299)

251 Notes payable (long-term)
255 Mortgages payable (noncurrent portion)
260 Bonds payable
265 Other noncurrent liabilities
270 Deferred income taxes

STOCKHOLDERS' EQUITY (300–399)

301 Preferred stock
302 Additional paid-in capital—Preferred
315 Common stock
316 Additional paid-in capital—common
325 Retained earnings (deficit)
330 Dividends
390 Income summary
393 Treasury stock

REVENUES (400–499)

400 Sales
430 Rentals
440 Sales allowances
450 Cash discounts

EXPENSES (500–599)

Departmental and Undistributed Operating Expenses (500–579)

500 Cost of sales
505 Freight-in

507 Purchase returns
509 Purchase discounts
511 Employee meals
513 Salaries and wages
515 Payroll taxes and employee benefits
517 China, glassware, silver, and linen
518 Uniforms
521 Contract services
523 Fuel
525 Laundry
527 Licenses and permits
528 Supplies
530 Other departmental expenses
532 Bad debt expense
534 Complimentary rooms, food, and other
536 Commissions
538 Management fees
540 Printing and stationary
542 Repairs and maintenance
544 Water
546 Electricity and gas
548 Postage
550 Contributions
552 General insurance
554 Cash short (cash over)
556 Advertising—outdoor
558 Advertising—print
560 Advertising—radio and television
562 Selling Aids—in-house
564 Selling Aids—point-of-sale
566 Public relations
568 Market research
569 Advertising agency fees
570 Music and entertainment
571 Franchise fees
573 Dues
575 Credit card commissions
577 Telephone expense
579 Miscellaneous expenses

Fixed Charges (580–589)

580 Rent expense
582 Property taxes
584 Property insurance
586 Interest
588 Depreciation and amortization

Other Revenue and Expense Accounts (590–599)

591 Gain or loss on sale of property
594 Income taxes

DEPARTMENTAL PREFIXES (00–90)

00 Hotel as a whole (no specific department)
10 Rooms department

15 Food department
20 Beverage department
25 Food and beverage department (combined)
30 Casino department
35 Telephone department
40 Garage–parking lot department
45 Golf department
50 Laundry department
55 Swimming pool–cabanas department
60 Tennis department
65 Other revenue-producing department
70 Administrative and general department
75 Marketing department
80 Guest entertainment department
85 Property operation, maintenance, and energy department

Instructions

Account numbers are assigned based on the chart of accounts above by combining a two-digit department prefix with a three-digit asset, liability, equity, revenue, or expense account number. Thus every account has a five-digit number. In the case of accounts applicable to the hotel as a whole, the first two digits are zeros. For example, the account number for rent expense would be 00580.

Glossary

Accelerated Cost Recovery System (ACRS). A system incorporated in the Economic Recovery Tax Act (ERTA) of 1981 that allows the recovery of the cost of property and equipment over a period shorter than its useful life.

Accelerated depreciation. Any depreciation method that allocates larger amounts of the depreciable cost of the property and equipment to earlier periods and lesser amounts to later periods of use.

Account. An individual record of effects of transactions on each asset, liability, owners' equity, revenue, or expense item.

Account balance. The difference between the total debits and the total credits of an account.

Account form. A form of balance sheet in which the assets are listed on the left-hand side and liabilities and owners' equity on the right-hand side.

Accounting. A system for collecting, summarizing, analyzing, and reporting, in monetary terms, information concerning an organization.

Accounting cycle. The processing of the raw material of the accounting system (business transactions) in order to get the output or end product of the system, which is information for management in the form of financial statements and other accounting reports.

Accounting period. The segment of time selected to measure the results of operations.

Accounting Principles Board (APB). A committee of the American Institute of Certified Public Accountants (AICPA) that was responsible for the formulation of accounting principles before it was replaced by the Financial Accounting Standards Board.

Accounts payable. Amounts owed to suppliers for goods or services purchased on credit.

Accounts payable subsidiary ledger. A subsidiary ledger containing a detailed breakdown of the accounts payable account in the general ledger and informing the manager how much is owed to each supplier.

Accounts receivable. Amounts owed by customers for goods or services sold on credit.

Accounts receivable aging method. A method used to develop an estimate of uncollectible accounts receivable.

Accounts receivable subsidiary ledger. A subsidiary ledger containing a detailed breakdown of the accounts receivable account in the general ledger and informing the manager how much is owed by each customer.

Accounts receivable turnover. A measure of liquidity that shows the number of times that accounts receivable are converted into cash during the period.

Accrual basis of accounting. The recognition of revenues when earned and expenses when incurred regardless of when cash is received or paid.

Accrued expenses. Expenses incurred during the accounting period not yet recorded.

Accrued revenue. Revenues that were earned but not recognized in the accounts during the accounting period.

Accumulated depreciation. A contra-asset account used to accumulate the total depreciation recorded on property and equipment; deducted from the corresponding assets on the balance sheet.

Acid-test ratio. *See* Quick ratio.

Additional paid-in capital. The portion of paid-in capital that exceeds the par value (or stated value) of the issued shares of both common and preferred stock.

Adjusted trial balance. A trial balance prepared after all adjusting entries were reflected in the accounts.

Adjusting entries. Journal entries made on the last day of the accounting period in order to update the trial balance accounts before the financial statements are prepared.

Aging of accounts receivable. The process of listing each account in terms of unpaid balances and due dates.

AICPA. *See* American Institute of Certified Public Accountants.

Allowance for doubtful accounts. A contra-asset account that shows the estimated amount of accounts receivable that will not be collected; shown as a reduction of accounts receivable on the balance sheet.

American Institute of Certified Public Accountants (AICPA). The national association of certified public accountants in the United States.

Amortization. The write-off of the cost of an asset over its estimated useful life. (Also used for allocating the premium or discount on bonds over the life of the bond.)

Annual occupancy percentage. A measure of the use of hotels' facilities through the generation of revenues from the sale of space.

Annual report. A yearly report for stockholders and other interested parties prepared by management.

APB. *See* Accounting Principles Board.

Arithmetic unit. The part of the central processing unit (CPU) in a computer system used for making calculations.

Assets. Future values or resources owned by the business.

Auditors' report. A report by a firm of independent CPAs that accompanies the financial statements and includes an opinion concerning the fairness of presentation of the financial statements.

Authorized capital stock. The number of shares of capital stock a company can issue according to its corporate charter.

Average food check. A widely used statistic in the foodservice industry that measures the ability of the food operation to generate revenues by relating the food sold to the number of customers served.

Average room rate. A measure of the rate structure and/or salesmanship ability of a hotel.

Bad debts. An estimate of accounts receivable that are uncollectible.

Balance sheet. A financial statement that reflects the financial position of a business at a particular date.

Beverage cost. *See* Cost percentages.

Board of directors. The governing board of a corporation elected by the voting stockholders.

Bonds payable. Long-term obligations normally requiring semiannual interest payments that can be issued or sold at par, at a discount (below par), or at a premium (above par) subject to the conditions stated on a bond indenture.

Bookkeeping. Record-keeping phase of accounting.

Business entity concept. An accounting premise that indicates that an organization is viewed as a unit independent from its owners.

Business transactions. The raw material of the accounting system involving an equal exchange of values between organizations.

Capitalize. To record an expenditure as an asset rather than as an expense of the period.

Capital lease. Long-term lease that transfers to the lessee the risks and benefits incident to ownership.

Cash basis of accounting. A basis of accounting under which revenues and expenses are recognized when cash is received or paid.

Cash disbursements journal. A special-purpose journal used to record transactions involving cash payments.

Cash receipts journal. A special-purpose journal used to record transactions involving money coming in.

Cash surrender value of officers' life insurance. The cash value accumulated up to the balance sheet date on the life insurance policies covering the lives of certain officers and other key members of an organization.

Central processing unit (CPU). A piece of hardware consisting of an arithmetic unit, a control unit, and an internal memory used by a computer in processing data.

Certified public accountant (CPA). The recognized professional accountant who provides auditing, tax, consultation, and advisory services.

Charge. Synonymous with the term "debit."

Chart of accounts. A numbering system in which a specific number is assigned to each account in the ledger in order to simplify the recording and posting processes.

City ledger. Credit charges by authorized persons or companies who are not registered hotel guests.

Closing entries. Journal entries made at the end of each accounting period to clear revenue and expense accounts, transferring the period's net income to the appropriate owners' equity account.

Commitments. Claims that may occur upon the future performance under a contract, such as a lease agreement.

Common-size analysis. The expression of all financial statement items in percentage form.

Common stock. The ownership rights given by a corporation evidenced by the issuance of shares of common stock.

Comparative financial statements. A firm's financial statements for two or more successive years used to detect trends.

Conservatism. When evaluating uncertainties, selecting the method of measurement that yields the least favorable immediate result in order to avoid self-serving exaggeration.

Consistency. An accounting concept that requires an entity to give the same accounting treatment to similar events in successive accounting periods.

Contingencies. Existing conditions involving uncertainty as to their ultimate effect; their resolution being dependent upon specific future events.

Continuity. *See* Going concern.

Contra-account. An account whose balance is subtracted from a related account on the balance sheet; for example, contra-asset accounts such as accumulated depreciation and allowance for doubtful accounts.

Control account (or controlling account). A general ledger account that summarizes the total balance of a group of related accounts in a subsidiary ledger. For example, the accounts receivable control account.

Controllable costs. Costs over which a particular manager or department head has direct control.

Convertible debentures. Bonds that are convertible into a specific number of common shares at the bondholder's option.

Corporation. A multiple-owner organization that is recognized as a separate legal entity by law.

Cost. Price paid to acquire the resources owned by the organization (or assets), representing the proper basis to account for those resources. *See also* Historical cost.

Cost center. A responsibility center that has control over the incurrence of cost.

Cost of sales. The cost of food or beverages sold to customers.

Cost percentages. Measures of the relative efficiency of the food and the beverage operations by relating the cost of food or beverages sold to the revenues generated from the sale of food or alcoholic beverages.

CPA. *See* Certified public accountant.

CPU. *See* Central processing unit.

Credit. Value(s) given in a business transaction. Decreases in assets and expenses, or increases in liabilities, owners' equity and revenues.

Creditor. A person or company to whom a debt is owed.

Current assets. Cash or other assets that can be converted into cash or consumed by the business within one year from the balance sheet date, the normal operating cycle.

Current liabilities. Obligations that are expected to be paid, or settled otherwise, within one year from the balance sheet date, the normal operating cycle.

Current ratio. A measure of short-term debt-paying ability computed by dividing total current assets by total current liabilities.

Debit. Value(s) received in a business transaction; increases in assets and expenses, or decreases in liabilities, owners' equity, and revenues.

Debt. An amount owed; an obligation.

Debt-to-equity ratio. The expression of the creditors' financing in relation to the owners' financing.

Declaration date. Time when dividend is declared by the board of directors of a corporation.

Deferred charges (or deferred expenses). Long-term prepayments recorded as assets and written off in future periods.

Deferred income. *See* Unearned revenue.

Deferred income taxes. The timing differences resulting from using different accounting methods for tax and financial reporting purposes.

Deficit. A negative balance in retained earnings.

Departmental income. The income of an individual operating department after departmental direct expenses have been deducted from revenue.

Depreciation. The periodic allocation of the cost of an asset over its estimated useful life.

Direct cost or expense. An expense that is distributed directly to an operating department since it is generally controllable by that department.

Direct write-off method. An accounting procedure whereby uncollectible accounts receivable are written off directly to an expense account.

Discounted notes receivable. Promissory notes sold to banks or other financial institutions.

Dishonored notes. Promissory notes not paid by makers on their due date.

Dividend. The distribution of corporate earnings to stockholders as a return on their investment in the company.

Dividend yield. The relationship of the current price of the company's stock to the annual dividend.

Double-declining-balance depreciation. An accelerated method of depreciation in which twice the straight-line rate is applied to the net book value of an asset in the determination of the asset's annual depreciation expense.

Dual-aspect concept. An accounting premise that is based on the fact that there are ownership claims to all things of value.

Earnings. The excess of revenues over expenses for an accounting period.

Earnings per share (EPS). A reflection of management's success in achieving earnings for the owners in which earnings are related to the weighted average number of shares of common stock understanding.

EPS. *See* Earnings per share.

Equities. Claims against resources owned by the business, consisting of liabilities and owners' equity.

Estimated useful life. The period of time in which an asset will be of value to a firm.

Expenditure. Payment of cash to obtain goods or services.

Expenses. Goods or services consumed in operating an enterprise.

Extraordinary items. Unusual and nonrecurring gains and losses.

FASB. *See* Financial Accounting Standards Board.

Federal income tax withheld. Taxes withheld from employees' gross pay that must be paid to the federal government.

FICA (Federal Insurance Contributions Act) taxes. Social security taxes.

FIFO. *See* First-in–first-out method of inventory valuation.

Financial accounting. Accounting information for both internal and external uses that is based on a set of principles and a number of ground rules designed to enhance and clarify communication between the business and parties external to the business.

Financial Accounting Standards Board (FASB). An independent board responsible, since 1973, for establishing generally accepted accounting principles.

Financial leverage. *See* Leverage.

Financial statement analysis. The use of tools and techniques to assist financial statement users in the interpretation and understanding of key trends.

Financial statements. The output or end product of the accounting system, representing means of transmitting to management and other interested parties a concise picture of the profitability and financial condition of a business entity.

First-in–first-out method of inventory valuation (FIFO). An inventory flow assumption by which ending inventory cost is based on the most recent purchases and cost of sales is determined from oldest purchases including beginning inventory.

Fiscal year. An annual accounting period that may not coincide with the calendar year.

Fixed assets. *See* Property and equipment.

Fixed charges. Noncontrollable indirect costs such as property taxes, fire insurance, interest, and depreciation that are deducted from income before fixed charges according to the income statement presentation of the Uniform System of Accounts for Hotels (USAH).

FOB. Free on board some location. For example, FOB shipping point and FOB destination.

Food cost. *See* Cost percentages.

Footing. Totaling of columns.

Franchising. A method of doing business by which the franchisor (party granting the franchise) confers to the franchisee the right to carry on a business in a specific location, in a prescribed manner over a particular period of time.

Full disclosure. A standard of financial reporting requiring the disclosure of all facts that might influence the decision of a user of the financial statements.

Fundamental accounting equation. Assets equal liabilities plus owners' equity.

Funds. Equivalent to working capital when used in connection with the statement of changes in financial position.

FUTA (Federal Unemployment Tax Act) taxes. A tax levied by the federal government to help subsidize the joint federal–state unemployment programs.

General journal. A book of original entry used to record business transactions.

General ledger. A book of final entry, consisting of a group of accounts that constitute an organization's accounting system.

Generally accepted accounting principles (GAAP). Set of ground rules or conventions that have received substantial support from an authoritative source.

Going concern. For accounting purposes, the assumption made is that the business will continue in operation indefinitely.

Goodwill. An intangible asset reflecting the cost of an acquired firm over the market value of the net assets acquired.

Gross margin (or gross profit). Revenue minus cost of sales.

Guest ledger. Accounts receivable due from customers currently registered at the hotel. Also called house accounts.

Historical cost. Original cost.

Horizontal analysis. The comparison of each account on one financial statement with the same account selected from a base year.

Income. *See* Earnings.

Income statement. A financial statement that reflects the results of operations of a company for a certain period of time.

Income summary. A temporary account into which revenue and expense accounts are closed at the end of the accounting period.

Indirect cost or expense. A cost not allocated directly to an operating department.

Intangible assets. Long-term assets that have no physical existence but have a value based on legal privileges or rights that have been acquired at a cost to a firm.

Interest. The cost for using money, frequently expressed as a rate per period, called interest rate.

Interest coverage. A ratio that measures the protection of creditors from a default on interest payments.

Interim statements. Accounting statements for periods shorter than one year.

Inventory. Goods (e.g., food, beverages) purchased but not yet used to generate revenues.

Inventory turnovers. A measure of how rapidly food and beverages are being sold and replaced during the period.

Investment centers. Departments whose managers are responsible for maximizing revenue, minimizing expenses, and minimizing investment.

Investment tax credit (ITC). A special tax credit allowed to businesses to encourage capital formation (i.e., investment in property and equipment).

Journal. A business diary used to record business transactions in chronological order.

Journal entry. The recording of a business transaction in a journal.

Journalizing. The chronological recording of business transactions in a journal by entering the value(s) received and value(s) given for each transaction.

Last-in–first-out method of inventory valuation (LIFO). An inventory flow assumption that results in an ending inventory priced at the earliest acquisition prices, whereas cost of sales is determined from the most recent purchases.

LCM. *See* Lower of cost or market.

Leasehold. The rights granted to a lessee under the terms of a lease agreement.

Leasehold improvements. Improvements to leased property made by a lessee.

Ledger. A book of final entry in which business transactions are entered after being journalized.

Leverage. The use of borrowed funds with the intention of improving the rate of return on capital invested by the owners of a corporation.

Liabilities. The claims of creditors against the assets of the firm; debts or obligations.

LIFO. *See* Last-in–first-out method of inventory valuation.

Liquidity. Measure of a firm's short-term debt-paying ability.

Long-term liabilities. Obligations that are expected to be paid or otherwise settled after one year from the balance sheet date. Examples are mortgages payable and bonds payable.

Lower of cost or market (LCM). An accounting convention for the valuation of final inventory and short-term investments in which the replacement value (or market value) is used if such value is lower than cost.

Management. The group of people in a firm who are responsible for planning, controlling, and directing business activities.

Management accounting. The accounting procedures primarily concerned with the internal uses of accounting information by management.

Marketable securities. Investment in short-term securities (e.g., stocks, bonds) that can be readily converted into cash.

Market value. The current value of an asset, sometimes called replacement value.

Matching. An accounting principle requiring that costs necessary for the generation of revenue are matched (offset) against the revenues they helped produced in the determination of periodic net income.

Materiality. An accounting concept that deals with significant information; accordingly, insignificant items might be ignored in applying the basic accounting concepts.

Maturity date. The date on which a note and any interest are due and payable.

Maturity value. Principal and interest due on a note's maturity date.

Minority interest. The portion of capital stock in a subsidiary corporation not owned by the controlling company (parent).

Money measurement. Accounting is only concerned with the recording of facts that can be expressed in monetary terms, as opposed to using physical or time units of measurement.

Mortgage payable. A long-term liability secured by designated property of the debtor.

Multistep income statement. Form of income statement that arrives at net income in steps.

Natural business year. An annual period, at the end of which the business activities are at their lowest point.

Net income. The excess of revenues over expenses.

Net loss. The excess of expenses over revenues.

Night auditor. The person responsible for the verification of postings of all guest charges and payments to clients' accounts.

Nominal accounts. *See* Temporary accounts.

Noncontrollable costs or expenses. Costs that are not under the control of managers or department heads in a company.

No-par stock. Stock that does not have a par value; a stated value may be assigned for accounting purposes.

Notes payable. Obligations evidenced by a promissory note.

Notes receivable. Claims evidenced by a promissory note from the borrower to pay a sum of money at some future date.

Objectivity principle. An accounting concept requiring that accounting measurements be free from bias and subject to verification by an independent third party.

Obligations. *See* Liabilities.

Occupancy percentage. *See* Annual occupancy percentage.

Operating efficiency ratio. Measure of the ability of a hotel to operate profitably.

Operating expenses. Expenses incurred in the normal course of activities of an enterprise.

Organization costs. Costs incurred in organizing a corporate business, such as legal fees, promoters' fees, and amounts paid to secure the corporate charter; such costs are recorded as intangible assets and are to be amortized over their estimated useful lives (not to exceed 40 years).

Organizations. Distinct entities with stated purposes operating in an environment.

Outstanding stock. Shares of capital stock held by stockholders.

Owners' equity. Owners' claims on the assets of the business after the creditors' claims have been fully satisfied; residual equity.

Paid-in capital. Sum of the balances in capital stock and capital contributed in excess of par (or stated value) accounts; also called contributed capital.

Parent company. A company holding a majority of the stock of another company, which is called a subsidiary company.

Partnership. An association of two or more persons to carry on as co-owners a business for profit.

Par value. An arbitrary value placed on a share of stock at the time the corporation seeks authorization of the stock; usually determines the legal capital of a corporation.

Payment date.   Date for payment of a dividend.

Payroll register.   A detailed listing of a firm's total payroll, prepared each pay period, showing each employee's earnings and deductions for the period.

Percentage of sales method.   A method of estimating bad debt expenses based on the determination of the percentage of current year's sales that will be uncollectible.

Periodic-inventory system.   An inventory system in which inventories and cost of sales are based on periodic physical counts of inventory items, usually done at least once a year.

Permanent accounts.   *See* Real accounts.

Perpetual-inventory system.   An inventory system in which inventories and cost of sales are based on book inventory records that reflect both purchases and sales of inventory at the time such transactions occur.

Physical inventory.   The actual counting, recording, and pricing of inventory.

Postclosing trial balance.   A trial balance prepared after the closing process has been completed.

Posting.   The transfer of the information recorded in a journal to a book of final entry known as the ledger.

Preferred stock.   A class of capital stock that possesses certain preferences over common stock in earnings distributions and in the event of liquidation of a corporation.

Prepaid expenses.   Items paid in advance that will benefit future accounting periods, for example, prepayments for insurance, rent, and licenses.

Price-earnings ratio.   An indication of how much the investing public is willing to pay for a company's prospective earnings.

Principal.   The amount of money borrowed in connection with the issuance of a note or bond.

Prior period adjustments.   Corrections of material errors made in financial statements of prior periods.

Profit.   *See* Earnings.

Profitability.   Measure of a company's ability to generate earnings from its available resources.

Profit centers.   Departments whose managers are responsible for maximizing revenues and minimizing expenses.

Profit margin.   Net income per dollar of sale.

Property and equipment.   Long-term assets used in the production of revenues; also known as fixed assets.

Proprietorship.   *See* Sole proprietorship.

Purchase journal.   A special-purpose journal used for recording credit purchases.

Quick ratio.   A measure of liquidity that relates cash, cash equivalents and receivables to current liabilities.

Quid pro quo.   Something for something; equal exchange of values inherent in business transactions.

Ratio.   A mathematical expression of the relationship between two financial and/or operating figures.

Ratio analysis.   The indication of the strengths and weaknesses of a firm by calculating strategic relationships (i.e., ratios).

Real accounts.   Balance sheet accounts.

Realization concept.   An accounting principle requiring revenues to be recognized at the time they are earned.

Recognition.   The process of formally recording or incorporating an item in the financial statements of a company.

Replacement value.   *See* Market value.

Report form. A form of balance sheet under which assets are listed at the top of the page and liabilities and owners' equity underneath assets.

Responsibility accounting. A system of accounting used to evaluate the performance of individual managers and supervisors within an organization.

Responsibility center. A department with specific goals that the manager is responsible for achieving and whose costs and expenses are controllable by a manager or supervisor.

Retained earnings. The cumulative earnings of a firm since its formation, net of any amounts paid out to shareholders in the form of dividends.

Return on assets. A measure of the return obtained on all the company's assets without consideration of the method used in financing those assets.

Return on equity. A fundamental measure of profitability from the standpoint of current and prospective investors that relates net income to average shareholders' equity.

Revenue. An inflow of assets in exchange for goods or services.

Revenue center. Responsibility center whose managers are responsible for maximizing revenues.

Reversing entries. Journal entries that reverse the adjusting entries pertaining to accruals, thereby permitting the routine recording of subsequent related receipts and payments.

Sales. *See* Revenue.

Sales journal. A special-purpose journal used to record sales transactions exclusively.

Salvage value (or residual value). The estimated value that property and equipment will have at the end of its estimated useful life (or estimated date of disposal).

Securities and Exchange Commission (SEC). A federal agency responsible for protecting the interests of investors in publicly held companies by regulating the sale and exchange of most securities.

Shareholders' equity. The owners' equity section of a corporate balance sheet.

Short-term liabilities. *See* Current liabilities.

Single-step income statement. A simple-form income statement with one section for revenues and one section for expenses and net income.

Sole proprietorship. An unincorporated business owned by one individual.

Solvency. The ability of a company to pay its long-term debts.

Source documents. Written documents that serve as evidence that business transactions took place, such as bank checks, purchase invoices, or cash register tapes.

Special-purpose journals. Books of original entry that are designed for recording specific types of business transactions (e.g., the cash receipts journal and the cash disbursements journal).

Specific identification method of inventory valuation. An inventory pricing method that keeps track of the specific cost of each inventory item.

Stated value. A nominal value assigned to no-par stock by a corporation.

Statement of changes in financial position. A basic financial statement that summarizes the financing and investing activities of management during the period by showing the sources and uses of working capital.

Statement of income. *See* Income statement.

Statement of retained earnings. A statement summarizing the changes in retained earnings during the period.

State unemployment tax. A payroll tax levied on employers by states in order to finance state unemployment compensation programs.

Stock dividend. Distribution by a corporation of shares of its own common stock, usually in lieu of a cash dividend.

Stockholders' equity. *See* Shareholders' equity.

Stock split. Increase in the number of common shares outstanding without a change in the total par value (or stated value) of the outstanding shares.

Stock subscriptions. Acquisition of shares of capital stock on a deferred payment plan according to the terms of an agreement.

Straight-line depreciation. A method of depreciation that allocates the cost of property and equipment evenly over the estimated useful life of the asset.

Subordinated debentures. Bonds that in the event of liquidation become payable only after all other liabilities have been discharged.

Subsidiary company. A company in which a controlling interest in its stock is owned by another company known as the parent.

Subsidiary ledger. A ledger that contains the details underlying the balance in a related control account of the general ledger such as accounts receivable.

Summary of significant accounting policies. A note to the financial statements that discloses which generally accepted accounting principles the company has followed in the preparation of said statements; usually the first footnote.

Sum-of-the-years' digits depreciation. An accelerated method of depreciation that allocates depreciation expense to each period in a fractional proportion, the denominator of which is the sum of the years' digits in the estimated useful life of the asset and the numerator is the years' digits in inverse order.

"T" account. A simplified form of a ledger account in the shape of the letter T; usually used for learning purposes.

Tax basis of income measurement. Income measured for tax purposes, which is governed by regulations established principally by congress, the tax courts, and the Internal Revenue Service.

Temporary accounts. The revenue, expenses, income summary, and withdrawals accounts.

Time period concept. An accounting concept stating that the results of operations of a company are to be measured over specific intervals of time.

Transactions. *See* Business transactions.

Treasury stock. Shares of outstanding stock that have been reacquired by the issuing corporation.

Trend analysis. Review of past performance in order to determine the direction that the business appears to be headed.

Trial balance. A list of the debit and credit balances from the general ledger to ensure that total debits equal total credits.

Undistributed operating expenses. Costs incurred for the benefit of the overall organization; not allocated to specific operated departments since they are typically noncontrollable costs, and not the responsibility of an operated department.

Unearned revenue. Payments received in advance for services to be provided in the future.

Uniform system of accounts. Presentation of financial statement information in order to facilitate comparability between hospitality firms.

Units-of-output depreciation. A method of depreciation based on the number of units used by the depreciable asset during an accounting period.

Unsecured debentures. Bonds that are issued on the general credit-worthiness of the firm.

Vertical analysis. The comparison of all financial statement figures with a base figure selected from the same statement.

Weighted-average method of inventory valuation. An inventory pricing system that spreads the total dollar cost of all goods available for sale equally among all units.

Withdrawals. Cash or property taken out by proprietors or partners for personal use.
Working capital. The excess of current assets over current liabilities.
Worksheet. An accounting tool used to bring together all the information needed in the preparation of financial statements, adjusting entries, and closing entries; also called financial statement worksheet.

Index